1968

1968

THE YEAR THE WORLD SHOOK

ALEXANDER BLOOM

OXFORD
UNIVERSITY PRESS

OXFORD
UNIVERSITY PRESS

Oxford University Press is a department of the University of Oxford.
It furthers the University's objective of excellence in research, scholarship,
and education by publishing worldwide. Oxford is a registered trade mark of
Oxford University Press in the UK and in certain other countries.

Published in the United States of America by Oxford University Press
198 Madison Avenue, New York, NY 10016, United States of America.

CIP data is on file at the Library of Congress.

ISBN 9780197793350

DOI: 10.1093/9780197793381.001.0001

Printed by Marquis Book Printing, Canada

The manufacturer's authorized representative in the EU for product safety is
Oxford University Press España S.A. of Parque Empresarial San Fernando de Henares,
Avenida de Castilla, 2 – 28830 Madrid (www.oup.es/en or product.safety@oup.com).
OUP España S.A. also acts as importer into Spain of products made by the manufacturer.

For Peggy
&

The Grandkids
Liza, Lucia, Mae, Jackson, Rufus, Sonya, and Vivian

Contents

Preface

This is not the first book about 1968, and it almost certainly will not be the last. A year as extraordinary as 1968 will always capture the attention of scholars and analysts of the twentieth century. My interest in this topic began with a conversation with Nancy Toff of Oxford University Press, about a volume in their splendid *Very Short Introduction* series. "You could do a book on a year," she suggested. "How about 1968?," I replied. When I sketched out my initial ideas for a book, I realized that what I envisioned would go well beyond the word limit of that series. I was hooked, however. My plan was to recount a number of the crucial events of the year, using cities as the anchors of the chapters—Saigon, Memphis, Prague, Paris, Chicago, Mexico City, and more. The interconnections among these moments would be developed, but each chapter would also stand as a brief history of the event. The more I began to work on the project, the more it became clear to me that in addition to the interconnections among the events, these moments often represented the culmination of movements that had evolved over the decade or were crucial in the evolution of newly emerging movements. The context for each of these moments needed to be developed—their place in the evolving history of its central issues—so as to locate and explain the 1968 eruptions.

The result is the book in front of you. It does not pretend to be the final word on 1968, nor does it contain a radical new analysis that negates all the previous works on this topic. As in all works of history, there are issues and understandings that I find essential and convincing, which others may not see as equally crucial. I have chosen examples that seemed the most compelling, knowing full well that I could have added many additional events and chapters. My idea was to have a complete but not massive work, filled with the most important moments, and for it be clear to the reader that these events were part of some larger, if uncoordinated, movement.

This book stands on the shoulders of the many works on 1968 that have come before. Each of these authors contributed to it. I am eternally grateful to those who ventured down this path before me, especially to David Caute, Robert Cottrell and Blaine Browne, the late Robert V. Daniels, Ronald Fraser, Charles Kaiser, Mark Kurlansky, Jeremi Suri, the late Jules Witcover, and David Wyatt. Their books (listed in the "Note on Sources") were beneficial in ways large and small. They have my heartfelt appreciation. So too many scholars of the 1960s, in general, some of whom I know personally and all of whom have my great respect, particularly Terry Anderson, Stewart Burns, the late David Chalmers, Todd Gitlin, Maurice Isserman, David Farber, Michael Kazin, Robert McElvaine, and James Miller.

A good part of this book was written as the pandemic froze the United States and the world, making the traditional form of archival research and haunting library stacks impossible. What I discovered was the vast array of sources available without ever leaving my desk— websites on particular topics, others filled with essential and often hard-to-find sources, databases of historical works, and so much more. I do not know the names of the countless archivists, reference librarians, historians, and digital humanists who put all these together and so cannot thank them by name. But they, and so many others, need to know just how crucial they are in the modern doing of history and other academic concerns.

During my last several years of teaching, I taught both first-year and senior seminars around the topic of 1968. I learned something from nearly all the research and papers of the students, including those by first-year students. The work of some was especially helpful, including that by Amy Bergquist, Elizabeth Faulkner, Josh Greenberg, Marissa Hexter, Quinn LaViolette, Maureen McCafferty, and Erika Prince.

Elizabeth Faulkner also did great work searching periodicals for popular culture references to the issues and themes of the year.

The American Studies community in Italy has been an open and supportive group, graciously incorporating me into their ranks when I first arrived to teach in Rome over 20 years ago. They remain a model of academic civility and mutual support, gracious and yet extremely serious about their endeavors. Among them, several have been particularly important for me and have my deepest thanks and appreciation: Fernando Fasce, Daniele Fiorentino, Cristina Giorcelli, Donatella Izzo, Gigiola Nocera, Paola Pierini, Paolo Pietromarchi, and, especially, Sabrina Vellucci.

I have been fortunate to have had Oxford as my publisher since my graduate school days, many years ago. The people I have encountered there over the years have always been, like Nancy Toff, enthusiastic, smart, and, most importantly, helpful. Susan Ferber offered initial enthusiasm about this project and remains a great editor and a dear friend. Timothy Bent grasped my sense of the book immediately and was both encouraging about the overall undertaking as well as carefully editing every line of the text, from big picture questions to thinking of better ways to say things or offering a more refined word choice. Tim has been an essential contributor to this work and an absolute pleasure to work with.

My amigos, Mary Beth Jarrad, Niko Pfund, Clark Dougan, and Christian Appy have not only provided quiet counsel and sound advice over the years but have also helped to maintain the balance between serious undertakings and just plain fun. Each of them is committed to their important work in publishing or as scholars, but never to the point of letting it dominate their life and missing its enjoyment.

Although she did not advise me on this book and has not yet even read a single word of it, a good deal of what I know about the 1960s came from my time working with Wini Breines over the years we edited and then revised our reader, *Takin' It to the Streets*. Wini has moved from academic life to a second career as a wonderful water colorist. Still, her contributions to anything I do on the 1960s are immense.

A number of friends read a chapter or two, bringing both their individual expertise and overall understanding of modern history to the effort. My gratitude to each of them for taking the time to carefully edit the text, to assess what was being said, to suggest what needed to be included and what was superfluous, and so much more is very great. They are all true friends as well as stellar historians: Dolita Cathcart, William Chase, John D'Emilio, Daniel Horowitz, Richard Immerman, Elaine Tyler May, Robert McElvaine, John McMillian, Amy Wright Nathan, Judith Smith, and Paul Spagnoli. In addition, my lunches with Dan Horowitz have served as a kind of regular reconnection with both the doing of history and being able to periodically talk about this book as well as his work.

My closest and longest continuous friend, the novelist and publisher Peter Warner, passed away as I was writing this book. Over many years, we talked so often about our own writing projects, as well as a thousand other topics, large and small. It is a great personal loss for me that Peter did not live to see the culmination of this book. I think he would have liked it.

My sons, Stefan Bloom and Zachary Bloom, have been constant sources of pride and pleasure since they were born, having become men with whom I can talk seriously about my work. They, along with my stepsons, Benjamin Stockman and Noah Stockman, and all their partners—Erin Boyle, Kali Lambson, Samantha Posey, and Leah Scandurra, respectively—are the central pieces of the family constellation that is central to my life. And they are the sources of our grandchildren, named in the dedication. The grandkids represent the lights on the horizon, the promise of a better future perhaps in keeping with the dreams of 1968, as well as the 1960s in general. On a day-to-day basis, they represent the most wonderful component of my life, the pinnacle of my happiness.

Peggy Stockman has been engaged in this project since its inception. She was the first person to whom I showed the outline that I initially sketched out for a book on 1968. Her enthusiasm led me to the next steps. Over the course of the writing, she has listened to my ideas and made numerous suggestions, large and small. She is the ideal reader for this work, someone who is not a professional historian but has some familiarity with the events of these years. In addition, she is an excellent editor. As each chapter came off the printer, Peggy read it meticulously, improving the syntax as well as suggesting what a reader needed to know to fully understand the arguments. Every line is better for her efforts. Similarly, every aspect of my life is likewise better for her daily efforts—or, actually, for her just being there.

The revolution is a festival of ideas and actions.

—*John Reed,*
Ten Days That Shook the World, *1919*

Time has come today
Young hearts can go their way
Can't be put off another day…
Time has come today

—*The Chambers Brothers*
"Time Has Come Today," 1968

Introduction

The Whole World Is Watching

*Children in the next century will learn about the year 1968
the way we learned about the year 1848.*

—*Hannah Arendt*
June 1968[1]

It is not clear if the children of the twenty-first century are being taught about 1968 in the way children in the twentieth were taught about 1848—the year when a wave of democratic revolutions swept across Europe, erupting in dozens of counties from France to Poland, Italy to Scandinavia. In fact, it is not clear that people younger than Hannah Arendt, who was born in 1906, were taught to understand the meaning of 1848 in the way she and her contemporaries had been. Regardless, there is no question that 1968 remains the most extraordinary single year of the twentieth century. Of course, there were other years when significant events erupted, years that only need to be named to evoke powerful images—1914, 1917, 1929, 1945. In these years, however, we can usually identify a single event that marked that year as exceptional—the Russian Revolution in 1917 (that shook John Reed's world), the Stock Market Crash in 1929—and that established the year as extraordinary. But in no year did so many events erupt in so many far-flung corners of the globe as in 1968. Hannah Arendt expressed her opinion about the year becoming momentous in June of 1968, *before* the Soviet invasion of Prague, the Chicago Democratic Convention, the boardwalk demonstrations at the Miss American Pageant, the massacre and Olympic Games protests in Mexico City, and more. Every month of the year brought new headlines about another world locale erupting around a local issue but seemingly connected to larger undercurrents circling the world.

Each event can stand on its own as a transformative and compelling moment of crucial importance to its people and locale. We nonetheless can also see connections among them, not all reacting to the impact of one specific event or spurred by some unicausal explanation but influenced by themes and impulses that rippled through society—enlightening people, connecting people, and moving people.

A number of analysts have pointed out that 1968 sits roughly halfway between the emergence of the Cold War after 1945 and its demise in the late 1980s. This is not accidental. By 1968, Cold War thinking and strategies had dominated the world stage for over two decades, with the two superpowers of the era—the United States and the Soviet Union—developing policies based on its presumptions. By the second half of the 1960s, the flaws in the Cold War thinking of both powers were becoming increasingly evident. The small cracks that began to appear almost immediately in the 1940s had grown to serious fissures.

One of the central stories of the post-World War II world was the end of colonialism and the creation of independent nations throwing off the bonds of imperial rule. At times, the transition was peaceful, more often the result of anti-colonial uprisings. Across Africa, Asia, and Latin America, peoples controlled by the Western powers (the United States and Europe) moved to secure their national freedom and autonomy. The arrival of these new, independent states created a series of arenas for competition between the Americans and the Soviets. It is often difficult to remember that along with the Cold War tension came a competition between utopian visions of the future. Both the U.S. and the USSR offered the world images of a brighter tomorrow—the American image of an affluent world of democratic, bourgeois capitalism and the Soviet's picture of a workers' paradise. Each of the superpowers laid out these visions for the countries emerging from colonialism. The best path lay with them, they each claimed. A new nation choosing to follow the path of one, however, became a threat to the other.

The actual motivations behind the rosy images put forward by the superpowers became apparent when each acted to respond to situations not to their liking. In 1956, reform impulses within Hungary led to anti-Soviet street actions and moves toward governmental reform. Within weeks, Soviet troops invaded Hungary, joining with troops already stationed there, to arrest the reform leadership and put down the insurgency. Instead of sending in ground troops, the U.S. had, over the first decade of the Cold War, covertly instigated actions masterminded by the Central Intelligence Agency (the CIA) in locales around the globe to topple governments and create change it believed beneficial to American interests, including in Iran (1953) and Guatemala (1954).

Despite his popularity with the American public, Fidel Castro's assumption of power in Cuba in 1959 almost immediately led to plans within the Eisenhower Administration to overturn the Cuban revolution. In the first months of the new Kennedy Administration, barely two years after Castro's coming to power, CIA-trained and equipped Cuban exiles landed at the Bay of Pigs, intending to spark a counterrevolutionary uprising among Cubans. The uprising never materialized; the landing proved a fiasco. The CIA continued to pursue anti-Castro programs, including various plans to assassinate the Cuban leader, which were made public during Congressional investigations into CIA activities in the 1970s. To anti-imperialists throughout the world, the Cuban leadership appeared to represent the new, youthful, anti-imperial forces emerging in the post-colonial world. Castro was depicted as a kind of "Robin Hood in the Caribbean,"[2] the coterie around him seeming as dynamic and romantic as Fidel, himself, including the Argentinean-born revolutionary Ernesto "Che" Guevara.

When the newly independent Congo appeared to be heading down a path that threatened American interests, the U.S. again intervened. The CIA, according to one internal document declassified in 2014, "conducted a series [of] covert action operations...to stabilize the government and minimize communist influence."[3] Fearing that the new Congolese Prime Minister, Patrice Lumumba, might be too sympathetic to the communists, CIA director Allen Dulles concluded that his "removal must be an urgent and prime objective and that under existing conditions this should be a high priority of our covert action." The plan was not only to remove Lumumba from office but facilitate his assassination. He was arrested and executed in January 1961, only seven months after first being sworn in. A few years later Dulles did admit, "I think that we overrated the Soviet danger . . . in the Congo.[4] Power ultimately ended up in the hands of Mobutu Sese Seko, the leader of the armed forces that had deposed Lumumba. Mobutu initially helped install a new government but then took control in a second coup a few years later. Somewhat more congenial to American interests, he would serve as absolute leader for the next 35 years.

In Vietnam, the U.S. initially tried the same kinds of behind-the-scenes actions to support the French in their failed war to retake their former colony after the Japanese surrendered in 1945. When the French effort collapsed, the U.S. supported the pro-American government it had created in the southern half of the country and stood against the Communist government that controlled the north. As we will see in Chapter 4, over the first half of the 1960s, it became increasingly clear to the U.S. government that covert actions, including the plot against and ultimate assassination of its own hand-picked leader of South Vietnam, Ngo Dinh Diem, as well as its supporting role in the South Vietnamese government's battle against the National Liberation Front (the Viet Cong), were insufficient. By 1965, American "advisers," as they were called, were replaced by ground troops. The American effort in Vietnam was now as publicly overt as the Soviets had been in Hungary.

As U.S. involvement in Vietnam began to grow, so too did an organized opposition to that involvement. An antiwar movement, as we shall see, developed in the U.S. and would help shape much of the history of the second half of the decade. In addition, opposition began to emerge around the world. Demonstrations against American policies and actions in Southeast Asia erupted in capitals from London and Paris to Ottawa and Tokyo. This put American foreign and military policy at the center of what was perceived as a worldwide struggle against capitalism and imperialism and created an international solidarity among students and protestors across national boundaries. A 1966 anti-Vietnam war rally in Europe, for example, included participants from France, Sweden, Norway, Italy, the Netherlands, West Germany, and Austria, all declaring their solidarity with the anti-war protestors in the United States. On the day of a major demonstration at the Pentagon in October 1967, rallies of support were held in numerous cities across Europe and in Japan.

While Che Guevara held a number of positions in the new post-revolution Cuban government, he also became, a "revolutionary statesman of world stature."[5] Before the United Nations in 1964, he castigated the organization for its failure to deal with South African apartheid, as well as criticizing the American treatment of its own Black citizens. In the same speech, he described Latin America as a "family of 200 million." He critiqued not just "Yankee monopoly capitalism," but the union of northern hemisphere nations, including the Soviet Union, which had colonized and exploited the nations of the Southern hemisphere.[6] Following his UN speech, Che's travels included stops in Paris, Prague, Ireland, Beijing, North Korea, and a number of African capitals. Soon after returning to Cuba, Guevara disappeared from public life. He reappeared in the Congo in 1965, where he joined pro-Lumumba rebels opposed to the new government. In 1966 he joined rebels in Bolivia, where he was ultimately captured and executed by government troops in 1967. Che would become an icon of rebellion and revolution throughout the world of 1968, his recognizable portrait on countless placards and walls.

Che proved a central voice in making left-wing politics global. In 1966, Havana hosted the Tricontinental Conference, a gathering of 500 delegates from 82 Asian, African, and Latin American liberation movements, aimed at creating a united front of anti-colonial and anti-imperial forces. Among the delegates were Chile's future president Salvador Allende, who would himself be deposed and executed in a covert CIA plot several years later as well as a representative of the Viet Cong. Che sent a long message from Bolivia, in which he assessed the international situation, titled "Create two, three...many Vietnams."[7] That phrase would become a rallying cry not only for anti-colonial struggles but also, as we shall see, echoed in a variety of confrontations in 1968.

One compelling element of the confrontations that grew in the postwar years, especially among those supporting the liberation and autonomy of the colonized states, concerned the racial basis of the struggles. The colonizers had been white Europeans; the oppressed black, brown, and yellow. The emergence of what was coming to be called a Third World consciousness was built on both the post-colonial reality and the racial identity of the colonized. This coincided with the growing international prominence of the American civil rights movement. Martin Luther King became a figure of global renown. He symbolized the heroic struggle in the United States against its institutionalized racial discrimination. But King's association with Gandhi and with the tactics of nonviolence connected him and the civil rights movement to the international anti-colonial struggle. As early as 1960, King had identified the American civil rights movement as part of "a worldwide struggle" centered on Africa and Asia, which African Americans watched, he noted, "with rapt attention." It was "a drama being played on the stage of the world with spectators and supporters from every continent."[8]

Another element crucial to the confrontations was generational. The postwar baby boom did not just occur within the United States but across the developed world. In France, for example, a third of the population in 1963 was under the age of 20, which meant they had no direct memory of the Second World War, a pattern that was replicated in numerous countries, including Britain, Mexico, and Czechoslovakia. This also meant that the student population of many nations grew significantly in the postwar years. As a university education became more widely available to young people, and as their numbers continued to grow, students became a distinct social element in their country's population. Students and young people, in general, became a self-conscious group focusing on both the limitations of their own situations as well as coming together to deal with larger social and political problems. "We are people of this generation," began the Port Huron Statement (1962), the organizing document of Students for a Democratic Society (SDS), "bred in at least modest comfort, housed now in universities, looking uncomfortably to the world we inherit." They defined themselves by their age more than their class position or race. Young civil rights activists in the early 1960s declined becoming an adjunct of an older civil rights organization, including a direct invitation from King's Southern Christian Leadership Conference (SCLC), and instead created the independent Student Nonviolent Coordinating Committee (SNCC). And in 1964, students at the University of California, Berkeley, organized the Free Speech Movement (FSM) to confront issues on their campus, leading to the first major confrontation of the student movement. These developments not only had a profound impact on American student life, as we shall see, but found sympathetic ears throughout the world as well. In 1966, for example, students at the French University of Strasbourg published, *De la misère en milieu étudiant* (*On the Misery of Student Life*). It became one of the most widely read tracts of the decade. Young people would be central to virtually all the actions and movements of 1968, within the United States and around the world.

By the 1960s, the world was increasingly linked by various media forms, none more prominent than television. People no longer had to wait to read about events in other cities, other countries, or far-flung world locales. Images appeared within hours on television screens everywhere. Of course, these were not the instantaneous imagery of contemporary media but, compared to what was possible only a few years before, they made awareness and participation more immediate and more personal. Vietnam came to be called the "living room war," as footage from Southeast Asia appeared on television news programs within 24 hours. Images from the confrontations on the streets of Chicago at the Democratic Convention were broadcast a few hours after they occurred. This did more than inform the public. It created bonds of solidarity. French student leader Daniel Cohn-Bendit, for one, came to feel a sense of comradeship with student leaders around the world. "We met through television, through seeing pictures of each other. We were the first television generation . . . we had a relationship with what our imagination produced from seeing pictures of each other on television.[9] It was not just hyperbole that led the demonstrators at the 1968 Democratic Convention to chant, "The whole world is watching!"

The expanded media forms carried the images and the messages of the emerging counterculture that, while not limited to the young, found its most receptive audience and its more prominent practitioners among them. Counterculture expressions occurred in virtually all the artistic forms, but none more powerful or ubiquitous than rock 'n' roll. The music was written for the young, made by the young, listened to and purchased by the young. It defied national boundaries, again creating solidarity among young people the world over. As one music critic put it, "The closest Western Civilization has come to unity since the Congress of Vienna in 1815 was the week" in June of 1967, "when the [Beatles'] *Sgt. Pepper* album was released...In every city in Europe and America the stereo systems and radios played [it] and everyone listened."[10] The kids in Prague weren't listening to the Voice of America or Radio Free Europe. They were listening to music programs on Western European radio stations. The artistic forms within the counterculture fed one another and created bonds with the political movements of the era. Barry Melton, lead guitarist of the San Francisco Bay Area psychedelic rock band Country Joe and the Fish, later identified his group as "one of the house bands of the antiwar movement."[11]

As might be expected, government officials from Washington to Paris to Moscow responded to the student movement and the growing activism and militancy of young people with explanations and critiques that had been repeated for years. In the U.S., the villains were communist agitators who had infiltrated and provoked the movements. Or it was the fault of permissive child rearing practices in the 1950s that created a generation of undisciplined and irresponsible young people. These attitudes would find expression in the views of political leaders finding fault with the student movements, from Charles de Gaulle to Richard Nixon to George Wallace.

But the governments actually knew better. Surprisingly, perhaps, two of the most clear-headed analyses came from the intelligence networks of the superpowers, the CIA and the KGB. On September 1968, the CIA sent Lyndon Johnson's National Security Adviser, Walt Rostow, a confidential analysis titled "Restless Youth," which Rostow forwarded to the president. "Youthful dissidence, involving students and non-students alike," the report concluded, "is a world-wide phenomenon." While admitting that local conditions shaped the activities, "there are striking similarities." And, the CIA feared, "as the underdeveloped countries progress, these similarities are likely to become even more widespread." The CIA fully understood the new reality. "Communications, the ease of travel, and the evolution of society everywhere," had changed student behavior forever. It would never again "resemble what it was when education was reserved for the elite. The presence in the universities of lower- and lower-middle-class students has resulted in an unprecedented demand for relevant instruction." What the students and other young people had felt was developing, the CIA confirmed. "Today's students are a self-conscious group; they communicate effectively with each other outside of the institutional framework, read the same books and savor similar experiences." Despite public dismissal by the powers that be, intelligence organizations understood the new reality. "Increasingly, [the students] have come to recognize what they take to be a community of interests." The report went on to analyze movements across Europe, from France and West Germany to Poland and the USSR. In addition, analysis covered non-European states in Africa, the Middle East, and Asia.[12]

Two months after LBJ read the CIA's analysis, Leonid Brezhnev received a similar report from his intelligence service. The KGB found that among students, "the very word 'opposition' is something students find appealing, and even the most thoughtful of them regard the creation of an opposition party as a solution." While some students shared the Soviet government's attitude toward the events that had transpired in Czechoslovakia in 1968 and the harsh Soviet response, most "generally take pleasure in anything that causes problems for or conflicts with the official line...They are impressed by the Czech students, who have become a major social force. Some even contemplate (albeit hypothetically) the possibility of repeating the Czech experience in our own country."[13]

Whatever the nature of the confrontations, the struggles of 1968 were clearly played out on a world stage created by the Cold War. And they also dramatically revealed growing weaknesses and limitations within the Cold War vision. To many, the events and impact of the Tet Offensive— the massive North Vietnamese and Viet Cong military offensive of January 1968—and the Prague Spring—the anti-Soviet reform uprising in Czechoslovakia—served as perfect representations of the growing failures of the ideologies of the two superpowers.[14] And there is much truth to that conclusion. But it is also clear that there is more to understanding the year than the playing out of the problems and conflicts of a world created by the US and the USSR. There were just too many elements of confrontation that did not fit neatly with the Cold War model. A few years later, a map of the world was published with a star at the site of every student disruption of 1968 and 1969. There are stars in countries on every continent, with so many overlapping in Europe, across the Eastern seaboard and the West Coast of the Unites States, and in Japan that they are impossible to count. And the rest of the world—Latin America, South and Southeast Asia, Australia, and Africa—was not far behind.[15] While the superpowers of the era shaped policy and practice in the world and created the arena of struggle, the wave of so many disruptions in places so far flung, and all within the same short period, suggest other factors—social, political, and demographic—at play.

What follows traces many of the crucial moments of 1968 from an American perspective. While several of the crucial moments occur in other countries, and certainly reflect issues central to that nation, they remain connected, in ways that will be explained, to the currents and actions that took hold in the United States. This proved to be true for much of the world. America was just too powerful—militarily, economically, and culturally—and what happened in the United States always seemed to have some measure of impact abroad. Often it was direct and intentional, as American economic investment or military involvement were intended to shape the world in ways the U.S. government found most pleasing. But in other areas, especially cultural, it was more indirect. Culture was big business in America—especially with movie studios and record companies—and part of that business was to market it internationally. People around the world might see films made by their own filmmakers, but everyone saw the movies that Hollywood produced. Local musicians might make music that their fellow citizens heard and appreciated, but everyone listened to Elvis Presley.

Looking back at the decade of the 1960s, it is clear many of the social and political movements within the United States had reached an explosive point by 1968. The civil rights movement had expanded to include Black Nationalism and Black Power. The once genteel anti-Vietnam War movement's critique grew increasingly strident, reacting not just to individual events or even to the overall Southeast Asian engagement but also to the entire basis of American foreign policy. In addition, the antiwar movement's tactics grew much more militant and sometimes violent. New constituencies, such as American women, began to challenge their secondary status more openly and to organize for their liberation. As the decade progressed, the efforts gained momentum, grew exponentially, and moved increasingly toward more direct action. Things developed over *time* to a point where people began to use the word "revolution" or terms such as "social transformation." And that point seemed to be 1968.

And things began to move across what I would call the *space* of late sixties America, as well, linking one movement with others, individuals feeling stronger and stronger connections with one another, both in terms of ideas and tactics. People had come to believe they were part of an effort to transform the very nature of American society—what many began to call "The Movement."

It was the convergence of these two—the interrelation of the movements as well as the emergence of "The Movement" over time and space—that helped create the explosive context of 1968, that led Hannah Arendt to conclude, just halfway through the year, that this was to be the most important year of the twentieth century.

This book falls into two parts. The first part, "The Movements," briefly traces the evolution of some of the movements of the era over the 1960s, indicating where they had arrived by 1968. These provide the 1960s context for the events of 1968. The second part, "When the World Shook," deals with the events of '68, themselves. In some cases, one significant moment would come to frame the context for another, becoming links in a chain—the reaction to the Tet Offensive fueling the insurgency in the Democratic Party around Eugene McCarthy that led to the campaign and tragedy of Robert Kennedy and on to the Chicago Democratic Convention. At other times the impact of one larger movement emerged elsewhere in a less direct way, such as the complementary motives and sense of connection that developed among students in Prague, at New York's Columbia University, and in Mexico City.

Taken together, all these events—directly and indirectly connected— and all the people caught up in them, as well as the way the rest of the world looked at what was going on around them, combined to create an extraordinary year. For so many the earth beneath their feet began to tremble. Political and social transformation seemed to be at hand across the country and around the world. The earth shook and people began to wonder whether what they were witnessing would bring about a new day and a new reality. Regardless of what we know about the ultimate outcome of all these tremors, to live through it all was to live through a year when the world seemed to be shaken to its roots.

PART
I

The Movements

I

Rumblings Beneath the Surface Calm

The 1950s as Prologue to the 1960s

They seem to stand in marked contrast in the popular imagination.*

The Fifties: white middle-class families, suburban homes, backyard barbecues, big cars with tail fins, "Leave It to Beaver," Little League and Girl Scouts, peace, prosperity, and stability.

The Sixties: civil rights sit-ins, students seizing college buildings, urban violence, anti-war demonstrations, Black Power salutes, hippie love-ins, draft card burnings, death and destruction in Vietnam, police riots in Chicago, obscenities, hostilities, and killings at Kent State and Jackson State.

As the periods receded in memory, these depictions hardened into stereotypes rather than accurate representations of the complexity of the times. We look back on the harmonious 1950s and the turbulent 1960s and remember them in stark opposition—snapshots that have come to symbolize these decades.

Yet if we look more closely at these decades, we can see them as more complicated and interrelated. The obvious tensions and anxieties of

---

* This chapter is a revised version of the introduction, "Past as Prologue," to Alexander Bloom & Wini Breines, eds., *Takin' It to the Streets: A Reader.* New York: Oxford University Press, 4/e, 2015, 1–10.

postwar America—the Cold War, fear of the atom bomb, McCarthyism—undermine the image of the calm and peaceful fifties. Concerns about race and gender further demonstrate that this era was not nearly so harmonious for minorities and women. We now understand more clearly the fault lines within family life, the pressures on men and women resulting from rigid gender roles, the large numbers of Americans—of all races—who felt left out of the suburban dream of the good life. All these suggest an era far more anxious, questioning, and discordant than commonly understood.

Conversely, much of what emerged in the 1960s does not seem to reflect a country torn by discontent and division: the counterculture's focus on "love," the hedonistic embrace of new lifestyles, the excitement of the 1968 presidential campaigns of Eugene McCarthy and Robert Kennedy. These enthusiasms intertwine with the intense anger over the Vietnam War, the tragic losses of assassinations, and the turbulence in the streets and on college campuses. Instead of a picture of society in upheaval, we find a mixed portrait—optimism coupled with hostility, visions of a "greening of America" jumbled with fears about an emerging quasi-fascist "Amerika." Again, all this suggests a decade more complex than the snapshot suggests.

Memory compresses the past, so that it seems as if the nation was pacific at one moment, then exploding in the next. But deeper analysis of the two eras reveals continuities between them. The civil rights movement began in the 1950s. Little Leaguers and Girl Scouts of the fifties grew up to become the college activists of the sixties. The unhappiness over the prescribed roles postwar housewives were asked to play in their "suburban utopias" proved a crucial impetus for the women's movement of the late sixties. Younger women sought new roles beyond limits that had been drawn for their mothers.

These decades are more tangled, more ambiguous, and more interconnected than popular imagery suggests. The events and perspectives of the sixties did not spring full blown and brand new into American life. For the 1960s, the 1950s are the past as prologue.

Throughout the 1950s, signs of the tumultuous days to come appeared amid the apparent harmony of postwar America; ripples in the seemingly calm waters of the era, which would grow to swells and ultimately torrents. A number of critics and iconoclasts, such as political analyst C. Wright Mills or poet Allen Ginsberg, offered critical analyses of American life in the 1950s or led their own lives in ways that were shocking to mainstream America. In a society that valued homogeneity, they were attacked as atypical outsiders. But in the 1960s, as nonconformity and radicalism grew more commonplace, these 1950s apostates found new audiences, and their work took on new significance.

The Cold War was at the heart of postwar America, springing from the international rivalry that developed between the United States and the Soviet Union, a rivalry based on the clash of economic systems; their emergence as the two nuclear-armed superpowers of the period; and their competition to convince the emerging nations of the underdeveloped world to join with one or the other in the postwar binary world of East vs. West. The degree to which Cold War ideology, imperatives, and necessities permeated American life proved extraordinary. The Soviet threat precipitated an enormous buildup in America's defenses. Immediately after World War II, the government had scaled back military spending dramatically. Within a few years, however, it had grown to monumental size for a nation not at war. This arms buildup had a significant impact on domestic life as well. No longer protected by the oceans that separated them from most of the world, and with constant reminders of the perceived Soviet threat, Americans came to believe that atomic war was not only possible but likely. Local citizens and school children practiced nuclear attack drills, and localities tested their civil defense sirens regularly. Some people built fallout shelters in their backyards, in which a family could take shelter for long periods of time during and after an atomic attack.

Foreign upheavals seemed to represent not the expression of local domestic issues, but a manifestation of the larger world struggle. Conflicts in Guatemala, Iran, the Congo, and many other sites were viewed only as Cold War outposts, perceived primarily as how they would fit into struggle with the Soviets. Nowhere was this viewpoint more apparent, or more misconceived, than in Vietnam.

In the U.S., fears of Soviet bombs raining from the skies were matched by the specter of Soviet agents penetrating the fabric of American society. These supposed subversives were not only the spies of the KGB, but American leftists purportedly working for Soviet interests. Beginning soon after the end of World War II, extraordinary measures were taken to root out these suspected traitors. Investigations into "communist activities" were initiated by various forces, from congressional committees to internal investigations by universities, school systems, labor unions, and the entertainment industry. Civil liberties were constricted, thousands lost their jobs, books were banned, passports lifted—all rationalized as necessary to protect the home front in the fight against communism.

Public trials focused attention on the issue. American Communists were tried and jailed for sedition. Former State Department official Alger Hiss ran afoul of the House Un-American Activities Committee, especially one of its members, California freshman congressman Richard Nixon. Accused of passing secrets to a Soviet agent in the 1930s, Hiss proclaimed his innocence and denied ever having even been a communist. After two trials, he went to jail for perjury. When the Soviets detonated their own atom bomb in 1949, cold war panic rose to new heights. The fears of pervasive Soviet espionage led to accusations that America's nuclear secrets had been stolen. Americans Julius and Ethel Rosenberg were charged with stealing one of those secrets. Tried in an atmosphere of intense anticommunism, they were, despite serious questions about the evidence presented, convicted in 1951 and, ultimately, executed in 1953. At their sentencing, the judge not only cited their supposed espionage and treason but held them responsible for the Korean War— illustrating the degree and intensity of anti-communist sentiment.

In 1950, searching for an issue to spark his reelection bid, Wisconsin Senator Joseph McCarthy announced that he possessed the names of numerous individuals within the State Department who were "known communists." (Never actually identifying any single individuals, the number McCarthy cited shifted over time as his assertions came under scrutiny.) McCarthy tossed unsubstantiated accusations wildly. His final charge, that the U.S. Army was trying to stop McCarthy's investigation of communist infiltration of American army posts, led to the 1954 televised public Congressional investigation known as the "Army-McCarthy Hearings," during which McCarthy's questionable tactics and mean spiritedness were exposed. Condemned by the Senate, McCarthy faded from public view and died in 1957. But his demise did not mark the end of the anti-communist crusade.

Anti-communist prerogatives remained at the heart of American foreign policy as well as a central concern of domestic American life. Institutions outside the government—Hollywood, labor unions, school districts, colleges and universities—had moved to follow the federal lead. Throughout the 1950s, anticommunism shaped American events in international relations, domestic politics, and local activities. It precipitated a view, reinforced by the tensions of the Cold War, that the world was a troubled place rife with agents of foreign powers bent on undermining American life. This mindset proved to hold little sway, however, with the emerging younger generation.

A crucial domestic issue of the 1950s proved much more important for this younger group. Beginning in the middle 1950s, the movement to end the legalized segregation of the races that existed in a large portion of the country sprang to public prominence. In the late nineteenth century, institutionalized segregation in many Southern and border states had created separate facilities for Black and white people in schools, hotels, waiting rooms, restaurants, restrooms, drinking fountains, buses, and more. African Americans had been systematically disenfranchised as voters, excluded from juries, and prohibited from marrying white people. Ruling in 1896 that facilities could be "separate" as long as they were "equal," the Supreme Court had deemed all of this constitutional. Legal segregation spread not only throughout the Deep South but also into Kansas, southern Illinois, Missouri, Delaware, Maryland, and even the nation's capital.

While movements to attack segregation had begun early in the twenti-eth century, often spearheaded by the National Association for the Advancement of Colored People (NAACP), their success was limited. Focusing on education, the NAACP Legal Defense Fund had won a series of small victories in the 1930s and 1940s. Its assault on school segre-gation culminated in the 1954 Supreme Court decision, *Brown v. Board of Education of Topeka, Kansas,* which declared school segregation unconstitutional. While Southern school districts managed for years to block or stall much of the desegregation of their schools, the decision nonetheless marked both a turning point in civil rights activities and the most important civil rights decision in the Court's history.

A new consciousness began to grow among many Southern Black people who were no longer willing to tolerate the unpunished physical abuse visited upon them by white people. The brutal murder in 1955 of fourteen-year-old Emmett Till in Mississippi epitomized the situation for many. His two white assailants were acquitted in a matter of minutes by an all-white jury, despite being identified as Till's abductors. Future civil rights activist Anne Moody recalled, "I was fifteen years old when I began to hate people. I hated the white people who murdered Emmett Till…But I also hated Negroes. I hated them for not standing up and doing something about the murders."[1]

This growing sense of resistance prompted many Black people to adopt new behavior with regard to their rights. In December 1955, riding home from work on a Montgomery, Alabama bus, Rosa Parks refused to give up her seat to a white man. Parks' case became the springboard for the organization of the Black community of Montgomery into collective action to boycott the buses until the situation improved for Black riders. It also catapulted a young Montgomery minister, Martin Luther King, Jr., to national prominence. During the year-long boycott, King refined his philosophy of nonviolent direct action as the means for battling seg-regation. Ultimately victorious, the boycott initiated a series of direct confrontations with segregated institutions, often spearheaded by King's new civil rights organization, the Southern Christian Leadership Conference (SCLC).

School desegregation battles frequently captured national headlines. The 1957 order to desegregate Central High School in Little Rock, Arkansas, led to a clash between state and federal authorities. When school opened on September 4 of that year, white mobs threatened the Black students. Arkansas governor Orval Faubus called out, and then withdrew, the National Guard. This left the students at the mercy of the mob that had gathered. President Eisenhower, feeling he had been double-crossed by Faubus, sent federal troops to Little Rock to facilitate desegregation and to ensure the students' safety. The troops remained stationed in Little Rock for the entire school year.

By 1960, civil rights had become the nation's most pressing domestic issue, capturing the attention of the young. Young Blacks, and then young whites, found their first real political cause.

Throughout the postwar years, America's political, social, and religious leaders had trumpeted what they saw as the many virtues of contemporary society. No matter what one's class or race, the values they saw embodied in the white middle-class American family were hailed. Traditional gender-differentiated roles of American adults provided the structure within which children matured, leading to an era of domestic tranquility. Celebrated in popular novels, movies, and, especially, on television, the stereotypical white nuclear family appeared to offer prosperity, harmony, and security for everyone.

The images were continually reinforced. Situation comedies, developed for the exploding television medium, offered one "typical" American family after another: the Cleavers on *Leave It to Beaver*, the Nelsons of *The Adventures of Ozzie and Harriet*, the Stones of *The Donna Reed Show*, and the Anderson clan who believed that *Father Knows Best*. White, middle-class, and suburban, these television families and countless others created by the media suggested that "real life" was to be found at home and not at the workplace. In these depictions, men served as breadwinners, women ran the household, and children's issues emerged as their major concern. Fathers monopolized the earning power of the family as well as possessing the rationality to settle family issues.

They "knew best." Fathers would return home from work to find slightly hysterical mothers unable to cope with the latest domestic crisis and calmly settle the matter.

Subsequent analyses suggest that this model of family life was not as widespread as the media made it appear. The number of working wives grew steadily during the 1950s, from 25 percent in 1950 to 32 percent in 1960. Urban families, families of color, poor families, single-parent families, gays and lesbians, and many white, middle-class families shaped their lives—by choice or by necessity—differently.

Even as the realities of their lives differed starkly from those depicted on television, the image of the cheerful white, nuclear family shaped plans and dreams. Those who constructed their lives around it often found it less fulfilling and more problematic than anticipated. Postwar home life had been arranged to serve the new children, the Baby Boomers, who populated postwar America at an amazing rate. They were, however, the first to rebel.

Thousands of suburban housing developments sprang up, offering many American families the chance to own their own homes. These communities attracted young white couples with small children—working fathers, mothers at home, and kids at school. Fearing that unregulated childhood activities might lead the kids into that most-feared snare for fifties youth, juvenile delinquency, structured activities grew rapidly: Little League, Cub Scouts, Boy Scouts, Brownies, Girl Scouts, music lessons, dance classes, and so on. Mothers had to add chauffeur to their other domestic tasks, shuttling children from one activity to another.

It was young people who first began to resist culturally, even before they took a political turn. This can best be clearly seen in the eruption of rock 'n' roll and in the person of Elvis Presley. Hardly understood as a cultural revolution at the time, the ascendancy of rock 'n' roll in mainstream culture in the middle 1950s, epitomized by the enormously popular success of Elvis, marked the clearest differentiation between parents and children of the decade. Growing out of various cultural roots, but especially African American music, rock 'n' roll grabbed white teenagers

with its youth concerns—dating, cars, sex, school, summer, dancing—
and the physical drive of its music. When Elvis Presley first appeared on
The Ed Sullivan Show, in October 1956, camera operators were instructed
to show him only from the waist up, as his swiveling hips were thought
to be too sexual. Parents looked on, aghast; girls swooned; and boys grew
their sideburns longer and slicked their hair into ducktails. Over the
years, rock music would stitch itself into the American cultural fabric—
first, as a sign of teenage rebellion and then, in the 1960s, of generational
identification.

For many, the 1950s were not an era of harmony but anxiety. Poor and
ghetto youths found their adolescent issues joined with concerns about
education, after-school work, both parents working outside the home,
and generally by how little their lives matched that of the "typical" media
families. Young people throughout the culture began to question their
place and their prospects, albeit in different settings. And everywhere
music punctuated youth culture. While adults frequently predicted the
end of these music "fads," one group, Danny and the Juniors, spoke for
many young people when, in their 1958 hit song, they proclaimed, "rock
'n' roll is here to stay." The sixties would prove them right.

As young people grew older, they subjected the assumptions of their
parents' lives to direct questioning. Without a background of depression
and war, the desire for material possessions and family stability proved
much weaker for the postwar generation. The virtues of suburban life
seemed less appealing; the problems of America more compelling.

In the immediate postwar world, the only socially acceptable path
available to a young, white middle-class woman was to become a wife
and mother. For young women, the eventual goal was to find a husband.
They were not encouraged to think of their futures in terms of work or
careers. While some were expected to go to college, the question became
to what end. The cliché that young women went to college to get their
"M-R-S Degree" was increasingly thought of as patronizing and insult-
ing. In addition, while television and mainstream culture glorified
domesticity, other messages emerged—such as the flamboyant lives of
female movie stars—that conveyed suggestions of feminine sexuality

outside of marriage. Finally, by the late 1950s, women had been joining the labor force in increasing numbers, making it much more difficult to conform to life as a full-time mom. Although the change was not yet obvious, young women's links to their families and adherence to notions of domesticity were loosening.

Middle-class men increasingly found their assigned roles less than fulfilling. The pressures to provide for their families brought about extraordinary strains. Rates of divorce, alcoholism, heart disease, ulcers, and other personal and social disorders all increased. Many housewives likewise found their prescribed places stifling and depressing. When Betty Friedan interviewed other Smith College alumnae 15 years after their graduation, she found many of them unhappy with their lives despite having achieved most of the goals they had once thought would bring happiness— husband, family, home, affluence. Feeling alone in their disappointment, they rarely spoke to anyone about their concerns, considering it a personal failing. Their daughters, part of the college-bound generation already questioning the assumptions of fifties America, often recognized that following in their mothers' footsteps would not bring them happiness.

Among the pervasive images of the 1950s is the picture of the American intellectual—often dismissed as an "egghead." Earlier in the century, intellectuals often gathered in bohemian and radical coteries, standing outside of American culture and offering an array of critical analyses. In the postwar years, spurred by economic prosperity and the GI Bill, which provided educational assistance to veterans, colleges and universities expanded in size and influence. Along with thousands of new college students, intellectuals, artists, and writers moved to college campuses. This coincided with a shift in intellectual temperament, as well. Once critics standing outside mainstream American society, many intellectuals now became supporters of the shape of American life, becoming central players in the postwar American consensus.

As with political and social life, intellectual and cultural life in the 1950s reflected the same divided sense of surface harmony and subterranean rumblings. Where once many intellectuals and artists had reveled in their Bohemianism and marginality, along with their postwar respectability came derision for younger intellectuals and cultural figures claiming to be part of a new avant-garde. These radical cultural eruptions were met with mainstream antagonism including doubts about the authenticity of the endeavor. The most prominent group to endure this scorn was the Beats, the cluster of poets and novelists who gathered in Greenwich Village in the late 1940s and early 1950s. With the publication of Allen Ginsberg's *Howl* (1956) and Jack Kerouac's *On the Road* (1957), the Beats gained wider public attention and accolades. They rejected materialism, 9-to-5 jobs, families, monogamy, and respectability, embracing instead explorations of feelings, sexuality, and immediate experience. The mass media dismissed them as self-indulgent, bongo-playing "Beatniks" (the "-nik" added as their coming to prominence coincided with the orbiting of the Russian satellite Sputnik). Many leading intellectuals took equally harsh aim. One older literary critic, Diana Trilling, dismissed the Beats as being equivalent to kids in a nursery school, their clothes and personal style merely a pose. They, in fact, "desperately wanted to be respectable," she declared. A younger literary critic, Norman Podhoretz, labeled them "know-nothing bohemians," claiming that the Beats' claims of "primitivism" served as "as a cover for an anti-intellectualism so bitter that it makes the ordinary American's hatred of eggheads seem positively benign."[2]

Despite this scorn, Beat life attracted many young people. Living for immediate experience and a disdain for making money, the Beats were progenitors of the youth revolts of the 1960s. Allen Ginsberg became an important figure, while Kerouac's books continued to inspire youthful readers. Neal Cassidy, the model for Kerouac's hero in *On the Road*, would reappear among the Merry Pranksters who followed novelist Ken Kesey in the drug culture of late sixties San Francisco.

There were other rumblings beneath the surface complacency of fifties culture—stirrings either ignored or dismissed by mainstream critics—that would find new adherents in the tumultuous world of sixties culture. In 1947 an avant-garde theatrical group, The Living

Theatre, began putting on plays in living rooms and later in very small performance spaces. By the 1960s, however, its notions of radical theater meshed with the emerging cultural vision of the new era. A holdover from the fifties avant-garde, the Living Theatre became one of the most central and infamous artistic institutions of the decade that followed.

In the visual arts as well, new modes appeared to contest the prevailing forms. When Pop Art sprang to public attention in the late 1950s, it was initially derided as simplistic and silly. Cartoon figures, soup cans, soft sculptures of everyday objects—all these seemed unlikely and unserious subjects for artistic representation. Initially, few appreciated the implicit critique of materialism embedded in these works. Pop Art and it practitioners, especially Andy Warhol, would find growing audiences in the 1960s.

Some young novelists who began to write in the postwar years found few readers and little critical response, as their work appeared alien to prevailing sensibilities. Novels set in World War II offered one example. The satiric wartime vision of Joseph Heller in *Catch-22*, which Heller began in 1953 and published in 1961, contrasted with the searing realism of other World War II novels, such as Norman Mailer's *The Naked and the Dead* (1948) or James Jones's *From Here to Eternity* (1951). By the mid-1960s, however, Heller's view of war found ever-larger audiences as it connected with contemporary attitudes, in general, and with the growing cynicism about Vietnam, in particular. Similarly, the offbeat sensibilities expressed in the early novels of Kurt Vonnegut, Jr., such as *Cat's Cradle* (1960), confounded critics and readers. Relegated to the science fiction section of bookstores, Vonnegut's view of American life would, like Heller's, acquire increasing numbers of devotees in the new decade.

A different literary corpus grew out of the African-American community: novels and plays that mirrored the growing prominence of racial concerns. Ralph Ellison's *Invisible Man*, published in 1952 and frequently cited as the most influential American novel of the postwar years, swept across twentieth-century Black history, from the segregated South to the Black colleges and, finally, to the radical movements of

Harlem. James Baldwin's novels explored the northern Black experience and homosexuality. On the stage, Lorraine Hansberry's "A Raisin in the Sun" (1959) depicted contemporary Black family life, while LeRoi Jones's (later Amiri Baraka) plays offered even more searing portraits of American racism.

The 1950s spawned iconoclasts, critics, and artistic movements at odds with prevailing notions of American life. Despite being viewed as angry or misguided, or ignored altogether, we can see these postwar artistic rebels as representing early stirrings of the cultural transformations to come. In body and spirit, they began to develop perspectives and styles that would attract disciples and audiences in the new decade, a decade they would play a major role in shaping.

By the early 1960s the postwar consensus—that shared sense of American beneficence, of the harmonious nature of a prosperous American society, as well as general agreement on the essential elements of American domestic and foreign policy—had run its course. National and world events, from college campuses to Vietnam, brought many of its basic tenets of American life into sharp consideration. The students who founded Students for a Democratic Society (SDS) in 1962 clearly felt themselves to be different from their parents, to be "people of this generation." These students and countless others—women, African Americans, Latinos, Native Americans, gays—found common cause and little in 1950s mainstream culture and politics to explain inequalities, restrictions, and discontent or to enable them to analyze the new world. The underground critiques of the 1950s, as well as important movements such as civil rights, offered the first hints of new perspectives and new possibilities, and began to emerge above ground. The young and some of the old—critics of the 1950s consensus, or apostates from it—would join to confront the new realities of the era. And the "Sixties" began.

2

Civil Rights

On Monday, February 1, 1960, just one month into the new decade, four African American students from North Carolina A&T University in Greensboro purchased several items at the local F. W. Woolworth's five-and-dime, then sat down at the lunch counter and ordered coffee. When they were refused service, they vowed to stay until served and remained seated until the store closed that day. Thus began the "sit-in movement." And, in a very real sense, announced that the Sixties in America had begun.

In fact, as we have seen, there was great continuity between the postwar years and what came to be known as the Sixties. It is also clear, however, that the currents that had begun in the 1950s gained speed, gathered many new adherents, staked out new areas of action, and moved from the margins—both left and right—to the center as the years of the decade progressed. Across the landscape—cultural, political, social, legal—new issues emerged, as older issues rose to the surface. People began to organize and act collectively, the ideology and methodology of the movements began to evolve, and—maybe most importantly for our purposes—the movements themselves began to connect with one another, activists sharing ideas and strategies, beginning to feel they were all part of some larger effort. People began to talk about "The Movement" as though there was some seismic shifting of the tectonic plates of American life, and that each of the individual movements and efforts became part of some larger, transformatory whole.

These eruptions, the seeming tectonic shifts, were happening all over the political and cultural terrain—left and right—responding to issues of the place and moment but also connecting with other eruptions. While it is impossible to talk about them all at the same time, jumping back and forth among them would only add confusion to the narrative. What I will do here is to lay out the major areas within American society where the eruptions took place, one by one, and suggest the overlap and interconnections among therm. The hope is to show how these movements evolved over the course of the 1960s, reflecting the development of ideas and strategies over the decade and showing how eruptions in one area created sparks that caught fire in others.

Even before the four A&T students had returned from Woolworth's to campus that Monday night, word had spread of their exploits. The next day, 23 additional students joined them when they returned to Woolworth's. The following day, sit-in demonstrators filled every seat at the lunch counter. By week's end, they were joined by a number of white students from local colleges as well. Hostile white crowds gathered outside the store, brandishing Confederate flags. Unsure of what to do, the Greensboro Woolworth's decided to temporarily close.

Word spread not only in Greensboro but also across the South, especially at the traditionally Black colleges. "I was sitting in a café near my college campus in Atlanta," future civil rights leader Julian Bond later recalled. A student he knew approached him, holding a newspaper with the headline, GREENSBORO STUDENTS SIT-IN FOR THIRD DAY! "Don't you think it ought to happen here?" Bond's friend asked him. "I'm sure it will," Bond replied. "Why don't we make it happen," his friend answered. They each took one side of the cafe and began to talk with other students. Ultimately students from several of Atlanta's Black colleges became involved. They organized and set out to replicate the Greensboro example at Atlanta's downtown lunch counters. "Within a few weeks," Bond recalled, "seventy-seven of us had been arrested."[1]

Nowhere did the sit-in movement stir Black students more than in Nashville. The Nashville Christian Leadership Council (NCLC), an affiliate of Martin Luther King's organization, the Southern Christian Leadership Conference (SCLC), had begun sponsoring civil rights workshops in 1959, led by James Lawson. These proved especially attractive to several students at Fisk University and other local Black colleges. Among the workshop participants were some who would go on to play significant roles in the civil rights movement, including Marion Barry, James Bevel, Bernard Lafayette, John Lewis, Diane Nash, and C. T. Vivian. In late 1959, they even attempted a few small sit-ins at the lunch counters of downtown department stores.

The Greensboro sit-ins galvanized their effort. On February 13, 1960, 124 Nashville students sat in at their local Woolworth's and other downtown establishments. Refused service, they returned—200 strong—five days later. Two days after that 350 sat in. Finally, during the fourth sit-in, a week later, police ordered the demonstrators to leave; and when the students did not, they arrested 81 of them.

By spring, sit-ins had sprung up in over 50 Southern cities. In response to this explosion, SCLC invited 200 student activists, including Julian Bond and the Nashville activists, to come to Raleigh, North Carolina that April. The idea had been to create a kind of student auxiliary of SCLC, but following the suggestion of SCLC's Acting Executive Director, Ella Baker, the students opted to create their own organization. Baker, a longtime civil rights activist, had felt slighted by the young male ministers who ran SCLC and believed they wished to exert too much control over the students.* James Lawson, the influential adviser of the Nashville students, supported Baker. Agreeing with them, the students chose to form their own organization, the Student Nonviolent Coordinating Committee (SNCC).

Beyond the important work that SNCC would do over the following years, its mere founding also suggested something that was new to the political arena. Making "Student" the first word of their name, they were declaring students to be a central and unique entity in the contemporary struggle—akin to workers, farmers, or other groups. The idea of a central

* See chapter 8 for background on Ella Baker.

role for students expanded well beyond civil rights. "Student" would appear in the names of many Sixties organizations. The decade seemed saturated by youth culture, reinforcing the idea that students, and young people in general, were a crucial element—in fact, often at the core of the social transformation. Like never before, age mattered in political and cultural life, and in the 1960s, the age that mattered most was that of the young.

Nineteen sixty was also an election year, one in which race and youth (or at least youthful energy) would play a significant part. The Democratic nominee, John F. Kennedy, projected a youthful image. He was not of the college-aged generation but was, at 43, the youngest nominee any major party had offered in the twentieth century. Despite his personal physical problems, he projected the energy and vigor of an even younger man. His campaign also decided it wanted to make a strong pitch to African American voters but without alienating the white Southern Democrats who were committed to segregation.

Kennedy was able to achieve some measure of Black support by his campaign's response to the arrest of Martin Luther King during a sit-in in Atlanta that fall. When King was sentenced to four months of hard labor, JFK expressed his concern for King's safety to Coretta Scott King. Robert Kennedy, the campaign manager, telephoned the judge in Georgia and was able to achieve King's release, winning the very public support of Rev. Martin Luther King, Sr., a lifelong Republican, who declared, "I've got all my votes and I've got a suitcase and I'm going to take them up there and dump them in his lap."[2] The campaign publicized all of this within the Black community, especially what the Kennedy brothers had done and how Vice President Richard Nixon, the Republican nominee, had done nothing. Again, they tried to spread the word among African Americans but without antagonizing Southern whites. Leaflets were printed describing what the Kennedys had done, which were distributed at Black churches. The 1960 election was one of the closest in U.S. history. Kennedy's gaining 70 percent of the Black vote—up 10 percent from what Adlai Stevenson had received in 1956— proved an essential piece of his winning coalition.

Once inaugurated, Kennedy continued to walk a fine line, trying to placate two major elements of his base, Black voters and Southern white Democrats. He initially tried to reward the Black community through appointments, such as nominating NAACP Legal Defense Fund head, Thurgood Marshall, to the U.S. Court of Appeals and choosing Robert Weaver to head the Federal Housing Authority.

Events in the coming months and years would, however, push the president and his brother Robert, now the Attorney General, to commit more directly to the question of civil rights. The Kennedys would wrestle with the dilemma of ultimately having to decide which constituency, Blacks or Southern whites, was more crucial to the future of their party.

One of the events that would immediately confront the Kennedys was the Freedom Rides. In 1961 another civil rights organization, the Congress of Racial Equality (CORE), decided it was going to test a recent Supreme Court decision that barred segregation in facilities, such as bus stations, that served the interstate transportation network. In 1946, the Court had declared that segregation on interstate buses was unconstitutional. In 1960, in a case argued before the Court by Thurgood Marshall, they extended their ruling to include the local facilities that served those buses. Neither the outgoing Eisenhower administration nor the incoming Kennedy one appeared eager to enforce this ruling. CORE decided to press the matter. Chartering two buses, CORE recruited Black and white volunteers who would ride the buses from Washington to Atlanta and then from Atlanta to New Orleans, attempting to desegregate the lunch counters, waiting rooms, restrooms, and other facilities along the way. A number of the riders, including John Lewis, came from SNCC.

In May, the two buses carrying 13 Freedom Riders, left DC and headed south. Save for one rough encounter in South Carolina, the first leg went relatively smoothly. But as the buses left Georgia and crossed into Alabama, violence escalated. In Aniston, a mob attacked one bus, smashing its windows. On the road out of town, the bus was stopped, a firebomb thrown through a window. The mob first held the doors shut as the bus filled with smoke and then beat the choking Riders as they escaped. The bus burst into flames. The press corps who had been covering the Freedom Rides reported all this. Photos of the burning bus appeared on newspaper front pages across the country.

The second bus pressed on to Birmingham, where it was greeted by yet another angry mob who mercilessly beat the Riders with fists and metal pipes. Though their headquarters was only a few blocks away, police did not arrive at the bus terminal until 10 minutes after the violence began. Later testimony suggested an arrangement for the delay had been worked out between the Birmingham police and the local Ku Klux Klan.

Traumatized by their encounters with violence, the original Riders were offered a flight out of Birmingham on a plane arranged by the Justice Department. CORE leaders feared that their entire initiative was being defeated by the violent actions of Southern whites. But the publicity had spurred various responses in and out of government. U.S. Marshals were ordered into Alabama. The SNCC student contingent in Nashville organized replacement Riders for the battle wearied. Chillingly, as these volunteers gathered in Nashville, many filled out their wills or wrote letters of what was to be done if they were killed. Then they headed to Birmingham. Arrested when they arrived, they were driven to the Tennessee border and released on an empty road in the middle of the night. Rather than heading back to Nashville, they found their way back to Birmingham.

Pressure began to mount on the Kennedy Justice Department to respond to the attacks. In addition to the federal marshals, DOJ official John Siegenthaler was dispatched to meet the bus in Montgomery. When it arrived, the terminal was filled with another mob but no police. Once again, the mob set on the Riders. John Lewis was beaten and left in a pool of his own blood. Others suffered broken bones, concussions, lost teeth, and other serious injuries. Two female Riders, fleeing the mob, ran towards Siegenthaler, who stood by his rental car. Signaling them to get into the car for safety, the mob attacked him, knocking him unconscious and sending him to the hospital. Echoing Birmingham, the Montgomery police arrived 20 minutes after the violence had begun.

All the national publicity resulted in many new volunteers. Robert Kennedy sent additional marshals as well as National Guard troops. When the remaining bus left Montgomery for Jackson, it was provided with a police escort. Peacefully arrested in Jackson, many Riders spent a few months in Mississippi jails. The Freedom Rides never made it to New Orleans but had succeeded in other important ways. The Interstate Commerce Commission would, later that year, ban all segregation in interstate transportation terminals. And, as one civil rights historian put it, they helped create "a self-consciously radical southern student movement."[3]

Over the next several years, as confrontations erupted across the South, the Kennedys kept trying to walk their fine line. But it would become harder and harder. When a federal court ordered the admission of James Meredith, a Black Air Force veteran, to the previously all-white University of Mississippi, the state's governor, Ross Barnett, blocked his admission. Kennedy sent in the National Guard and DOJ officials to escort Meredith to campus and arranged his admission. In response, riots broke out on campus, including the burning of cars and the pelting of National Guardsmen with rocks and bricks. Small arms fire, all coming from the white rioters, resulted in the deaths of two innocent bystanders. The rioting prompted the Kennedys to send additional federal troops to restore calm and guarantee Meredith's safety.

As civil rights events gained momentum, the student groups seized the initiative. Some of the students had become critical of Martin Luther King, thinking his movement was built too strongly on a cult of person-ality and that SCLC had failed to establish grass roots organizations. Black students often sarcastically referred to King as "Da Lawd." As King felt his centrality to the movement slipping, he and SCLC decided to mount a major campaign in Birmingham, a totally segregated city with a history of racial violence. The Black population accounted for 40 percent of the citizens of the city. And Birmingham had, in Police Commissioner Eugene "Bull" Connor, a real-life embodiment of the Hollywood stereotype of a Southern racist sheriff. The plan was to demonstrate for the desegregation of downtown commercial areas, including lunch counter sit-ins and a boycott of the downtown merchants during the Easter shopping season, as well efforts to improve the employment prospects of African Americans whose only opportunities had been jobs at the most menial level.

The first march through downtown resulted in numerous arrests, although Connor had ordered that they were to be carried out in a quiet and restrained manner. King was among those jailed for violating a court injunction and, while held in solitary confinement, he penned a response to local clergymen who had objected to the demonstrations. Writing on the margins of copies of the *Birmingham News*, as well as scraps of paper supplied him by a Black jailhouse worker and a legal pad left by one of his lawyers, his reply became his famous "Letter from a Birmingham Jail." He laid out the basic steps of a nonviolent political campaign, as well as answering the charges that he and his movement were too impatient. "For years now, I have heard the word 'Wait!'" This, in fact, "almost always meant 'Never.'"[4]

What raised the intensity of the Birmingham crusade was the decision to create the Children's March. On May 2, a month after the first marches had begun, thousands of mostly high school-aged students took to the streets, singing as they marched. When arrested, they sang and skipped their way to jail. Connor understood that images of these marches would only unify and enlarge their support. The next day, when thousands more students, including some much younger than the first group, took to the streets, they were met by high-pressure fire hoses and snarling police dogs. Images of these nicely dressed children bloodied by the intense jets of water and fending off vicious attack dogs, shocked the nation. It also enraged the older Black citizens of Birmingham. They took to the streets, confronting the police who again brought out fire hoses and dogs, creating dramatic images that were once more all over the national news.

The national outcry led to hundreds of demonstrations throughout the South. RFK sent Burke Marshall, head of the Civil Rights Division, to negotiate a settlement. While some felt the final settlement was too mild, it did achieve the desegregation of Birmingham's public facilities and increased the opportunities for Black workers to find employment. JFK called the agreement "fair and just" but also ordered troops to Alabama to maintain order. He was still trying to walk that fine line.

But Kennedy and the Democrats could no longer accommodate the two antagonistic constituencies within the base of their party. The time had come to choose. On June 11, JFK went on national television. "We preach freedom around the world, and we mean it, and we cherish our freedom here at home...now the time has come for this Nation to fulfill its promise. The events in Birmingham and elsewhere have so increased the cries for equality." Kennedy then announced that he would introduce a Civil Rights Bill to end discrimination in public facilities. "Next week I shall ask the Congress of the United States to act, to make a commitment it has not fully made in this century to the proposition that race has no place in American life or law."

Many, including Martin Luther King, were cheered by Kennedy's announcement. Southern whites were furious. One segregationist senator called it a "blueprint for a totalitarian state." Walking from his car to his front door that night, Mississippi NAACP field secretary Medgar Evers was shot in the back and died on his front lawn. Evers had been active in Mississippi race issues for a decade, involved in the investigation of the murder of Emmett Till in 1955 and the effort to enroll James Meredith at Ole Miss in 1962. In 1963, he had demanded that the Federal Communications Commission's "equal time" guideline allow him to reply to a televised speech by the segregationist mayor of Jackson. In this talk that May, Evers spoke of both being a "native Mississippian" who fought "in the war against Hitlerism and Fascism"—enlisting at 17 and ultimately taking part in the landing at Normandy—but also as being one of the many Black Americans who "knows from his radio and television" what is going on in the world. "He knows about the new free nations of Africa and knows that a Congo native can be a locomotive engineer but in Jackson he cannot even drive a garbage truck."[5] This speech made Evers an even greater target among Mississippi whites. He survived two attempts on his life, one in late May and the other in early June. But on June 12, a lone gunman was successful. The assassin, Byron

De La Beckwith, a well-known Ku Klux Klan member, was apprehended and tried twice, but both trials ended in a hung jury. (He was finally rearrested and retried in 1994 and found guilty. He died in jail.)

Despite the settlement and the national commitment to civil rights, racial tensions in Birmingham remained high. In September, Klansmen planted explosives at the 16th Street Baptist Church, which were set off on a Sunday morning, killing four young girls, ages 11 and 14, and injuring a number of others.

For several years, various civil rights leaders led by long-time labor organizer A. Phillip Randolph and his associate Bayard Rustin, had been attempting to organize a coalition of race leaders to sponsor a march on Washington for "jobs and justice," planned for the summer of 1963. While the more moderate elements of the civil rights movement, like the NAACP and the Urban League, were cautious, the young and more activist groups, like SNCC and SCLC had signed on. Birmingham and the reaction of the Kennedy Administration changed things. The focus of the march was changed to "jobs and freedom," reflecting the civil rights bill the administration had introduced.

Over the course of the sixties, Washington became a frequent site for large-scale political marches and rallies. But in 1963 this was something new. The logistics were staggering, the planning monumental. Rustin assigned individuals to coordinate everything, from transportation to medical services, parking to restroom facilities. Opposition from the FBI and Southern senators only added to the pressure. Bayard Rustin, who was gay, had been arrested a decade before on sex charges. The organizers had to fend off attacks on its leaders being labeled Communists as well as over Rustin's homosexuality. But the civil rights momentum and general press support limited the impact of these attacks.

Plans had been made to bring marchers from across the country. The DC police commissioner had assigned two-thirds of his force to cover the march, supplemented by 5,000 reservists, National Guardsmen, and Park Service Police. The Washington Senators baseball team cancelled two of their home games, and many businesses shut for the day.

People poured into the nation's capital. Early estimates of 100,000 marchers swelled to 200,000 as the day progressed.

The plan was for Randolph to open the ceremonies, followed by speeches from each of the civil rights leaders. When a copy of John Lewis' planned speech circulated among the organizers, they felt it too harsh and incendiary. Lewis was critical of Kennedy's civil rights bill as being too mild and not dealing with voting rights or police brutality. "Mr. Kennedy is trying to take the revolution out of the street and put it into the courts," Lewis argued. "All of us must get in the revolution. Get in and stay in the streets…the black masses are on the march…We will march through the South…the way Sherman did. We shall pursue our own 'scorched earth' policy and burn Jim Crow to the ground— nonviolently."[6] Lewis agreed to soften his speech, but only a bit. The reference to Sherman was taken out. Even in its revised form, however, Lewis's words suggested that elements of the civil rights struggle had moved beyond traditional liberal approaches.

It had been agreed that King would speak last, as no one wished to follow him. And that was a wise choice. King was at his finest, as history has recorded. His "I Have a Dream" speech soared and is remembered as one of the great American speeches of the twentieth century—or likely ever. Despite the acclaim, King was still viewed with wariness by some of the student activists. "We never had time to sleep, much less dream," Anne Moody would later write.[7]

With the program completed, the leaders went to the White House for a meeting with the president. The day had been historic. Rustin later recalled, "everyone who was there knew that the event was a landmark." It was "one of the great days in American history."[8]

In Congress, Kennedy's Civil Rights Bill, while generally popular with members of both parties, was running into roadblocks thrown up by some Southern senators and representatives, whose seniority gave them committee chairs. The bill was stalled in the House when JFK was assassinated in Dallas on November 22. In his first speech before Congress, after he became president, Lyndon Johnson declared that the greatest memorial they could erect to the fallen president was an early passage of the Civil Rights Bill. Using his considerable legislative skills and powers of persuasion, Johnson was able to secure passage of the bill. This included persuading Republicans to join in the June vote to end a 72-day filibuster by 19 Southern senators.* The Senate then voted to pass the bill, 73 to 27. (The House had voted to pass it 290 to 130 in February). In July, Johnson held a televised White House event to mark the signing of the bill, with hundreds of invited guests including Martin Luther King.

By that July, SNCC was already on the ground in Mississippi, part of a larger strategy to register voters. Called "Freedom Summer," SNCC recruited Black and white, Northern and Southern students, training them in Ohio and then sending them into Mississippi to live in communities, assist in registering voters, teach in Freedom Schools, and support civil rights actions. While still in training in Ohio, the volunteers learned that three civil rights workers—Michael Schwerner, a CORE organizer; Andrew Goodman, a Queens College freshman; and James Chaney, the one African American and, at 21, already a veteran of several civil rights actions—had disappeared in Neshoba County, Mississippi, a Klan stronghold. Their burned-out station wagon was found several days later. After six weeks of searching, the bodies of the three were discovered buried beneath an earthen dam, having been beaten, shot, and, in Chaney's case, mutilated.

Despite their fears, the volunteers pressed on. "I'm so shook up that death just doesn't seem so awful anymore" one volunteer wrote her father. "If they're risking their lives, then so must I."[9] Facing constant harassment, arrests, beatings, and being shot at, the nearly 1,000 volunteers continued their work. They stayed with Black families, tried to convince Black residents to register to vote, and accompanied those who were willing to face the hostile voting registrars. Seventeen thousand people attempted to register, but only 2,000 actually made it onto the

* Of the 19 senators who joined the filibuster, 18 were Democrats. The lone Republican was, ironically, the new senator from Texas, John Tower, who was elected to replace Johnson when LBJ became vice-president in 1961.

voting rolls. The volunteers also worked in Freedom Schools not only teaching literacy and basic skills but also Black history and culture.

Nevertheless, the anxieties remained. Another volunteer wrote home, "Yesterday while the Mississippi River was being dragged looking for the three missing civil rights workers, two bodies of Negroes were found...Mississippi is the only state where you can drag a river any time and find bodies you were not expecting."[10]

The strategy ultimately developed was the creation of an alternative Democratic Party, one that was not closed to African Americans. The plan was to choose a slate of delegates to the National Democratic Convention that August in Atlantic City and to challenge the all-white Mississippi regulars. The new party, the Mississippi Freedom Democratic Party (MFDP), enrolled 60,000 members, held a state convention, and chose 44 "freedom delegates." Before the credentials committee of the national convention, which televised these hearings, they laid out their case in compelling testimony. Among the MFDP's powerful speakers was Fannie Lou Hamer, who powerfully described the enormous hardship of a sharecropper's life as well as the brutal treatment by police that she and others experienced when they were arrested for civil rights' actions. She was joined in testifying by Rita Schwerner, widow of Michael Schwerner, one of the three slain civil rights workers. Lyndon Johnson, who stood unopposed for nomination and planned a smooth and harmonious convention, wanted these hearings and this dramatic testimony off national television. Calling an impromptu news conference, which the networks felt obliged to cover, LBJ made a relatively minor announcement about his vice-presidential choice.

Like his predecessor, Johnson tried to walk a fine line. He feared antagonizing white Southerners in his fall campaign and Southern committee chairs with the power to undermine his Great Society programs. But he did not wish to antagonize the civil rights community either. He instructed his operatives at the convention, including Minnesota Senator Hubert Humphrey to broker a compromise. Humphrey, who had been the floor sponsor of the Civil Rights Bill, desperately wanted to be vice-president. Working out this compromise appeared to him to be a requirement for Johnson giving him the nod. The deal ultimately offered would give two "at-large" seats to the MFDP, with the promise that delegates to all future conventions would be chosen without any racial biases.

While some race leaders, including King and Rustin, thought it the best deal they could get, others, especially the younger activists in SNCC as well as the Mississippians themselves, rejected the offer. "We didn't come all this way for no two votes," proclaimed Fannie Lou Hamer. Sympathetic delegates let the MFDP delegates use their floor passes and they sat-in on the convention floor, in the seats reserved for the all-white Mississippi delegation, before being removed by the sergeant-at-arms. They held a vigil on the boardwalk on the convention's final night, singing freedom songs and chanting civil rights slogans. And then they went home to Mississippi, chastened by their experience.

In a few short years, the movement for racial equality had captured the attention of mainstream America, led to front-page confrontations where injustice was challenged and defeated, saw its leaders elevated to positions of national and international prominence and renown, and forced at least one of the major political parties to seriously reconsider its commitment to civil rights and to pass the most sweeping civil rights legislation in a century, if not ever. Yet, just as the nation seemed to be on verge of a major social transformation, the failure of the Mississippi Freedom Democrats at the 1964 Democratic Convention led many in the civil rights community to question just how deep was the commitment of the federal government and of white political leaders to their cause.

3

The Student Movement and
the New Left

While the events of the civil rights movement proved exceptionally compelling for most Americans during the late 1950s and early 1960s, they held special attraction for young people. The baby boomers of postwar America had grown up in a society their parents' generation praised as the "best of all possible worlds." But among the young, especially those of college age, concerns and critiques about American society in general—and about their own place within it—began to surface, as we have seen.

The civil rights movement demonstrated to them with powerful clarity that their society was steeped in inequality, discrimination, and racist violence. For those looking for an obvious example of where it needed to be reformed and recast, one needed to look no further than institutionalized segregation and American race relations.

The sheer hypocrisy and ugliness of segregation moved many of the young, especially after 1960 and the Greensboro sit-ins, to embrace the civil rights struggle, with its commitment, its courage, and its idealism. The images of people facing down the threat of violence and harm, in nonviolent forms, proved incredibly inspiring. And when self-identified students became a part of the civil rights mix, the call to the young became even clearer. Many of those who would later be identified as leaders of the student movement, the anti-war movement, and the emerging New Left, gained their first major political experience from participation in the civil rights movement, which had direct impact on the other emerging movements of the Sixties. As reporter Jack Newfield concluded, "one word, above all others, has the magic to inspire blind loyalty and epic myth. SNCC."[1]

The young had been a preoccupation of postwar American society, from suburban life to situation comedies to juvenile delinquency. We have seen how youth culture—from Elvis Presley to James Dean—became a significant part of mainstream culture. Adolescent rebellion—inevitable in every generation—took on added weight in a society so focused on the young, especially as there were so many of them. The population of the United States in 1960 was 180 million—50 million of them, or approximately 35 percent, were baby boomers, the highest percentage in U.S. history.*

It was not just popular culture that reflected this shift. John Kennedy had called on young people to commit to making American society and the world at large a better place, from his inaugural call to "ask not what your country could do for you, but what you can do for your country" to the creation of the Peace Corps, sending young Americans around the world to work to improve the lives of people in developing countries. Soon the government added the Volunteers in Service to America (VISTA) program to send young teachers into poverty-stricken areas. Kennedy's call tapped into a wellspring of idealism. "I really believed that I was going to be able to change the world," remembered one baby boomer. Phone calls flooded the White House switchboard after the initial Peace Corps announcement. Queries poured in even before the program was established. And one official recalled that no one asked anything about the salary.[2]

It was the young who first began to feel and then articulate their concerns with the presumptions of postwar America, from the ideology of

---

* Direct comparisons with earlier American populations are difficult to make, as lower overall life expectancy meant a smaller percentage of older Americans. But comparisons to the present day are easier. In recent years, only about 20 to 25 percent of the population has been identified as young.

the Cold War to the limitations of gender roles. It was the kids of the 1950s who became the college students of the 1960s. They had absorbed their sense of power and centrality within the culture and, combined with typical adolescent bravado, would confront the wrongs they perceived and the constraints imposed by authority that they felt. All around them, their generation seemed to wake up to a new day, most often attracted to left-wing movements and ideas. As student leader and civil rights activist Tom Hayden would later put it, "I didn't get political. Things got political."[3]

The American Left, as noted, had been an integral part of 1930s political culture but had been decimated and driven into silence by the Cold War and the pressures and persecutions of McCarthyite America. It had also been plagued by internal warfare with factions squaring off against one another—Socialists against Communists, Stalinists against Trotskyists, and so on. A pillar of postwar intellectual life was the belief that the West had entered a period marked by an "end of ideology."[4] But in the left-wing margins of American political life in the late 1950s, discussions had begun about replacing the moribund left, now characterized as the "Old Left." The need for a "New Left" began to emerge in a number of quarters, although people were unsure of exactly what this meant.

In 1960, the sociologist C. Wright Mills published a "Letter to the New Left" in the British journal *The New Left Review*. Critical analysts had derided the left's "utopianism," Mills claimed; but mirroring the idealistic emotions developing among the young, he declared "is not our utopianism a major source of our strength?" He asked rhetorically, who had become "fed up" with older leftist analysis? Mills answered, "All over the world...the answer is the same: it is the young intelligentsia." It was students and young professors—from the Soviet bloc to Western Europe to the United States—who were challenging their societies. And to critics who dismissed it all as merely "utopian," Mills retorted, "tell that to the Negro sit-ins."[5]

On the margins of student life in the fifties, political activity was quietly developing in the new decade, especially among students at several major universities. The transgressions they perceived in Cold War America stirred them, including the investigations into the personal lives and political ideas of individuals accused of being Communists by the House Un-American Activities Committee (HUAC). When HUAC arrived in 1960 to hold hearings in San Francisco, crowds of student demonstrators, many from UC Berkeley, confronted them. A few years earlier, students at the University of Michigan had demonstrated when a young instructor was suspended and then dismissed for refusing to testify before the same committee. The atomic bomb also stirred political action, with calls for test ban treaties and, as the name of one group suggested, Sane Nuclear Policy. Women organized themselves in Women's Strike for Peace, founded by future Congresswoman and feminist icon Bella Abzug, among others. On November 1, 1961, 50,000 women demonstrated against nuclear weapons in 60 American cities.

In June 1962, 60 members of a small student organization called Students for a Democratic Society (SDS), gathered at Port Huron, a retreat on Lake Michigan lent them by the United Auto Workers. While representatives came from all over the country, the majority were either students at the University of Michigan or had come from New York City. The new activism among students, especially in the civil rights movement, inspired and spurred them. Intending to invigorate their movement and set it in a new direction, they gathered with a great sense of optimism. "We were launching something that had not happened among university students, ever," recalled one attendee.[6] The central task of this meeting was the creation of a manifesto for the developing student movement. It fell to SDS Field Secretary, Tom Hayden, to write the first draft. Hayden, a Michigan student and a veteran of the civil rights movement, had been beaten and jailed in the South. "I didn't want to go from beating to beating, jail to jail," Hayden later wrote. "SNCC could not go on alone. There was an entire generation to arouse."[7] The meeting at Port Huron would be the place to begin this work. Over the course of several days, the delegates worked on Hayden's draft, ultimately agreeing on what became known as the Port Huron Statement.

The statement opened with a telling declaration, "We are people of this generation, bred in at least modest comfort, housed now in universities, looking uncomfortably to the world we inherit." Even before getting to specifics, this opening suggested that this was a left-wing movement very different from the ones that had come before. We are the young ("of this generation"). We are middle class ("bred in at least modest comfort"), following a typical bourgeois path ("housed now in universities"), questioning the life path that they were expected to follow. This was not a revolt of the "have-nots" against the "haves"—workers against bosses, peasants against lords, colonized peoples against imperialists, the dispossessed against the possessors. This was a revolt among the "haves" themselves. And despite, or even because of, their privileged position, the young would be the coming force of revolution and change.

There was something else that was new for the left. The aura of existentialism—the postwar French philosophical movement that believed that people must create meaning in their own lives—hung over this vision. The personal was political, but not merely in the issues being raised. It was the *personal* meaning of joining a *political* movement. At the 1960 meeting of the National Student Association (NSA) Hayden had fallen hard for a graduate student from Texas, Sandra (Casey) Cason. Cason had been deeply involved in the civil rights movement. During a debate on whether to support civil disobedience, she connected the personal with the political. "I am thankful for the sit-ins if for no other reason than they provided me with an opportunity for making a slogan into a reality...It seems to me that this is what life is about." For her, the struggle carried in it "the possibility of becoming less inhuman humans through commitment and action."[8]

The introduction to Port Huron goes on to identify the sources of "discomfort" for the young, particularly the bomb, civil rights, the Cold War—vestiges of postwar America. Crucial to the struggle was the idea of merging the political with the personal. The coming change would be both socially transforming and personally liberating. "We seek the establishment of a democracy of individual participation governed by two central aims: that the individual share in the social decisions determining the quality and direction of his life; that society be organized to encourage independence in men and provide the media for common participation."*

---

* The continual use of male nouns and pronouns reflects the year in which this was written and not a sexist perspective. This grammatical form did not change until the emergence of the women's movement some years later.

The statement was filled with idealism and hope, including a deep-rooted belief in the potential of democracy. But this potential needed to be actualized in new political forms. "We would replace power rooted in possession, privilege, or circumstance by power and uniqueness rooted in love, reflectiveness, reason and creativity. As a *social system* we seek the establishment of a democracy of individual participation." The document went on to discuss a number of crucial areas, from "Colonialism," "Anti-Communism," and "Discrimination" to "Values" and "The University and Social Change." It was the concept of "participatory democracy" that most drew in the young. Over the years, the idea of participatory democracy would be widely debated and its ambiguities and problems highlighted. At the outset, however, the young radicals found a powerful phrase that captured their idealism and enthusiasm, a phrase to ground their emerging left critique of the United States and to describe how to solve these problems.[9]

Leaders within SNCC began to encourage young white activists to try to organize poor whites. SDS leaders agreed. They organized the Economic and Research Action Project (ERAP) to work in white urban neighborhoods and help create an "interracial movement of the poor." Leaving their campuses, SDS organizers moved in among the poor, living in group housing and organizing their lives according to the principles of Port Huron, combining the personal and the political. Various difficulties, ranging from neighborhood resistance to the cumbersome nature of trying to live in a totally democratic environment, plagued the program. ERAP never achieved its idealist goals of organizing these neighborhoods and creating a powerful movement among the working poor. Several years later, former SDS president Paul Potter noted, we "had seen a chance to go directly for the jugular vein of our system. We leapt and missed.[10] Youthful arrogance likely led to unreasonable expectations, but the issues and the lessons in community organizing would help inform future movements.

On university campuses themselves the desire for change that began to percolate up among the young came into direct conflict with the status quo. Colleges and universities had operated under the notion of *in loco parentis*, literally "in lieu of the parent." Campus rules reflected this attitude, from restrictions on students of opposite sexes visiting each other's dorm rooms to limitations on campus political activity.

When students returned to the University of California, Berkeley in the fall of 1964, for example, they discovered that the university had banned students from setting up tables on the city sidewalk just outside the main campus gate, where for years student organizations had been able to solicit donations and recruit members. Among those most shocked by the new policy were the students returning from Mississippi who had hoped to raise funds and distribute literature for the civil rights movement. But the cause extended beyond supporting efforts in the South. "Last summer I went to Mississippi to join the struggle for civil rights," one student leader, Mario Savio, wrote. "This fall I am engaged in another phase of the same struggle, this time in Berkeley."[11]

The civil rights experience had also brought a new attitude. "A student who has been chased by the KKK in Mississippi," one declared, "is not easily scared by academic bureaucrats."[12] Activists continued to set up tables in the disputed location, ultimately escalating their opposition by moving some tables inside that campus gate to Sproul Plaza, the center of campus activity and located in front of the administration building. On October 1, campus police drove on to the plaza, stopping at a table that had been set up by CORE, intending to arrest the student manning the table. As he was being put into the squad car, a crowd surrounded it, creating a standoff between students and police. For 32 hours, Jack Weinberg, a graduate student from Buffalo, New York, sat in the back of the police car. Students stood on the roof of the car to speak to the huge crowd, commenting on everything from the ban on the tables to their own sense of powerlessness and infantilization by the university. The most compelling of the speakers proved to be Mario Savio, a junior just back from Mississippi, where he had taught in a Freedom School. Savio was adept at mixing the personal and the political, suggesting that the university "emasculated" students. "The Bible says what knowledge is when it writes that a man knows a woman. Knowledge and action are inseparable."[13] Finally, negotiations between students and UC President Clark Kerr defused the situation. The space for the tables was restored. Savio informed the crowd, the students began to disperse, and the crisis appeared to be over.

Out of this encounter sprang the Free Speech Movement (FSM), a coalition that included radical Maoist groups, the conservative Students for Goldwater, and many in between. Just as passions seemed to be calming in subsequent weeks, the administration reignited them, deciding to press on with disciplinary action against some of the students who had been involved in the initial incident. FSM responded, holding daily rallies in Sproul Plaza, sometimes drawing crowds of 5,000. The rallies would include the singing of civil rights anthems and old labor songs as well as original sarcastic songs that mocked vapid aspects of campus life. Ultimately, they began to talk about a sit-in in the administration building.

At noon on December 2, Savio spoke to a large crowd with words that captured many of the issues swirling among students and that would become famous in years to come. He declared, "There is a time when the operation of the machine becomes so odious, makes you so sick at heart, that you can't take part...you've got to put your bodies upon the gears...and you've got to make it stop." And echoing the calls for freedom emanating from the civil rights movement and Port Huron, Savio told students what they needed to do. "You've got to indicate to the people who run it...that unless you're free, the machines will be prevented from working at all."[14] Joan Baez, a rising star in the folk movement, sang Bob Dylan's "The Times They Are A-Changin'" and closed the rally with the civil rights anthem, "We Shall Overcome." And then a large part of the crowd, estimated at over 1,000, walked into Sproul Hall and sat down.

The students moved to all four floors of Sproul and settled in. Some areas were used to distribute food, others became spaces to watch old movies, hold a Hanukah service, or just as a study hall. At 3 a.m., the Berkeley chancellor announced over a bullhorn that unless the demonstrators left, they would be arrested. When no one moved, nearly 400 police officers came in to literally drag the students out, bouncing them down the marble stairs. It became the largest mass arrest in California history, with about 800 taken into custody. Word quickly spread across campus. FSM called for a student strike. Graduate students also went on strike, which shut down the university, as graduate teaching assistants taught so many of the undergraduate courses. A week later, the faculty Academic Senate voted overwhelmingly in support of FSM. Ultimately, the regents and administration accepted the faculty recommendations to lift the free speech ban. The students had clearly triumphed.

FSM came to mean much more than a victory of free speech at Berkeley. American college students and, in fact, students throughout the world, as we shall see, had come to feel like products produced by a university system that resembled, in Savio's words, a machine. They felt their personal rights constrained by *in loco parentis*, their civil rights limited, and their own participation in the educational decisions that affected their lives minimal or nonexistent. Over the course of the next years, the student movement sprouted on campuses large and small, in the United States and around the world, confronting local issues but all reflecting these generational frustrations. They demanded the transformation of everything from the restrictive rules about dorm visitations to student participation in educational policy, demanding things like student course evaluations and student seats on university committees. The final section of the Port Huron Statement was titled, "The University and Social Change." FSM and the subsequent student movements had demonstrated just how prescient that was.

The ultimate potential of the student movement, despite these victories, would never be fully known. In the spring of 1965, a new form of campus activity emerged. On March 17, the first Vietnam teach-in—responding to the escalating conflict in Southeast Asia—occurred at the University of Michigan, sponsored by Michigan faculty and SDS. Over the next two months, teach-ins followed at a number of other schools, including Columbia, Penn, Rutgers, and in May at Berkeley—the largest teach-in to date. Like so many aspects of American life, the war in Vietnam came to envelop existing structures and to siphon much of the energy of the emerging student movement.

4

Vietnam

The War in the Rice Paddies

The United States experienced an amazingly rapid transition from its hot war with Germany and Japan, which ended in 1945, to a cold one with its World War II ally, the Soviet Union. By 1947, the America political leadership saw itself involved in a life-and-death struggle against an international communist enemy, controlled by the Soviets and, after its Communist Revolution, the Chinese. To American policymakers, any internal uprising revolution in which local communists took part was considered to be part of this larger struggle. This view made knowledge of local history and indigenous cultural issues irrelevant, the insurgents seen merely as pawns of Moscow or Beijing. A successful communist revolution anywhere in the world would be seen as enhancing the overall communist effort, regardless of regional or internal political tensions, such as Vietnamese antipathy toward China or the growing rift between the Soviets and the Chinese.

The emerging American policy of "containment"—stemming all Soviet expansionism and keeping the Soviet sphere within its current borders—necessitated responding to any conflict in the world that threatened it. The Vietnam conflict could have happened anywhere—in Africa, Asia, or Latin America. It did not really matter to American policymakers. "I had never visited Indochina, nor did I understand or appreciate its history, language, culture, or values," Defense Secretary Robert McNamara later admitted. "The same must be said, to varying degrees, about President Kennedy, Secretary of State Dean Rusk, National Security Advisor McGeorge Bundy, military adviser Maxwell Taylor, and many others. When it came to Vietnam, we found ourselves setting policy for a region that was *terra incognita*."[1]

"[He was] an awfully sweet old guy," a former American Office of Strategic Services (OSS, the wartime precursor of the CIA) officer recalled of a meeting he held during World War II. "If I had to pick out one quality about that little old man sitting on his hill in the jungle, it was his sweetness."[2] By 1945, the sweet little old man, Ho Chi Minh, had been working to expel foreigners from his homeland for decades. The Vietnamese people had been trying to oust them for centuries—Chinese, French, Japanese, and, in subsequent years, Americans. Fiercely nationalistic, the Vietnamese cared little if the foreigners were Asian or European.

During their colonial control of Vietnam, the French had sought to destroy Vietnamese culture and institutions, dividing the country in three, declaring French the national language, and bulldozing Buddhist pagodas to build Roman Catholic churches. They outlawed the word "Vietnam," fearing it would be a rallying cry for protest and insurrection, and insisted the nation be called French Indochina.

Just before World War I, the young Ho Chi Minh had left his homeland. He traveled to the West, working in Boston, New York, and London before arriving in Paris in 1918, where he became active in anticolonial political movements. As the victorious allied leaders met in Versailles to hammer out the peace, Ho electrified fellow Vietnamese expatriates by issuing a set of demands that called for individual rights and political equality.

Embracing communism as the only logical anti-imperialist ideology, Ho moved to Moscow and then on to Canton, China. In China he became the rallying figure for forces committed to Vietnamese independence. When the Germans conquered France in June 1940, Vietnam became especially vulnerable to Japanese expansion. By the middle of 1941, the Japanese had taken control of most of Vietnam, creating a puppet state, with the last Vietnamese emperor, Boa Dai, at its head. The Japanese now replaced the French as the object of Ho's enmity. For the first time in 30 years, he returned to Vietnam, taking refuge in the mountains, which is where the OSS found him. Together with other Vietnamese nationalists, including the teacher-turned-revolutionary, Vo Nguyen Giap, Ho formed the Viet Minh, which emerged as the central group dedicated to Vietnamese independence.

Anxious for good intelligence sources among Southeast Asian groups and willing to work with anyone opposed to the Japanese, the OSS developed a relationship with Ho and the Viet Minh, supplying them with arms. At the surrender of Japan in 1945, Ho proclaimed Vietnam independent, the opening lines of his declaration reflecting his debt to and admiration of American history. "All men are created equal. They are endowed by their Creator with certain inalienable rights; among these are Life, Liberty, and the Pursuit of Happiness . . . In a broader sense, this means: All peoples on the earth are equal from birth, all the peoples have a right to life, to be happy and free."[3]

During World War II, Franklin Roosevelt had signaled that the United States would not be interested in helping European nations restore their lost colonies, seeing the next arenas for American economic development in the newly independent countries of Asia and Africa. Near the end of his presidency, FDR had begun to move away from this position, in part due to the exigencies of ending the war. His successor, Harry Truman, abandoned it entirely.

The new realities of the Cold War, the overarching struggle between the United States and the Soviet Union, with a divided Europe as the central line between East and West, as previously discussed, altered American policy. The U.S. hoped that reestablishing colonial empires would aid the economic recovery of the Western European nations, including French claims to retake Indochina, which led to a renewal of the French-Vietnamese conflict. The 1949 victory of the communists in the Chinese civil war added intensity to this position. A newly articulated "domino theory"—the fear that Asian nations would fall to communism one after another like a row of dominoes set on end—became a rationale for deeper involvement in Asia.

These concerns destroyed Ho Chi Minh's hopes for an independent Vietnam. British, Chinese, and Japanese troops had engaged the Viet Minh, even before the French returned. The French restored Bao Dai as a puppet emperor and planned to conclude a quick military victory over the Viet Minh. Ho and Vo Nguyen Giap understood the situation differently. While the Europeans assumed their military superiority would easily prevail, Ho and Giap planned a guerilla war, believing from the outset that victory would come in political terms, when they had sapped the French will to persevere.

By the end of the 1940s, the United States had committed itself wholeheartedly to the main elements of its cold war strategy, including the containment of communism. A communist victory could not be allowed in Vietnam. As the cost of the France's Indochina War escalated and as economic difficulties continued to plague postwar France, American aid to the French grew steadily. By 1954, the United States was underwriting between 75 and 80 percent of the cost of the Indochina war.

Giap set about raising an army, while continuing to harass the French. It soon became clear to all that while the French may have controlled the major cities, the Viet Minh controlled the countryside. The French military leadership, trained in Western war strategy and frustrated by Giap's tactics, itched for a direct confrontation with the Viet Minh. A new French commander came to Vietnam in 1953, intending to implement a decisive, new strategy, building impenetrable garrisons deep in the Vietnamese countryside from which to engage and destroy the enemy. The first of these was to be a fortification in the valley of Dien Bien Phu.

The new French strategy was based on a number of faulty assumptions. The French assumed that the way the Koreans had fought in the Korean War, which had just ended in a stalemate—with soldiers attacking in a human wave—was how all "Orientals" fought, including the Vietnamese. Instead, Giap set about digging tunnels and trenches that moved steadily toward the French fort. The French assumed that, as there were no roads up the steep mountains that surrounded the valley, the Viet Minh could not bring artillery into positions to threaten them. Giap had the artillery pieces disassembled, gave a piece to each of his soldiers, and had the parts walked up the mountain. The guns were then reassembled at the summit. The valley terrain, itself, turned impassable when the rains came and, even when dry, proved exceedingly inhospitable to French vehicles.

Meanwhile, Giap moved many more men into position than the French had believed possible. By April 1954 Viet Minh troops outnumbered French by ten to one, while the steady progression toward the garrison had reduced the perimeter drastically. On May 6, Giap made his final push, seized the garrison, and the French surrendered. In Paris, the French government fell, with the new prime minister promising a ceasefire within a month. The French Indochina War was over.

Once again, the Vietnamese looked forward to the establishment of an independent Vietnam.

That same April, an international conference had opened in Geneva. Even before the fall of Dien Bien Phu, the French had put Indochina on the agenda. The meeting was underway when news of the defeat arrived. Negotiations over the next few months led to a final accord on Vietnam, including a declaration of a ceasefire and the framework for what was to come. Vietnam was temporarily divided in two "regrouping" zones—those loyal to the Viet Minh would retreat north, while the French and Vietnamese loyal to the French would move to the south. The temporary nature of this "demarcation line" was made explicit. It "should not in any way be interpreted as constituting a political or territorial boundary," the final accords declared. Further, the accords called for general elections for a unified Vietnam to be held in July 1956.[4]

Representatives of the United States attended the Geneva Conference, but they were never happy with the Indochina outcome. Secretary of State John Foster Dulles instructed the American delegates to leave the final accord unsigned, though the Americans did promise to "refrain from the threat or the use of force" to undermine it. Every American intelligence assessment pointed to an overwhelming victory by Ho Chi Minh, should the 1956 elections be held. So, despite its public pronouncements, the U.S. sought to undermine the Geneva Accords almost from their inception.

What the Americans sought was a figure to take over the south, some-one who would provide the locus for government strong enough to keep that half of the country separate. They thought they had found such a figure in Ngo Dinh Diem, a member of a prominent family of Vietnamese Catholics. The fact that the vast majority of the Vietnamese were Buddhists and that, to the Vietnamese, Catholicism was associated with French colonial rule, did not occur to the Americans as an impediment to Diem's acceptance. Diem had lived for several years in the U.S., where he had acquired influential friends, among them the powerful arch-bishop of New York, Francis Cardinal Spellman, and Senators John Kennedy and Lyndon Johnson.

He also had a friend in CIA Saigon station chief Edward Lansdale. Lansdale saw in Diem the nationalist leader the U.S. sought, believing that despite his Catholicism, Diem's longstanding opposition to the French would stand him in good stead with the Vietnamese. Diem returned to Saigon in June 1954, technically as Bao Dai's prime minister and, with American assistance, began to transform the "temporary demarcation" of the Geneva Accords into a permanent one. Opposition political groups were systematically crushed and a new system of village control was introduced—replacing local leaders and elected officials with appointees loyal to Diem. In October 1955, Diem declared the South a republic, and he and the U.S. were now beginning to refer to the two halves of the country as separate nations, South Vietnam and North Vietnam. Diem cancelled the upcoming general elections, replacing them with an election strictly in the South, between himself and Bao Dai. Diem's overwhelming victory—98.2 percent of the popular vote—has always been seen as fraudulent. In Saigon, for example, he gathered over 600,000 votes out of 450,000 registered voters.[5]

These developments left the northern half of the country in a quan-dary. Hesitant to begin armed hostilities again so quickly, Ho once more thought that a political victory was preferable to a military one, intend-ing to consolidate the government in the north, while supporting insur-gency in the south. Many Southern Vietnamese, who had retreated north with the Viet Minh, began to migrate home. Once there, they joined with other opponents of the Diem regime in a small guerilla group, which Diem labeled "Viet Cong"—"cong" a Vietnamese pejorative for "commie." These "Viet Cong" always saw themselves as Viet Minh.

In 1960, the anti-Diem groups formed a coalition to liberate the South, calling themselves the "National Front for the Liberation of South Vietnam," or the NLF. The NLF included communists, Buddhists, Catholics, professionals, and peasants, all sharing their opposition to the Diem regime, the American presence, and the impoverished situation of most Southern Vietnamese. First among the NLF's demands was the removal of "the camouflaged colonial regime of the American imperialists." With hostilities against Diem mounting in the countryside, the American government sent 1,000 advisers to arm and train the Army of the Republic of South Vietnam (ARVN). As Viet Cong pressure increased, so did the number of advisers, climbing to 3,200 by 1961 and 16,000 by 1963.

By 1961, America had a new president. John Kennedy surrounded himself with advisers anxious, like the new young president, to be more proactive in foreign policy. Still resistant to sending ground troops to Vietnam, they searched for strategies to undermine the rising influence of the Viet Cong. Focusing on the idea of counterinsurgency, they created the Strategic Hamlet Program, relocating Vietnamese peasants to barbwire-enclosed villages. American pilots were then free to fire on all the abandoned areas, under the assumption that anyone remaining was Viet Cong. The Americans believed this would eventually crush the movement. The campaign did just the opposite. The Viet Cong promised that a victory over the Americans and Diem would mean that the peasants could return to their homes. Further, Diem gave control of the program to his brother, Ngo Dinh Nhu, head of the secret police. Nhu's brutal tactics only further incensed Vietnamese citizens, as did the massive and indiscriminate American air power.

Most of these events remained back-page news, at best, in the U.S. Other foreign flashpoints—from Suez to Berlin to Cuba—took center stage. If there was a moment when Americans woke up to the situation in Vietnam, it was June 11, 1963, when an elderly Buddhist monk sat down in the middle of a Saigon intersection, was doused with gasoline, and set himself on fire in a ritual suicide to protest the Diem regime. Photographs of this event were splashed across the American media—the lead story on the nightly news and with front-page pictures in newspapers across the country—as well as spurring widespread demonstrations in South Vietnam. For several months, Buddhists had protested against the government, but the suicide moved the debate to a new plateau.

Within the halls of the Kennedy Administration, it became increasingly clear that Diem was a major liability. The U.S. Ambassador, Henry Cabot Lodge, initiated discussions with the South Vietnamese military about the overthrow of Diem. By August, Lodge cabled Washington that there was "no respectable turning back" from this path, in part, because there was "no possibility of the war being won under a Diem Administration."[6] On November 1, Diem and his brother tried to flee but were apprehended. When their vehicle returned to command headquarters, they were dead. Before Kennedy could receive a full report on these events, he too was dead. And Lyndon Johnson was now president.

Unlike John Kennedy, Lyndon Johnson's heart was in domestic politics, not foreign policy. His Great Society programs—rolled out over the next several years, including things like anti-poverty legislation, social welfare programs, and aid to education—were intended to do for the postwar U.S. what Franklin Roosevelt's New Deal had done for Depression America. But as a dedicated cold warrior, Johnson also feared that defeat in Vietnam would destroy his domestic agenda. So he turned to his foreign policy advisers to chart a path that would ultimately prevail.

The militarists of the Kennedy Administration—Defense Secretary Robert McNamara, National Security Adviser Walt Rostow, Secretary of State Dean Rusk—moved into ascendancy. Still unwilling to commit formal U.S. ground troops, they looked for new strategies to bring the Viet Cong and the North to their knees. Despite Pentagon war gaming and intelligence analyses that suggested victory was nearly impossible, they pressed on. The development of new, highly powerful herbicides, like Agent Orange, offered the possibility of a program to defoliate forests and therefore expose the enemy to air attack. Believing that operations in the South were controlled by Hanoi, they initiated a covert program to begin to punish the North with air assaults. The hope was to make the cost of continuing the war too high. Forgetting the lesson of the French—a lesson repeated over and over during these years—these actions only strengthened the resolve of the Vietnamese.

In 1964, Johnson dispatched General Maxwell Taylor, one of the strongest advocates of counterinsurgency, to South Vietnam as the new ambassador and chose a new field commander, William Westmoreland. Almost from the day he arrived, Westmoreland began to request ground troops. With proper troop levels, he believed, American military and technological superiority would easily crush the enemy.

There was also an American presidential election in 1964, pitting Johnson against the hawkish Arizona Senator Barry Goldwater. Anxious to appear firm but moderate, Johnson claimed that he sought no wider war. In August, he got to show his "moderate" style, when he informed the American people that North Vietnamese patrol boats had committed unprovoked attacks on American ships in the international waters of the Gulf of Tonkin, off the coast of North Vietnam. Johnson ordered a one-time retaliatory air attack against the North and asked Congress for broad powers to wage war in Vietnam.

The Gulf of Tonkin Resolution, as it came to be called, passed overwhelmingly, by voice vote in the House and with only two dissenting votes in the Senate. Subsequent revelations suggest that much about the entire episode remains suspect, including where the ships were as well as whether some of the attacks had even occurred. Further, the resolution had been drafted months earlier, with Johnson waiting for the opportune moment to introduce it. When subsequently asked why no formal Vietnam war declaration had even been introduced, Johnson (and later Richard Nixon) responded by citing the Tonkin Gulf Resolution as providing all the authorization he needed.

Johnson won a landslide victory in November 1964. Yet by that point, officials in Washington knew that their Vietnam strategy was failing. In February of the new year, the Americans embarked on Operation

Rolling Thunder, a new sustained series of air attacks on the North. The idea was a kind of carrot-and-stick strategy—bombing on the one hand, diplomatic overtures on the other. Once again, the Americans failed to understand the Vietnamese mindset. The U.S. might calculate the costs in immediate monetary terms. The Vietnamese took a much longer political view, as well as determining the best way to resist and rebuild. At the same time, Viet Cong strength had grown markedly. Westmoreland continued to ask for ground troops. In Washington and Saigon, American officials began to agree. On March 8, 1965, American troops came ashore at Danang in full battle regalia.

And, in response, on March 17, the first Vietnam Teach-In occurred at the University of Michigan. The American War, as the Vietnamese called it, had entered a new phase.

The commission of ground troops to Vietnam required a marked change in U.S. strategy. It had become increasingly clear that the ARVN was not going to develop into an effective fighting force. Some of the troops had been bribed to join. Others were conscripted, but the desertion rate at draft centers often reached 50 percent. The U.S. could rely neither on the South Vietnamese troops or their government. It had to take the lead in the field just as it had in Saigon.

The problem for the Americans was that most independent analyses suggested the chances for victory over North Vietnam still remained extremely low. Military personnel, like Gen. Westmoreland, were eager for direct combat moments, but the enemy avoided these, preferring their tested guerilla tactics. The American strategy that emerged argued that if the enemy could not be defeated directly, they could be weakened over time. A war of attrition became the central American approach, demoralizing the enemy in the North through bombing raids, weakening the Viet Cong in the South, and providing the Saigon government time to stabilize.

The problems with this strategy were several. It would require more and more troops; it ran counter to conventional attitudes about how one achieves victory in war; and it failed to understand the approach that

Ho, Giap, and the other leaders in the North brought to the conflict. Nevertheless, Westmoreland periodically asked for and received greater numbers of American troops, the total rising beyond 300,000 in 1966 to over 500,000 in 1968. This was a far cry from the 3200 advisers of 1961. And as there was still a military draft in place, this meant that more and more young men found themselves facing the possibility of either going to war or developing a strategy to avoid it.

The weekly body counts that were broadcast to the American people—numbers that seemed to show a causality rate among the enemy many times higher than among the Americans—at first seem to indicate success. But after several years with little else to suggest that victory was any closer, the American people began to grow skeptical. The Saigon press corps had always been incredulous. They started to refer to the daily press briefings at the U.S. Embassy as the "Five O'Clock Follies."

Finally, it proved almost impossible to present to the American people a strategy that promised the kind of military victories they expected, with conclusive battles and white-flag surrenders. Instead of realistic assessments about strategy and progress, the government continued to issue optimistic pronouncements based on unproven assumptions and specious explanations, often phrased in clichés such as seeing "a light at the end of the tunnel." Exposing the government's faulty logic or deliberately misleading assessments only added to growing feelings of pessimism and cynicism among the American people.

Several times Lyndon Johnson had ordered pauses in the bombing and signaled his willingness to negotiate an end to hostilities. But the basis of any American agreement rested on an underlying principle Ho would never accept. To LBJ, it made sense that both the Americans and the North Vietnamese should withdraw, seeing them both as foreign powers inside South Vietnam. To Ho, the Northern troops were Vietnamese fighting within their homeland and bore no relationship to the "American invaders." Ever the political dealmaker, Johnson even offered massive renewal projects for the Mekong Delta as part of his peace offering. But where a local American politico might jump at the chance for these kinds of public works projects, Ho Chi Minh was no local American politico.

After each pause, the bombing would resume, with increased intensity. In 1965, the Americans flew 25,000 sorties over North Vietnam. That number increased to 79,000 in 1966 and 108,000 in 1967. Despite the increased numbers and massive destruction, the bombing never achieved its intended impact. Bombed-out roads and bridges were quickly rebuilt, often overnight. Meanwhile, over 900 American aircraft were shot down over the North. Most American POWs in Hanoi were downed pilots.

Many, inside and outside of Washington, began to articulate their doubts. A cluster of prominent senators, Democrat and Republican, expressed criticisms more and more publicly. Privately, a number of Johnson Administration insiders grew skeptical, including Robert McNamara. Coming to realize just how wrong he had been, McNamara resigned as Defense Secretary in November 1967, though he kept his misgivings private for nearly 30 years.

Westmoreland, however, continued to offer optimistic estimates and plans to Washington. Each seemed to require additional troops. The remaining hardliners in the government—like Rostow and Rusk—supported him. By 1967, despite opposite views from many quarters, Westmoreland believed "the tide had turned" and he envisioned the long-desired final battle to bring an American victory. In Vietnam, he declared, the U.S. had reached the "crossover point."

5

Vietnam

The War at Home

If the ritual suicide of a Buddhist monk on a Saigon street in 1963 woke Americans up to the depth and the effects of U.S. involvement in Vietnam, 1965 marked the year they became aware that resistance and opposition had grown to significant size—that the war had come home. American escalation in early '65, with Operation Rolling Thunder and the introduction of ground troops, merged with the surge in the student movement and the New Left to a turn anti-war sentiment into a major national movement.

While there had certainly always been pacifist groups in the U.S. and there had been some opposition to the Vietnam War itself, even from its earliest days, it is unsurprising that the antiwar movement caught fire among the young. It was from the young that most of the GIs were drawn, a great many involuntarily, again mixing the political and the personal. And the young, especially those in college, had become increasingly organized and motivated to challenge what they saw as a flawed and corrupt system.

All these elements converged in the spring of 1965 with the advent of the first teach-in, unsurprisingly at the University of Michigan. Co-sponsored by faculty members and Students for a Democratic Society (SDS), the first teach-in was an all-night gathering of over 3,500 people—mainly, but not exclusively students—who listened to talks and debates, watched movies, and heard music. While both pro- and anti-war viewpoints were heard, it was clear that the audience was decidedly anti-war. The teach-in idea caught fire. There were dozens held just that week—and by year's end, well over a hundred. The largest teach-in was held at Berkeley in May. By this point, the political orientation of the audience had become clear, and the pro-war voices began to dwindle. The State Department declined to send a representative to Berkeley. Two pro-war professors withdrew. But the roster of those who did appear read like a Who's Who of the growing antiwar gallery—beloved pediatrician Benjamin Spock, ageing Socialist leader Norman Thomas, veteran political activist David Dellinger, Student Nonviolent Coordinating Committee (SNCC) leader Robert Moses, and Free Speech Movement's Mario Savio. Renowned British philosopher Bertrand Russell sent a taped message. Progressive California political officeholders agreed to speak. And there were voices from the cultural side of the movement—novelist Norman Mailer, Buddhist philosopher Alan Watts, Black comedian Dick Gregory, folksinger Phil Ochs, and many others. The antiwar movement was showing, in one of its first public demonstrations, that it was a movement drawing adherents from all across the political and cultural landscape.

In April 1965, SDS had organized the first major national demonstration against the war, to be held in Washington. The call for the march argued that the war was "self-defeating," "dangerous," "never declared," and "immoral." It urged "the participation of all students who agree with us that the war in Vietnam injures both Vietnamese and Americans, and should be stopped."[1] Organizers were stunned when 25,000 people showed up, far exceeding their expectations. This was, to that point, the largest anti-war demonstration in American history. In addition, it was not just students who came but also many older Americans. The program again exhibited an emerging pattern of music and talk. Gathering at the Washington Monument, the audience heard peace songs from Joan Baez, Judy Collins, and Phil Ochs. The speakers included Alaska Senator Ernest Gruening, one of the two Senators who had voted against the Tonkin Gulf Resolution; SNCC's Moses; and radical journalist I.F. Stone.

The most memorable of the speeches, however, came from SDS President Paul Potter. Potter pushed beyond a critique of the Vietnam War, itself, to a larger frame. While arguing that neither Johnson nor his advisers were "evil men," their decisions had led to the "mutilation and death of thousands of people." And then Potter tellingly asked, "What kind of system is it that allows good men to make these kinds of decisions?...We must name that system. We must name it, describe it, analyze it, understand it, and change it."[2]

The teach-ins and the DC march put the antiwar movement on America's front pages. SDS membership expanded. Campus chapters doubled. A national coordinating committee was developed to plan subsequent actions. October's "First International Day of Protest" witnessed events in nearly a hundred cities, across the nation and around the world, with thousands of demonstrators participating. The war became the catalyst for bringing disparate protest elements from around the country into a political coalition. SNCC argued that the murder of Black Americans in the South "is no different than the murder of peasants in Vietnam," as they both "sought and are seeking to secure their rights."[3] "A new generation of radicals has been spawned from the chrome womb of affluent America," Jack Newfield wrote in *The Nation*. "They are a new generation of dissenters, nourished not by Marx, Trotsky, or Stalin but by Camus, Paul Goodman, Bob Dylan, and SNCC."[4]

In February 1966, Senate Foreign Relations Committee Chair J. William Fulbright launched a series of televised hearings about Vietnam policy. Not only had Fulbright been close to LBJ but he had also been the floor sponsor of the Tonkin Gulf Resolution. Now the Arkansas senator set out to publicly question the war. Appearing before the committee were Johnson administration officials, retired military officers, and respected former government officials, like George Kennan, once a key architect of Cold War policy and the author of the policy of containment but now questioning Vietnam policy. Pro- and anti-war senators on the committee were each allowed to question the witnesses and argue their own position on the war, but the net impact of the Fulbright hearings was a kind of national teach-in. Fulbright would become a steady antiwar voice and critic of American foreign policy as the years progressed.

In November 1965, a Quaker activist and father of three from Baltimore, Norman Morrison, sat down in a small garden outside the Pentagon, beneath an office window of Defense Secretary Robert

McNamara. And then, like the Buddhist monk in Saigon two years earlier, doused himself in kerosene and lit himself on fire, dying within minutes. A week later, a 22-year-old member of the Catholic Workers, did the same in front of the United Nations. Earlier that year, an elderly refugee from Nazi Germany set herself aflame in Detroit, choosing, she said, "the illuminating death of a Buddhist."[5] While the antiwar numbers were growing overall, among some the tactics and actions were ratcheting up in intensity.

Anti-war sentiments began to surface within the American military, epitomized by the 1966 actions of three soldiers at Fort Hood in Texas. Scheduled to be shipped to Vietnam in July, they appeared at a press conference at the end of June declaring they would not go. "We consider [the war] immoral, illegal, and unjust." Representing a cross-section of the nation—an African-American, a Puerto Rican, and a working-class white—they further declared, "We have been in the army long enough to know that we are not the only G.I.s who feel as we do…We want no part of a war of extermination…We refuse to go to Vietnam!!!!!"[6]

The Fort Hood Three saw their stance as connected to other sixties issues, including the arguments emerging from the Black Power movement. In fact, at their next scheduled appearance, SNCC chair Stokely Carmichael was to stand at their side. They were arrested just before that event took place. Court-martialed that September, they argued that the war was immoral and illegal, citing the Nuremberg Trials of Nazis at the end of World War II and the case of the more recently captured Nazi Adolf Eichmann in their defense. Rejecting this argument, a court officer declared that the war in Vietnam was legal, and forbid them to argue that it wasn't. They were dishonorably discharged and sentenced to three to five years at hard labor.

Their case led folksinger and activist Pete Seeger to pen, "The Ballad of the Fort Hood Three." Its final verse read,

> Now if you don't believe me, you can read about it more,
> About the Fort Hood Three who have refused to fight this war;
> We can help them set our country straight on the right track again,
> When a man can hold his head with pride and say: "I'm an American!"[7]

Gatherings were held around the country in support, including one in New York that October, at which, among others, David Dellinger and cartoonist Jules Feiffer spoke. Seeger sang his ballad as well as his anti-war song, "Bring Them Home." A reporter for the *Columbia Spectator* summed up the sentiments of the evening. "The pardoning of [the three] would be a step towards justice. The time has passed when one can kill for peace."[8]

Of all the newly emerging forms of protest, the ones that seemed to most capture American interest were the strategies developed to resist and avoid the draft. The United States had, in the past, only employed a draft system—involuntarily conscripting young men into the military— during wartime. This changed with the advent of the Cold War. In 1949, the government instituted a peacetime draft. The Selective Service System, which ran the draft, offered deferments to men who fit particular categories—from severe health concerns to educational status to participating in crucial occupations. At 18, young men registered at their local draft boards and received their draft classification, ranging from 1-A (available to be drafted) to 4-F (physically unable to serve.) But as the demand for troop levels rose in Vietnam, available deferments shrunk. Once being married provided a deferment, but that ended on August 26, 1965. LBJ announced on that day that the deferment would end at midnight, leading to a rush of marriages, especially on the West Coast, where people could get to Las Vegas, as quick marriages were common there.[9] Soon, college students not making "normal progress" (falling behind in credits, taking a semester off, going on academic probation) found themselves reclassified to 1-A. In 1966, the Selective Service System announced that class ranking would now determine one's status. Those at the bottom could be made available to the draft. Colleges and universities were instructed to submit a student's rank to his draft board. Many schools resisted, arguing that it made them complicit with the war effort. At places where a clear ranking could not be determined, such as those with a pass-fail grading system, men were to take a national examination, like the SAT, to determine their ranking. Some schools refused to participate.

Stories began to spread of individuals who had faked medical conditions to stay out of the military, sometimes supported by friendly medical professionals; of school counselors and religious leaders who helped young men to become conscientious objectors; of men choosing career paths only because they led to deferments; and of those opting to cross the border to Canada to avoid conscription. Beyond these, there were also those who publicly declared that they would refuse to be drafted. One of the first to refuse, David Mitchell, who had dropped out of Brown University, was sentenced to five years in prison.

At a 1965 anti-draft action in New York, some young men dropped the paper identification card issued to them by the Selective Service System into a flaming pot. A photograph of this incident that appeared in *Life* created a public uproar. Burning one's draft card was now made a federal offense, punishable by five years' imprisonment and a $10,000 fine, even though the paper card had no bearing on whether one would be drafted or not. Draft-card burners were part of a "sleazy beatnik gang," one congressman declared; to another it was an insult to our men in Southeast Asia. "No government can condone this kind of defiance and govern," *Newsweek* magazine editorialized. Anti-draft protestors were often punished by losing their deferments and being reclassified 1-A. The generational divisions emerging across the sixties landscape only added fuel to the fire. "I'm one of those old-fashioned fathers who never let pity interfere with a spanking," argued General Lewis Hershey, the 72-year-old head of the Selective Service System.[10]

More than a spanking was, however, at stake. A classified memo that circulated within the Selective Service System in 1965 (but not made public until 1967) outlined the "process of channeling" young men as a secondary goal of the draft system. The draft created "the inducement of manpower for civilian activities...in the national interest." The draft system steered young men to choose particular college majors or occupations that benefited society beyond military activity. While teachers' salaries had been "historically meager, many young men remain in that job, seeking the reward of a deferment," the memo noted. If a young man is trained in a particular field, "the loss of deferred status is the consequence for the individual...[who] does not use it or uses it in a non-essential activity." The bottom line, the memo argued, was that this is the "American or indirect way of achieving what is done by direction in foreign countries where choice is not permitted." It achieved the same result, without the resentment that "he has been told what to do."[11] Young American men were being sent to Southeast Asia to fight, the U.S. government maintained, to oppose authoritarian governments whose citizens had no rights and where the government made all the personal decisions of an individual's life. It turned out the U.S. was, though more subtly, coercing its young citizens in much the same way.

Debates about war were not confined to op-ed pieces, public rallies, or campus teach-ins. They erupted around dinner tables across the country. "Like many of my friends," recalled one Pentagon official, "my evenings...were spent listening to my wife and children screaming about how awful the war was." Nicholas Katzenbach who, when with the Justice Department, had heroically stood with civil rights demonstrators challenging segregation. Now in the State Department, he became a target of antiwar activists, including his own family. One aide remembers going to dinner at Katzenbach's house, only to hear his kids "really mau-mau him" on Vietnam. "His back would be up against the wall." These conflicts emerged in family after family, regardless of the prominence of the patriarch. But none was more compelling than Robert McNamara and his son Craig. Craig taped a small National Liberation Front flag on his bedroom wall, as well as hanging an American flag upside down, a symbol of distress. The growing tensions led to a rift between father and son that lasted for years.[12]

This pattern was repeated at all levels across the country. Fathers who glorified their World War II experience could not understand their sons and daughters questioning of American policy and their resistance to serving their nation. Their children could not understand their parents' blind allegiance to a mythologized vision of the United States, which bore little relationship to its foreign policy and international military adventures. In a smaller number of families, however, parents moved to the antiwar side, helping their sons avoid the draft. They hired lawyers to help win conscientious objector applications, worked to find sympathetic physicians and medical practitioners to support medical deferments, or aided their child's move to Canada. The phrase, "the war at home," no longer only meant "home," in the sense of within the United States, but "home" in the sense of one's own family.

Throughout 1965 and 1966, voices in the U.S., and increasingly around the world, heatedly debated the war. Most of the mainstream press still castigated and patronized the antiwar forces. *Life* called them "chronic showoffs"; another major newspaper saw them as "Communist-incited beatniks, pacifist and damned idiots" who should be tried for treason. To another, "this is the time for police brutality if there ever was one."[13] Articles tried to show how limited were the anti-war voices among the young and spotlighted pro-war student rallies and individual support for the soldiers in Vietnam. But the numbers did not matter. Looking back at the 1930s, sociologist Daniel Bell had concluded, in the postwar years, that despite the small number of Thirties radicals, "like a drop of dye that suffuses the cloth, this number gave the decade its coloration."[14] So, too, the antiwar activists of the 1960s. Their ideas and actions are what we remember and what proved essential to defining the era.

6

Race Politics at Mid-Decade

Three events, spread over a period of six months in 1965, marked changes in the United States in the struggle for racial equality and race thinking nationwide.

- On Sunday, February 21, el-Hajj Malik el-Shabazz, the Muslim minister formerly known as Malcolm X, stood before his congregation in Harlem. A scuffle appeared to break out among a few members of the audience. One rushed the stage and fired a shotgun. Two other men shot at Shabazz with handguns. Struck by 21 bullets, he was pronounced dead later that afternoon.

- Two weeks later, on Sunday March 7, 600 marchers gathered in downtown Selma, Alabama to begin a march to the state capital in Montgomery in support of voting rights. Crossing the Edmund Pettis Bridge, they were confronted by state troopers and local police, some on horseback, who gave the marchers two minutes to disperse. They then rushed the crowd, firing tear gas, swinging clubs, using cattle prods, and inflicting concussions and splitting heads open.

- Six months later and 2,000 miles to the west, Los Angeles police officers patrolled the African American neighborhood of Watts. Spotting a drunk driver, they stopped their patrol car to investigate. As neighbors gathered around, words were exchanged, the police called for backup, and the incident escalated into an urban riot that lasted for several days, with as many as 10,000 Black citizens taking to the streets. By the time peace was restored, 34 people were dead, nearly 4,000 had been arrested, and damage estimates were placed at $40 million (the equivalent of $400 million in today's dollars).

These three incidents—the death of Malcolm X, the Selma March, and the Watts Riot—emerged at the crossroads at which racial movements had come and highlighted the issues that would underpin the discussions that developed over the next few years.

The path that took Malcolm X to Selma on February 4, 1965, intersected with the ones that had brought SNCC workers and Martin Luther King, Jr. to the Alabama city that same day. While not fully understood at the time, this convergence spoke much about the current state of civil rights activism.

For Malcolm Little, the journey had begun in his youth in Omaha and Detroit, where his father Earl had been a Baptist lay minister but also a disciple of Marcus Garvey and his back-to-Africa movement, as was Malcolm's mother. Earl Little died in a suspicious streetcar accident that many, including Malcolm, always felt had been the result of violence by a white mob but which Earl's life insurance company had ruled a suicide—and thus refused to pay a significant part of his life insurance policy. The death of his father as well as his mother's hospitalization for mental issues, forced Malcolm to drift from foster home to foster home, before ending up with his sister in Roxbury, Massachusetts. He wandered into petty crime, mostly in New York and Boston, ultimately being arrested in Boston for burglary and sentenced to prison in 1946.

While in prison, urged by one of his own brothers and influenced by other inmates, Malcolm began to take an interest in the Nation of Islam, often called the Black Muslims. Soon he began calling himself Malcolm X, "my 'X' replaced the white slave master name of 'Little' which some blue-eyed devil named Little had imposed upon my paternal forebears," he later wrote.[1] He had begun corresponding with Elijah Muhammad, the cofounder of the Nation of Islam. Upon being paroled in 1952, Malcolm was placed by Muhammad in a series of Nation of Islam temples around the country, before being chosen to head the Harlem Temple in 1954. Malcolm's charismatic style meshed with the already growing community interest in the Nation of Islam, and memberships began to grow nationally, nowhere more than in Harlem. Much of the Nation's appeal was to race pride and a focus on inner strength and ultimate redemption. "Mr. Muhammad teaches us the knowledge of our own selves, and of our own people," Malcolm told an interviewer.

> He cleans us up—morally, mentally and spiritually—and he reforms us of the vices that have blinded us here in the Western society.... He's cleaning up the mess that white men have made...And Mr. Muhammad teaches us love for our own kind. The white man has taught the black people in this country to hate themselves as inferior, to hate each other, to be divided against each other. Messenger Muhammad restores our love for our own kind, which enables us to work together in unity and harmony.[2]

Although the FBI began to take notice of the Black Muslims and Malcolm X in the early 1950s, they were virtually invisible to white America until at least 1959. That July, newsman Mike Wallace coproduced and narrated a five-part television documentary series, "The Hate That Hate Produced," about black nationalism, in general, and Black Muslims, specifically. The tone was set by Wallace's opening words.

> While city officials, state agencies, white liberals, and sober-minded Negroes stand idly by, a group of Negro dissenters is taking to street-corner step ladders, church pulpits, sports arenas, and ballroom platforms across the United States, to preach a gospel of hate that would set off a federal investigation if it were preached by Southern whites.[3]

Malcolm X combined powerful ideas with a very compelling presence and soon became a widely sought after speaker and commenter. Much of white American society discovered Malcolm X's ideas in 1963, when *Playboy* magazine featured him in its monthly "*Playboy* Interview." These very long interviews with prominent individuals were a part of the magazine's attempt, along with contributions from notable fiction writers, to confer respectability to what was, essentially, a slickly produced girlie magazine. Running to nearly 8,000 words, the interview offered Malcolm a place to spell out his ideas fully—on history, international events, religious differences, the sins of white America, and the place of the Black man in modern U.S. society.*

Perhaps the Nation of Islam's biggest publicity coup came when, in March 1964, newly crowned heavyweight champion Cassius Clay announced that he was converting to Islam, joining the Nation, and changing his name to Muhammad Ali. Ali had been interested in the Black Muslims for several years and, by the early sixties, had grown close to Malcolm X, whom he considered a spiritual adviser.

Yet, while Ali was moving closer to the Nation of Islam, Malcolm X was moving away from it. By the same spring of 1964, personal disagreements with Elijah Muhammad, as well as a widening of his political and religious perspective, led Malcolm to leave the Nation. He traveled to the Middle East and Africa, where he met Muslims of all skin colors, and began to view issues from a wider perspective. Converting to true Islam, he adopted the Muslim name el-Hajj Malik el-Shabazz. Back in the U.S., he founded the Organization of Afro-American Unity. Incorporating much of the emerging discussion of Third World consciousness and the place of African Americans in it, he sought to "expand civil rights to the level of human rights."⁴ Both he and King began to soften their views of the other, not fully embracing one another but coming to see the utility of the other man in the overall struggle.

Malcolm continued his sharp critiques, but with significant modifications. "I'm not an American," he proclaimed in April 1964. "I'm one of the 22 million black people who are victims of Americanism...I don't see any American dream; I see an American nightmare." For him, Black Nationalism meant that "the black man should control the politics and the politicians in his own community." This was not, he argued, very different from what civil rights organizations and even the churches had been teaching. It was just time to take personal control. "There's no white man going to tell me anything about *my* rights." While he still

---

* The interview had the added element of introducing Malcolm to Alex Haley, the journalist *Playboy* hired to conduct the interview. Malcolm would eventually invite Haley to coauthor his *Autobiography*, which Haley completed after Malcolm's death.

rejected nonviolent resistance as a tactic, he did declare, "We will work with anybody, anywhere, at any time, who is genuinely interested in tackling the problem head-on, nonviolently as long as the enemy is nonviolent, but violent when the enemy gets violent."[5]

During the rest of 1964, Malcolm met with members of SNCC, including its chair John Lewis, and members of the Congress of Racial Equality (CORE). In early 1965, as they were planning for the voting rights march from Selma to Montgomery, King had been physically assaulted by a member of a neo-Nazi organization. Malcolm had responded with an open letter, promising that "if your present racist agitation against our people there in Alabama causes physical harm to Reverend King or any other black Americans who are only attempting to enjoy their rights as free human beings, you and your Ku Klux Klan friends will be met [by] those of us who are not hand-cuffed by the disarming philosophy of nonviolence, and who believe in asserting our right of self-defense—by any means necessary."[6] Invited by SNCC members to visit Selma, he arrived just as King had been arrested. Enthusiastically greeted by the SNCC volunteers, he met with Coretta Scott King, assuring her that he had come to aide King's cause, not "to make his job more difficult. I really did come thinking I could make it easier."[7]

Malcolm X traveled back to Harlem where, two weeks later, he was assassinated. For those still unable to understand his importance and the meaning of his message, Malcolm remained, as *The New York Times* editorialized, "an extraordinary and twisted man" who turned "many true gifts to evil purpose." White America was stunned when tens of thousands, mostly African American but with some whites, filled the streets of Harlem on the day of his funeral. In his eulogy, actor Ossie Davis called Malcolm "one of [Harlem's] brightest hopes." And to those who "revile him" and call him a "demon," Davis asked, "Did you ever talk to brother Malcolm?...Did he ever do a mean thing? Was he himself associated with violence?...Malcolm was our manhood, our living, black manhood!" And he concluded, "we will know him then for what he was and is—a Prince—our own black shining Prince!"[8]

With the publication of his *Autobiography* later that year, Malcolm X's stature would grow to a level on par with Martin Luther King.* What we would never come to see were the accomplishments that might have developed from the enlarged perspective of the last phase of his life.

From his jail cell in Selma, Martin Luther King sponsored an ad in the *New York Times* of February 5, the day after Malcolm X had come to town.

This is Selma, Alabama
There Are More Negroes in Jail With Me
Than There Are on the Voting Rolls[9]

SNCC had tried to register voters in Selma for several years. In 1965, it was joined by King and SCLC. In mid-February, tensions escalated when a peaceful rally in the neighboring town of Marion ended with state troopers shooting and killing a young Black man, Jimmie Lee Jackson, who was trying to shield his mother from harm. The shock of Jackson's murder and the beatings of other peaceful demonstrators led SCLC to plan a march from Selma to Montgomery, to dramatize their plight and to confront Alabama Governor George Wallace directly. After some internal bickering among the civil rights organizations, SNCC declared that its members were free to do as they chose. John Lewis was among those who chose to participate.

On Sunday the 7th, the 600 marchers left Selma's Brown AME Chapel and headed across the Edmund Pettis Bridge, where they encountered the state troopers and police in what became known as "Bloody Sunday." "I was hit in the head by a state trooper with a nightstick," John Lewis later recounted. "I had a concussion at the bridge. My legs went out from under me. I felt like I was going to die. I thought I saw Death." The violence was indiscriminate—victims included senior citizens and children, with everyone battered and bloodied. Lewis could not remember how he even got back to the church. Someone from the press "asked

---

* Barack Obama recently referred to Martin Luther King and Malcolm X as "the yin and yang of the liberation movement in this country." https://storage.googleapis.com/pr-newsroom-wp/1/2021/04/RENEGADE_Ep-8_Looking-Towards-American-Renewal.pdf.

me to say something... And I stood up and said something like: 'I don't understand it, how President Johnson can send troops to Vietnam but cannot send troops to Selma, Alabama, to protect people whose only desire is to register to vote.'"[10] This was not merely hyperbole. As Lewis was speaking, the very first American ground troops in Vietnam were preparing to come ashore.

Newsreel footage of the police attack was rushed to New York, where ABC News interrupted its movie of the week to show 15 minutes of unedited footage. That week's movie was the network premiere of *Judgment at Nuremberg*, an Academy Award winning film about Nazi war guilt and the postwar war crimes trials. The irony was not lost on millions of viewers.

Bloody Sunday stirred many to become involved. Volunteers headed to Selma to join whatever the next steps would be. After eating dinner in a restaurant in the Black part of town, one of the volunteers, James Reeb, a white Unitarian minister and father of four from Boston, was attacked by four Selma whites. Uttering racial slurs, they struck him in the head with a wooden club. Reeb collapsed on the sidewalk and died the next day, further infuriating national opinion. Picketers gathered in front of the White House, and members of Congress denounced George Wallace. SCLC and SNCC planned their next moves. And Lyndon Johnson decided this was time for action. Once cautious about pushing for a second civil rights bill so soon after the first in 1964, he now went on television on March 15. Speaking before Congress, he announced that he would submit "a law designed to eliminate illegal barriers to the right to vote... What happened in Selma is part of a far larger movement which reaches into every section and state of America." We all must, he said, join this cause. "Their cause must be our cause too... it is all of us who must overcome the crippling legacy of bigotry and injustice. And we shall overcome..."[11]

John Lewis remembered sitting with Martin Luther King, watching LBJ's speech. When LBJ echoed the words of the civil rights anthem, Lewis recalled that he and King broke into tears. After some internal disagreements over procedures, marchers again left Selma for

Montgomery. This time federal authority protected them, and they had in their ranks politicians, labor leaders, well-known academics, religious leaders, and Jimmie Lee Jackson's grandfather. On their last night before arriving in Montgomery, celebrities joined the crowd including conductor Leonard Bernstein, former heavyweight champion Floyd Patterson, actors Sidney Poitier and Paul Newman, singers Tony Bennett, Sammy Davis, Jr., and Harry Belafonte. Ella Fitzgerald, gospel legend Mahalia Jackson, comedian Dick Gregory, folk singers Joan Baez and Peter, Paul, and Mary, and SNCC's Freedom Singers provided entertainment.

Before a crowd of 30,000 in Montgomery the next day, King, flanked by civil rights leaders including Rosa Parks, spoke of how "Selma has become a shining monument in the conscience of man." A day of redemption was at hand, he declared. When he asked, rhetorically, "How long?" he answered, "Not long. Because the arm of the moral universe is long, but it bends toward justice."[12]

Among the listeners was Viola Liuzzo, a Detroit mother who had been so moved by the previous events that she got in her car and drove to Alabama to volunteer. She had worked tirelessly all week and, when the rally ended, drove marchers back to Selma. Returning to Montgomery, she was trailed by four Klansman, who opened fire and murdered her.

By August, the Voting Rights Act was on Lyndon Johnson's desk, awaiting his signature. Despite its passage, the events of 1965, adding to the frustrations over the fate of the Mississippi Freedom Democrats at the 1964 Democratic Convention, had begun to move many members of SNCC in new directions. Soon after the march to Montgomery, Stokely Carmichael led a group of SNCC workers into rural Alabama to form the Lowndes County Freedom Organization (LCFO), a third party focusing on African-Americans voters. They chose as their symbol the black panther and, supported by the new voting rights act and federal registrars, began to sign up voters and nominate candidates for local office.

SNCC, itself, faced serious internal disputes over its direction, pitting its initial style, that of Ella Baker and John Lewis among others, against the new approach of Carmichael. In addition, outside events began to adjust their perspective. Vietnam demanded attention. Bob Moses had spoken at early anti-war rallies and in January 1966, as we have seen, SNCC came out against the war, connecting their struggle with those of other peoples of color, including the Vietnamese. The war even had its influence on SNCC's electoral strategy. In 1965, SNCC Communications Director Julian Bond had been elected to the Georgia state legislature, but, in January 1966, legislators refused to seat him over his opposition to the war. Appeals went all the way to the U.S. Supreme Court, where a unanimous decision in December gave Bond his rightful seat.

In May 1966, SNCC held its spring conference, at which the group's direction and leadership would be decided. John Lewis, who had been SNCC's chair since 1963, represented the older nonviolent strategy that some younger members thought was growing out of touch. The new energy seemed to sit with Stokely Carmichael. Carmichael's work in Lowndes had staked out electoral politics as the next phase, and even members of SNCC had begun to talk about limiting or resisting white involvement in the newest efforts. As left-wing journalist I. F. Stone summarized a month later, "the battle has shifted from the simpler symbolic acts of sitting at a segregated lunch counter or in a segregated waiting room to the harder and more complicated tasks of winning economic and social equality." The initial struggles had needed the "wonderful white boys and girls who went South," Stone concluded. But the new job "will have to be done by Negroes themselves."[13]

In the final vote for SNCC chair, Carmichael handily defeated John Lewis. Typically, Lewis later saw the change in philosophical terms. "More than anything else, what happened in 1966 can be traced to what happened [at the Democratic Convention of 1964]. Stokely and I were symbols about the sense of direction...I didn't take it personally. Change is bound to come in any movement where you don't have a top down structure."[14]

A month later, James Meredith, who had desegregated the University of Mississippi in the fall of 1962, announced that he would embark on a one-man "March Against Fear." His plan was to walk the 220 miles from

Memphis to his home in Mississippi without marshals to protect him. Covering the 12 miles to the Tennessee state line the first day, he was 14 miles into Mississippi on the second day when a man shouting "I only want James Meredith" stepped into the road and fired his shotgun three times at Meredith. Reports first circulated of his murder, but these were later corrected to say he was only in surgery.

There was an immediate nationwide reaction to the shooting, including from Lyndon Johnson, Senator Robert Kennedy, and the major forces of the civil rights community. CORE first proposed that others take up the "March Against Fear," and King received permission bedside from Meredith to proceed. On the day after the shooting, King locked arms with Stokely Carmichael and Floyd McKissick, the new, more militant head of CORE, leading a group of marchers who resumed the march. Stopping at night to camp along the highway, crowds gathered and rallies were held. And the compelling presence was Carmichael. "I ain't going to jail no more…The only way we gonna stop the white men from whuppin' us is to take over," he declared one night. "We have been saying freedom for six years and we ain't got nothing." And then he uttered a phrase that caught fire. "What we gonna start saying now is Black Power!" At this point, SNCC field organizer Willie Ricks, often called "the Reverend" because of his powerful oratorical style, leaped on to the stage and shouted to the crowd, "What Do We Want?" to which the audience shouted back, "Black Power!"—a call-and-response repeated a number of times with increasing volume and enthusiasm.[15]

The Los Angeles neighborhood of Watts did not look like the stereotypical image of an urban slum, with its single-family homes on tree-lined streets. But its appearance masked decades of residential segregation and economic discrimination. And despite the national attention to desegregation efforts in the South, things were only growing worse in Los Angeles. Large segments of real estate in the city were off-limits to citizens of color. In 1963, the California state legislature had passed a fair housing act to eliminate residential segregation. In 1964 voters forced the measure onto the ballot. That November, while California voters were giving 60 percent of their vote to Lyndon Johnson, they overturned the fair housing law by a 2-to-1 majority. By 1965, the first hints of a white backlash had begun to surface. Even before the problems of Northern urban communities could be addressed, white America was beginning to turn away.*

On Wednesday, August 11, 1965 two brothers from Watts were celebrating the discharge of one of them from the Air Force. Weaving in traffic, they were pulled over by police close to home. Their mother rushed to the scene to berate her sons for drinking but also to protect them from being arrested. She ended up in the back of the police cruiser. One of her sons refused to follow, shouting, "Go ahead, kill me!" Onlookers grew restive. Motorcycle police appeared, driving on to the sidewalk to push the crowd back. Shouted insults resulted in further arrests, as the crowd swelled. Rocks were thrown; stores began to be looted. And the largest urban riot to date in the postwar years was underway.[16]

The riots waxed and waned for several days, often calming in the day-time and reigniting at night. Rumors spread in both the Black and white communities. Police were supposed to have indiscriminately beaten African Americans, including a pregnant woman. Stories in the *Los Angeles Times* quoted the crowds as chanting "Get Whitey!" and "Burn, Baby Burn."

Martin Luther King flew to Los Angeles to try to calm the situation but also to reinforce nonviolence as the best method of change. But he found an ambivalent audience. "Sure, we like to be nonviolent," one man shouted to Kin, "but we up here...will not turn the other cheek." "All we want is jobs," shouted another. "We get jobs, we don't bother nobody. We don't get jobs, we'll tear up Los Angeles, period." Evidencing

---

* I recall a high school mathematics teacher telling my white, suburban Los Angeles class a year or two earlier that he was planning to organize a group called SPONGE, "The Society for the Prevention of Negroes Getting Everything." I am sure he did not come up with this idea or even the name on his own but was only repeating something he had heard and liked.

his growing awareness of the change in the national conversation on race, King declared, "Elijah Muhammad is my brother, even though our methods are different," which was greeted by a thunderous ovation from the crowd. And perhaps most tellingly for his own future plans, King declared, "We are not free in the South, and you are not free in the cities of the North...We all go up together or we go down together."[17]

The city of Los Angeles responded to the unrest by calling out over 15,000 police and National Guardsmen to restore order. A curfew was declared for all the Black neighborhoods. L.A.'s police chief issued an order for mass arrests. By Sunday the 15th, some sense of calm had been created. But the Watts Riots proved a wake-up call for a nation that thought its racial problems had been on the way to being solved. California's governor appointed a commission to investigate the riots, with former CIA chief John McCone, as its chair, and future Secretary of State Warren Christopher as its vice-chair. The Commission's report, issued in December, proved a stinging indictment of the situation in Los Angeles, including recommendations on how to prevent a "recurrence of the nightmare," as they put it, for every American city. These included improvements in employment, housing, education, and more. Acknowledging how complex and costly their suggested improvements would be, the commissioners argued that "the consequence of inaction, indifference, and inadequacy, we can all be sure now, would be far costlier in the long run than the cost of correction."[18]

While issues of race, discrimination, and segregation still plagued the South, it was clear that, by 1965, the movement for racial equality had begun to move north, or as the eloquent Taylor Branch later put it, "up the Mississippi heartland, from the Delta's primitive soil to Chicago's granite expanse."[19] Watts initiated a series of summers filled with urban violence. In 1966 alone, riots erupted in Cleveland, Dayton, Milwaukee, Omaha, and San Francisco. Similar images were repeated from city to city—smashed windows, streets on fire, stores looted. It became difficult for audiences at home to distinguish between the cities set ablaze.

Martin Luther King, already in the process of expanding his perspective to include national economic issues and foreign policy concerns, followed the northward transition. He joined the struggle for open housing in Chicago, organizing marches through white neighborhoods that had systematically kept out people of color. The white backlash was staggering. Racist signs and chants greeted the marchers. In one neighborhood, the crowd waved Confederate flags, held signs that said, "Nigger Go Home," and hurled bricks and bottles. One projectile hit King, dropping him to his knees. "I have never seen such hate," he said, "not in Mississippi or Alabama as I see here in Chicago."[20]

The fallout from the Meredith March and the public announcement of "Black Power" stirred Black people and alarmed whites. An article in the *New York Times* concluded that a new "black consciousness" was "sweeping the civil rights movement" with "Mr. Carmichael as its leader and the late Malcolm X as its prophet." The appeal, the *Times'* reporter felt, was mostly to Black youth "ages 15 to 30, but it also provides emotional release for older Negroes." It noted that after the emotion of the speeches are over, Carmichael and other SNCC leaders "spend hours explaining they are not anti-white but are simply trying to make the Negro feel pride in his race."[21]

SNCC attempted to spell out its new mentality in a position paper "The Basis of Black Power." While acknowledging the role of whites in the previous civil rights efforts, the time had come for "white people who desire change...[to] go where...racism is most manifest. The problem is not in the black community. The white people should go into white communities." "We had fallen into a trap whereby we thought that our problems revolved around the right to eat at certain lunch counters or the right to vote," they admitted. But "the problem is much deeper." And to deal with these deeper problems, "we must cut ourselves off from white people. We must form our own institutions, credit unions, co-ops, political parties, write our own histories...We must determine our own destiny."[22]

In speeches around the country, Carmichael linked Black Power to economic and diplomatic concerns, to existential philosophy and the notions of a Third World consciousness being argued by intellectuals like Frantz Fanon, to Western colonialism in Africa and Southeast Asia. Black people could no longer allow whites to determine the path of racial politics or allow them to identify the appropriate solutions. "How can white people who are the majority, and who are responsible for making democracy work, make it work?" asked Carmichael. "They have never made democracy work, be it inside the United States, Vietnam, South Africa, the Philippines, South America, Puerto Rico, or wherever America has been."[23]

It was not merely the young militants of SNCC who embraced the idea of Black Power. On July 31, the National Coalition of Negro Churchmen published a full-page statement in the Sunday *New York Times*, signed by nearly 50 Black Protestant clergymen from across the country. "The fundamental distortion facing us in the controversy over 'black power' is rooted in a gross imbalance of power and conscience between Negro and white Americans." This leads to the unstated "assumption that white people are justified in getting what they want through the use of power, but that Negro Americans must...make their appeal only through conscience." The need was to develop "group power." "We must not apologize for the existence of this form of group power; for we have been oppressed as a group, not as individuals. We will not find our way out of that oppression until both we and America accept the need for Negro Americans to have and to wield group power."[24] Black Power was much more than a phrase to inspire the young. It was an idea penetrating deep into the thinking on race of many Black Americans.

Among those moved by the calls for Black Power and the expanding perspective of the movement for racial awareness, were two young men from Oakland, California, both college graduates, Bobby Seale and Huey Newton. In the fall of 1966, they founded the Black Panther Party for Self Defense, choosing its name and symbol from the LCFO party in Lowndes County. Their platform, "What We Want, What We Believe," echoed the arguments surging across the country. "We want freedom. We want power to determine the destiny of our Black Community," the platform began. They went on to demand "full employment" and "decent housing," but "an end to robbery by the CAPITALISTS of our Black Community," the exemption of all Black men from military service, freedom for all Black people currently in prison, and "an immediate end to POLICE BRUTALITY and MURDER." Their final call was for a United Nations-supervised plebiscite "throughout the black colony…for the purpose of determining the will of black people as to their national destiny."[25]

To reinforce their message, the Black Panthers adopted a compelling visual style—black pants, black leather jackets, and black berets. To raise money, they bought bulk copies of Mao's *Little Red Book* and sold them on the streets of Berkeley. And they began to develop ways to confront police brutality directly, patrolling Oakland neighborhoods at night to challenge police actions. This was a new form of Black activism, echoing the self-defense message of Malcolm X and expanding the ideas embedded in Black Power.

Civil rights activism stretched back to the early 1950s and well before. But in a few short years in the mid-1960s, the struggle and direction of racial efforts changed radically. Race would no longer be ignored, and anyone concerned with the progress of racial justice in the United Sates was forced to pay attention.

7

The Counterculture

There is probably no more stereotyped or misunderstood aspect of Sixties' life than the counterculture. The persistent typical caricature is of a vaguely inarticulate, drug-addled, long-haired hippie spouting vacuous phrases about seeing magical visions, entranced by psychedelic music, or rapturously praising some aspect of the counterculture lifestyle unavailable to the straight world. Sometimes the counterculture is patronizingly dismissed with the clichéd trinity of "sex, drugs, and rock 'n' roll," ignoring all its actual complexity. This paragraph from *America: Land I Love*, an eighth-grade textbook for Christian schools, suggests just how far one of these stereotyped depictions can go.

> Many young people turned to drugs and immoral lifestyles; these youth became known as hippies. They went without bathing, wore dirty, ragged, unconventional clothing, and deliberately broke all codes of politeness or manners. Rock music played an important part in the hippie movement and had great influence over the hippies. Many of the rock musicians they followed belonged to Eastern religious cults or practiced Satan worship.[1]

Yet, there is much to be taken seriously in the counterculture, its influence moving well beyond easily dismissive cliches. It offered a critique of contemporary American society framed in personal expression as well as in the manner in which people shaped their lives. It's effect on American culture would prove profound.

Often, when people think of the1960s, it is as a something fully formed and static. Yet, it is clear that there were a variety of developments over the course of the era, some emerging early in the decade, some much later. It was not until the last third of the decade that people began to take note of a coherent counterculture, one linking various social and artistic trends. But the roots of the counterculture stretch back to the first years of the decade and often into the 1950s.

In fact, even amid all the self-satisfied praise of the early postwar years about the beneficence of American life, there was significant resistance to the basic tenets of postwar life. Everyone did not see this as the best of all possible worlds. The praised literary outpouring of the postwar years rested heavily on novels whose central premise was built on a critique of the zeitgeist. From J. D. Salinger to Philip Roth, John Updike to John Cheever, Sylvia Plath to Richard Yates, postwar literature became defined by alienation from the mainstream and resistance to conformist and materialistic premises of the times. While some, like the heroes of Jack Kerouac's *On The Road*, actively rebelled against the norms of the era, the main characters in many novels just lived lives of quiet (and not-so-quiet) desperation.

Many observers concluded that postwar life was insufferable, even for those presumed to be the beneficiaries of the period—men, women, and children. Yet, if they rebelled, the overall social response to these critiques was usually one of disdain and dismissal, refusing to take any of the questioning seriously. The young were "rebels without a cause," as James Dean's 1955 movie was titled. In *The Wild One* (1953), Marlon Brando's character is asked, "What are you rebelling against?" He replies, "Whaddaya got?" The critic Diana Trilling, writing about a famous Beat poetry reading at Columbia in 1958, patronizingly dismissed the audience as juvenile. "There's nothing dirty about a checked shirt or a lumber jacket and blue jeans," she wrote, "they are standard uniform in the best nursery schools." And she concludes that while Allen Ginsberg presented himself as a bohemian, he had really "always desperately wanted to be respectable."[2] Taking the critiques seriously would only suggest that there was substance to their arguments. Better to dismiss it all as juvenile or posturing.

Social analysts began to develop assessments that reinforced the literary ones. Sociologist David Riesman, in *The Lonely Crowd* (1950), depicted middle-class Americans as feeling the need to conform to the society around them; but this led to a lonely, personal emptiness. Social critic Paul Goodman told American youth that they were *Growing Up Absurd* (1960), encouraged to favor conformity and professional ambition, which led to lives lacking passion and meaning. Both books became bestsellers.

The sexual values of the era seemed epitomized by the characters Doris Day played in a series of 1950s films where the plots revolved around her trying to stay out of her male costar's bed until they wed. Sexuality was to be contained within marriage. The age when people married went down,* and the culture continually reinforced a sexual double standard. Television programs and movies were controlled by a strict code of what could and could not be depicted. And very little could be depicted, including the requirement that married couples on TV had to sleep in separate, twin beds and women's navels could not be shown. Yet the reality was actually much more tumultuous than movies, television, or society at large would acknowledge. The Kinsey Reports—one on male sexuality (1948) and one on female sexuality (1953)—had demonstrated that Americans were more sexually active than people believed. (These books also became bestsellers, despite their dry, academic tone.) The releases for suppressed sexuality were channeled into socially acceptable outlets, such as *Playboy* magazine, which first appeared in 1953. As discussed above, *Playboy* sought respectability by offering serious fiction and interviews along with its pictorials of naked young women. And even those Doris Day movies were, in fact, all about sex, although there wasn't any actually taking place.

All these tensions and the double standard in American society and culture were not lost on the young. Traditional youthful rebelliousness and the typical desire to diverge from the patterns of one's parents were reinforced by what was understood about the limitations of the adult

* In 1900, the median age at which men married was 26, for women it was 22. In 1940, the ages were 24 and 22, respectively. By 1960, the median age for men had declined to 22 for men and 20 for women. https://www.census.gov/data/tables/time-series/demo/families/marital.html

world. It seems obvious why the Beats would offer such a compelling example of an alternative way of life. Rather than the lives of quiet desperation depicted in the prominent novels of the era, the characters in *On The Road*, as was stated above, rejected materialism, 9-to-5 jobs, families, monogamy, and respectability, embracing instead explorations of feelings, sexuality, and immediate experience—all antidotes to the limitations of postwar life.

In addition, a separate youth culture began to emerge in the fifties, catering exclusively to the young as never before. And the central element of this culture was rock 'n' roll. Young people became an identifiable consumer market. One can clearly see the existence of two vastly different cultural spheres—one for adults, one for the young—by simply looking at the Billboard music charts. In 1956, for example, Elvis Presley had the #1 and #2 bestselling singles of the year, "Heartbreak Hotel" and "Don't Be Cruel." But the #3 spot was an instrumental by bandleader Nelson Riddle, "Lisbon Antigua." In fact, six of the year's Top Ten were from mainstream musicians like Dean Martin and Doris Day. Even as youth-orientated songs began to dominate the charts, there would always be records aimed at the adult market.

Rock 'n' roll confounded older America for many reasons. They found the lyrics incomprehensible, foolish, or nonsensical, and the sexual undertone of the music or the overt sexuality of the male singers problematic. This was in addition to rock 'n' roll's troubling connections to Black music. Often labeled "jungle music," one music periodical wrote in 1956 that teens were "definitely influenced in their lawlessness by this throwback to jungle rhythms." "DON'T BUY NEGRO RECORDS," the segregationist White Citizen's Council of New Orleans declared. "The screaming, idiotic words, and savage music of these records are undermining the morals of our white youth in America."[3]

But to the kids, rock music offered something that spoke to their concerns and desires, and it was something their parents hated. The subjects of the songs—school, summer, cars, dating, sex, dancing—were enhanced by a pounding beat. It was their music, and they could dance to it. For both the parents and their children, rock 'n' roll began to define a generation.

Another music trend that emerged in these years was the folk revival. Folk music had moved the American left in the Depression years, especially labor songs and music emanating from the Black South. The New Deal's WPA had created projects to collect folk songs. Folk musicians, like Woody Guthrie and Pete Seeger, became associated with leftwing causes. In the late 1950s, as record companies began to come to terms with the rock 'n' roll explosion and exercise greater control over its production and distribution, some young people began to see folk music as more authentic. Further, it connected with the political movements of the day, especially civil rights.

Greenwich Village had been the magnetic center of bohemianism in America for decades and no less so in the 1950s and early 1960s. And part of the postwar bohemian scene included folk music. Coffeehouses symbolized fifties bohemian life—Beat poets read their work, politicos debated, and folk singers performed. Coffeehouses began to spring up in cities across the country. Many of the musicians in the first popular American bands of the sixties, like the Grateful Dead, Jefferson Airplane, Country Joe and The Fish, The Byrds, and the Lovin' Spoonful, began their music careers in the folk clubs of New York, San Francisco, and Los Angeles.

As the 1960s dawned, these various cultural currents began to merge. In early 1961, a young folksinger from Minnesota began to appear in Greenwich Village clubs. To some older Village habitués, like socialist Michael Harrington, the Village he knew ended "the night a gawky kid named Bob Dylan showed up...I heard the future and I didn't like it."[4] But younger people did. Dylan joined a new generation of folksingers, like Joan Baez, Phil Ochs, Judy Collins, and Peter, Paul, and Mary, some of whom wrote their own songs and many of those songs tapped directly into the political and social issues of the day. Dylan's first album, made up of mostly traditional folk songs, received a tepid response. But his second, *The Freewheelin' Bob Dylan*, contained mostly his own songs, on topics including nuclear war and civil rights, as well those about personal issues and experiences. The album opener, "Blowin' In The Wind," became a radio hit for Peter, Paul, and Mary. One critic later wrote, "These were the songs that established [Dylan] as the voice of his generation—someone who implicitly understood how concerned young Americans felt...his mixture of moral authority and nonconformity was perhaps the most timely of his attributes."[5] A year later, Dylan's third album was tellingly titled, *The Times They Are a Changin'*. The songs again mixed the political and the personal, with the title song containing the prophetic verse,

> *Come mothers and fathers*
> *Throughout the land*
> *And don't criticize*
> *What you can't understand*
> *Your sons and your daughters*
> *Are beyond your command*
> *Your old road is rapidly aging*
> *Please get out of the new one*
> *If you can't lend your hand*
> *For the times they are a-changin'*

Here was a perfect distillation of what many of the young people were feeling.

In July 1965, Dylan appeared at the Newport Folk Festival carrying not an acoustic guitar but a Fender Stratocaster and with a backup band of rock musicians. Dylan "going electric" became a staple of rock mythology, the symbolic merger of the two genres. Reports said many in the crowd booed, that a furious Pete Seeger tried to cut off the sound, but that others danced and cheered. One song from his set, "Like a Rolling Stone," was released as a single a few weeks later and, despite its six-minute length, became a radio hit, peaking at #2. (A shorter, more Top 40-friendly edited version was also released to increase radio play.)

When the mid-fifties explosion of rock 'n' roll, epitomized by Elvis, Chuck Berry, Jerry Lee Lewis, Little Richard, and others, subsided (in part due to personal issues of some of the artists*), rock music became

---

* In 1958 Elvis Presley was drafted and spent two years in the military. In 1957, Jerry Lee Lewis married his 13-year-old cousin, the scandal undermining his popularity. Chuck Berry was arrested in 1959 for transporting a 14-year-old girl across state lines for the purpose of engaging in a sexual encounter. He was ultimately sentenced to three years in prison. In 1957, Little Richard abandoned rock 'n' roll for five years after becoming a born-again Christian.

more managed by record companies and Top 40 radio stations. The acts were deemed "safer," the sexuality toned down, the racial implications defused. While some very good music was released in this period, such as the early Beach Boys' records, the industry did not feel it was riding a hurricane, as it had before. But soon people began to hear about, often even before they actually heard, the music explosion that was shaking the United Kingdom. Crowds were screaming for a band from Liverpool, reminiscent of how young people had screamed for Elvis or, a generation before, for Frank Sinatra.

The Beatles had, evidently, decided that they would not tour America until they had a #1 hit in the U.S. They had seen too many British bands go to America, be placed at the bottom of the bill at a rock concert, and fade into obscurity. So they waited. While they had several #1 UK hits, it was not until February 1964 that "I Want to Hold Your Hand" claimed the top spot in the U.S. The record was not just a hit but also a phenomenon, for both the song and the band. Capitol Records could not keep up with the demand for copies. And when, after spending seven weeks at #1, it was only dislodged from the top spot by another Beatles record, "She Loves You."

People seemed to understand that something new had arrived. "They were doing things nobody was doing," Bob Dylan later recalled. "Their chords were outrageous, just outrageous, and their harmonies made it all valid." Brian Wilson, the musical genius behind the Beach Boys, later recalled that upon hearing "I Want to Hold Your Hand," "I flipped. It was like a shock went through my system...I immediately knew that everything had changed."[6]

On February 9, it became staggeringly clear just how much things had changed. Nearly 74 million Americans, about 40 percent of the entire U.S. population, tuned in to the Ed Sullivan Show to see and hear the Beatles. The band opened the show with three songs, to a torrent of screams. Other acts followed, but the screaming persisted and proved distracting for the performers and the audience. The Beatles closed the show with two more songs.

And the world seemed to turn. People, especially young people, long remembered where they were the night the Beatles appeared on Ed

Sullivan. Years later, one young man remembered he felt as if he had been "struck by lightning. I had never been so excited by any musical group or performance like that."[7] "From the moment I saw them, my life was changed forever," recalled another. For one young woman, "That day in February affected the person I became…Life in general was never the same again." "I was awe struck. I had never seen anything like them," one young man recalled. "I was blown away by them—in absolute awe!"[8]

Suddenly, the hottest spot in the general culture emanated from youth culture itself. It was not just what the kids were listening to. Everyone was listening. The Beatles were more than a band. They were a cultural phenomenon. They may have been selling more records than anyone in the world, but they rooted their personae within the world of youth culture. As one writer in the *Los Angeles Free Press* put it at the time, "They are hip, disrespectful, carefree, anti-patriotic, irreverent…They challenge older generations to earn the respect they demand from kids—and so seldom deserve."[9] In the struggle between adult culture and youth culture, the Beatles arrived and decided the issue. Mainstream artists would still exist—with artists like Barbra Streisand, Andy Williams, and Louis Armstrong continuing to release albums—but they would be pushed to the margins. Center stage now belonged to the kids.

The Beatles ushered in what became known as the British Invasion. Bands from the UK, like the Rolling Stones, the Who, the Yardbirds, the Kinks, and many more, joined the Beatles to dominate the airwaves and turntables. Rock music was revitalized by this infusion of fresh and exciting new music, that seemed to exemplify the excitement of contemporary Britain. The irony was most of these British bands traced their musical roots back to American rhythm and blues.

Beyond their staggering musical success, the Beatles helped create and popularize the new look of youth culture. One female viewer of the Ed Sullivan showed recalled, "I screamed!…We loved their 'long' hair and their accent." But many parents dissented. "The Beatles looked like girls and their hair was too long," one parent complained. Another called them "long haired freaks." The musical director of the Ed Sullivan show was unimpressed. He told *The New York Times*, "The only thing that's different is the hair, as far as I can see. I give them a year."[10]

In retrospect, it is quite amazing to consider the cultural reaction that accompanied something as seemingly superficial as the length of men's hair. When we look at the pictures of the Free Speech Movement demonstrators at Berkeley or those of the first Vietnam Teach-Ins, it is surprising to see just how traditional the students looked, including the men's hair length. Even the Beatles on Ed Sullivan hardly seem the "long-haired freaks" that would characterize the counterculture hairstyles by the late sixties. There was just something so telling and so challenging in the choice of young men to grow their hair longer, a clear rejection of the well-kept, crew cut style of the fifties. The mainstream reaction was not merely distaste or even disparaging comments. Legal battles ensued from men and boys who felt they'd been discriminated against in the work place or in school because of their hair length. It was cultural warfare, mirroring the political conflicts taking shape. And it was a battle fought from within families all the way to the courts.[11]

Hair length was only the most prominent symbol of the emerging cultural rebellion, all of which reflected a rejection of the prevailing postwar norms, especially its perceived crass materialism. In 1962, the Port Huron Statement had noted that too many Americans exhibited a "cheerful emptiness" amid "national doldrums." "Beneath the stagnation of those who have closed their minds to the future, is the pervading feeling that there simply are no alternatives, that our times have witnessed the exhaustion...of Utopias."[12] Many young people now sought to break out of the "emptiness," to develop "alternatives," and to create "utopias." If the personal was political, one could start with one's own appearance and lifestyle.

There is always more to fashion than what a magazine declares to be "in style" each year. It is how one presents oneself to the world. And how did the kids drawn to the counterculture present themselves? In second-hand clothes, sometimes bought in Army surplus stores, with men in work shirts and blue jeans, women in clothes made from Asian bedspreads or long, flowing paisley dresses. Men began to wear jewelry beyond the wristwatch and class ring, which was about all that adorned men in the fifties. Everyone started to wear beads, flowers, and other body decorations. Their self-presentation announced their rejection of all the styles of postwar America. One writer later declared that hippies "will not play the straight game of camouflage." Their "disregard of straight taboos of dress makes them seem to be capable of anything and therefore a danger."[13] If the goal was to overcome the perceived grayness of modern life, what better place to start than with how one looked? And to declare your difference in bold patterns and bright colors.

Or in how one lived. Kids who grew up in suburbia with bedrooms decorated with Little League trophies, athletic team pennants, and stuffed animals, now put mattresses on the floor, made bookcases out of boards and bricks, and bought items at a brand-new business venture, the head shop. Here one could secure not only drug paraphernalia but also objects promising to enhance drug experiences, from lava lamps to black light posters to incense burners.

How one looked and where one lived announced how you were going to live your life. "Many people cannot understand the hippies' rejection of everything that is commonly expected of the individual," wrote hippie and later gay activist Guy Strait, especially "in regard to employment and life goals." Hippies dressed the way they do "because they have thrown a lot of middle-class notions out the window."[14]

Sexual behavior that had been shaped and controlled by postwar social norms was also an easily identifiable target for those seeking a new, more meaningful existence. And they were aided by the introduction of new birth control methods, particularly the birth control pill. Researchers, such as birth control pioneer John Rock, understood the potential pitfalls of constraining sexual energy in the fifties. It was "the greatest menace to world peace," he argued in 1954, greater than atomic weapons. Oral contraception would be "the greatest aid to the happiness and security of individual families." By 1960, the FDA had approved "The Pill," as it came to be called. The response was staggering. "By 1964, 6.5 million married women and untold numbers of unmarried women" were using it. And its social implications were viewed as much wider than family security.[15]

The sexual double standard could now be dismantled, allowing both men and women to pursue sexual lives without fear of unwanted pregnancies. As part of the emerging counterculture lifestyle, men and women began to openly live together, even before marriage, a situation that announced a sexual relationship. And it allowed for more casual sex encounters, sometimes with newly found acquaintances and sometimes with total strangers. Much has been made of the "free love" aspect of the counterculture life, but this was only a very small part of a much larger transformation of sexuality that accompanied the overall social transformation.

There had always been non-conformists in American society, those who fled the social constraints of modern society, often living in isolated communal settings, from the Oneida and Brook Farm communities of the nineteenth century to religious and socialist ones of the twentieth. Once disdained as irresponsible or weird, these escapees now became the heroes and role models of a new behavior. The constant refrain of many of the young was their sense of alienation from modern society and their personal desire to resist its conformist aspects. To these alienated young people, those non-conformists were pioneers.

Beyond how one looked or where one lived, the central intention was to think differently. Postwar personal experience had been reduced to what was felt to be a black-and-white existence proscribed by unfulfilling social norms. The aim was to replace it with a technicolor reality. A variety of means were available—from drugs to religious experiences to a deeper connection with nature. Each would bring a fuller understanding of life, a more meaningful existence, and a profound appreciation of the beauty and pleasures of the world's sights and sounds. Drugs, from marijuana to LSD, became the most popular vehicle that might lead toward this nirvana. But so too was a reinvigoration of religious enthusiasm. Eastern religions offered one path, redefined Christianity, another. Beat poet Gary Snyder told how "Buddhist philosophy sees the world as a vast interrelated network in which all objects and creatures are necessary and illuminated... the mercy of the East has been individual insight into the basic self/void." This would not only lead to personal transformation, but a move "toward a free, international, classless world...If we are lucky," Snyder concluded, "we may eventually arrive at a totally integrated world culture with free-form marriage...less industry...and lots more national parks." In 1965, Malcolm Boyd, an Episcopal priest, published *Are You Running With Me, Jesus?*, a series of prayers and ruminations, including "Prayers for the Free Self," "Prayers for the Free Society," "Prayers for Racial Freedom," and "Prayers for Sexual Freedom." Learning to see the world at its fullest would not only offer personal salvation, but it would initiate a social transformation that would usher in a utopia. Again, the personal became the political.[16]

Indigenous peoples began to be credited with a more intimate understanding of nature—be they in India or New Mexico—undistorted by modern society. All the better if these understandings were enhanced by the use of mind-altering drugs. Carlos Castaneda, an anthropology grad student at UCLA, published a series of articles, culminating in *The Teaching of Don Juan: A Yaqui Way of Knowledge* (1968), in which the hallucinogenic drug peyote, provided by a Mexican shaman, led to deeper connections with nature.[17] But more often, the drugs were seen as a self-sufficient means of transcending the constraints of modern life. Marijuana became ubiquitous, offering an easy path to relaxation and heightened experience. LSD, which was not illegal until 1968, was hailed as the ticket to paradise. The LSD experience—or "trip" as it came to be called—promised a mental journey of discovery. "You are apt to feel like an explorer who landed on Mars with no return fuel," wrote one advocate. "The ceiling above me," wrote another, "became a black sky filled with universes, red, white and blue, whirling at incredible speeds...a very beautiful religious experience happened to me then...I wept for all the people I have hurt in my life, including myself."[18] There proved to be many problematic personal experiences with LSD (called "bad trips"), but the promise of the experience, especially when LSD first gained wider acceptance, seemed to offer the perfect vehicle by which to transcend the dull reality of contemporary life and to embrace the deeper meaning of the universe.

By this point, LSD had its guru, former Harvard professor Timothy Leary. Leary had followed a peripatetic path to Harvard, but in 1960 he convinced the psychology department to form the Harvard Psilocybin Project with him at its head, assisted by a young psychology professor, Richard Alpert (later Baba Ram Dass). Both were ultimately dismissed from the university for using undergrads in their psychedelic experiments, but by then they had developed a national reputation as advocates of the possibilities of psychedelics, specifically LSD. From very early on, Leary was in tune with the emerging mentality of the era. "I speak to you," he told a conference in 1961, "from a point midway between the Western and Eastern hemispheres of the cortex." He felt his approach combined Chinese, Indian, and Western approaches.[19]

Offered the use of an enormous estate in Dutchess County, New York, Leary and Alpert created a utopian commune based in Millbrook, the mansion on the property, and built around psychedelic explorations. Numerous individuals were attracted to Millbrook, from jazz musicians Charles Mingus and Maynard Ferguson to writers Allen Ginsberg and Alan Watts. In 1964, Leary wrote the introduction to an edited volume, *LSD: The Consciousness Expanding Drug*, which included essays by many well-known individuals.* In his introduction, Leary wrote of his own drug journey. "Instead of fleeing *from* reality, I flew more deeply *into* it. I had never before seen, touched, tasted, heard, smelled, and *felt* so profound a personal unity and involvement with the concrete material world." This was heady stuff in these days—"mind-blowing," acolytes might have said. In 1964, Robert Anton Wilson wrote in *The Realist* magazine that he thought Albert Einstein and Leary might be "the two greatest thinkers of the twentieth century." Einstein had shown "how to create atomic fission in the physical world." Leary showed how to do it in "the psychological world."[20]

---

* Among the contributors to this volume were novelists Dan Wakefield, Aldous Huxley, and William Burroughs; Alan Watts, the popular American writer on Buddhism and Eastern religions; and a number of academic psychologists and medical professionals. David Soloman, ed., *LSD: The Consciousness Expanding Drug* (New York, G.P. Putnam's Sons, 1964).

All these investigations—whether through drugs, spirituality, or exercises in self-awareness—would not only enhance personal experience but add to an emerging artistic sensibility. Ken Kesey's 1962 novel *One Flew Over the Cuckoo's Nest* fit perfectly into this new style. Set in a mental hospital, the novel questions who—the patients or the staff—is sane and who insane. It connected to a growing sense that madness was not mental illness but deep insight. And this corresponded to the belief in the insights that drugs elicited. Kesey, himself, had begun using hallucinogenic drugs a few years before. While a graduate student at Stanford in the early 1960s, he had attracted a following, "a court" one fellow student called it, of others interested in hanging out and consuming LSD-spiked food and drink, including future novelists Robert Stone and Larry McMurtry, as well as a young folk musician named Jerry Garcia. With the royalties from *Cuckoo's Nest*, Kesey purchased a large ranch south of San Francisco, to which many friends flocked. The community became known as the Merry Pranksters. Having read Kesey's novel, Neal Cassady, Jack Kerouac's friend and the model for one of the characters in *On the Road*, decided it was the place for him. "We're on the verge of something very fantastic," Kesey declared in 1963, "and I believe our generation will be the one to pull it off."[21] Kesey purchased an old school bus, which the Pranksters painted in psychedelic colors and symbols, and, with Cassady at the wheel, headed out on a cross-country journey of LSD-enhanced experiences, including a stop at Millbrook.

Other artists, forced to the margins of cultural life in the 1950s, found their artistic sensibilities much more in tune with the new developments. As discussed in chapter 1, this included groups such as the Living Theatre, which sought to push the boundaries of theatrical presentations; novelists like Joseph Heller and Kurt Vonnegut, whose fiction defied easy categorization when they first appeared; or Andy Warhol, who had added filmmaking to his pop art painting, including "Sleep" and "Empire" (both in 1964), which featured hours-long footage of a man sleeping or of the Empire State Building, respectively. As the 1960s progressed, these works found new, receptive audiences who felt the connections between this art and the new zeitgeist.

By late 1965, the counterculture began to go public. People would gather at an "Acid Test," where they would eat, drink, dance, and take LSD. Five hundred people showed up to such a "happening" in Los Angeles in November. A number of "tests" sprang up in Northern California. In January two thousand people came to the Fillmore Auditorium, where the Warlocks (the band that would morph in The Grateful Dead) played, LSD was dispensed, lights shimmered, and Allen Ginsberg sang Buddhist mantras. The Merry Pranksters showed a film they had made of their cross-country bus trip. The culmination of this first wave of these events came with the Trips Festival, a three-day happening in January 1966 at the Longshoreman's Hall on San Francisco's Fisherman's Wharf. Estimates of attendance ranged between six and ten thousand. The Grateful Dead and the newly formed Big Brother and the Holding Company played, but it was hardly a typical concert. Strobe lights and black lights illuminated the space. Microphones were available for any-one to use. People could jump on trampolines. Multiple projectors offered a constant variety of films. Tom Wolfe, in his popular history of the San Francisco counterculture, *The Electric Kool Aid Acid Test* (1968), called the Trips Festival "the first national convention of an underground movement that had existed on a cell-by-cell basis."[22]

San Francisco was clearly the capital of the emerging counterculture, though offshoots were sprouting all over the country, in major cities like Los Angeles, New York, Boston, and Seattle; in university oases like Madison, Wisconsin and Austin, Texas; and even in Midwestern work-ing class cities like Detroit. As people began to flock to neighborhoods that seemed receptive or merely available to those now being called "hip-pies,"* a kind of model of community organization began to emerge. Places where people could sleep, known as "crash pads," became avail-able. Free food was distributed. And a sense of community began to

---

* The term "hippies" derives from the postwar use of "hip" and "hipsters," frequently asso-ciated with the Beats. The first direct use of the term to describe the new young people congregating in San Francisco appeared in an article in the *San Francisco Examiner*, on September 5, 1965, "A New Paradise for Beatniks." The author used the term hippie to identify this new generation of beatniks.

emerge, rooted in the rejection of postwar American values and an embrace of possibilities of a new era.

Music usually accompanied and often defined these counterculture outposts, with the new bands marking the development of the American counterweight to the British Invasion. Along with the Dead and Big Brother, San Francisco produced the Jefferson Airplane, Country Joe and the Fish, and numerous others, who, as mentioned above, were often folk musicians who had moved to electric instruments. They would play in the new counterculture music venues, like the Fillmore Auditorium or the Avalon Ballroom, where the trappings of events like the Trips Festival would accompany the music—light shows, incense, dancing. The posters advertising the coming shows were marked by a new artistic style and were hung all over the city, making the poster artists important figures in the counterculture.

Each city had its defining bands, like the Byrds and the Doors in Los Angeles or the Fugs and the Velvet Underground in New York. The Velvet Underground, a band with avant-garde tendencies, was taken up by Andy Warhol and folded into his 1966 multimedia show, the Exploding Plastic Inevitable, which included projections of Warhol films and strobe lights. Members of the Doors had been students at the UCLA Film School and took their name from the title of the book *The Doors of Perception* by Aldous Huxley (1954). Huxley had been an early proponent of mind-expanding drugs. Elements of the counterculture approach to life and to art seemed to weave themselves into both artistic endeavors and personal lifestyles.

All this—the attempts to construct redefined lifestyles, new relationships with social and economic structures, and new expressions in one's personal life—suggested something deeper than the stereotypical media depictions. And these swirling currents, both in the artistic and the social sense of the counterculture, connected strongly to the various ideas and impulses emerging from the more overtly political side of 60s life, fighting racism and challenging foreign policy presumptions. But in a larger sense, the counterculture proved a direct challenge to the constraints and rules imposed on one's life and one's art, alternatives to what many felt were stilted lives and a gray existence.

By 1966, the counterculture was no longer underground or on the periphery, an escape or a hidden refuge for those wanting to drop out of traditional American life. Signs of the counterculture were everywhere, from Top 40 radio to musical guests on television variety shows, from changes in men's fashion to long-haired kids walking down the streets of most American cities. To those wed to postwar social norms, these challenges felt nightmarish. To the young, it seemed the dawning of an exciting new world.

8

The Women's Movement
Arrives

Not until the late 1960s did a clearly identifiable women's movement join the swirl of Sixties activism. In fact, one of the crucial events of 1968 was essential in leading the nation to understand that women's concerns were demanding their place on the stage of social and political movements. As with other social movements of the era, its roots stretched back through the decade, on into the postwar world, and often further. It did not arise from a single impulse but a variety of sources. This proved especially true among Black women, some of whom had begun to articulate what would later be identified as "feminist" viewpoints years before their coming to common recognition. But they were not alone. From a variety of positions on the landscape, a number of currents relating to women's experiences developed and came together by the late 1960s.

The postwar social construct painted a particular picture of the place and role of women. This was reinforced in the public imagination by the depiction of women in the situation comedies that proliferated on television in the 1950s. These TV women, who were always white, were painted as patient homemakers, committed to the maintenance of their family and to the support of their husbands. The only ripples in the tranquil lives of television domesticity were the occasional complicated home front problems that required Dad to solve when he came home from work. When non-white women—most often Black—would appear they were usually domestic workers. In fact, however, we have come to understand just how complicated, conflicted, and often unfulfilling these lives were for all these women, including the middle-class housewives.

Despite the powerful emphasis during the postwar years on a woman's place being in the home, women's participation in public sector activities, most notably employment, rose steadily over the 1950s. The number of working women grew by 35 percent between 1950 and 1960. This included married women, who accounted for 80 percent of the increase. Unsurprisingly, the greatest increases occurred in the rapidly populating areas of the Sun Belt—California, Arizona, New Mexico, Texas, and Florida—where the postwar boom was most pronounced. The growth of women in the workforce would continue through the 1960s. Women accounted for about 37 percent of the workforce in 1960 and 44 percent by 1970.[1]

In fact, economic and political conditions had spurred women to enter the workforce for several decades. The Great Depression forced more women, including married women, to seek work outside the home. During World War II, women had been called upon to join the war effort by going to work. This was often depicted as a woman's patriotic duty, replacing the men who went off to war, especially in the munitions and other war-related industries. But it was also clear that many women found the experience a rewarding one, beyond their feelings of aiding the war effort, for both personal and economic reasons. For working women, the chance to enter positions previously prohibited to them, along with better wages and a more positive work experience, proved attractive and fulfilling. They came to discover, however, that they were still being paid less than their male coworkers.

Non-white women had always worked, or at least a significant percentage of them did—in good times and hard times, non-white women worked at a rate slightly more than twice that of white women.[2] During the war, they too often were able to perform jobs once barred to them. But this did not mean they escaped racist discrimination as well as the sexist discrimination white women also experienced. Black women often earned less than white women, both of whom earned less than white men.[3]

At war's end, there was a desire on the part of many Americans, especially the white middle class, to return to an era that seemed to only exist in a mythic distant past—before the war, before the Depression, back when life was "simple and good"—at least for their class. This led to various efforts to push women out of the workforce. Sometimes they were merely let go, told they were no longer needed and that returning veterans required jobs. In other instances, social attitudes pressured women who wished to work outside the home. However, changing social and economic factors challenged the assumptions that defined women's roles. Media imagery, political pronouncements, and the advice of so-called psychological "experts" all pointed women in one direction. Other forces of social change and personal outlook would push in another.

Popular magazine articles talked about the problems that children experienced when mothers worked or how disappointed husbands would become with their partners, helping coerce women out of the workforce. Paid work was also perceived to be harmful to the woman herself. "The more importance outside work assumes, the more are the masculine components of the woman's nature enhanced and encouraged," argued a 1947 bestseller, *Modern Woman: The Lost Sex*, co-authored by a female medical doctor. "In her home and in her relationship to her children, it is imperative that these strivings be at a minimum...She is in the dangerous position of having to live one part of her life on the masculine level, another on the feminine." Living with this duality would prove difficult. The result is that "we are observing the masculinization of women and with it enormously dangerous consequences to the home, the children (if any) dependent on it, and to the ability of the woman, as well as her husband to obtain sexual gratification."[4]

The GI Bill had been hailed as a godsend for young men who could now finance a college education. It also contributed to an enormous growth in American higher education, in general, as universities expanded rapidly in the postwar years. Part of this growth would mean increasing numbers of young women who could now go to college. Some, including the authors of *Modern Woman: The Lost Sex*, worried about its social and psychological impact. "The more educated a woman is, the greater chance there is of sexual disorder, more or less severe. The greater the disordered sexuality in a given group of women, the fewer children they have."⁵ College curricula were adjusted to incorporate the perceived needs and limits of young women, steering them away from "masculine" professions and into areas of study felt to be compatible with female attributes, such as elementary education or home economics. Ultimately, women's place in academe was justified by increasing a woman's chance of finding a mate: It was "the world's best marriage mart," one college administrator declared.⁶ The great middle-class female fear of this era was to end up an unmarried "old maid."

The family was depicted as the central social institution of postwar life, and there was an assigned place for everyone within this fantasized vision. And it was clear from every angle that the place assigned to women was decidedly secondary.

Occasionally a contrary voice among the white middle-class was raised, such as that of Edith Stern, whose 1949 article "Women Are Household Slaves," anticipated later feminist critiques. Appearing in *The American Mercury*, Stern, a novelist, editor, and author of books on mental health, satirized the modern woman's plight.

HELP WANTED: DOMESTIC: FEMALE: All cooking, cleaning, laundry, sewing, meal planning, shopping, weekday chauffeuring, social secretarial service, and complete care of three children. Salary at employer's option. Time off if possible.

Stern goes on to say that despite laws providing workers with protections, none applied to women working at home. And she suggests that those who make arguments about the "joys of housewifery" are "those who have never had to work at it." If one provides personal services in a democracy, she declares, one is paid for them. "It is neither freedom or democracy" when one is not paid and when "such service is based on color or sex."⁷

While not widely embraced (or even widely read) when it appeared in its English edition in 1953, Simone de Beauvoir's *The Second Sex* (which had been published in French four years earlier) was still reviewed in many major publications, like *The New Yorker* and the *Saturday Review* as well as newspapers and academic journals. De Beauvoir's work was the first to identify women as "The Other," a concept that proved crucial in coming years. The book prompted intellectual debate, some of it on televised panels and talk shows, mostly as connected to discussions on the emerging topic of human sexuality inspired by books, like *The Kinsey Reports*, and the work of anthropologist Margaret Mead and others.[8] The Kinsey Reports, *Sexual Behavior in the Human Male* (1948) and *Sexual Behavior in the Human Female* (1953), had challenged puritanical beliefs about adult sexuality. The reports suggested that homosexuality was far more prevalent among Americans than anyone had believed as were premarital and extramarital sexual experiences. Kinsey estimated that 50 percent of American men and 26 percent of American women had had at least one extramarital sexual experience. Nearly 50 percent of American women had engaged in premarital sex.[9] While the numbers in the Kinsey reports were refined over the coming years, as people began to question aspects of their research methodology, their general conclusions remained unchallenged. The American sexual experience—for men *and* women—was nothing like the innocent imagery depicted in popular culture or championed from pulpit and political platform.

Largely ignored by American society, in 1955 several San Francisco women founded Daughters of Bilitis, the first lesbian civil and political rights organization—"A Woman's Organization for the Purpose of Promoting the Integration of the Homosexual into Society." Their aim was to promote education and public awareness of lesbians, as well as seeking to change the psychological conclusions about gay women and the legal limitations and penalties they faced.

Over the next few years, Daughters of Bilitis chapters appeared in a number of major American cities. Always cautious about being publicly identified, members nonetheless held their first national convention in San Francisco in 1960 often using pseudonyms. The 200 delegates did have to face police who made sure that none of them were wearing men's clothing, a crime in many states and localities. All the delegates arrived in dresses, stockings, and heels.[10]

As in so many other areas of 1950s life, we can see seeds of various discussions that would blossom into full-blown debates in the 1960s. While they would come to dominate the discourse a decade later, serious works like *The Second Sex* or sarcastic ones like Edith Stern's article, as well as reconsiderations of women's (and men's) sexuality including the first stirrings for lesbian rights, swam against the very strong currents of post-war attitudes about gender relations and female sexuality.

As mentioned, we can see even stronger undercurrents of frustration and earlier critiques of the prevailing order among Black women. Some of these women emerged as leaders in the early phases of the civil rights movement yet had begun their activism back in the 1930s, expressing what would later be identified as feminist sentiments. Facing what Frances Beal would later label "double jeopardy,"[11] these Black women, because of their "collective confrontation with white supremacy," writes historian Carol Giardina, were "positioned to grasp the systemic nature of male supremacy and the need to fight collectively. They understood sexism sooner than most white women."[12]

Ella Baker had been engaged in civil rights work since the Great Depression, often with a particular focus on Black women. As part of the Harlem Young Women's Christian Association, she had developed relationships with other young Black women activists, including Dorothy Height, Anna Arnold Hedgeman, and Pauli Murray. In 1960, Baker counseled the young sit-in students to create their own organization, SNCC, instead of becoming an auxiliary of SCLC. This was in part motivated by Baker's own treatment in the organization. She always felt that the younger male ministerial leadership of SCLC never fully appreciated her because she was a woman. She was never promoted beyond "interim" executive director, despite her age and years of civil rights experience.

Pauli Murray began confronting segregation and sexism in the 1930s. She had lost a legal challenge to be admitted to the all-white University of North Carolina in 1938. In 1940, 15 years before Rosa Parks, Murray and a friend were arrested and charged with disturbing the peace when they refused to move from their seats in the white section of a North Carolina bus, because the seats in the Black section were all broken. As a student at Howard, one of the historically Black colleges, she had begun to think and write about the legal justifications for segregation and how to counter them. But when she entered Howard's law school, as the only woman in her class, she was often treated as a second-class citizen. Some professors would not even answer her questions in class. It had been traditional for the top graduate from Howard's law school to be awarded a scholarship to Harvard. But this prize was denied to Murray—her class's top student—because she was a woman. "I entered law school preoccupied with the racial struggle," she later wrote, "but graduated an unabashed feminist, as well."[13] All of these personal experiences, plus her study and analysis of the segregation system, led her to coin the phrase "Jane Crow," which would become a rallying cry for Black women in the sixties.

Dorothy Height had graduated from New York University in the early 1930s, after being barred from entering Barnard College, even though she had been accepted, because Barnard had an unofficial rule of admitting only two African American students each year. Graduate study in social work at NYU and Columbia led Height to work with the Harlem branch of the YWCA. At a meeting of the Nation Council of Negro Women (NCNW), she met both Eleanor Roosevelt and Mary McLeod Bethune, the famed Black educator, founder of the NCNW, and confidant of Mrs. Roosevelt. One of Height's most noteworthy actions was leading a protest in 1939 against the "Bronx Slave Market." Women, mostly of color, seeking day work, would stand on street corners waiting to be chosen. They often were underpaid and faced sexual harassment and assault.[14] Height continued her civil rights work into the postwar years.

Trinidad-born Claudia Jones had migrated to New York in 1924 at age eight. Extremely intelligent, winning various academic awards in high school, Jones could not afford to go to any college and instead began a series of poorly paid menial jobs. She also joined the Young Communist League, ultimately moving into positions on the staff and then editing various Communist Party publications. The American Communist Party had been an early advocate of rights for African Americans, well before any of the other political parties. Jones sought to expand the Party's position on women, with particular focus on Black women. In 1949, she published "An End to the Neglect of the Problems of the Negro Woman!", merging a Marxist perspective with her racial awareness, and a clearly feminist argument. "Negro women—as workers, as Negroes, and as women—are the most oppressed stratum of the whole population."

> It is not accidental that the American bourgeoisie has intensified its oppression, not only of the Negro people in general, but of Negro women in particular. Nothing so exposes the drive to fascization in the nation as the callous attitude which the bourgeoisie displays and cultivates toward Negro women.

It was the responsibility of all women to address this indignity. "White women, today, no less than their sisters in the abolitionist and suffrage movements must rise to challenge this lie and the whole system of Negro oppression."[15]

Jones' immigrant status made her vulnerable to the rising tide of McCarthyism. Charged with violating provisions in several anticommunist pieces of legislation, Jones was imprisoned several times and ultimately deported to Great Britain in 1955. Never in good health, she continued her work until her death in London in 1964 at age 49. She was buried in Highgate Cemetery near the tomb of Karl Marx.

As a young girl growing up in Kansas City, Florynce Kennedy, who was always known as Flo, had experienced segregation, racist taunts, and Klan violence and intimidation. But she had also been encouraged by her mother to be independent in matters both political and personal. Moving to New York during World War II, Kennedy took a government job and enrolled in Columbia's School of General Studies, a program for nontraditional students of all ages who often worked full-time. With so many men off at war, the restrictions against women applicants had been loosened. Throughout her undergraduate career, she frequently investigated the comparative disadvantages faced by African Americans and women. Understanding that white women were better treated than Black men or women, she nonetheless found that both groups faced discrimination. As her biographer Sherie Randolph concluded, "she called upon white women and African Americans to join together to disrupt 'social peace' and 'revolutionize' the U.S."[16]

Initially rejected by Columbia Law School in 1948, Kennedy appealed the decision, arguing that she had been denied admission because "I was a negro." She later recalled meeting with one of the school's deans. He tried to reassure her by saying "they had rejected me because of my sex and not because of my race." Hardly pacified, she replied, "if you have admitted any white man with lower grades than mine I want to get in too!"[17] The law school ultimately relented and accepted her.

Kennedy's 1951 law school class had 205 members, 195 of whom were men. She found the environment both inside and out of class riddled with sexism and racism. "Women were openly ridiculed," she recalled. Social events, where class cohesion and future connections were established, were barred to all Black and women students. She graduated into a world in which the prospects for Black women lawyers were slim. In 1950, there were over 6,000 women lawyers in the U.S., but only 83 were African American. A few were able to work for their fathers or brothers, but most found clerical jobs in larger law firms. Kennedy was one of these, taking a job assisting the bookkeeper at a small Manhattan firm. "I did shit work, I ran errands. I got people sandwiches, researched their dull little cases."[18] White women lawyers at the firm found their situation little better than Kennedy's.

Finally able to open her own small practice a few years later, Kennedy became the only Black woman in New York City with her own office. (There were only 19 in the entire state.) Her firm was so small that she wrote her own briefs, did her own typing, and answered her own phone. But she did begin to take on civil rights cases, gaining some notoriety when she defended Billie Holliday in several cases involving the singer's use of narcotics. She also represented the family of jazz great Charlie Parker in their fight over his royalties. Kennedy began to write a weekly column, "Once Upon a Week," in a local Black newspaper, where she commented on a variety of issues, including police brutality, the injustices of the legal system, and abortion, arguing that it was a woman's basic right to have access to safe and legal abortions.[19]

At the dawn of the 1960s, Patricia Robinson, an African American social worker and therapist who had worked with Planned Parenthood in Mt. Vernon, New York, organized the Mt. Vernon/New Rochelle women's group. She was particularly concerned with teenage pregnancy. Black women—from grandmothers to teens—joined. Employing what would later be titled consciousness raising, Robinson's group generated cross-generational discussions, the young women feeling especially empowered. The group began to argue for expanded availability of birth control, especially the oral contraceptives that were coming into wide usage in the early sixties. This was an early example of the call for women to maintain control over their own bodies.

As civil rights began to force its way onto the national agenda, it became increasingly clear that the particular situation of Black women spurred an array of individual women and small groups to begin to identify the burdens and limitations that plagued the lives of African American women.

During his campaign for the White House in 1960, John Kennedy had actively solicited the support of women's groups, especially women labor leaders like Lillian Hatcher. Hatcher had been one of the African American women who gained factory employment during World War II, working as a riveter (a real-life "Rosie the Riveter"), where she joined the United Auto Workers. She soon moved into various union staff positions, usually dealing with women workers. In 1960, she helped mobilize women labor leaders to support JFK. Hatcher was joined by Esther Peterson, who had traveled a very different path to the campaign. The daughter of Danish immigrants, Peterson had been raised in a conservative Mormon household in Utah. Teaching in a prep school and volunteering at the YWCA in Boston, she confronted both gender and class issues. No Black women were allowed in the Y where she volunteered. She pointed out that this violated the organization's claims of equality and justice. A strike by piecework garment workers enabled her to see firsthand their poverty and exploitation. She untimely joined their picket lines. Peterson went on to become an organizer for the American Federation of Teachers and then a Washington lobbyist for the Amalgamated Clothing Workers Union. By the end of the 1950s she had become the first woman lobbyist for the Industrial Union Department of the AFL-CIO.

John Kennedy had known Peterson since his early days as a member of Congress and, in 1960, put her in charge of the labor desk at the Democratic National Committee, where she organized the "Committee of Labor Women for Kennedy and Johnson." Once elected, he appointed her the director of the U.S. Women's Bureau and, then, assistant secretary of labor. From that position, Peterson began to meet with various female labor leaders to discuss the idea of a presidential commission on the status of women. In December 1961, Kennedy announced its creation.

Peterson served as executive vice chair of the commission, having convinced Eleanor Roosevelt to serve as chair. FDR's widow remained the most admired woman in American life in the postwar years, having been named that in surveys of the American people every year but one from 1948 to 1961. Among the commission members were Dorothy Height and Pauli Murray, as well as the heads of the National Council of Jewish Women, the National Council of Catholic Women, the President of Radcliffe College, and various women labor leaders. Roosevelt would pass away in November 1962, while the committee was still at work on its report.

The final report of the commission, *American Women*, was presented to Kennedy on what would have been Eleanor Roosevelt's 79th birthday, in October 1963, a month before Kennedy's own death. Focused heavily on women's economic situation, the report called for "full equality of rights," and discussed such topics as paid maternity leave and childcare as well as upgrading the status and remuneration for the jobs that were mostly performed by women. In addition, it called for a stronger government commitment to workers' organizing and collective bargaining as well as programs to further women's political and civil leadership.

Even before receiving the commission's final report, Kennedy had signed The Equal Pay Act, a limited attempt to balance wages. This act proved to be a symbolic victory more than one that actually transformed lives. Regardless, it was clear that feelings had been stirred and new objectives imagined. *American Women* sold 64,000 copies in its first year. Various states created their own state commissions and women's bureaus. And the report constituted an official U.S. government document that chronicled women's discrimination.[20]

By 1963, the civil rights movement had become the nation's most pressing domestic issue within the United States. As we have seen, John Kennedy and his brother Robert, the Attorney General, had finally been forced to choose which constituency of their party to stand behind, African Americans or Southern segregationists. They chose the former, and in June, JFK went on television to announce his introduction of a civil rights bill to Congress. And, as we have seen, the plans for a major march for racial justice planned for Washington that summer continued, spurred by the administration that seemed to have joined the general effort.

But even the shining vision behind the March on Washington was not expansive enough to include the participation of African American women. Anna Arnold Hedgeman, whose work on the issues of Black women also stretched back to the 1930s when she worked with the Harlem Young Women's Christian Association along with Ella Baker, Dorothy Height, and Pauli Murray, was the only woman on the planning committee for the march. Hedgeman had worked with labor leader A. Phillip Randolph for years, including his first plan to hold a Washington march during World War II. In 1963, Hedgeman recruited Height and Murray to join her in pushing for women's inclusion in the 1963 march. Despite the crucial role of a number of Black women in the emerging civil rights movement, including Montgomery's Rosa Parks, Little Rock's Daisy Bates, and Nashville's Diane Nash, no women were among the speakers planned for the ceremony at the Lincoln Memorial. Protesting this exclusion, they met with resistance. Bayard Rustin told them that the men did not really know which women to choose and that women were already represented by gospel singer Mahalia Jackson. Plus, he said, there were already too many speakers on the program. Finally, after continued pressure, small adjustments were made to the program, but they limited women to a few very small roles—brief introductions, with little time to say anything meaningful.[21]

Progress on Kennedy's civil rights bill had slowed in the fall of 1963 because of the legislative tactics of Southern segregationists. After JFK's murder, Lyndon Johnson made passage of the bill his top domestic priority, and its passage seemed promising. In an effort to undermine the bill's support, the Virginia Congressman Howard W. Smith proposed adding the word "sex" to Title VII of the bill, banning discrimination on the basis of sex, in addition to the race, ethnicity, and religion categories already in the measure. Smith believed this would torpedo the entire bill, assuming chauvinist members of Congress would not go along. Further, it split women's groups and leaders, some strongly endorsing the idea, others fearing the loss of gender-specific protections in other legislation. Ultimately the amendment and then the entire bill passed, only after significant resistance.

By 1964, SNCC was deeply committed to its Freedom Summer project, recruiting students and sending them to Mississippi to register voters. One female SNCC member called Dorothy Height to report the beatings, harassment, and assaults that the Black and white female volunteers faced after being arrested and jailed in Southern towns. She hoped that Height's organization, the National Council of Negro Women, might help organize some action that would bring older and middle-class women of both races into the fray, helping to protect these younger women. Height contacted Polly Spiegel Cowan, a well-to-do white New York activist. Height and Cowan proposed organizing small teams of prominent middle- and upper-class white and Black women to venture into Southern towns, hoping to have a "quieting influence" on the situation. What became known as "Wednesdays in Mississippi" (WIMS) launched in the summer of 1964, with 48 volunteers. Each week interracial teams of women would arrive in Jackson on Tuesday night. On Wednesday they would spend the day in a smaller town, returning home on Thursday. Flo Kennedy was on one of these teams.

Some of the women bridled at the WIMS leadership's insistence that they dress like traditional white or Black women in the South, but they ultimately agreed. The Black women stayed with Black families in Jackson. The white women stayed in segregated hotels. On her first trip to Mississippi, Kennedy and her team met Fannie Lou Hamer, who told them harrowing stories of her beatings while in the hands of the authorities. This was similar to the compelling testimony Hamer would give only weeks later, on national television, at the Democratic National Convention in Atlantic City.[22]

The message and the vocabulary of the civil rights movement resonated with the experience of many women of all races. Discussions about equal access, opening closed doors, ending segregation, all became more common. But for many in the emerging women's movement, the national focus on civil rights, amplified by television and front-page images of horrible violence, kept many women preoccupied with the racial questions. When Mary King and Casey Hayden, two deeply committed white SNCC workers, asked a set of questions in 1964 about women's roles in the civil rights movement, they did so anonymously, they later recalled, fearing ridicule. "Why is it that in SNCC," they asked, "women who are competent, qualified, and experienced are automatically assigned to the 'female' kinds of jobs such as: typing, desk work, cooking...but rarely the 'executive?'" Their answer was to suggest that within SNCC there existed "the assumption of male superiority."[23]

By 1965, King and Hayden were ready to become more public with their criticism. They circulated a signed document, "Sex and Caste: A Kind of Memo," to a group of female activists in SNCC, SDS, and other organizations. The internal dynamics of these organizations, they argued, mirrored society at large, placing women "in the same position of assumed subordination...It is a caste system which, at its worst, uses and exploits women." Men in the movement, when confronted with this issue could not, they felt, "respond non-defensively, since the whole idea is either beyond their comprehension or threatens and exposes them. The usual repose is laughter."[24]

Late one night at a SNCC retreat in 1964, a small group began cracking jokes, often at each other's expense. Stokely Carmichael launched into a comic monologue, roasting everyone including himself. Amid it all, he asked rhetorically, "What is the position of women in SNCC? The position of women in SNCC is prone!" Mary King was among the gathering, and she recalls that everyone "collapsed with hilarity...he was poking fun at his own attitudes."[25] Over the next years, Carmichael's joke, regardless of its initial context, appeared less and less funny and seemed to encapsulate the way women felt they were viewed.

As more and more women began to question their assigned roles in the movements, the more they heard similar responses. In 1965 when a small group of women at the SDS national conference sought to raise questions about women's inferior roles, they were greeted with boos and catcalls from the men. "She just needs a good screw," one male SDS delegate yelled. At the following year's conference, those arguing for a motion on women's liberation were pelted with tomatoes.[26]

In the early 1960s, Pauli Murray lived and taught in Ghana, returning to the U.S. to continue her legal education. In 1965, she became the first African American to receive a Doctor of Juridical Science from Yale. During her time at Yale, she refined her argument about the discrimination Black women confronted, culminating in her landmark article "Jane Crow and the Law," co-authored with Mary Eastwood, a white lawyer with whom Murray had worked on JFK's Commission on Women. Women, they wrote, belong to a "large, permanent, unchangeable, natural class. No other kind of class is susceptible to implications of innate inferiority...Discriminatory attitudes toward women are strikingly parallel to those regarding Negroes." They continued, "most men have accepted as self-evident, until recently, the doctrine that women had inferior endowments in most of those respects which carry prestige, power, and advantages in society." These prejudices were based on false theories about "smaller brains, scarcity of geniuses and so on. The study of women's intelligence and personality has had broadly the same history as the one we record for Negroes. As in the case of the Negro, women themselves have often been brought to believe in their inferiority of endowment." This ultimately led to "the myth of the 'contented woman,' who did not want to have suffrage or other civil rights and equal opportunities, [and] had the same social function as the myth of the 'contented Negro.'" Systematically reviewing a century's worth of legal arguments, court decisions, and political actions, Murray and Eastwood concluded that both The Equal Pay Act and Title VII of the Civil Rights Act made all workplace limitations illegal.[27]

Implementation of the 1964 Civil Rights Act included creation of the Equal Employment Opportunity Commission (EEOC), established to investigate job discrimination. Despite the addition of sex to

Title VII, the EEOC seemed disinterested in pursuing any claims of discrimination against women. Its first executive director called women's inclusion "a fluke...conceived out of wedlock." One commissioner labeled the entire issue "the Bunny problem," sarcastically dismissing women's complaints by suggesting how absurd it would be for men to complain about not being hired as Playboy Bunnies.[28] At the June 1966 National Conference of State Commissions on the Status of Women, delegates were blocked from presenting a motion calling on the EEOC to enforce Title VII with regard to women. The angry women walked out. Joined by others, they regrouped that evening in Betty Friedan's hotel room.

In 1963, Betty Friedan published what proved a very popular book, aimed at raising the awareness of middle-class women to the social and political structures that limited their lives. A Smith College graduate, Friedan had worked as a freelance journalist in the postwar years, as she raised her family. Interviewing members of her Smith class for their fifteenth reunion led her to the realization that many of these women were deeply unhappy, despite having achieved all they thought they had wanted to achieve—marriages, children, nice homes, comfortable lifestyles. In the interviews Friedan heard time and again about how unfulfilled they felt. Despite doing everything she was "supposed to do," one woman concluded, "I'm desperate. I begin to feel I have no personality. I'm a server of food and a putter-on of pants and a bed maker...But who am I?"[29]

Searching for the sources of this quiet despair—which she titled "the problem that has no name"—Friedan researched this question for the next several years, which culminated in *The Feminine Mystique*, published in 1963, the same year as *American Women*, the report of the Commission on Women. Friedan's work hit the bestseller lists with sales topping one million copies in its first year. As African American women like Height and Murray were part of the efforts to bring Black women into the developing movement that focused on women, Friedan's book was crucial in encouraging white, middle-class women to also see themselves as a part of it.[30]

Among the several dozen women who gathered that June night in Friedan's hotel room was Pauli Murray. By 1966, she was keen to create a new organization, "an NAACP for women."* Others shared Murray's desire. On a hotel napkin, Friedan scribbled the acronym NOW, for the organization they were about to create—The National Organization of Women. By October they were ready to hold their first conference. "The time has come for a new movement toward the true equality for all women in America," they declared, "and toward a fully equal partnership of the sexes, as part of a world-wide revolution of human rights."[31] Issuing a "Bill of Rights," they called for passage of the Equal Rights Amendment, as well as demands for equal educational and employment opportunities, childcare programs, maternity leave, and women's control over their reproductive lives.[32] In the growing constellation of groups focused on the situation of women in America, NOW staked out the moderate feminist position.

While no one was yet using the term "women's movement"—or even as it was first called, "women's liberation"—the momentum of other Sixties movements, especially the civil rights movement, as well as the critique of postwar life, had spurred serious thinking about the place and rights of women. As the decade progressed, women's organizations would proliferate and social and cultural analyses would venture into nearly every aspect of contemporary life. In retrospect, we can see the fermenting antecedents of this "world-wide revolution of human rights," as NOW labeled it, bubbling up across the landscape, out of the other simmering movements of the 1960s and from the decades-old critiques of the place of African American women in U.S. society.

---

* After several years as an academic, in her sixties, Murray left to enter a theological seminary. In 1977 she became the first African American woman ordained as an Episcopal priest.

9

The "Crossover Point"

1967—Coming to Terms with the Sixties

On January 6, 1967, *Time Magazine* announced its annual Man of the Year. Rather than choosing a world leader as it typically did (the previous two winners had been Lyndon Johnson and William Westmoreland), it instead anointed "a generation: the man—and woman—of 25 and under... Never have the young been so assertive or so articulate, so well educated or so worldly... This is not just a new generation, but a new kind of generation." The accompanying essay identified the "congruent culture" the young had already staked out. "No Western metropolis today lacks a discotheque or espresso joint, a Mod boutique or a Carnaby shop. No transistor is immune from rock 'n' roll." This "minisociety" had gone on to influence adults as well. "What started out as a distinctively youthful sartorial revolt... has been accepted by adults the world over."

Instead of the usual stark contrast between Vietnam soldiers who understood their obligation to the nation as opposed to the cowardice of those who avoided the war, *Time* instead suggested that "among the fighting men, there is a good deal of the Peace Corps ardor that animates their peers back home... Today's youth appears more deeply committed to the fundamental Western ethos—decency, tolerance, brotherhood— than almost any generation since the age of chivalry." It linked modern youth culture with previous idealistic endeavors. "Henry David Thoreau would have felt at home with the young of the 60's," *Time* argued, "they are as appalled as he was at the thought of leading 'lives of quiet desperation.'"

After years of disdain and dismissal of the young, it seemed a moment of acceptance, as if the simmering critiques of postwar society and the enthusiasms of the young had merged into an optimistic vision. "With his skeptical yet humanistic outlook...the Man of the Year suggests that he will infuse the future with a new sense of morality, a transcendent and contemporary ethic that could infinitely enrich the 'empty society.' If he succeeds (and he is prepared to) the Man of the Year will be a man indeed—and have a great deal of fun in the process."[*][1]

No one can claim that 1967 witnessed the end the political and social tensions that marked the decade. But it did seem that the decade-long emergence of a new political and social mentality—"the worldwide revolution of human rights," as NOW had put it—along with the growing place of the youth culture in American society, was finally beginning to penetrate the mainstream and suggested that a new enlarged consensus, encompassing previously antagonistic camps, might be on the horizon.

Clearly tensions remained and confrontations erupted. Most prominent were those around racial issues and around the continuing war in Southeast Asia. Sometimes these two intertwined, creating compelling political moments.

On April 28, Heavyweight Champion Muhammad Ali appeared at the Army induction center in Houston, Texas. Refusing to step forward when his name was called, he was ultimately arrested. That same day, his New York boxing license was suspended, and he was stripped of his title. In the next days and weeks, most boxing organizations followed suit. But Ali remained unbending. "Why should they ask me to put on a uniform and go ten thousand miles from home and drop bombs and bullets on brown people in Vietnam while so-called Negro people in Louisville are treated like dogs and denied simple human rights?"[2]

---

[*] Once again, the language had not yet adjusted the use of male pronouns to speak for all. This appraisal is not as sexist as it reads today.

In June, former Cleveland Browns running back Jim Brown organized a gathering of Black athletes to respond to Ali's situation. After privately questioning Ali about the sincerity of his beliefs, they held a press conference to support the dethroned champion. Sitting alongside Ali were Brown, basketball great Bill Russell, and up-and-coming phenom Lew Alcindor (later Kareem Abdul-Jabbar), at this point only a UCLA sophomore. Standing behind the four were a number of Black athletes from several NFL teams, as well as attorney Carl Stokes, who that November would be elected Cleveland's mayor, the first African American to become mayor of a major American city. Under the leadership of Jim Brown, for the first time, Black athletes began to assert their distinct identity. And Ali's situation galvanized this effort. "Muhammad Ali was one of my heroes," Abdul-Jabbar later observed. "He was in trouble and he was someone I wanted to help because he made me feel good about being an African-American." "We were unified," former Cleveland Brown John Wooten remembered. "We knew we were doing something for the betterment of all."[3]

There was so much urban racial unrest in the summer of 1967 that it has often been characterized as the "Long Hot Summer of 1967." Cities across the country, from Boston and Milwaukee to Atlanta and Tampa, likely over 150, all erupted. The two most volatile eruptions occurred in Newark and Detroit. The arrest and beating of a taxi driver by Newark police in July led to protest marches and then four days of rioting. Buildings were torched, stores looted. By the time calm had returned, 26 people, mostly African Americans, were dead, and nearly 1,500 were under arrest.

Two weeks later in Detroit, simmering tensions between the police and the Black citizens exploded. The attempted arrest of over 80 celebrants at an unlicensed drinking club, attending a celebration for two returning Vietnam soldiers, led to the riot. Again, rocks were thrown, stores looted, buildings torched. The police responded with brutal force, most infamously when they raided the Algiers Motel and shot, beat, and otherwise assaulted the residents.[4] The governor called out the Michigan National Guard, and Lyndon Jonson sent in two U.S. Army divisions.

When the dust settled, 43 people were dead and over 7,000 under arrest. More than 400 buildings had been severely damaged or destroyed. Detroit was the worst urban riot to date in the twentieth century. Newark and Detroit were central to Lyndon Johnson's decision to create a special commission to investigate racial conflict in the U.S., the National Advisory Committee on Civil Disobedience, ultimately known as the Kerner Commission, after its chair, Illinois Governor Otto Kerner.

That fall, in an incident whose details remain unclear to the present day, Black Panther founder Huey Newton and a friend were involved in a confrontation with Oakland police that led to the death of one policeman and the wounding of Newton and another officer. Newton was charged with first-degree murder (which carried the death penalty), assault, and kidnapping (for commandeering a car to take the wounded to the hospital.) As Newton faced trial and imprisonment, the rallying cry "Free Huey" became part of the political lexicon of the day.*

Demonstrations against the war in Vietnam continued and grew throughout 1967, as opposition mounted. Polls showed public approval of the war declining. The Gallup organization determined, based on their survey data, that twenty-five million adults had changed their minds about Vietnam over the previous two years. One newspaper survey of members of the House of Representatives identified 43 members whose position on the war had shifted. And it was not just Democrats and liberals whose attitudes were changing. Kentucky Senator Thruston Morton, former national chair of the Republican Party, told reporter Dan Oberdorfer, "I was an all-out hawk," but "I was wrong." He subsequently called Vietnam polity "bankrupt."[5] Other members of Congress joined suit, including Massachusetts Congressman Thomas (Tip) O'Neill, who was part of the Democratic leadership and would eventually rise to Speaker. The critiques of his son and daughter, both students at Boston College, prompted him to dig more deeply into Vietnam

---

* Newton was ultimately convicted of voluntary manslaughter and sentenced to 2 to 15 years. But the conviction was reversed on appeal. Two subsequent trials ended with hung juries.

policy, beyond the standard official briefings he received. He also discovered that not only were the liberal academic enclaves of his Cambridge congressional district changing, so too his middle-class Irish constituents. "I've decided that Rusk and McNamara and the rest of them are wrong." O'Neill declared. "We are dropping $20,000-bombs every time somebody thinks he sees four Viet Cong in a bush. And it isn't working."[6]

On April 15, the Spring Mobilization Committee—a coalition of anti-war groups that had been formed the previous fall—staged massive marches in New York and San Francisco, attracting hundreds of thousands. Speakers at the New York rally included Martin Luther King, singer and activist Harry Bellefonte, and beloved pediatrician Benjamin Spock. San Franciscans heard Coretta Scot King, Black Panther leader Eldridge Cleaver, and SNCC's Julian Bond, among others. In addition to the speeches, the day's events included marches through the streets, musical performances, and draft card burnings. Just as the number of troops in Vietnam continued to "escalate"—in the Pentagon's term—so too did the size of the anti-war actions on the home front.

That spring, student leaders from Stanford and Berkeley had come together to form "The Resistance," whose intention was to counsel and convince young men to resist the draft. While intentionally leaderless, David Harris emerged as the group's leading spokesperson. Harris had been the Stanford student body president, having won election on a platform of student rights, marijuana legalization, elimination of the Board of Trustees, and the severing of all ties between Stanford and the Vietnam War.[7] He and others moved from campus to campus, meeting with young men and quietly encouraging them to join the movement. During the San Francisco march, they announced that the group would sponsor a nationwide draft-card "turn-in" in October.

By this point, prominent figures from across the movements had joined the anti-war actions. Civil rights groups and individuals like King, Cleaver, Bond, James Bevel, and others had wedded their agenda to the anti-war one. So too the Yippies, the guerilla theater cohort that merged political ideology and counterculture sensibility. Their numbers included Berkeley radical Jerry Rubin, who in 1966 appeared before the House Un-American Activities Committee in an American Revolutionary War uniform, claiming to be the heir of Jefferson and Paine, and blowing soap bubbles at the committee members; Abby Hoffman, the former Brandeis University tennis player who had studied with New Left theorist Herbert Marcuse at Brandeis, and then became part of the civil rights and antiwar movements; and Paul Krassner, a former Merry Prankster and founder and editor of *The Realist*, the irreverent and controversial magazine he described as a *Mad Magazine* for adults.

In August, even before they had taken the Yippie name, Hoffman and several others entered the viewing gallery high above the trading floor of the New York Stock Exchange. From this position they threw hundreds of dollar bills down onto the floor of the exchange, causing the stockbrokers to stop trading and scramble to catch the falling money. They proclaimed their stunt as "the death of money." The *New York Times'* story about the event ran the next day on page 23, under the headline "Hippies Shower $1 Bills on Stock Exchange Floor." The story did report that a number of cameramen and reporters had been waiting in the gallery, having been told that a stunt was planned. An essential element of the Yippie approach was to do things that garnered press coverage. It was, one contemporary analyst suggests, "the first display of Hoffman's zany Marx Brothers style of politics, which undermined the system by mocking it."[8]

As plans coalesced for the general fall anti-war campaign, it took on the name "Stop The Draft Week." On October 16, 200 protestors stood in front of the doors to the Army induction center in Oakland, blocking the entry of young recruits. "I am going to try to talk with the young men going in, talk with them against all wars," Joan Baez said. Police swooped in and arrested them all, including Baez, her sister singer Mimi Farina, and their mother.[9] That night David Harris, who would marry Baez the next year, addressed a crowd of 2,000 in San Francisco. As he spoke, a basket was passed into which men were encouraged to drop their draft cards. By the time the basket returned to the stage, it was filled to the brim.[10]

That same day, Boston's Arlington Street Church became the scene of another resistance gathering. Standing before the crowd, Harvard graduate student Michael Ferber spoke of the meaning of the personal decision to resist the draft. "We have come here to show that we are united to do one thing, to say No." But he continued, "Albert Camus said that the rebel, who says no, is also one who says Yes, and that when he draws a line beyond which he will refuse to cooperate he is affirming the values on the other side of that line." Despite the day's efforts, Ferber knew that "Tomorrow the world will be in pretty much the same mess as it is today." He knew bombs would still fall on innocent Vietnamese, "ghettos will continue to be rotten places to live...And the American Selective Service System will continue to send young men out to slaughter." Yet there was cause for hope. "Today is not the End. Today is the Beginning."[11]

The tone of news coverage of anti-war activities was beginning to shift. Sander Vanocur, an NBC news commentator, told one of the Boston speakers, "What a country this would be if something like this were now to take place in every church." NBC news anchor John Chancellor quietly concluded that night's story on the Boston gathering. "If men like this are beginning to say things like this, I guess we had all better start paying attention."[*][12]

Three thousand demonstrators returned to the Oakland induction center Tuesday morning, and this time they were met by a brutal police force response. Many were injured, others arrested. At the University of Wisconsin, students entered the building where job interviews were being held, demanding that representatives of Dow Chemical (which manufactured the napalm being used in Vietnam) leave the campus. The local police SWAT team violently drove the demonstrators out of the building and into a waiting company of more police who beat them a second time. Two thousand student onlookers jeered at the police,

* On January 5, 1968, Ferber was arrested along with famed pediatrician Dr. Benjamin Spock, Yale Chaplin William Sloane Coffin, social critic and activist Marcus Raskin, and writer and activist Mitchell Goodman. They were charged with conspiracy to violate the Selective Service Act. Known as the "Boston Five," they were convicted, but the verdicts were overturned on appeal.

shouting "Sieg heil," pelting them with rocks and bricks. Using Mace, tear gas, and police dogs, the police bloodied and dispersed the crowd.

On Friday morning, some 10,000 demonstrators gathered in the streets around the Oakland induction center. This time they were more prepared. Many wore headgear. Leaders communicated by walkie-talkie. When the police moved in to attack, the marchers retreated to pre-planned positions. They barricaded streets, overturning cars and dragging things like garbage cans into the street. Sometimes they surrounded policemen. Surprisingly, there were fewer arrests and serious injuries than on previous days.

Three thousand miles away, the Resistance collected draft cards on the steps of the Capitol. Yale chaplain William Sloane Coffin and Benjamin Spock led a contingent into the Justice Department to present Attorney General Ramsey Clark with 992 returned draft cards. The following day a 100,000 people gathered at the Lincoln Memorial and, after a series of speeches, began their march to the Arlington Memorial Bridge and on to the Pentagon. Police and army units had been called out. When one small group managed to enter the Pentagon through a side door, waiting troops brutally responded. Blood-splattered floors testified to how far the demonstrators had come and what they had encountered. Even as March leaders tried to calm the situation, police continued to assault them. "You are our bothers," pacifist David Dellinger called to the soldiers, "Join us." In reply, Dellinger and others received kicks, rifle butts, and arrest. Staring down at the demonstrators from their office windows, several Pentagon officials realized that friends, relatives, and even their own children were in the crowd.[13]

For all the violence, the Pentagon March was not without its political theater. Back in August, Abbie Hoffman had announced, "We're going to raise the Pentagon three hundred feet in the air." In fact, they made an official application to raise the building off the ground. Officials humorously negotiated, countering that they should limit the levitation to ten feet. Hoffman also claimed that in reaction to Mace they had developed a substance called "Lace," which would lead its victim to tear off their clothes and have sex with the person closest to them.[14] On the Saturday of the March on the Pentagon, a contingent broke off from the main crowd. Hoffman, poet Allen Ginsberg, and Fugs singer Ed Sanders performed an exorcism, chanting "Out, demon, out!" People dressed as everything from witches and warlocks to Uncle Sam and Roman senators, some played flutes and bongos. A carnival atmosphere prevailed. They sang, built campfires, and smoked marijuana.[15]

In his award-winning chronicle of the March on the Pentagon, *The Armies of the Night*, Norman Mailer concluded, "one did not march on the Pentagon and look to get arrested as a link in a master scheme to take over the bastions of the Republic." Instead "a generation of the American young had come along different from five previous generations," believing in "technology more than any before it, but the generation also believed in LSD, in witches, in tribal knowledge, in orgy, in revolution." Their radicalism, he argued, "was in their hate for the authority." Their challenge was not systematic, but personal, political, and liberating all in one. "The future of the revolution existed in the nerves and cells of the people who created it and lived with it."[16]

By 1967, the demonstrations, happenings, and new lifestyles, as well as the emotions and impulses that underlay them, had begun to merge into something that felt coherent but remained indescribable. They had become "The Movement."

Despite the continuing confrontations and harsh rhetoric, there also seemed, as in the choice of *Time's* "Man of the Year," something new in the air. Some believed there finally was a "light at the end of the tunnel" in Vietnam. Oppositional politics and counterculture styles seemed to have found their way into the global mainstream. It was not as though everyone had accepted the changes. Hardly. It was more that after years of cultural and political antagonism, living in a world of divided perspectives had become accepted. And while some of the manifestations remained confrontational, some appeared to possess a tone that seemed milder, gentler.

On a sunny Saturday morning in January 1967, people began to file into the Polo Field in San Francisco's Golden Gate Park, to join in a

"Gathering of the Tribes" or, as it was known ever after, "The Human Be-In." On the surface, the Be-In seemed a logical extension of events, like the Trips Festival of the previous year. But the differences were telling. Advertisements for the Be-In had been plastered on walls all over San Francisco and Berkeley. "Bring food to share, bring flowers, beads, costumes, feathers, bells, cymbals, and flags." There would be music—the Dead, the Airplane, Big Brother, and more—and speakers—Allen Ginsberg, Gary Snyder, Timothy Leary, Jerry Rubin. But as one observer put it, the aim was a union of the "Berkeley political activists and his community and the San Francisco's spiritual generation." This convergence would result in a transformative moment. "We declare and prophesy the end of wars, police states, economic oppression and racism…In unity we shall shower the country with waves of ecstasy and purification. Fear will be washed away, profits and empire will lie dying…violence will be submerged and transmuted to rhythm and dancing."[17]

Ginsberg and Snyder had begun the day with a Hindu blessing ritual. All morning people streamed onto the grounds. What greeted them was "mind-boggling," as one participant later recalled. "A seemingly endless sea of people, tens of thousands. And all were present for a purpose too important for words." Food was passed out, as was free LSD. The bands played, but this was not a music festival. People spoke, but this was not a typical rally. People dressed in colorful hippie garb or in casual student dress. They brought food, flowers, incense, tambourines, bells. People had never seen an event like this. "All most people could do was walk around and amaze themselves with all the faces that were present," wrote *Rolling Stone* editor Charles Perry.[18]

The California motorcycle gang, The Hell's Angels, took charge of protecting the bands' sound equipment and of finding lost children and retuning them to their parents. A call would go out, one attendee recalled, "The Hell's Angels have a little girl here behind the platform and she has curly hair. She says her name is Mary." The Hell's Angels caravan, this observer felt, looked like a "heavenly nursery" and that "the formidably dressed young men were angels." The day seemed "the end of something and the beginning of something else," wrote Helen Swick

Perry, author and Managing Editor of the journal *Psychiatry*. "There was clearly a renewal of the spirit of man...it was people being together, unprogrammed, uncommitted, except to life itself and its celebration."[19]

Be-Ins spread across the country that spring. Events were held in Chicago, New York, Los Angeles, Boston, Detroit, Philadelphia, Houston, and elsewhere, all with the same vibe. New Yorkers held theirs on Easter Sunday. The *Times* ran side-by-side pictures atop its front page of the traditional Fifth Avenue Easter Parade and the Central Park Be-In. "L-O-V-E, L-O-V-E, L-O-V-E," its story began. "They circled policemen and shrieked it. They strummed guitars and sang it. They painted their foreheads pink with it. And they jumped up and down and hollered it." According to one of its organizers, it was a "celebration of being alive...It's an affirmation of love and happiness." The wife of Mayor John Lindsey was bicycling through the park. She stopped to take in the event, her six-year-old son running to join a group playing drums and bells. "'Fantastic!' she exclaimed."[20] Across the country the news stories were similar—confused reactions to the participants' garb and childlike activities, but in a tolerant tone that proved accepting rather than antagonistic.

The Be-Ins joined the ever-expanding place of popular music on the cultural landscape, leading to the first major music festival of the decade, the Monterey International Pop Festival in June. Crowds were estimated at between fifty and one hundred thousand. Most of the major San Francisco and L.A. bands performed, as did others from across the country and the oceans. Indian sitar master Ravi Shankar shared the bill with Otis Redding and Britain's The Animals and The Who. Rolling Stone Brian Jones introduced Jimi Hendrix.* The concert took on a festival atmosphere. "Be happy, be free, wear flowers, bring bells," the publicity read. The bands performed for free, with all profits going to charity.

---

* The performers at Monterey read like a who's who of contemporary music acts, including: The Animals, Big Brother and the Holding Company, Booker T. and the M.G.s, Buffalo Springfield, the Butterfield Blues Band, the Byrds, the Grateful Dead, Jefferson Airplane, Jimi Hendrix, The Mamas & the Papas, Moby Grape, Otis Redding, Simon and Garfunkel, the Steve Miller Band, and The Who.

Stalls sold everything from jewelry to hashish brownies. San Francisco's Diggers, the radical community-action group, served free food. Free tabs of LSD were distributed. The police looked away as people smoked marijuana. "Everyone seemed to be smiling," one observer noted.[21]

For several years young people had been descending on the Haight-Ashbury, a neighborhood that had long welcomed avant-garde and cultural émigrés: rents were cheap, neighbors more tolerant, it's politics progressive. Now it became a national phenomenon. Novelist Mark Harris, then teaching at San Francisco State, assessed the San Francisco hippie scene for *The Atlantic*. The "visual" impact of the hippies was what confronted people initially—males with long hair, earrings, "weird-o granny glasses"; young women who looked "unwell, pale, sallow"; "everyone barefoot or in sandals"; and "generally dirty." The tour buses had begun to include the Haight in their San Francisco itineraries. Tourists drove through the neighborhood, snapping pictures.

But Harris goes on to develop a textured picture of this supposedly exotic world and its inhabitants. They possessed "the ennobling idea of hippies... they were middle-class American children to the bone... boys and girls with white skins from the right side of the economy in all-American cities and towns from Honolulu to Baltimore... if they'd only wanted them, they could commute to fine jobs from the suburbs, and own nice houses with bathrooms, where they could shave and wash up." But instead they flocked to San Francisco. Back east—across the Bay Bridge—lay the "wider United States whose values the hippies were testing... They had theories of community, theories of work, theories of child care, theories of creativity." And while other forms of dissent seemed to be increasingly antagonistic and potentially violent, these hippies possessed an "unwavering adherence to the ideal of nonviolence," Harris reminded his readers. "If they did not oppose the war in Vietnam in the way of organized groups, they opposed it by the argument of example, avoiding violence under all circumstances."

Harris remained critical of the hippie belief that LSD might offer "breathtaking panoramic visions of human and social perfection accompanied by profound insights into the user's own past." He feared it might also lead to suicide, at worst, to "self-destructive or antisocial behavior" or, at the least, to inarticulateness among users' unable to explain its full impact to non-users.

Yet, Harris concludes his piece quoting a long-time Haight resident, a teacher at a Catholic high school. "The new community by its rejection of certain middle-class attitudes of comfort, security, position, and property has pointed out to us our exaggerated concern for these material distractions.... They make us more aware of the over-looked pleasures of colors, sounds, trees, children, smiles." The older and the younger were learning to live together, to appreciate one another. "Not all middle-class people are squares," this teacher continued. "Generally speaking, upon close, personal examination of any square by any hippie, the sharp corners soften and the image of a human being appears."[22]

San Francisco and the Hippies became the subjects of global media attention. Stories about them appeared on the cover of national magazines, on the national nightly news. The tour buses continued to roll through the Haight. Tourist trinkets now included Day-Glo posters and other faux hippie paraphernalia. In May, singer Scott Mackenzie released "San Francisco (Be Sure to Wear Some Flowers in Your Hair)," written by Mamas and Papas' leader John Phillips.

> *If you're going to San Francisco*
> *Be sure to wear some flowers in your hair*
> *If you're going to San Francisco*
> *You're gonna meet some gentle people there...*
> *If you come to San Francisco*
> *Summertime will be a love-in there*

The song moved up the charts, reaching #4 in the U.S. and #1 in the UK. For many, especially those on the outside looking in, it captured the image of all that was positive in San Francisco. For others, including many in the Bay Area, it signaled the end of the building of a harmonious community and the beginning of the end of San Francisco as the counterculture mecca.

· The young did pour into the city—some estimates putting the number as high as seventy-five to one hundred thousand—in what became known as "The Summer of Love." The streets of the Haight were filled with joyous celebrants and alienated runaways. Many of the original Haight residents began to make plans to find their utopian community elsewhere. But there was no question that the counterculture, in general, and the Bay Area, in particular, had become central preoccupations within American and global culture.

Hollywood seemed to be incorporating this new sensibility, as well. Among the year's biggest hits were Mike Nichols' *The Graduate* and Arthur Penn's *Bonnie and Clyde*, both of which felt to audiences as if something new had come to American cinema. *The Graduate* seemed to be telling the young to reject the world of their parents. *Bonnie and Clyde* told people about the presence of violence at the heart of American mythology. While the more mainstream *In the Heat of the Night* took the Academy Award for Best Picture, as well as Best Actor (Rod Steiger), it was about an African American police detective from Philadelphia, confronting racism and a racist sheriff in a Mississippi town. Even the very traditionally styled *Guess Who's Coming to Dinner*, a fairly conventional comedy of manners, concerned an interracial romance between a successful Black physician and a young white woman.* The couple needs to convince both sets of parents that their marriage is a good idea. It too was nominated for Oscars in most of the major categories, with Katherine Hepburn winning Best Actress. *The Graduate* and *Bonnie and Clyde* also received nominations in all the significant categories, including Best Picture, Best Lead and Supporting Actor and Actress, and Original Screenplay. Mike Nichols won the Oscar for Best Direction.

The CBS television network tried to make its programming more youth-oriented when they debuted *The Smothers Brothers Comedy Hour* that February. The show hired a group of young, hip comedy writers, including Steve Martin, Albert Brooks, and Rob Reiner. They showcased musical guests like George Harrison, The Doors, Simon and Garfunkel, Cream, and The Who. Famously the show ran afoul of CBS

---

* Six months before the film's release, while it was being shot, the Supreme Court had handed down its verdict in *Loving v. Virginia*, which finally struck down all laws banning interracial marriage.

censors when the Smothers Brothers planned to have Pete Seeger sing his anti-Vietnam song "Waist Deep in the Big Muddy" in September 1967. Seeger was not allowed to appear. Public outcry against his removal led to him performing the song on the show in 1968.*

While rock music had become central to global youth culture, it was still mostly heard on Top-40 radio stations. But a changing pattern began in San Francisco, when station KMPX-FM, which was running on a shoestring budget, gave its midnight to six o'clock slot to a rock DJ. There were no set playlists; no need to push the top hits of the major labels. The DJ played everything from Bob Dylan to Ravi Shankar to deep album tracks. A few months later, a second rock DJ took the eight-to-midnight slot. And FM radio, which had mostly played classical, jazz, and easy listening music, became the place where counterculture sensibilities, musical tastes, and public media fully came together. Stations like KMPX sprang up all over the country.[23]

Other elements of youth culture and the counterculture began to penetrate the mainstream, suggesting, again, that a new consensus was developing. "The closest Western Civilization has come to unity since the Congress of Vienna in 1815 was the week" in June of 1967, "when the *Sgt. Pepper* album was released," recalled rock critic Langdon Winter. "In every city in Europe and America the stereo systems and radios played [it] and everyone listened."[24] *Sgt. Pepper's Lonely Hearts Club Band* was more than a rock phenomenon. The Beatles were the most famous people in the world, and young people around the globe shared in the experience. And beyond this, as author and journalist Charles Kaiser later concluded, "it forced even the most skeptical adult critics to admit that rock and roll could be art. For the first time ever, we had proved to the world, and to ourselves, that we really could be as perceptive as our parents."[25]

As if to give academic and social legitimacy to the counterculture, in its Autumn 1967 issue, *The American Scholar*, the quarterly literary magazine of the Phi Beta Kappa Society, published Ralph Gleason's article,

---

* The Smothers Brothers continually pushed against the limits of network censorship. Despite their ratings success, by 1969 the combination of network frustration and, supposedly, pressure from the new Nixon Administration led to their cancellation.

"Like a Rolling Stone." The journal had published articles by Albert Einstein, W.E.B. DuBois, Saul Bellow, Sinclair Lewis, Thomas Mann, Bertrand Russell, and a long list of other notables. To include an article on rock music therefore marked a significant moment of recognition of its cultural place. Gleason was the music critic of the *San Francisco Chronicle* and had been a major voice in promoting rock music and the San Francisco scene. He began his piece with several epigrams.

> *Forms and rhythms in music are never changed without producing changes in the most important political forms and ways.*
> Plato said that.

> *For the reality of politics, we must go to the poets, not the politicians.*
> Norman O. Brown said that.

> *For the reality of what's happening today in America, we must go to rock 'n' roll, to popular music.*
> I said that.

Gleason praised Dylan—"he took poetry out of the classroom...and put it right out there in the streets for everyone"—and the Beatles—"a declaration in favor of love and of life, an exuberant paean to the sheer joy of love." But it was more than simply about the sound. "In almost every aspect of what is happening today, this turning away from old patterns is making itself manifest." This is a generation that is not for sale, he argued. "Money doesn't talk it swears," he quotes Dylan. "'Make Love, Not War' is one of the most important slogans of modern times, a statement of life against death...the New Youth is finding its prophets in strange places—in dance halls and on the jukebox." "Youth is wise today," Gleason concluded. "'Hail, hail rock 'n' roll,' as Chuck Berry sings. 'Deliver me from the days of old!' I think he's about to be granted his wish."[26]

For mainstream America, William Westmoreland looked like central casting's idea of a general. His regal bearing, perfectly combed hair, piercing eyes, and Southern drawl suggested a man steeped in military tradition and a life spent in the most important outposts of his era—West Point,

Germany, Korea, Vietnam. He had taken on the toughest assignment any modern U.S. general had been assigned—commanding the U.S. forces in the Vietnam War—and despite the private misgivings of many policy planners and military strategists—had finally come to believe that victory was at hand.

Standing before the National Press Club in Washington, in November 1967, Westmoreland stated that he had, during the year, become "absolutely certain that whereas in 1965 the enemy was winning, today he is certainly losing." There were indications, he added, "that the Vietcong and even Hanoi know this... we have reached an important point when the end begins to come into view.... It lies within our grasp. The enemy's hopes are bankrupt."[27] His confidence was based on estimates of enemy troop strength, enemy casualties, and evaluations of how secure the South Vietnamese countryside had become, statistical reports that suggested that the longed-for "crossover point" had finally been reached. One U.S. evaluation concluded that 75 percent of the South Vietnamese population was pacified.[28]

For years, Americans had watched as the nation became ever-more deeply involved in a war whose point they failed to understand, whose citizens had begun to oppose the war in greater and greater numbers, and whose sacrifices had divided families, communities, and the nation as a whole. The war still raged, but perhaps optimistic assessments such as Westmoreland's might be signs that there were finally bright spots on the horizon.

By the end of 1967, Americans looked to the year ahead, sober but resolute, still feeling internal divisions but beginning to believe that these divisions might be accommodated in a new national sense that incorporated the differing perspectives. "Each generation has had to face its crisis of conscience over the means of establishing and preserving the Nation," the *Washington Post* declared in its 1968 New Year's Day editorial. "Domestic and foreign problems well may occasion some discouragement and distress," it observed, "but they do not justify despair and resignation... The world ahead looks like a hard world; but it's always been a hard world." When the nation would look back on the year 1968, the *Post* predicted, "the country will remain intact and its people will still be undaunted and undismayed."[29]

When he stood before Congress on January 17, 1968 to deliver his State of the Union Address, Lyndon Johnson echoed this sense that the nation, as well as the war, had reached a crossover point. He was optimistic about Vietnam. The enemy "has been defeated in battle after battle." This enemy "continues to hope America's will to persevere can be broken. Well—he is wrong…Our patience and our perseverance will match our power." Beyond Vietnam, America was on the move—annual production growing, paychecks rising, factories humming, "a new college is founded every week." Of course there was restlessness, but "when a great ship cuts through the seas," Johnson declared, "the waters are always stirred…Our ship is moving…toward new and better shores."

Johnson felt confident about what 1968 would offer—for the nation and for him. The political reporters from the *New York Times* concluded in their end-of-the-year assessment that despite difficulties, the president and his advisers had come to feel that "from here on out their fortunes would be going mostly up."[30] With this sense of optimism and confidence, Johnson concluded his address to the nation. "If there ever were a time to know the pride and the excitement and the hope of being an American—it is this time."

Halfway around the world, as North Vietnamese and Viet Cong soldiers were steadily moving into positions throughout South Vietnam, a different reality and a different future were taking shape, one that would shatter the optimism of the crossover point, replacing those sentiments with a sense felt around the globe that the world seemed to be coming undone.

PART II

When the World Shook

10

Saigon

The Tet Offensive

Monday, January 29, 1968 marked the beginning of the Vietnamese Lunar New Year known as Tet.* To commemorate it, the U.S. Embassy in Saigon decided to host a party that evening, inviting a large number of Vietnamese and American guests, who gathered on the Embassy lawn, drinking and socializing. The South Vietnamese Prime Minister sent a long string of fireworks as a gift. Setting off fireworks on Tet was a common occurrence, said to drive away evil spirits. When the Prime Minister's gift string was set off in the middle of the evening, "it had been the longest, loudest and fiercest series of explosions that anyone had heard for quite a while at the American Embassy or anywhere else in the secure city of Saigon," *Washington Post* reporter Don Oberdorfer later recounted.[1] Matching a growing optimism about the war against the North Vietnamese was the feeling that Saigon had become a safe haven, emblematic of the growing allied success. That sense of security, along with the quiet of Saigon, would be shattered in a matter of hours.

In the days following his State of the Union Address on January 17, Lyndon Johnson's immediate Asian problem did not focus on Vietnam but Korea. On the 23rd of January, North Korean ships had intercepted an American research and surveillance vessel, the *USS Pueblo*, and forced it into port. The next day the *New York Times* announced the seizure

* "Tet" is a shortened form of "Tết Nguyên Đán," or "celebration of the day."

with a five-column headline, and the *Pueblo* continued to be its lead story for days. On Friday, January 20, the *Times*' headline repeated the U.S. Government's belief that a "Grave Situation" now existed in Korea. Johnson later spoke on television to the American people about the incident, as the United States took the issue to the United Nations. News from Vietnam was reduced to secondary stories or fell off the front page entirely.

On Tuesday, January 30, the day after the Tet holiday, the *Times* reported on its front page that the Viet Cong had attacked seven cities. "American sources seemed dismayed by the success of the closely coordinated attacks." But it was not the paper's lead story that day. The following day, however, Vietnam grabbed the *Times'* lede:

> **FOE INVADES U.S. SAIGON EMBASSY;**
> **RAIDERS WIPED OUT AFTER 6 HOURS;**
> **VIETCONG WIDEN ATTACK ON CITIES.**

The fighting continued to be the lead story all week, displacing the *Pueblo*. On Thursday, the *Times* reported that, "in one suburb, northwest of the capital, South Vietnamese sources reported, families were serving meals to guerillas who had routed police forces from the area."

Friday's front page felt like the culmination of the week's gathering storm.

> **STREET CLASHES GO ON IN VIETNAM,**
> **FOE STILL HOLDS PART OF CITIES;**
> **JOHNSON PLEDGES NEVER TO YIELD.**

Just below this five-column headline, the Times ran the soon-to-be infamous photo of the South Vietnamese national police chief holding a handgun to the head of a handcuffed Viet Cong prisoner and assassinating him at close range.[2]

From the outset, the war in Vietnam had always presented a dilemma for U.S. military planners. The conflict was nothing like any they had fought previously. Schooled in Western military tactics based on traditional encounters, they frequently found their strategies ineffective or misguided. The events preceding Tet followed this pattern. There were numerous troop movements and other signs that might have hinted at what was to come. American commander William Westmoreland noted mainly that North Vietnamese regular army troops were moving toward Khe Sanh, a base near the Demilitarized Zone (DMZ) and the Laotian border. He paid little or no attention to the guerilla forces (the Viet Cong) fanning out across South Vietnam. At one point, an exasperated CIA analyst declared, "Here we are in the middle of a guerilla war and we haven't even bothered to count the number of guerillas!"[3]

Westmoreland began to amass troops at Khe Sanh, determined that this would not be his Dien Bien Phu, the crucial battle the French had lost back in 1954—and with it, their war. Ultimately, the U.S. committed 50,000 soldiers to Khe Sanh. During the week of January 30, as attacks were underway across the country, Westmoreland kept his central focus on Khe Sanh, where the *Times* reported, "only scattered contacts and light shelling was reported." By Friday, the *Times'* Tom Wicker was reporting that the Offensive had dealt Washington "a hard blow." To the hawkish Mississippi senator John Stennis, it was "embarrassing and humiliating." Still, Wicker quoted another Democratic senator who "predicted that American forces would win a major victory in the battle now developing at Khe Sanh. 'Then it will look like a different ball game.'"[4] But Khe Sanh turned out to be only a diversionary maneuver by the North Vietnamese, pulling American troops and material away from the major scenes of the fighting.

There were other signs the U.S. had missed in the months preceding Tet. Famously, in his memoir two decades later, cited above, former Secretary of Defense Robert McNamara noted, "I had never visited Indochina, nor did I understand or appreciate its history, language, culture, or values." Had McNamara or any of the other military planners known more about Vietnamese history, they would have known about the number of previous military actions that had begun during Tet. In 1789, the Emperor Quang Trung had launched a surprise Tet attack against the Chinese, driving them from Hanoi, an event widely celebrated by the Vietnamese. In fact, Westmoreland had been given a statuette of Quang Trung, which he displayed in his living quarters in Saigon.

He seems, however, to have never bothered to discover just what it was that made the Emperor a national hero.[5]

In the months before the attacks, the decision had been reached in the North to proceed with the offensive, though it diverged from the guerilla tactics that had been used for years. Since the days of the French, a dichotomy seemed to define the Vietnamese situation: The communists controlled the countryside while the government controlled the cities. Now the North and the Viet Cong were contemplating a single, massive campaign, directed at the cities. This would require enormously detailed planning but promised both literal and symbolic victories. The cities would no longer be seen as refuges for thousands of South Vietnamese fleeing the horrors of war but an arena of the action. The added national insecurity would further strain the relations between the U.S. and South Vietnamese government. And so, beginning August 1967, massive amounts of North Vietnamese weaponry were shipped into South Vietnam, hidden in trucks, ox carts, and sampans (flat-bottomed river boats). Thousands of new troops were recruited. While Westmoreland remained focused on Khe Sanh, men and material moved into positions all over South Vietnam, including almost 100 tons of weapons and thousands of Viet Cong soldiers into the Saigon area. Much of this material was stored in the tunnel complex in the Mekong Delta, twenty-two miles south of Saigon and was ultimately brought into the city in carts carrying vegetables to markets.[6]

Elsewhere around the country the same kinds of careful preparations were taking place in the lead-up to Tet. Near one Marine base in Cam Lo, along the coast close to the DMZ, Tuan Van Ban remembers that, before the assaults, he and his small battalion had "crawled and cut our way through the mines and barbed wire to get a close look at the base." They drew maps "including the positions of all the bunkers and buildings so our mortar men could preplan their targets...As much as possible we wanted to take the battle right into the enemy bunkers and grab the Americans by the belt buckle."[7]

The Americans did note a few signs that some kind of offensive was being planned, but they chose to ignore them. Doris Allen, a Black Army intelligence officer, warned higher-ups about the massing of enemy troops preparing to attack targets in the South. "We'd better get our stuff together because this is facing us, this is going to happen." Allen was ignored. She always felt that she was not taken seriously because she was not an officer and was also a Black woman.[8] One document captured in November indicated plans for a major direct conflict involving coordinated uprisings, including taking Saigon. American intelligence officers concluded it was merely a "propaganda document" intended to "boost Communist troop morale." Chairman of the Joint Chiefs of Staff Earle Wheeler concluded that if a major assault occurred, it would be like the German effort at the Battle of the Bulge toward the end of World War II—the last desperate attempt of a combatant facing its likely defeat. Lyndon Johnson told allies that he expected some "kamikaze" attacks, again suggesting that the Communists knew their days were numbered. One U.S. intelligence officer later admitted, "If we'd gotten the whole battle plan, it wouldn't have been believed. It wouldn't have been credible to us."[9]

Despite American military claims that the South Vietnamese Army had the "upper hand completely" throughout the Delta, as the *Post*'s Oberdorfer put it, "Hundreds, perhaps thousands of ordinary citizens in the Mekong Delta knew that the Viet Cong were about to attack...Simple people were building bunkers in previously secure neighborhoods. Wealthy folk were quietly leaving town. The American advisers knew nothing."[10]

On January 29, the Viet Cong and North Vietnamese launched attacks throughout the country. Five of the six largest cities, thirty-six of the forty-four provincial capitals, and numerous smaller towns came under siege. It is estimated that 70,000 to 80,000 Communist troops engaged in these battles, but it was a handful of them who became the symbols of the Offensive. Insinuating themselves into Saigon and waiting in an auto repair shop, they launched a middle-of-the-night attack on the U.S. Embassy, blowing a hole in the main gate and entering the Embassy grounds. Within minutes, four American soldiers had been killed—two guarding the gate and two others who responded immediately to the attack. Several rockets tore through the main doors of the Embassy building. Those stationed or sleeping inside the compound grabbed whatever weapons they could find, everything from handguns to grenades to, in one desperate case, a coat hanger.[11]

While it was the middle of the night in Saigon, it was the middle of the afternoon in the U.S., with the nightly news programs planning their evening programs. With two minutes until airtime, NBC News' hastily written copy was handed to anchor Chet Huntley. While some of the factual details proved to be wrong, Huntley's ninety-second report captured the intensity of the moment. It was, he declared "the enemy's biggest and most highly coordinated offensive of the war."[12]

U.S. Marines retook the Embassy the next day, its grounds littered with debris and bodies. But the damage had already been done. There was likely no building more protected or one more symbolic in South Vietnam than the U.S. Embassy. The Embassy assault became big news in the U.S. That night, *The Huntley-Brinkley Report* ran footage of the Embassy attack. Huntley asked his reporter, "Would you say they are trying for some psychological Dien Bien Phu?" Saigon was too large to capture, the reporter replied, but "they are certainly trying for a psychological splash and making it." Later that night both NBC and CBS ran primetime news specials about events in Vietnam.[13]

After the Marines had ended the Embassy siege, Westmoreland came to inspect the grounds. Surveying the Viet Cong dead, as well as the Americans who died, he concluded, "The enemy exposed himself by virtue of his strategy and he suffered great casualties." The U.S. had prevailed, he continued, because "American troops went on the offensive and pursued the enemy." One journalist recalled, "The reporters could hardly believe their ears. Westmoreland was standing in the ruins and saying everything was great." The *Washington Daily News* ran a front-page editorial, "WHERE WERE WE? WHERE ARE WE?" Accompanying the editorial was a political cartoon in which Westmoreland turns a corner at the Embassy and runs directly into a Viet Cong soldier. Westmoreland's uniform is in disarray, he has dropped his gun, and the Viet Cong soldier has his rifle pressed against the general. The caption read, "We've turned the corner...—Gen. Westmoreland."

While the Embassy siege lasted only about six and a half hours, "it seemed to many," Don Oberdorfer recalled, "the most embarrassing defeat the United States had suffered in Vietnam. Even though the scale was small, this was a big, big story, very big."[14]

Although gaining the most initial attention, the battle at the Embassy was hardly the only, or even the most brutal, clash that occurred. Saigon, itself, experienced attacks from three directions, including assaults on its major airport, Tan Son Nhut, and the government radio station. Carrying tapes they intended to broadcast to the nation, Viet Cong troops seized the station but were unable to play their messages. Instead they destroyed the control room. After fierce and deadly fighting, South Vietnamese government troops drove out the Viet Cong, then looted whatever equipment remained undamaged.

As was typical of the entire Vietnam war, sometimes a victory wasn't always a victory. What the Americans declared as a win ended up a different kind of defeat. In one area of Saigon, District Eight, populated primarily by middle-class Catholics, the Viet Cong shot at a few policemen and fired a few other rounds. They knew, recalled the combat photographer Philip Jones Griffiths, "the Americans would overreact. And indeed, within hours, U.S. helicopters were killing everything that moved." Where the Americans had always assured the South Vietnamese "they'd be safe in the cities," Griffiths continues, "the Viet Cong said, 'You're not safe in those cities.'" The Tet Offensive, "disillusioned many Vietnamese who had been loyal to the government." Where was the "highest concentration of pro-American Vietnamese? It was District Eight. And that's the district the Americans destroyed."[15]

The government-imposed curfew in Saigon made the city look, to journalist Michael Herr, like the final images of the post-nuclear apocalyptic landscape in the film *On the Beach*, "a desolate city whose avenues held nothing but refuse, windblown papers, small distinct piles of human excrement and dead flowers and spent firecracker casings of the Lunar New year."[16]

The battles in Saigon ended relatively quickly. Not so in the ancient imperial capital at Hue. As with most of the assaults, the North Vietnamese and Viet Cong began their attack on Hue in the middle of the night. By dawn they had the run of the city, including the walled center, the Citadel. The Americans believed that, as in Saigon, the enemy had dispatched only a small force to Hue. They sent a single company to respond, then soon came to realize just how large were the forces they were confronting. The enemy held not only the old Imperial palace but also important buildings throughout the city. Each side began to augment their forces, the Communists mostly moving under cover of darkness and eventually adding ten battalions. The Americans countered with nine battalions, supplemented by eleven South Vietnamese battalions.[17]

For twenty-five days, the Viet Cong flag flew from the Citadel's flagpole. One French journalist described the Viet Cong moving through the occupied city, "joking and laughing...without showing any fear...Numerous civilians brought them great quantities of food." The diversity of the Viet Cong force suggested its popular roots. "There were local country girls in black pajamas," one reporter recalled. "Some were city boys...with long hair and American-style blue jeans. One Viet Cong soldier was the girl elected queen of her senior class at a local high school. She wore a revolver on each hip."[18]

The American counter-offensive was long and brutal. Massive aerial bombardment and strafing were later joined by street-by-street fighting. By the time the assault ended, 10,000 civilians had been killed, over half of the houses had been destroyed, and eighty percent of Hue's inhabitants had lost their homes.

In addition to the battles in the major cities like Saigon and Hue, there were countless smaller encounters. Tuan Van Ban, who was among the Viet Cong forces who crawled close to the base in Cam Lo in preparation for the attack, recalled that his small force knew from the start that they would be unable to sustain an assault for long. When they launched their attack, they moved in as quickly as they could, so that when artillery began to be fired against them, "most of us had penetrated the perimeter and the shells landed behind us." Understanding their limitations, "we just destroyed as much as we could and gave the signal to withdraw. We were in and out, all well before daybreak."[19]

Events in the Mekong Delta mirrored encounters around the country: the battles were fierce, the death toll high, the destruction widespread.

But U.S. participants in this region expressed another sense, common to the entire experience. Tobias Wolfe, a Green Beret officer, recalled in his 1994 memoir *In Pharoah's Army: Memories of the Lost War*, that the U.S. response in My Tho, a city in the Delta, epitomized the American mentality. "We knocked down bridges…leveled shops and bars…pulverized hotels…I didn't think of our targets as homes where exhausted and frightened people were praying for their lives. When you're afraid you will kill anything that might kill you. Now that the enemy had the town, the town was the enemy."[20]

When asked by an American journalist why such devastation had been visited upon Ben Tre, another Mekong Delta town, an American major responded with an observation that many would later come to believe epitomized the American attitude in the entire war. "It became necessary to destroy the town in order to save it."[21] To Michael Herr, all of Vietnam became "a dark room full of deadly objects, the VC were everywhere at once like spider cancer, and instead of losing the war in little pieces over the years we lost it fast in under a week."[22]

At this point, two Tet Offensives emerged: The first was the one in which the American military declared victory. The second was the perception Tet created at home and around the world. They could not have been more different. To the U.S. military, the enemy had given it its best shot and had failed. By the end of Tet, Westmoreland felt "like a boxer who has his opponent on the ropes," he later recounted.[23] And by traditional military standards, Tet was "a tactical disaster for the communists," as two historians assessed it. "They achieved none of their major objectives." But "tactical disasters did not mean a strategic defeat." For one eminent Vietnam historian, Ngo Vinh Long, the most important objectives of Tet were "to force the United States to de-escalate the war against the North and to go to the negotiating table." In this way, Tet was a strategic victory for the North Vietnamese.[24]

A different perspective emerged among many of the American soldiers in Vietnam. The generals' reassurances flew in the face of what soldiers began to feel. "The country came back under what we called control," Michael Herr later observed, but "it remained essentially occupied by the Viet Cong and the North." In Hue, Herr found that "the grunts [slang for soldiers] were whistling, and no two were whistling the same tune, it sounded like a locker room before a game that nobody wanted to play." In one unit, he noted, "a despair [had] set in among members of the battalion that the older ones, veterans of two other wars, had never seen before." A joke began to circulate among the soldiers. "What's the difference between the Marine Corps and the Boy Scouts? The Boy Scouts have adult leadership."[25]

Tet shook the American public deeply. And nothing had a greater impact than the image of the execution of the Viet Cong soldier on the street in Saigon. The *New York Times* took the unprecedented step of not only running the horrific photo on its front page—four columns wide and five inches deep—but reprinted it on page 12, along with other images taken moments before and after the assassination.*

While Lyndon Johnson characterized the Offensive as "a complete failure," his Democratic rivals offered powerful rebuttals. "If taking over sections of the American Embassy, a good part of Hue, [and elsewhere] constitutes complete failure," Minnesota Senator Eugene McCarthy replied sarcastically, "I suppose by this logic that if the Viet Cong captured the entire country, the Administration would be claiming a total collapse." Robert Kennedy was more direct. Tet "has finally shattered the mask of official illusion from which we have concealed our true circumstances even from ourselves," he observed, "but for twenty years we have been wrong." He continued, "The history of conflict among nations does not record such a lengthy and consistent chronicle of error. It is time to discard so proven a fallacy and face the reality that a military victory is not in sight, and that it probably will never come." Republicans joined Democrats. "If what we have seen in the past week is a Viet Cong failure," GOP candidate George Romney of Michigan proclaimed, "then I hope they never have a victory." Even the hawkish Richard Nixon began to tone down his rhetoric.[26]

---

* The photo won photographer Eddie Adams that year's Pulitzer Prize for photography, plus numerous other prizes and awards.

Most Americans seemed to agree with these critiques. The optimistic promises of 1967 had left Americans equally divided on the war. A December 1967 poll showed forty-five percent thought Vietnam a mistake, forty-six percent thought it was not. Tet sent the favorable numbers tumbling. By February, the split was forty-six percent against to forty-two percent in favor. In March, it was forty-nine to forty-one, and by August fifty-three to thirty-five. The number of Americans who believed the U.S. was making progress in Vietnam plummeted from fifty to thirty-three percent.

The reaction around the world echoed the feelings on the U.S. home front. "In an amazing week," one British Labour Party commentator recalled, "the offensive completely destroyed the political image and confidence of the U.S. It was a shattering blow for the U.S. globally—the most important event of 1968 because it changed the course of history." To one West German, "It was a world-shaking event that allowed me to imagine what the Russian revolution must have meant for people with socialist ideas...There was no doubt now—the world revolution was dawning."[27]

Despite all this, Westmoreland came back to Washington with a request for additional troops, as he had done frequently since assuming command in 1965. Each request for a troop escalation had come with a promise of victory. Post-Tet was no different. So committed to his belief that Khe Sanh was the focal point of the entire endeavor, Westmoreland undervalued the centrality of Tet in his depiction of the enemy's overall strategy. Early attacks along the Cambodian border in 1967 were its first phase, he argued. Tet was its second. But Khe Sanh, he believed, remained their central intention.*

On March 10, the *New York Times* reported that Westmoreland was requesting 206,000 additional troops, to augment the 510,00 already there. The Selective Service system was already strained to its limits in supplying

---

* Westmoreland continued to concentrate more and more troops at Khe Sanh. Ultimately there were 50,000 American troops stationed there, soldiers that might have been used elsewhere during Tet. The Americans dropped 60,000 tons of napalm and 40,000 tons of other weaponry on the mountains around the base. The North Vietnamese assaults continued for several months and then, their diversionary necessity completed, in March the siege ended.

troops. Westmoreland's new request would require mobilizing most of the reserves, which would only add to the war's growing unpopularity.

Johnson administration officials played down the *Times'* story, never firmly denying it but emphasizing that it was only a request. What had begun inside the halls of government was a reassessment of overall policy. Newly appointed Defense Secretary Clark Clifford created a task force of high government officials to evaluate the troop request. The discussions proved troubling for Clifford. "I could not find out when the war was going to end, could not find out whether the new requests for men and equipment were going to be enough…All I had was the statement, given with too little self-assurance to be comforting, that if we persisted for an indeterminate length of time, the enemy would choose not to go on."[28]

For several years Johnson had relied on a group of unofficial senior advisers, sometimes tagged The Wise Men, all major figures in the foreign policy establishment, whose expertise dated back to the Truman administration. In November 1967 they had gathered at the State Department and had been supportive of the Administration, thinking its Vietnam policies were on the right track. In March 1968 they returned to the State Department, meeting along with a number of other government officials. Attitudes of group members had shifted. Dean Acheson, Harry Truman's Secretary of State and one of the key architects of the Cold War, said his view had changed since November. He now did not think it was possible for the U.S. to achieve its aims through military means. Others also began to speak of their hesitations or new perspectives, including Clifford. When they finally had their private meeting with Johnson, men who had themselves shaped Vietnam policy only a few years before—people like JFK's National Security Advisor McGeorge Bundy and former Ambassador to South Vietnam Henry Cabot Lodge—began to counsel shifts in goals and tactics, essentially as LBJ saw it, "to initiate disengagement."

Johnson was shocked by this new turn among these trusted advisers. He "could hardly believe his ears," Clifford recalled, "he thought somebody had poisoned the well."[29] Within the corridors of American power, Vietnam strategy began to change. LBJ plotted a new course. Westmoreland was not going to get his troops. In fact, on March 22,

LBJ summoned reporters to the Oval Office and announced a shake-up in the senior military staff. Westmoreland was reassigned to Washington, where he would become Army Chief of Staff. In the immediate aftermath of Tet, Westmoreland remembered that, as noted above, he felt "like a boxer who has his opponent on the ropes." But he added that at that very point, "[the boxer's] seconds threw in the towel."[30]

The home front reaction to the Tet Offensive dramatically changed Americans' attitudes toward the war in Vietnam. This was especially striking in the reactions of some of the most mainstream voices in media. The *New York Times'* columnist James Reston asked, "What is the end that justified this slaughter? How will we save Vietnam if we destroy it in the battle?" The widely syndicated columnist (and former JFK speechwriter) Joseph Kraft wrote on February 1, "The war in Vietnam is unwinnable, and the longer it goes on the more the Americans...will be subjected to losses and humiliations." The usually conservative *Wall Street Journal* believed "the American people should be getting ready to accept, if they haven't already, the prospect that the whole Vietnam effort may be doomed." On February 12, the *Times* editorialized, "The Administration's organized optimism over the 'failure' of the Viet Cong's Tet offensive is unfortunately ill-founded. It compounds the harm already done." *Time* magazine concluded that, "between the Red offensive and North Korea's seizure of the U.S.S. Pueblo, the mighty U.S. suddenly seemed as impotent as a beached whale. Even those nations that normally delight in American embarrassment refrained from crowing openly."[31]

Art Buchwald, the popular syndicated humor columnist, took sarcasm deep into the Tet debate. His column of February 6, opened with the dateline, "Little Big Horn, Dakota."

> Gen. George Custer said today in an exclusive interview with this correspondent that the Battle of Little Big Horn had just turned the corner, and he could now see the light at the end of the tunnel. "We have the Sioux on the run," Gen. Custer told me. "Of course we will have some cleaning up to do, but the Redskins are hurting badly and it will only be a matter of time before they give in."[32]

Perhaps no media figure loomed as large in the post-Tet discussions as did Walter Cronkite. The anchor of the *CBS Evening News,* Cronkite was, by 1968, the "most trusted man in America." The unbiased anchor with the reassuring demeanor, Cronkite had grown somewhat troubled by the reports he was reading about the war and the growing opposition among some of his respected colleagues. But he had been reassured by the government several times, including three private meetings with Johnson and senior officials. When the first reports of the Tet attacks made it to Washington, Cronkite was preparing for his evening broadcast. "What the hell is going on?" he declared, "I thought we were winning the war!" He decided he needed to go to Vietnam himself. Arriving less than two weeks after the first assaults, he toured the country, met with soldiers and strategists, generals and Vietnamese civilians. By the end of February, he was back in the U.S., and on February 28, CBS offered a special, "Report from Vietnam by Walter Cronkite." After showing footage from his tour and clips from his interviews, Cronkite ended with his personal assessment. "Who won and who lost the great Tet Offensive against the cities? I'm not sure...history may make it a draw." However, he concluded, "It seems now more certain than ever that the bloody experience of Vietnam is to end in a stalemate...It is increasingly clear to this reporter that the only rational way out then will be to negotiate, not as victors, but as an honorable people who lived up to their pledge to defend democracy and did the best they could."[33]

The impact of Cronkite's report was enormous. "It was the first time in American history," David Halberstam later wrote, "that a war had been declared over by an anchorman."[34] Watching Cronkite's report at the White House, Johnson declared, "If I have lost Walter Cronkite, I have lost Mr. Average Citizen." Events of the next few weeks would demonstrate just how right Johnson was.

II

Portsmouth

The Democrats Splinter

The events of January and February in Saigon and across Vietnam reverberated throughout the United States and around the world. Far from the battlefields of Southeast Asia, in the hills and small towns of New Hampshire—a landscape as unlike Indochina as there might be—the rumblings and reactions created by the Tet Offensive intensified the already growing movement within the Democratic Party to challenge its leadership over the issue of Vietnam—the "Dump Johnson" movement.

In 1967, two political activists Allard Lowenstein and Curtis Gans had created the movement, seeking a candidate to take up the call. Lowenstein was the political organizer, moving among Democratic circles, looking for support. He had to walk a fine line between New Left radicals and leaders of the antiwar movement, who saw him as a middle-class reformer, on the one hand, and anti-communist liberals, like Hubert Humphrey and major union leaders, who saw his movement as threatening the postwar order. Lowenstein and Gans, who excelled in statistical analysis, really had only one individual in mind—Robert Kennedy. Kennedy, they felt, could not only create a national debate about Vietnam but also, unlike a more typical protest candidate, stood a chance of winning the nomination and then the general election.

Relations between Johnson and Robert Kennedy had long been strained, with their intensity increasing since JFK's assassination. Johnson knew full well how many of the hopes engendered by JFK, all of which grew exponentially with his death, had become attached to Bobby. LBJ resisted calls to make RFK his running mate in 1964, but could not restrain the overwhelming response to Kennedy when he appeared at that year's Democratic convention, following a filmed tribute to his late brother. The standing ovation lasted an extraordinary twenty-two minutes.

Although the heir apparent to the Kennedy mystique, RFK's reputation alternated between social reformer and ruthless, ambitious politico. After the assassination, he became more philosophical and had begun to embrace the counterculture a bit. He met and talked with poets Allen Ginsburg and Robert Lowell, read Camus, Emerson, Aeschylus, and Sophocles. He grew his hair longer, began listening to Bob Dylan, turned up now and then at Andy Warhol's Factory, and, occasionally, wore what had become known as "love beads." His political interests widened to concerns about social justice and poverty, including connections with Cesar Chavez and the United Farm Workers.

In 1966, Kennedy traveled to South Africa to give the "Day of Affirmation Speech" to students opposed to apartheid. He had contacted Allard Lowenstein to help revise the initial draft of his speech. Kennedy's talk began with a semi-humorous but trenchant opening. "I come here this evening because of my deep interest and affection for a land…in which the native inhabitants were at first subdued…a land which defined itself on a hostile frontier…a land which was once the importer of slaves, and now must struggle to wipe out the last traces of that former bondage. I refer, of course, to the United States of America." But he went on to frame the current situation in South Africa in international terms. "It is a revolutionary world we live in, and thus, as I have said in Latin America and Asia, in Europe and in the United States, it is young people who must take the lead. You, and your young compatriots everywhere, have had thrust upon you a greater burden of responsibility than any generation that has ever lived." While his final call went out to individuals in the audience, it could have equally been proclaimed at rallies in the U.S. and around the world. "It is from numberless diverse acts of courage and belief that human history is shaped each time a man stands up for an ideal or acts to improve the lot of others or strikes out against injustice. He sends forth a tiny ripple of hope...those ripples build a current that can sweep down the mightiest wall of oppression and resistance."[1]

Kennedy still had all the main strategists of his brother's world working on his future—including Theodore Sorenson, Arthur Schlesinger, and his brother Ted. Younger, enthusiastic staffers, whose hair length suggested they came from the next generation, had joined them. For these Young Turks, as they were sometimes called, the days of JFK seemed a distant memory. "Those New Frontier cats were out of the fifties," one observed. "Don't forget that JFK campaigned in '60 on Quemoy and Matsu and that Cold War crap, and on some mythical poll about how our prestige was down in Europe."[2] There was little doubt among them that the 1972 Democratic nomination could be Bobby's. But the question became "What about 1968?"

Throughout the early fall of 1967, the Kennedy camp fiercely debated his entry. After much discussion, among themselves and then with Lowenstein, with advisers arguing strongly for each side, Kennedy finally decided to wait until 1972. While he had grown increasingly skeptical about Vietnam War policy, Kennedy told Lowenstein that he "would have a problem if I ran against Johnson...People would say I was splitting the party out of ambition and envy." "That's too bad," Lowenstein replied, "because you could have become President of the United States."[3]

By this point, a number of prominent Democrats had emerged as critics of the war. But they either demurred from Lowenstein and Gans' appeal or were not the kind of candidate to whom the masses might rally. In October 1967, Minnesota Senator Eugene McCarthy told Lowenstein he would explore the possibility of running. McCarthy had come from the same progressive Minnesota Farm-Labor background as Vice President Hubert Humphrey. Unlike the voluble Humphrey, McCarthy was reserved and intellectual, but also sarcastic and often aloof. A devout Catholic, he had once attended a seminary, but had left because he found it too narrow intellectually. He taught sociology at a small Minnesota college and then entered politics after World War II, winning election to the

House in 1948. He moved on to the Senate in 1958, where his mentor became Majority Leader Lyndon Johnson. He was supportive of his party, but sometimes rankled at the praised attributes of its leaders. "I'm twice as liberal as Hubert Humphrey," he told *Time* magazine in 1960, "and twice as Catholic as Jack Kennedy." He was on Johnson's vice-presidential short list in 1964 and had been a loyal supporter of the Vietnam War.

McCarthy's view began to shift in 1967. Testimony before the Senate Foreign Relations Committee, on which McCarthy sat and whose chair, J. William Fulbright, had emerged as a leading critic of the war, seems to have moved him. Under Secretary of State Nicholas Katzenbach, the once-lauded U.S. Attorney General associated with leading desegregation efforts in the South, now argued that because of the Tonkin Gulf Resolution there were no limits to presidential authority in Vietnam. Senators replied that when they voted for the resolution they thought they had voted for a much more limited scope of presidential authority. Katzenbach argued back, "There is no limit to what he says the President can do." "There is only one thing to do," McCarthy concluded. "Take it to the country. Someone's going to have to take them on."[4]

By the end of November he was ready to be that person. He was, however, emphatic that he was challenging a policy not a person.

Despite McCarthy's somewhat scholarly demeanor, his campaign soon generated tremendous excitement. For years, opponents of the war—especially the young—had been told to stop complaining and to work within the system to foment change, but those avenues had usually been blocked. Neither party appeared ready to participate in a serious challenge to Vietnam policy. Office holders and party leaders who grew too critical usually found support from the national party evaporating. Now there appeared an opening. While some in the antiwar movement feared that the McCarthy campaign would minimize or ignore important radical political and social issues, others felt that they finally could do more than loudly declare their grievances. They could act.

The McCarthy campaign had little organization and few volunteers when the small group of Dump Johnson operatives arrived in New Hampshire. Gerry Studds, soon to be a Congressman from Massachusetts, later told an interviewer, "We sort of looked at each other and said, 'God, there are ten weeks to go. What are we going to do?'"[5] There were volunteers arriving from the beginning, but after Tet exploded, they streamed into New Hampshire in greater numbers than the Granite State had ever seen. Many agreed to become "Clean for Gene," the men shaving their beards and donning sports coats, the women trading their jeans for skirts. New Hampshire is a small state, and its politics, including its famed presidential primary, is built on personal contact. Curtis Gans told one interviewer, "We had coffee at shopping centers and town dumps. We had six pieces of literature for every man, woman, and child…two phone canvasses and two door canvasses…we had transportation to and from the polls…we had Polaroids of everyone who shook hands with McCarthy." A group of Yale students even wrote pro-McCarthy pamphlets in French for French-Canadian voters.[6]

And they also had the continuing fallout from Tet. On Sunday, March 10, two days before the New Hampshire primary, the *New York Times* reported that Westmoreland had requested 206,000 additional troops. Reactions erupted across the country but especially in New Hampshire. More volunteers poured into the state, adding to all those already on the ground. "We have four times as many people as we need," remarked one McCarthy staffer.

The energy that flowed into the campaign seemed to stir the candidate himself. He began to campaign more intensely, though never abandoning the pragmatic style of his rhetoric. He would be compelling without being off-putting to more traditional voting blocs, and they responded— not just the kids but also small business people and working-class voters. It was the LBJ forces that raised the volume—a full-page newspaper ad declared, "the Communists are watching the New Hampshire primary." Thomas McIntyre, the state's pro-LBJ Democratic senator, called McCarthy "a friend of draft-dodgers and deserters."[7] By contrast, McCarthy's slogan was "New Hampshire can bring America back to its senses."

Despite feeling the surge growing under the McCarthy candidacy, no one was ready for the results. He polled 42.4 percent of the vote, to Johnson's 49.5 percent. In fact, when write-in votes were added, LBJ had won the state by only 230 votes. Despite the hairline numerical loss, both McCarthy and the press who covered the campaign saw the result as a victory for the Minnesota senator and a serious defeat for LBJ. During his "victory" speech, McCarthy echoed a sentiment beginning to be felt around the country. "People have remarked that this campaign had brought young people back into the system. But it's the other way around: The young people have brought the country back into the system."[8]

No sooner had McCarthy exceeded expectations so spectacularly than attention turned back to Robert Kennedy. *Village Voice* columnist Jack Newfield, who had covered Kennedy's 1964 Senate campaign, had become friendly with RFK in the subsequent four years. Newfield had gladly voted for LBJ in 1964, but had become, like many others, deeply disillusioned with the President, famously comparing him in one column to former heavyweight champion Sonny Liston, "a bully with a quitter's heart...he will not run if he thinks he cannot win." Newfield had been one of the "Run in '68" contingent of Kennedy's friends and advisers and had been acutely disappointed when Kennedy had opted out. In a December column, Newfield had warned, "If [Robert] Kennedy does not run in 1968, the best side of his character will die. He will kill it every time he butchers his conscience and makes a speech for Johnson next autumn." Even more painful for Kennedy, evidently, was a placard held aloft at Brooklyn College, "BOBBY KENNEDY: HAWK, DOVE, OR CHICKEN?"[9]

The day after the New Hampshire primary, Tom Wicker's front-page analysis in the *New York Times* noted that Kennedy was "more than ever on the horns of a dilemma." McCarthy's strong showing had reignited the debate within the Kennedy circle. But the same fears again emerged. This time it was not about taking on the president of his own party. It was about shoving the winner of the New Hampshire primary out of the way, once he had shown the President's vulnerability. A meeting between Kennedy and McCarthy went nowhere. McCarthy repeated that he was not getting out of the race. He had, after all, just massively exceed expectations in the nation's first primary. The best he might do, he suggested, was pledge to be a single-term president and then endorse Bobby in 1972. That was not what the Kennedys had hoped to hear, and the meeting adjourned.[10]

The Kennedy camp was as divided as ever. Some thought his career would be over if he ran. Others though it would be over if he didn't. Ted Sorenson said he should stay neutral between McCarthy and Johnson, while former JFK press secretary Pierre Salinger feared neutrality would look "opportunistic." RFK, himself, seemed to be moving ever closer to getting in the race. Still worried about dividing the party, he and Sorenson arranged a meeting with Defense Secretary Clark Clifford. They proposed that Johnson appoint a commission to reconsider Vietnam policy and make Kennedy a member. If the commission proposed a reasonable path to end the war, and if Johnson supported it, then Kennedy world not enter the race and instead support LBJ in the fall. If not, Kennedy told Clifford, he was going to run.[11]

Johnson rejected the offer. Kennedy put Sorenson to the task of drafting his announcement, scheduled for Saturday morning, March 15, a mere four days after McCarthy's strong showing in New Hampshire.

They had one final plan to keep from splitting the antiwar movement within the party. Ted Kennedy was dispatched for a Friday late-night meeting in Green Bay with McCarthy, where he suggested that McCarthy and RFK should each run unopposed in all but one of the remaining primaries. In California, in June, they would square off to see who would be the party's anti-war challenger to LBJ. McCarthy declined, never letting Teddy explain the plan fully. Teddy returned to RFK's house at 6:00 a.m. Saturday morning to tell him the news. By 10:00 a.m., his brother was standing before cameras in the same Senate Caucus Room where JFK had declared his candidacy in 1960, announcing that he too was seeking the Democratic nomination for president.

The tragic ending of Robert Kennedy's campaign would obscure the political turmoil that developed from the day of his announcement until his victory in the California Democratic primary three months later.

While many of McCarthy's volunteers had joined because of an issue, as journalist Charles Kaiser was later to conclude, many "had fallen in love with the man."[12] For many, Kennedy seemed an ambitious interloper. "Kennedy thinks that American youth belongs to him at the bequest of his brother," wrote colonist Mary McGrory. "Seeing the romance flower between them and McCarthy, he moved with the ruthlessness of a Victorian father whose daughter has fallen in love with a dustman."[13]

In 1968 there were many fewer presidential primaries than today. Fifteen states held primary elections that year, but only about half were essential contests. McCarthy had already shown strength in New Hampshire; and the next contest, in Wisconsin, was both a state even more receptive to his message and one in which Kennedy had missed the filing deadline. When Kennedy announced, he talked about only entering three of the primaries—Nebraska, Oregon, and California. Kennedy supported McCarthy in Wisconsin and tried to reiterate that the aim was to make it clear that they were not running against each other but against Johnson and his Vietnam policy. McCarthy told the *New York Times*, however, that he feared Kennedy could "have a divisive effect within the party" and that he "may cause some trouble." "An Irishman who announces the day before St. Patrick's Day that he's going to run against another Irishman," McCarthy suggested, "shouldn't say it's going to be a peaceful relationship."[14]

Both candidates began to infuse the campaign with fresh enthusiasm. Of Kennedy's first campaign trip to California in mid-March, British journalist David Caute later recalled, "The Kennedy magic sprang to life. Often he was surrounded by teenage girls in Day-Glo toreador pants and emitting 'Beatle' squeals." He campaigned in the Watts ghetto. "Perched on the back of a car, Bobby drove among blacks and Mexicans and college kids."[15] The crowds were huge, diverse, enthusiastic, seeming to want to touch the candidate as much as hear him. He frequently lost his cufflinks or shirt buttons. A crowd of seven thousand, predominantly Mexican American, turned out in San Jose. One reporter equated the frenzy at an appearance at the Los Angeles Greek Theater to a Rolling Stones concert.[16]

Still, resentments bubbled. Some McCarthy supporters heckled RFK or held signs questioning his integrity. Journalist Murray Kempton, long-time veteran of liberal political wars, took aim at Kennedy in the *New York Post*, calling him a coward who had come "down from the hills to shoot the wounded." He had in a single gesture, Kempton continued, "confirm[ed] the worst things his enemies have ever said about him."[17] Some of his left critics did have to admit there was something more to the Kennedy campaign than mere protest. "It is impossible to reject the Bobby phenomenon," Andrew Kopkind concluded in an otherwise scathing piece in *The New Statesman*, "Kennedy is real. The radical protests...and even the McCarthy campaign are not. Bobby alone can make it."[18]

Meanwhile, McCarthy's youthful supporters moved to Wisconsin, site of the next primary on April 2. This was a state more in tune with McCarthy, who represented neighboring Minnesota and had come out of the same Farm-Labor background as many Wisconsinites. Further, the University of Wisconsin had been a center of anti-war and student activity. Volunteers did not have to be bussed into the state. Many lived there and went to school there. As soon as the votes from New Hampshire had been counted, McCarthy became the favorite in Wisconsin.[19] The campaign had caught fire. Newspaper endorsements began to roll in. Campaign rallies were jammed. Thousands filled Veterans Memorial Coliseum in Madison—students, workers, and farmers; the young, the middle-aged, and seniors.

The polls were showing that Johnson would lose.[20] By the end of the month, even Johnson's Wisconsin aides were telling reporters that the President would be defeated.[21] On Sunday, March 31, the *New York Times* quoted one Johnson campaign aide. "Ten days ago we were predicting McCarthy would get 60 per cent of the vote so the President would look good when McCarthy only got 53...Now we're afraid he really may get 60 per cent."[22]

The *Times* also reported on its front page that day that Johnson would address the nation that night "to deal 'rather fully' with the situation in Vietnam, including further troop build-ups, the possibility of reserve call-ups and the additional costs thereof." These were the issues that had developed after Tet, and now Johnson, two nights before the Wisconsin primary, was going on TV to tell the nation what he had decided about them. Referencing the reaction that accompanied reports that Westmoreland was asking for an additional 206,000 troops, Johnson assured Americans that the new deployments would not be "anything like the hundreds of thousands mentioned in speculation."[23]

At 9:00 p.m. Lyndon Johnson looked into the television cameras and began what seemed to be another call for Hanoi to come to the conference table. "Tonight I want to speak to you of peace in Vietnam and Southeast Asia. No other question so preoccupies our people. No other dream so absorbs the 250 million human beings who live in that part of the world. No other goal motivates American policy in Southeast Asia," he began. This was something we had been doing for years, he argued. And yet, the enemy would not reciprocate. Instead, they attacked during the Tet holidays. But contrary to the feelings of most Americans, Johnson declared that the attacks "failed to achieve its principal objectives... The Communists were unable to maintain control of any of the more than 30 cities that they attacked. And they took very heavy casualties."

He then renewed his call for peace talks but only "serious talks on the substance of peace." He declared that he would halt the bombing of North Vietnam, would only send new troops of support and to replace those already there (and not the 200,000 Westmoreland had asked for), and initiate a process to create meaningful peace talks. Veteran diplomat Averill Harriman was assigned the task of conducting talks with the North Vietnamese toward that end. To a number of McCarthy staffers, all these concessions and moves were a clear victory for them and their campaign, even though they feared they might enhance LBJ's chances in the upcoming primary.

Johnson had added a final section to his address, which he had written himself, and of which only he and Lady Bird knew. He had not even fully decided whether he would give this last part, although he had had it added to his teleprompter text. He and Lady Bird had a signal. If he was going ahead with this section, he would raise his right hand a bit. After praising American troops and the will of the American people, Johnson turned to the debates erupting at home. He lifted his right hand. "What we won when all of our people united must not now be lost in suspicion, distrust, selfishness, and politics among any of our people." To limit these developments, "I have concluded that I should not permit the Presidency to become involved in the partisan divisions that are developing in this political year." And then to nearly everyone's astonishment, he concluded, "I do not believe that I should devote an hour or a day of my time to any personal partisan causes or to any duties other than the awesome duties of this office—the Presidency of your country. Accordingly, I shall not seek, and I will not accept, the nomination of my party for another term as your President."

Viewers across the nation sat up in shock. LBJ had dropped out, quit the race, thrown in the towel. McCarthy volunteers poured into the hallways of their hotel, screaming and dancing. A group of anti-war protestors gathered outside the White House and sang, "We *have* overcome."[24]

At the beginning of the year, reporters thought Johnson's candidacy would only grow more popular in 1968. Just three months later, he declared himself out. Whatever else would happen in the course of the presidential election of 1968—and very much more would happen—the national tumult that had begun with the Tet Offensive had already claimed its first casualty. Lyndon Johnson, who strode across the American political stage like a giant, was trying for one last grand gesture—to bring peace to Vietnam—and would then head home to Texas.

12

Martin Luther King—The Road to Memphis

In April of 1967, a year before Lyndon Johnson would be driven from office in a wave of anti-Vietnam opposition, Martin Luther King, Jr. stood at the podium of New York's Riverside Church and delivered a speech that moved him into new and uncharted territory. For over a decade, King had been the conscience of the nation and the prime spirit of the civil rights movement. Certainly other groups and individuals had joined the effort, leading to important victories for racial justice. King, however, remained the central focus, and his efforts had marked him as a target of groups from white supremacists to the FBI. But it had also made him a gigantic presence on the American and global landscape. In 1965, he had been awarded the Nobel Peace Prize, the youngest recipient up to that point. By 1967, however, King's reputation, even within the movement, had begun to decline. For many younger and more militant voices, he seemed too mild, even a bit anachronistic. To one left-wing journalist, King "has been outstripped by his times, overtaken by events" and "poor blacks have stolen the stage from the liberal elites, which is to say the old order has been shattered."[1]

Over the years since his emergence as a national civil rights leader, beginning with the Montgomery Bus Boycott of 1955 and 1956, as other political and social issues swirled, King had remained steadfast in keeping his focus essentially on civil rights and race issues. He had generally avoided speaking out about other concerns—such as Vietnam or larger economic questions—fearing it would distract and weaken his central focus. By the time of the Riverside church address he was rethinking this tactic. "I come to this great magnificent house of worship tonight because my conscience leaves me no other choice," King told the Riverside congregation. "A time comes when silence is betrayal...That time has come for us in relation to Vietnam." King was quite powerful in his critique of American policy, his empathy with the Vietnamese people, and his general concern for American soldiers.

He was, however, most compelling when he linked the Vietnam War to what was going on in the U.S. and, especially, in the communities he thought he served most directly. Just a few years earlier there had been optimism and hope engendered by government programs and policies, creating a sense of promise among the dispossessed. Vietnam had undermined all that. The promise had been "broken and eviscerated as if it were some idle political plaything of a society gone mad on war." The poor were being asked to send "their sons and their brothers and their husbands to fight and to die in extraordinarily high proportions relative to the rest of the population." The hypocrisy was too glaring. "We [are] taking the black young men who had been crippled by our society and sending them eight thousand miles away to guarantee liberties in Southeast Asia which they had not found in southwest Georgia and East Harlem...I could not be silent of such cruel manipulation of the poor."

King went on to talk about the young men he had seen in the Northern ghettos in which he had worked for the last three years. Here his words reflected the changes that had been taking place in the movement for racial justice and equality. More militant approaches and certainly more militant rhetoric had become the order of the day. "And why not?", King asked. "As I have walked among the desperate, rejected, and angry young men, I have told them that Molotov cocktails and rifles would not solve their problems. I have tried to offer them my deepest compassion while maintaining my conviction that social change comes most meaningfully through nonviolent action," he asserted. But they asked, and rightly so, "What about Vietnam?"

King admitted, "Their questions hit home, and I knew that I could never again raise my voice against the violence of the oppressed in the ghettos without having first spoken clearly to the greatest purveyor of violence in the world today: my own government. For the sake of those boys, for the sake of this government, for the sake of the hundreds of thousands trembling under our violence, I cannot be silent."

As ever, King connected the personal to the political, once again emphasizing human values in relation to the larger struggle. This time his words had a new context. "If we are to get on the right side of the world revolution," he proclaimed, "we as a nation, must undergo a radical revolution of values." And echoing yet another attitude emerging from the young, he noted, "we must rapidly shift from a 'thing-oriented' society to a 'person-oriented'" one."[2]

Opposition to the war represented a widening of King's agenda. The victories over segregation, while beginning to undo the apartheid system of the South, had done little for those African Americans and other minorities living elsewhere in the country. Instead of the "beloved community" of the civil rights movement spreading across the nation, racial violence had erupted—from urban neighborhoods going up in flames to individual acts of violence directed at non-whites. King had increasingly begun to articulate what he had likely always known: that poverty and class divisions only exacerbated the racial situation in the U.S.

King's expanded vision did not find an immediately receptive audience. The response, especially from mainstream voices, was surprisingly harsh. The *New York Times* editorialized that King was "fusing two public problems that are distinct and separate. By drawing them together, Dr. King has done a disservice to both." This might end up being "disastrous for both causes." To the *Washington Post* editorial board, King's talk was "filled with bitter and damaging allegations." He had inflicted "a grave injury to those who are his natural allies...Many who have listened to him with respect will never again accord him the same confidence." The speech was a "demagogic slander," *Life* magazine asserted, slamming King for "a proposal that amounts to abject surrender in

Vietnam." Brandeis professor John Roche, who had become LBJ's White House academic liaison, told Johnson in a private memo that King, "in desperate search of a constituency…had thrown in with the commies." He was "destroying his reputation as a 'Negro leader'…He is painting himself into a corner with a bunch of losers." Even others in the civil rights world chastised him. Black columnist Carl Rowan warned, "Millions of black people would suffer for his insults." The national directors of the NAACP voted 60-0 in opposition to King's proposal, calling it "a serious tactical mistake" that would "serve the cause neither of civil rights or of peace."[3]

The summer of 1967 had witnessed two major urban upheavals—in Newark and Detroit—as well as many smaller ones. These only deepened King's resolve to address the issues that underlay them. In August of 1967, King wrote a report for the Southern Christian Leadership Conference (SCLC), "The Crisis in America's Cities," which he saw as applying his ideas about nonviolence and civil disobedience to the national stage. King cited a number of underlying causes of the violence—the white backlash, unemployment, discrimination, the Vietnam War, and the conditions of urban life. "The riots are not simply a reign of terror or a splurge of crime, though both elements are partially present. They are also a wildly emotional protest and a desperate attempt to display the utter desperation that has engulfed many."[4]

King's report included a plan of action. "Civil disobedience has never been used on a mass scale in the North," King declared. If actions are "developed as weekly events at the same time that mass sit-ins are developed inside and at the gates of factories for jobs, and if simultaneously thousands of unemployed youth camp in Washington, as the Bonus Marchers did in the thirties, with these and other practices, without burning a match or firing a gun, the impact of the movement will have earthquake proportions."[5]

At a retreat that November, King told the SCLC staff that he was planning a "camp-in" of poor people in Washington. "I'm on fire about this thing," he exclaimed. In December, King went public with his plan.

SCLC "will lead waves of the nation's poor and disinherited to Washington, DC next spring." Three thousand "pilgrims" he called them, "trained in nonviolence" would stay in the capital until the country responded." The *New York Times* reported the story under the front-page headline:

DR. KING PLANNING TO DISRUPT CAPITAL IN DRIVE FOR JOBS.[6]

During the winter and spring of 1968, a series of events gave focus to King's plans. In early February, in the small South Carolina town of Orangeburg, a group of students from two local Black colleges attempted to integrate the local bowling alley, four years after the Civil Rights Act of 1964 had banned such segregation. The bowling alley owner was able to have state troopers and National Guardsmen block the integration. Two nights later, the troopers moved to one of the campuses where a rally was underway. Opening fire on the students, they killed three and wounded twenty-seven. Initially reported as an exchange of gunfire, the corrections to the story—including that no students had fired any weapons and that half the victims were shot in the back—never even appeared in many of the newspapers that ran the initial report.

After the 1967 urban riots in Detroit and Newark, Lyndon Johnson had created the National Advisory Committee on Civil Disobedience, known as the Kerner Commission, named for its chair, Illinois Governor Otto Kerner. Composed of politicians from both parties, including Republicans John Lindsey, Mayor of New York, and Edward Brooke, Massachusetts' African American senator, as well as Roy Wilkins of the NAACP and Atlanta's police chief, among others. Despite its moderate make-up, the Commission's Report was harsh and stark. The commissioners issued its report at the end of February 1968, four months ahead of schedule, fearing that waiting until June would be too late to affect the issues that led to the usual summer uprisings. "Our nation is moving toward two societies," it famously argued, "one black, one white, separate and unequal." It went on to point out that segregation and poverty "had created in the ghetto a destructive environment totally unknown to most white Americans." This now threatened "the future of every

American." While most politicians paid lip service, at best, to the report, King was energized by it. He announced he would add its recommendations to his agenda. More than anything, it reinforced the direction in which he was already moving.[7]

King also began to test various strategies to expand his network to new communities. In early March, he held a closed-door meeting in Atlanta with seventy-eight "non-black" minority leaders—representatives of several Native American tribes, a deputy of Cesar Chavez, Reies López Tijerina, often called the "Chicano Malcolm X," and Puerto Rican organizers. Representatives from white Appalachia joined in the final days. This was beginning to look like the coalition that King envisioned.[8]

As plans were being developed, King became involved in a strike by the largely African American sanitation workers in Memphis. After failing to get Memphis authorities to discuss pay increases, safety and health issues, and to recognize their union, the workers called a wildcat strike, with eighty-five percent of the workers walking off the job. King traveled to Memphis on March 20 and found the solidarity impressive. "I've never seen a community as together as Memphis."[9] To those who thought that this was a distraction from the planning for the summer, King replied that Memphis was a "prelude" to the Poor People's Campaign.

King headed back to Memphis on March 28 to participate in a massive march down Beale Street in support of the garbage workers. King's flight had been delayed and he did not land until 30 minutes after the intended ten o'clock start. The crowd had grown impatient as they waited. King was hustled to the front at almost eleven. On all sides, order began to come undone. Students pushed past sanitation workers. Rocks flew into store windows, cars were overturned, tear gas canisters hurled. Organizers tried to turn the march around. Police ordered it dispersed. King was hustled down a side street and driven away. The police made 280 arrests. Sixty marchers were hospitalized. One looter was shot and killed by a policeman. The mayor declared a seven o'clock curfew, enforced by 3,800 National Guardsmen.

That night King was distraught. He told an aide that all this made him think of calling off the Poor People's March. "Maybe we just have to admit that the day of violence is here. And maybe we just have to give up and let violence take its course."[10] By the next day, King had calmed a bit.

He admitted that the march had lacked preparation. And he publicly reiterated his plans for the Washington march. "Nonviolence can be as contagious as violence," he declared. "I can only guarantee that our demonstrations will not be violent." He told his staff, "Memphis is the Washington campaign in miniature."[11]

The chaos of Memphis only stiffened opposition. The *New York Times* thought it had resulted in "solidifying white sentiment against the strikers." King's "descent on Washington is likely to prove even more counterproductive." His opponents pounced on King's departing the march. "He ran like a scared rabbit," one Tennessee congressman declared. Memphis' daily newspaper suggested that "King's pose as the leader of a non-violent movement has been shattered." From the *St. Louis Globe-Democrat*, "Memphis could be only the prelude to a massive national bloodbath in the nation's capital."[12] SCLC tried to counter the negative publicity with a statement that included: "The issue at stake is not violence vs. nonviolence but POVERTY AND RACISM."

A bomb scare stalled King's flight back to Memphis five days later. The FBI had discontinued informing King of any type of threatening notice about him they might intercept, including one local phone call that day to Eastern Airlines. "Your airplane brought Martin Luther King to Memphis, and when he comes again a bomb will go off, and he will be assassinated."[13]

King was scheduled to speak that night to a large congregation at Mason Temple. He was initially hesitant about going but was persuaded to attend. At about 9:30 p.m. he began. "If you allow me to live just a few years in the second half of the twentieth century, I will be happy." He recalled when African Americans "were just going around...scratching where they didn't itch and laughing when they were not being tickled...But that day is over. We mean business now, and we are determined to gain our rightful place in God's world." He then referenced some of the recent threats, finally declaring, "I don't know what will happen now...But it doesn't matter with me now." Then King uttered words that would come to haunt the nation. "I've been to the mountaintop," he declared, "and I've looked over and I've seen the Promised Land. I may not get there with you," but "we, as a people, will get to the promised land...I'm not worried about anything. I'm not fearing any man. Mine eyes have seen the glory of the coming of the Lord."

The next day, Kling readied himself for an early dinner before another evening's mass meeting, talking and joking with friends, movement associates, and his brother. At about 6 p.m., he stepped onto the balcony of his Memphis motel. A single shot rang out, striking King in the head. Rushed to the hospital, at 7:05 p.m. he was pronounced dead.

The next four days' headlines in the *New York Times* summarize the immediate effects of King's death.

Thursday, April 5:

MARTIN LUTHER KING IS SLAIN IN MEMPHIS

Friday, April 6:

ARMY TROOPS IN CAPITAL AS NEGROES RIOT; GUARD SENT INTO CHICAGO, DETROIT, BOSTON

Saturday, April 7:

MORE SOLDIERS SENT TO CONTROL WASHINGTON AND CHICAGO RIOTS; CAPITAL PUT UNDER 4 P.M. CURFEW

Sunday, April 8:

U.S. TROOPS SENT TO BALTIMORE; VIOLENCE EASES IN PITTSBURGH; DR. KING MOURNED IN THE NATION

The reaction to King's murder rapidly spread across the country. Lyndon Johnson went on TV to address the nation. He asked, "every citizen to reject the blind violence that has struck Dr. King, who lived by nonviolence." This was a message that many in the civil rights community and many African Americans, in general, found hard to hear. Floyd McKissick, the new more militant head of the Congress of Racial Equality (CORE) declared, "King was the last prince of nonviolence...Nonviolence is a dead philosophy, and it was not the Black people that killed it." Stokely Carmichael, who had moved the Student Non-Violent Coordinating Committee (SNCC) to a much more militant posture and had coauthored the book *Black Power*, proclaimed, "Now that they've taken Dr. King off, it's time to end this non-violence bullshit."[14]

Riots erupted in over a hundred U.S. cities. Mayor John Lindsey headed to Harlem, where he tried to calm the large crowds he found, before bodyguards pushed him into a car and drove off. In Washington, fires and looting spread to within blocks of the White House. Over 10,000 troops began to patrol the city. Machine gun nests appeared on the Capitol steps and in front of the White House.[15] The eruptions were repeated across the country—in Chicago, Baltimore, Kansas City, Memphis, Boston, San Francisco. The rioting in Boston may have been kept to a lower level because that night soul singer James Brown was scheduled to perform at the Boston Garden. Before the show, Brown, Boston mayor Kevin White, and a Black City Councilman spoke to the crowd about peace and unity. Subsequent Vietnam memoirs noted the impact on African American soldiers. "Black GIs went cold as stone," one recalled, as if leaving them "with no choice but to turn from non-violence to militant confrontation." Over 20,000 people were estimated to have participated in the riots. Seventy-six hundred had been arrested, most for curfew violations but some for looting and disorderly conduct. Twelve people were dead.[16]

LBJ's press secretary remembered that the rioting did not surprise the President. "What did you expect? I don't know why we're so surprised," the President observed. "When you put your foot on a man's neck and hold him down for three hundred years, and then you let him up, what's he going to do? He's going to knock your block off."[17]

Political efforts exacerbated tensions rather than lessening them. Maryland Governor Spiro Agnew had already begun taking a hard line on civil rights leaders, from SNCC's Rap Brown's militant rhetoric to King's anti-Vietnam sentiments. In the wake of the riots, Agnew assembled a group of what he saw as Maryland's moderate Black leaders. No "circuit-riding, Hanoi visiting type of leader," had been invited he said, no "caterwauling, riot-inciting, burn-America-down type of leader." He then excoriated those he *had* invited, charging them with capitulating to the more militant wing. "You were intimidated by veiled threats, you were stung by insinuations that you were Mister Charlie's boy, by epithets like 'Uncle Tom.'" Some leaders walked out. When an older African American civil rights pioneer, and matriarch of one of Baltimore's most prominent Black families, rose to speak, Agnew attacked her. "Answer me! Answer me!" he yelled. "Do you repudiate Stokely Carmichael and Rap Brown? Do you? Do You?"[18]

In Chicago, Mayor Richard Daley imposed a curfew on anyone under the age of 21, closed streets to automobile traffic, and suspended sales of guns and ammunition. Over 10,000 police were sent in to quiet the streets, supported by nearly 7,000 Illinois National Guardsmen and 5,000 regular Army soldiers. Daley gave police the authority "to shoot to kill any arsonist or anyone with a Molotov cocktail," as well as shooting "to maim or cripple anyone looting any stores in our city."

Sunday, April 8 was declared a national day of mourning by LBJ, and King's funeral was scheduled for Atlanta on Tuesday, April 9. The annual Academy Awards ceremony was to be held Monday night, but when many entertainers had refused to attend, the awards were postponed for several days. Perennial master of ceremonies Bob Hope, who had spent years entertaining the troops in Vietnam—and turning his annual visits into network TV specials—opposed the delay. When the ceremony was finally held on Wednesday, April 10, Hope's old-school opening monologue fell flat. The delay "didn't affect me," he joked, "but it's been tough on the nominees. How would you like to spend two days in a crouch?" When it came to his closing remarks, the best Hope could muster was, "The Man from Montgomery and today's young filmmakers have much in common. They, too, have a dream."[19]

King's funeral march was said to have numbered 50,000, with another 100,000 viewing the procession from the sidewalks. His casket was carried on a simple farm wagon pulled by two mules. Inside the church, people from across the political spectrum filled the pews. Many in Atlanta were critical of Lyndon Johnson's decision not to attend—which he blamed on the Secret Service who thought it too dangerous. All the major presidential candidates—Richard Nixon, Eugene McCarthy, Robert Kennedy, and Vice President Hubert Humphrey—were in attendance, as were former First Lady Jacqueline Kennedy, Senator Edward Kennedy, Governors Nelson Rockefeller of New York and George Romney of Michigan, New York Mayor John Lindsey, and representatives of all the major U.S. religious organizations. In addition, famous faces filled the seats: singer Harry Belafonte, actor Marlon Brando, entertainer Sammy Davis, Jr., singer Eartha Kitt, Supreme Court Justice Thurgood Marshall, singer Aretha Franklin, actor Sidney Poitier, baseball great Jackie Robinson, and newsman Mike Wallace. Conspicuous by their absence were Alabama governor George Wallace and Georgia governor Lester Maddox, both long associated with segregation and white supremacy. Maddox refused King a state funeral or to allow him to lie in state. He had even resisted lowering Georgia's flags to half-mast, but was ultimately overruled by other state officials who told him it was a federal mandate.

Coretta Scott King requested that King eulogize himself. A recording of his famous "Drum Major Instinct" sermon, first given in February, was played. "Every now and then I think about…my own funeral…And every now and then I ask myself, 'What is it that I would want said?'" He hoped that people would say that he "tried to give his life serving others…tried to love somebody…tried to be right on the war question…tried to feed the hungry…to clothe the naked…tried to love and serve humanity…I just want to be there in love and in justice and in truth and in commitment to others, so that we can make of this old world a new world."[20]

The pace of events in 1968 would, again and again, prove extraordinary. On a Sunday night, Lyndon Johnson had shocked the nation by withdrawing from the presidential race. The following Tuesday, Eugene McCarthy, whose quixotic campaign had only really begun a few months before, handily won the Wisconsin Democratic primary. And two days, later Martin Luther King, probably the most revered American of his time, was shot dead in Memphis.

If one week exemplified the explosive nature of life in 1968, it might be this one. But this would not, however, be the last shocking week of the year.

13

Prague Spring

The readers of the *New York Times* of Monday, March 11, paging through the morning paper, perhaps looking for the continuation of page 1 stories about the next day's New Hampshire primary or the revelation that General Westmoreland had asked for 206,000 more troops, might have easily missed the story atop page 2:

PRAGUE LEADER URGES NOVOTNY TO GO TO THE PEOPLE

The leader of the Prague Communist Party had suggested that the Czechoslovak president, Antonin Novotny, ask the people for a vote of confidence. "The call was made," the *Times* reported, "as political tension and agitation here continued to rise." Three thousand people, mostly students, had demonstrated at the grave of Czech martyr Jan Masaryk, son of the founder of Czechoslovakia, on the 20th anniversary of his suspicious death. "Conservative forces appeared to be rallying and counter attacking against liberal intellectuals."[1]

Two months earlier, Novotny had been the subject of a front-page story in the *Times*, which told of his being ousted as Communist Party Secretary, though retaining the presidency. His replacement as party leader, a post that he had held for 15 years, was Alexander Dubček. Inside the paper, a brief biography of Dubček focused mostly on the fact that he was the first Slovak, as opposed to Czech, to "achieve supreme power in the land." The expectation for the political changes that might come under Dubček mostly concerned the place of Slovakia in the Czechoslovak state.[2]

For a generation, the United States had looked at most of the world's events through the prism of the Cold War. Never was this more true than when it came to the Soviet Union and its Eastern European allies. American media culture was filled with images of "Iron Curtain countries," with their oppressed citizens huddling around a small radio, secretly listening to Voice of America or Radio Free Europe, the CIA-sponsored broadcasts emanating from West Germany. These "prisoners," as the media and politicians depicted them, were seen longing for freedom and occasionally risking life and limb to escape.

When news of the changes within Czechoslovakia began to filter west, this frame shaped the analysis. One Czech writer told *New York Times* editorial writer Harry Schwartz, "What a tragedy it is that George Orwell did not live long enough so he could have been here these last few weeks." These events might have led to a sequel to *1984*, he thought, envisioning what would happen "after Big Brother was overthrown." Schwartz's article went on to talk about how Czechoslovakia had been "a land of frozen terror," where Stalin's statue still loomed over Prague long after similar ones had disappeared in Moscow. A cartoon accompanying this article showed Soviet premier Alexei Kosygin tending to a series of garden stones, each engraved with the name of one Eastern European country. The "Czechoslovakia" stone has been raised up to a 45° angle, as a flower beneath it pushes toward the sunshine.[3]

As might be expected, however, the changes in Czechoslovak—embodied in Dubček's rise to prominence—sprang from deeper and more complex roots. Some of it had to do with internal dynamics within the Soviet sphere; some came from cultural currents flowing beneath the political landscape of Czechoslovakia; and some from international events like the Tet Offensive that were creating tremors throughout the world. Like so much of what happened in 1968, internal and local phenomena meshed with larger global developments. And all were spurred on by the improvements in communications that linked like-minded groups around the world.

Czechoslovakia held a unique place in the Soviet orbit. Geographically, Prague is located west of Vienna, and it citizens, especially the Czechs, had always felt themselves more a part of European culture than Warsaw

Pact nations. In contrast, Novotny's hardline rule had created an atmosphere much less culturally and socially experimental than in the West, especially among intellectuals and students. There had long been a Czech avant-garde, which in the 50s, as one Czech cultural scholar has noted, aimed to incorporate "that which was absolutely most up-to-date...what was being established on the New York avant-garde scene." In fact, she argues that "the first contacts across the Iron Curtain came through New Music and poetry."[4]

At the 1967 Czechoslovak Writers' Congress—a meeting that would figure significantly in the events that led to the "Prague Spring"—novelist Milan Kundera noted that for "Czech and Slovak literature, and probably for Czech art altogether" the previous four or five years had been "the best years since 1948, perhaps since 1938," the years when communism and fascism came to Czechoslovakia, respectively. Writers like Kundera, novelists Ludvík Vaculík and Pavel Kohout, and playwright Václav Havel had emerged. Films from what became known as the "Czech New Wave"—such as Milos Foreman's *Loves of a Blonde* (1965) and *Fireman's Ball* (1967) or Jiri Menzel's *Closely Watched Trains* (1966) played in art houses throughout Western Europe and the United States. *Closely Watched Trains* won the Academy Award for Best Foreign Language Film, while both Foreman films received nominations for that award.*

These writers and filmmakers sought to harness this recognition in the direction of social and artistic reform. Some pledged support for Soviet dissident Alexander Solzhenitsyn. Others lambasted the current Czechoslovak leadership for creating a cultural wasteland. Ludvík Vaculík's speech to the Congress rejected the leading role the Party took in cultural matters and criticized it for failing to address social issues. For this, Vaculik was expelled from the Party. "Who are the vandals today?", Milan Kundera asked in his talk. "Not your illiterate peasant setting fire to the

---

* In 1968, Foreman left Czechoslovakia and came to the U.S. In the 1970s he directed two films with strong counterculture connections, *One Flew Over the Cuckoo's Nest* (1975), based on the Ken Kesey novel, and *Hair* (1979), based on the hit Broadway hippie musical. *Cuckoo's Nest* swept the Academy Awards, including Oscars for Best Picture and Best Director.

hated landlord's mansion…The vandals I see around me these days are well off, educated people, satisfied with themselves and bearing no particular grudge. The vandal is a man proud of his mediocrity."[5]

Unsurprisingly, one group that began to challenge the cultural mediocrity of Czech society was the students. As in many Western countries, the student population had grown in the 1960s. And, as with many Western students, they began to break from their parents' paths. In Czechoslovakia, this meant a weaker affiliation with the Communist Party and its youth organizations. As in many Western countries, the authorities began to worry about the "youth problem."[6] What had moved American and Western European youth moved Czech youth as well. Jiri Josek, who was born in 1950 and later translated *On The Road* into Czech, remembers that after first reading some examples of Kerouac in Czech magazines in the 1960s, he was amazed how similar the lives and values of Kerouac's heroes were to his own. Josek and his friends "thought they had found their own authentic lifestyle and discovered that, somewhere in America, young people were living and feeling the same way," concluded one literary scholar.[7]

For the 1965 May Day celebrations, a delegation of students had invited poet Allen Ginsberg to Prague and crowned him King of May. Ginsberg's coronation speech involved chanting a Buddhist hymn while playing finger cymbals. Followed around by the secret service, Ginsberg was ultimately detained and deported. On the plane to London, he wrote the poem "Kral Majales" ("King of May").

> *The Communists have nothing to offer but fat cheeks and eyeglasses*
> *   and lying policemen*
> *and the Capitalists proffer Napalm and money in green suitcases to*
> *   the Naked…*
> *And when Communist and Capitalist assholes tangle the Just man*
> *   is arrested or robbed or has his head cut off.*
> *And I am the King of May, which is the power of sexual youth,*
> *and I am the King of May, which is long hair of Adam and*
> *   Beard of my own body*

For Ginsberg, the connections between the Czech students and those in the West were clearly evident. Their particular concerns remained beyond the ken of their respective governments, whether capitalist or communist.

It was not Radio Free Europe that young Czechs were tuning their radios to. Instead they listened to West European stations, especially Radio Luxembourg and its English language "Top Twenty" show. For years Czech youth had been listening to Elvis, 50s British sensation Cliff Richard, and others. Now they were hearing the Beatles, the Rolling Stones, and all the other bands filling airwaves throughout the Western world. In 1964, a Czech pop singer had released a cover, with Czech lyrics, of the Beatles' "From Me to You." While the authorities disparaged what they saw as the unruly behavior of British rock audiences, it strongly attracted the young. In 1965, they got their first live taste of this phenomenon when the English band Manfred Mann visited Prague and several other cities. "We then saw what these kinds of rock groups looked like," wrote one music journalist. "They weren't provocateurs but musically each better than the other. And we never heard anything like the way [Manfred Mann lead singer] Paul Jones performed."[8]

The Rolling Stones seemed to elicit Czech youth's greatest passion. One popular Prague band, Donald, became famous for covering Stones' songs. "Donald became literally Prague's Rolling Stones," wrote one rock historian, "not only in the material used and style, but also in the external gesticulations of both the band and the singer." Another band began to play a series of "rock programmes," each dedicated to a different British band—the Kinks, the Yardbirds, the Spencer Davis Group, and more. The number of local rock bands exploded, some singing in Czech, some in English. Predictably, and appropriately, one popular Prague band, The Golden Kids, sang Dylan's "Casey Se Meni" (an approximate translation of "The Times They Are A-Changin'").[9]

Václav Havel traveled to the U.S. in 1968, where his play *The Memorandum* was having its American debut at the New York Public

Theater.* "I took part in demos and rallies and student protests," he later recalled. "We wandered around Greenwich Village and [the] East Village." While in New York, Havel saw a performance of *Hair*, and attended shows at the Fillmore East, including Frank Zappa and the Mothers of Invention. He brought back rock posters, like the ones American students were hanging on their dormitory walls, and smuggled in the first album by the Velvet Underground, which included the famous banana cover art by Andy Warhol. This was the point in their careers when the Velvets were more than a band, but part of the Exploding Plastic Inevitable, the multimedia presentation orchestrated by Warhol, embodying all the sensual aspects of the counterculture. "The whole spirit of the 60s [in the US]," Havel remembered, "affected significantly the spiritual life of my generation and of the younger people."[10] As one might have expected, Czech youth began to dress like young people everywhere. They began to wear *Texasskis* (blue jeans). "Prague had more young people with long hair, beards, sandals than anywhere else in central Europe," Mark Kurlansky would later write.[11] As in the West, long hair on men became a symbol of one's political and social philosophy as well as a target for the authorities. Labeled *máničky*, which roughly translated as "mops," young men were often forced to cut their hair (one state-sponsored campaign led to 4,000 young men having their hair shorn) or were banned from bars, cinemas, theaters, and public transportation in many Czech towns. In a variety of ways, "Flower Power" can be said to have blossomed as much in Prague as in San Francisco.

Counterculture trends were not the only Western currents flowing through Czechoslovak society. Betty Friedan's *The Feminine Mystique* found a receptive audience among young Czech women. Friedan visited Prague in late 1967, meeting with members of the new Czechoslovak Union of Women. "I found developments there very fascinating," she

---

* *The Memorandum* had its premiere in May, staged by Public Theater director Joseph Papp, and featuring John Heffernan, Olympia Dukakis, and Raul Julia, among others. It earned positive reviews, including one from Clive Barnes, in the *New York Times*, who called it "witty, funny, and timely," while also demonstrating "the Eastern bloc's ideological thaw." *New York Times*, May 6, 1958. The play won the 1968 Obie Award as Best Foreign Play.

wrote to a friend. The Czech experience was adding "insight into the depth and importance of the unfinished revolution...all of us are fighting to complete."[12]

As in many locations in the U.S. and Europe, these currents would sometimes come to a head around a seemingly small issue. In Prague it was lights in the dormitories. In fall of 1967, power outages had repeatedly left dormitories dark. Finally, on October 31, students took to the streets—1,500 marchers carrying candles and chanting "We want light!" the double meaning of their plea lost on few.

The government dispatched the police to disperse the march. Using tear gas and clubs, they sent a number to the hospital. While the press called the students "hooligans," other students and sympathetic intellectuals responded like their Western counterparts. Students held a five-hour meeting at Prague's Charles University that resulted in a resolution demanding punishment of the responsible police officers and condemning the disputed press coverage. Students began to hand out flyers on the streets of Prague; debates began on street corners and in bars. As Kurlansky put it, by the end of the year "they looked very much like students in Berlin, Rome, or Berkeley. True they were being watched by secret police, but so were American and Western European demonstrators."[13]

Outsiders, like the *Times'* Henry Swartz, may have thought Czechoslovakia to be a "land of frozen terror," but the Novotny government was hardly the Stalinist monolith the West perceived. A thaw was already underway. Novotny found himself driven by the shifting political landscape of the Eastern bloc. When Leonid Brezhnev engineered the removal of Nikita Khrushchev in 1964, Novotny had been one of the only Communist leaders to publicly express his disapproval. This is one likely reason that Brezhnev failed to support Novotny in 1967 and 1968 when internal Party disputes erupted.

The tumult in the streets only exacerbated internal tensions within the Czech leadership. Party leaders who found fault with Novotny began to coalesce around Alexander Dubček, first Secretary of the Slovak Communist Party, who had grown critical of what he saw as the unnecessarily repressive approach of the government. In early December, Novotny had requested that Brezhnev himself come to Prague to help suppress the internal revolt. After meeting with various leaders, the Soviet leader determined that Novotny was in the wrong but wanted to maintain stability and party order. After a month of backstage maneuvering, Dubček assumed the role of party leader—the more important of the two positions—with Novotny remaining as president.

Dubček's ascendance was hardly the anti-Soviet counterrevolution that the Western press depicted. More reformer than radical, Dubček was seen as someone who might modernize the Czech communist government. Had he supported deeply profound change he would not have gained Brezhnev's support.

While he identified as a Slovak, Dubček and his family had actually led a peripatetic existence for much of his youth. His father, a deeply committed radical, had first tried to organize socialists in pre-World War I Budapest and then emigrated to the United States, settling on Chicago's North Side. Excited by the Russian Revolution and disappointed by the United States, he and his wife moved back to the newly established Czechoslovakia, where Alexander was born in 1921. Four years later they moved again, this time deep into the Soviet Union, settling on an agricultural cooperative, where they lived until Alexander was 17. In 1938, the Dubčeks returned to Czechoslovakia. With the coming of the war, Dubček joined the partisan underground, fighting against the Nazis. Because of his communist past, his father was deported to Mauthausen concentration camp, where, in an amazing coincidence, he would make the acquaintance of another political prisoner—Antonin Novotny.

With the defeat of the Nazis and the establishment of the Czechoslovak Socialist Republic, Alexander Dubček proved a hard-working party bureaucrat, steadily moving up in various Slovak posts, returning to the Soviet Union in the mid-1950s to study at the Moscow Political College. He led a new generation of Slovak Communist officials who initiated reforms aimed at moderate liberalization, much of it focused on promoting Slovak cultural identity as well as opening avenues for freer political and intellectual discussion. As a moderate reformer as well as a loyal Communist, it is unsurprising that Brezhnev would tilt in Dubček's direction. "Our Sasha," as Brezhnev often called him, seemed a safe choice to replace the discredited Novotny.

Dubček's first public statements as Party leader reflected both his work in Slovakia as well as responses to the growing unrest in the country. He called for "far greater encouragement of an open exchange of views" as well as a "true invigoration and unification of all constructive and progressive forces in the republic." He never questioned the leading role Communists were to play in all this, wanting to "implement the progressive objectives of socialist development and strengthen confidence in the Party." "The important thing is not to reduce our policy to a struggle 'against' but...to wage a struggle 'for'...We shall tackle these in a new and creative manner." He wanted his reforms both to put more attention on and encourage greater participation from the nation's youth. Rather than suppress youthful enthusiasm, Dubček thought he could channel it, and the young themselves, into the Communist Party.[14] "What are the guarantees that the old days will not be back," one student asked Dubček during a meeting he held with students. "You yourselves are the guarantee," he responded. "You, the young."[15]

The vehicle for this reform would be the Action Program, promised when he first took over as Party leader, but not announced until April. Dubček saw that a relaxation in press censorship and the restrictions on free speech were crucial to the success of his endeavor. This had worked for him in Slovakia. Why not the whole nation? Open discussions would not only help revitalize the economy and the society, but make citizens feel they were invested in the process and its outcomes. Writers like Ludvík Vaculík, previously expelled from the Party, were invited back. Editors and journalists could be trusted to know what to publish and what to withhold. Relaxing press restrictions led to a wide variety of investigations into an array of subjects, including political corruption. Television stations joined in the effort, including appearances by dissident writers. One investigation revealed that one of Novotny's chief lieutenants had used his position to enrich himself. He ultimately fled the country to avoid prosecution. Public pressure mounted on the Czech president and in March, without any direct pressure from Dubček, Novotny resigned.[16]

All of a sudden, Prague buzzed with life. Plays, independent newspapers, literary magazines all proliferated. Café life was energized. "Nobody talks about football at my local any longer," one taxi driver told a visitor.[17] One veteran of these days recalled it as a "growing sense of national resurgence, of a national destiny…the sudden joy at the end of a long period of despair…and the feeling of a new beginning."[18] This was exactly what Dubček had hoped to achieve. He continually reassured the Soviets of his commitment to socialism, and he meant it. He was careful to avoid provocative terms like "reform" and "revision," choosing instead "renewal" and "revival." And the Czech citizens shared his vision. From the American perspective, this flowering of personal and artistic liberties was seen as the first steps in a march toward Western democratic capitalism. But the Czechs thought differently. As one student leader put it, "I cannot seem to distinguish between capitalist freedoms and socialist freedoms. What I recognize are basic human freedoms."[19] A poll taken in late June and early July 1968 asked whether they thought the country should stick with communism or adopt capitalism. Only five percent responded that they wanted capitalism.[20] Czechs, unlike Americans, could distinguish between cultural liberation and economic systems. As H. Gordon Skilling concluded in his monumental work on Prague Spring, "1968 was not a confrontation with the past, but an attempt at a marriage of democracy and socialism."[21]

This "marriage" not only attempted to engineer reform within the Soviet system, but it also connected with one of the major themes of the global 1968: actualizing utopian dreams. It was just that the starting point was so different in Czechoslovakia. As Czech historian Jiri Suk has recently put it, the "original Communist utopia, based on simple Stalinist laws of development, was replaced by a reform utopianism…This was the basic framework of a 'new model of socialism.'" This new model would "gradually become stronger all over the world."[22]

Unsurprisingly, Czech students mobilized and pushed the reform movement. In March 1968, a gathering of 20,000 issued a Manifesto of Prague Youth, calling for free speech, a free press, and free assembly—but contained within a democratic socialist model. A new student organization was created to compete with the one controlled by the Party. A student newspaper reported on student activities in the West and began discussing left-leaning Western writers like C. Wright Mills, as well as Gandhi, and the works of banned Czech liberal thinkers. Echoing the desires of U.S. students, like those in the 1964 Free Speech Movement at Berkeley, Czech students called for an open curriculum and freedom of expression. In April, German New Left leader Rudi Dutschke lectured at Charles University.[23]

Despite his initial support of Dubček, many of these developments began to worry Leonid Brezhnev. Even before the Action Program was released, Dubček was called to a meeting in Dresden, with Brezhnev, Kosygin, and other Warsaw Pact leaders, where they voiced their concern about the direction in which Prague was heading. They reminded Dubček about what had happened twelve years before in Hungary, Brezhnev noting that major upheavals often begin with small, seemingly insignificant groups of writers. There was no need to go further than the mention of Hungary comparison, whose 1956 "uprising" had ended with a Soviet invasion.[24]

By April, the expectations for what the Action Program would bring had grown dramatically. Czechs looked for a bold statement detailing the utopian reforms for which they now clamored. Meanwhile, Soviet and other Eastern bloc leaders wanted a plan to moderate the reform enthusiasm, while limiting what they saw as growing "anti-socialist" elements. When it finally appeared, the Action Program contained some of the key ideas that Dubček had been developing since the new year. But its tone, to quote historian Kieran Williams, was "obtuse, contradictory, and bloated."[25] It seemed to please no one, even as it called for free speech, economic decentralization, a growing toleration of free markets, creating equality between the Czechs and the Slovaks, and adjustments in foreign policy. It did end on an optimistic note, reflecting current trends. "We want to create conditions so that every honest citizen, who concerns himself with the cause of socialism, the cause of our nations, should feel that he is the very designer of the fate of this country." Trying to satisfy both Czech citizens and the Soviet leadership, it declared, "let the Action Program become a program of the revival of socialist efforts in this country. There is no force that could resist the people who know what they want and how to pursue their aim."[26]

Despite its tone, the program, Dubček declared in a speech on April 1, "opens scope for basic structural changes in our society and the creation of a new dynamic of socialism."[27] Or, as it would come to be called, "Socialism With a Human Face."

The Czech people claimed they supported the program, but polls suggested that most had not read the entire document and only twenty-five percent had even read parts of it, relying on media reports to tell them what was in it. Few Party functionaries had apparently even read it. On the other hand, Brezhnev had, calling it a "bad program" that he feared might open a path for capitalism's return."[28]

As happens—and especially in 1968—popular attitudes raced ahead of government pronouncements. Václav Havel openly called for the creation of an opposition party. May Day, always an essential holiday in Communist countries, held special promise. People poured into the streets, some with painted faces, some carrying signs that spoke to a variety of desires, from "Fewer Monuments More Thoughts" to the ubiquitous global call, "Make Love, Not War;" from "Democracy at All Costs" to "I Would Like To Increase Our Population But I Have No Apartment."[29]

Called to Moscow to defend his plans, Dubček reasserted the leading role of the Party and suggested new oversight plans for the media. However, he was vague on the actual details of the proposals, frustrating Soviet leaders.

By June, Dubček announced, "One thing is clear; we must not and will not stop half-way."[30] He called for an Extraordinary Party Congress to be held in September. Delegates would be elected over the summer, and the reformers assumed their candidates would be chosen. The summer held the promise of consolidating the reforms of the past months. But it would also hold the risk of other harrowing possibilities.

14

New York

The Columbia Strike

"Grayson, I doubt if you will understand any of this," Columbia University SDS chair Mark Rudd declared in an Open Letter to the university's president, Grayson Kirk, on April 22, 1968. In early April, Kirk had accused students of rejecting "all forms of authority" and of "taking refuge in a turbulent and inchoate nihilism whose sole objectives are destruction."[1] "You might want to know what is wrong with this society," Rudd countered, "since, after all, you live in a very tight self-created dream world."

- We can point to the war in Vietnam . . .
- We can point to your using us as cannon fodder to fight your war.
- We can point to your mansion window to the ghetto below you've helped to create through your racist University expansion policies...
- We can point, in short, to our own meaningless studies, our identity crises, cogs in your corporate machines as a product of and reaction to a basically sick society.

Kirk's comments about the students had come before events at Columbia had erupted that spring. Rudd's came after. "Your cry of 'nihilism' represents your inability to understand our positive values," Rudd chided Kirk. "You call for order and respect for authority, we call for justice, freedom, and socialism." But there really was no way, by this point, for one side to understand the other. "There is only one thing left to say," Rudd concluded, with a flourish that captured both the meaning and the spirit of the year. "It may sound nihilistic to you, since it is the opening shot in a war of liberation. I'll use the words of LeRoi Jones, whom I'm sure you don't like a whole lot: 'Up against the wall, motherfucker, this is a stick-up.'"[2]

Columbia held a curious place in New York in these years, at least geographically. Its majestic campus stretched for blocks in upper Manhattan, its perimeter touching the then African American community of Harlem. The university had always had an ambivalent relationship with these neighbors, the elite Ivy League school and the most famous Black community in the nation, if not the world. New students were sometimes advised about how to take the subway up to Columbia from Midtown. If they got on the wrong train and ended up on the other side of Morningside Park, which bordered the campus to the east, for their own safety they should take the subway back downtown and take the correct train, rather than try to cross the park on foot.

It was precisely the university's plans for this park that served as the spark for the campus unrest that April. As early as the late 1950s, the University had begun making plans to build a gymnasium in Morningside Park. This was city land and did not belong to Columbia, necessitating complicated negotiations over several years. Responding to community concerns, the university agreed to add a neighborhood facility, but it was to be separate and much smaller than the $8+ million student gym. Rejecting a proposal that the community share the new facility with the students, Columbia then offered to build a public swimming pool. Again residents rejected the offer.[3]

Perhaps a decade earlier the residents might have been more open to Columbia's offer, but by the late 1960s, after years of civil rights actions in the nation and with the advent of Black Power and black nationalism, this kind of gesture could easily be dismissed as tokenism and, to Harlem residents and Columbia's students, as patronizing racism. Despite the disagreements, in February 1968, ground was broken for the new gym. Opponents began to refer to it all as "Columbia's Gym Crow."

The decision to begin building the gym was one of a series of events that coalesced to create an antagonistic atmosphere on the Morningside Heights campus that spring. Recruiters from the CIA and from Dow Chemical, who manufactured the napalm gel that had become a prominent symbol for American brutality in Vietnam, met with hostile receptions. In fact, demonstrations against military recruiters in 1967 had led Kirk to ban all demonstrations inside any Columbia building.

Columbia's relationship with the Institute for Defense Analysis (IDA), a think tank devoted to military and weapons research that Columbia had joined in 1959, became another point of conflict. President Kirk was Columbia's representative on the IDA board. Whereas other universities, such as Princeton and the University of Chicago, had withdrawn from IDA, Kirk refused to allow the Columbia faculty to even debate withdrawal.[4] Relationships such as this, which suggested that America's universities were in league with the military-industrial complex, had become hot campus issues across the country.

That spring, the Students Afro-American Society (SAS) chose as its new president, Cicero Wilson. Wilson, a native of Brooklyn's Bedford-Stuyvesant neighborhood, changed the tone of the SAS. He was, one undergrad recalled, "a tough, city black kid...he exerted a kind of moral force on the other guys. He wasn't a 'Negro'; he was the equivalent of Malcolm X."[5]

And then there was Mark Rudd and the SDS. Arriving at Columbia in 1965 from suburban New Jersey, Rudd immediately fell in with the campus SDS chapter, later writing that their main activities were opposing the war and fighting "racism on campus in the form of the university's refusal to allow mostly black and Latino cafeteria workers to organize a union." By 1968, another Columbia SDS veteran recalled the chapter had split between the "Praxis Axis" that "believed in door-to-door organizing and writing manifestos" and the "Action Faction" that "believed in brazen action and tools that electrified people." The Action Faction, which included Rudd, came to dominate the chapter.[6]

A visit by the New York City Director of the Selective Service System provided the opportune moment for their approach. The director was questioned about the legitimacy of the draft, but was then hit in the face with a lemon-meringue pie. During a university-organized memorial for Martin Luther King in April, Rudd commandeered the microphone and accused Columbia of hypocrisy by celebrating King while exploiting minority citizens in its neighborhood, paying its unskilled workers substandard wages, and blocking all their attempts to organize. He then led a walkout of a number of students.[7]

Despite this growing sense of campus tension, Columbia's administration still did not comprehend its ultimate meaning. Grayson Kirk, called a "walking anachronism" by one recent analyst, remained a distant figure for students, "more comfortable in the company of corporate executives than he was with undergraduates," a contemporary observer noted. "He hasn't spoken to anyone under thirty since he was thirty," chided literature professor and playwright Eric Bentley. Kirk was not alone in his attitudes. In the midst of the IDA debate, Provost and philosophy professor Herbert Deane declared, "A university is definitely not a democratic institution. When decisions begin to be made democratically around here, I will not be here any longer." He then went on to utter a phrase that became famous, even infamous, in many circles. "Whether students vote 'yes' or 'no' on a given issue means as much to me as if they were to tell me they like strawberries."[8]

Student activism had been a reality on campuses at least since Berkeley students organized the Free Speech Movement in 1964. Columbia's administration remained particularly tone deaf to what was simmering both on their campus and in the larger world around them. The students heard the events of late April loud and clear. Defying Kirk's ban against indoor demonstrations, six students gathered in Low Library to protest the university's connection to IDA. When ordered to report to their deans for disciplinary measures, they refused, instead gathering with supporters at noon on April 23. Unable to get into Low Library, Cicero Wilson led a group to the gymnasium site. James Simon Kunen, whose *Strawberry Statement* would become one of the first published works about the Columbia events, described what he saw that day. "There is an excavation cutting across the whole park. It's really ugly. And there's a chain link fence all around the hole. I don't like fences anyway, so I am one of the first to jump on it and tear it down."[9] The crowd tore down a section of the construction fence, had minor confrontations with the police, and made several speeches, including one by Rudd proposing that they go back to the sundial in front of Low Library to join with a large group of demonstrators already there.

Regrouping back on the main campus, Rudd is supposed to have shouted, "Hamilton Hall is right over there. Let's go!" Others recall how randomly events seemed to unfold. "The serendipity of it all has always been phenomenal to me," recalled one student activist, "the whole damn thing was such happenstance."[10] The students moved into Hamilton Hall, the main classroom building on campus, and decided to stay. "A group of us started scouting out the rooms on the first floor," one SDS member remembered, "and there's Dean [Henry] Coleman, in his office, and I said, 'You can't leave.' He said, 'What?' I said, 'You can't leave.'" But in keeping with the spirit of the times, "Coleman opened the venetian blinds of his window, which looked onto College Walk, and he got someone to get him an ice cream."[11]

The SDS and SAS leaders formed a steering committee, deciding they needed to develop a succinct set of demands, which ultimately included dropping disciplinary actions against those who protested IDA, stopping construction of the gym, and granting amnesty to all those who participated in that day's demonstrations.

Sometime between that afternoon and early the next morning, a decision was made for the white students to leave Hamilton Hall to the Black contingent, which now included community residents as well as African American students. There have been various interpretations as to why the Black students had asked the whites to leave. It seems mostly to have to do with their approaches to protest and actions. "We white kids were ragtag, messy, arguing constantly with each other. We were unsure of what to do once we had occupied Hamilton," Rudd recently wrote. "But the black students, inspired by the civil rights movement in the South and by their own parents' lifelong struggles, were certain that they had to barricade the building as their own disciplined statement." One SAS member remembers it similarly. "The white people didn't know what they were doing. Their hearts were in the right place, but logistically they didn't have it together at all." "The real reason why they asked us to leave, it turns out," Rudd concluded, "was that they couldn't deal with the SDS's lack of discipline."[12]

By dawn, the white students had moved out of Hamilton. Moving to Low Library, which was the administrative center of the University, they broke several windows to enter the building, including breaking a pane in the glass door to Grayson Kirk's office. "Things were moving so fast by that point," Rudd later recalled, "that I only dimly understood we had passed the point of no return."[13]

Once inside Kirk's office suite, the occupiers moved to settle in. One student found "a carnival atmosphere the first day, with press photographers and reporters from magazines... There was an unforgettable, Fellini-esque visit from a faculty member who swooped through the window in full academic regalia, Batman-like, to 'reason' with us."[14]

The first time the police arrived, many students inside Low jumped out of windows to avoid a confrontation, but the police rejected the idea of clearing Low while leaving the Black students in Hamilton, as the administration had requested, fearing a confrontation with the Black community. The Martin Luther King riots had occurred just weeks earlier, and the administration and New York mayor's office feared inciting a race riot if they moved on Hamilton Hall. Still a complaint of trespass, the police argued, could not be administered along racial lines. They moved through Low, took possession of a Rembrandt from Kirk's office, and abandoned the building. As the police receded, the students moved back in. James Kunen remembered a campus guard who told him, "As long as you think you're right, fuck 'em." He hoped something good might come out of it all. "He makes eighty-six dollars week after twenty years on the job," Kunen reported.[15]

Slowly, New York and the rest of the country began to be aware of what was happening at Columbia. The occupation of Hamilton Hall had warranted a below-the-fold story in the *New York Times*:

**300 Protesting Columbia Students
Barricade Office of College Dean.**

The next day, after the occupation of Low Library, the news stories moved above the fold:

Columbia Closes After Campus Disorders.

The following day:

Columbia Halting Work on Gym; Suspends Classes.

But alongside this story, another proclaimed:

Kirk Issues Statement Barring Amnesty to Student Protestors.

The occupation spread to three additional buildings: Fayerweather, Avery, and Mathematics. As each new building was occupied, an "OURS" label was attached to the scale model of the building in the campus diorama in Grayson Kirk's office. The students began to see their occupied spaces as communes and structured activities accordingly. "Contrary to popular belief and press reports, the President's suite of offices was kept immaculate and orderly after the chaotic first day," one occupier later wrote. "Cleanup detail included vacuuming, shaking out blankets, scrubbing the bathroom, etc. The administration's fears of vandalism (and their special concern for the Rembrandt hanging above President Kirk's desk) were poorly founded."[16] One SDS member took a picture for a freelance photographer of a fellow occupier smoking one of Kirk's cigars. The photo ran in *Life* the next week. More significantly, he recalled, "a few people who had done a lot of research on Columbia's relationship with the IDA went into Kirk's files and found evidence that Columbia had been directly supplying research on war material for the war in Vietnam." Some documents were photocopied and later published in a New York underground newspaper, *The Rat*.[17]

Each building became a commune, often reflecting the personalities of its occupiers. "The spirit was of cooperation; everyone had to make decisions together; everyone had to speak; everyone had to act as a group.

And it was men and women. Not only was Columbia College all male, but women and men were pretty much segregated on campus. So here are men and women, people from the neighborhood, radicals from different parts—all together."[18]

The lobby of Hamilton Hall was decorated with posters of Lenin, Che, and Malcolm X. Local stores and the Harlem chapter of CORE sent food and money that was raised by collection. The main campus switchboard was in Hamilton Hall, which the occupiers took over. They responded to calls from the press and parents. It was also the week when acceptance letters had gone out. "Parents were calling, saying, 'Is Columbia under siege? What will happen next semester?'" "I was snarky," one student recalled, replying, "We don't even know if there will be a university here next year!"[19]

Mini-societies began to emerge. Sympathetic physicians and medical students set up an infirmary. A Chopin concert was performed on a piano in Low. People brought in stereos and records. A radical theater group performed in Fayerweather. One student recalled that when he and his girlfriend moved into Fayerweather, they decided to get married there. Campus minister Reverend William Starr performed the ceremony. "At the end he didn't pronounce them husband and wife—he pronounced them 'Children of the New Age,'" one student noted. "Everybody started cheering and sobbing…It wasn't just a wedding—it became a statement of solidarity among the people who were there because of our collective beliefs. We felt that we put our lives on the line in that moment."[20]

New Left veteran Tom Hayden, in New York for a SNCC meeting, showed up on campus. "I had never seen anything quite like this," he later wrote. He eventually ended up joining the occupiers at Mathematics Hall. Stokeley Carmichael and H. Rap Brown, who had been central to the development of Black Power, came to visit Hamilton Hall. So did Florynce Kennedy, lawyer and civil rights activist, who had been a champion of women's rights for years. All these events led Kennedy to wonder if, "women may be the third force to link up with youth and black people."[21] But it was not only young radicals who were attracted to what was happening. Columbia professor and literary citric F.W. Dupee, veteran of the radical wars of the 1930s, found these student radicals so much more

exciting than his thirties' counterparts, who were "so stodgy and unin-
ventive." "You must come right up, Dwight," Dupee told fellow thirties'
radical veteran Dwight Macdonald. "It's a revolution! You may never get
another chance to see one." Initially resistant to the strike, Macdonald
did as Dupee suggested and was won over. He found "an atmosphere of
exhilaration, excitement," especially impressed with the way the "com-
munards" had established a working society within each building.[22]
Macdonald and Dupee were not alone among older leftists attracted to
this new enthusiasm. But Columbia sociologist Daniel Bell, another veteran of the old left, scoffed at his old brethren, accusing them of being
"ecstatic at having a real revolution on their doorstep."[23]

Other groups began to emerge. "A group of Columbia students created the Majority Coalition, which represented those of us who were
against the radicals shutting down the university," remembers future
New York Governor George Pataki, then a Colombia Law Student. "I
was not a leader, but I was very active in supporting it. We formed a ring
around Low Library to prevent radicals from getting in." One Majority
Coalition leader recounted, "We wanted to stop all food and water going
to the protesters inside to basically starve them out so they'd have to
leave."[24] Despite its name, the Majority Coalition did not represent a
majority, but was one of the smallest student groups, made up of mostly
conservatives and athletes, "jocks" to radicals. Among the tactics used to
transcend their barrier, a Low occupier remembered, "one day a tall
stranger with waist-length hair appeared at the distant fringe of the
crowd and began to hurl five-pound bags of home-made fried chicken
our way, one after another, with perfect aim, over the jocks' heads and
right into our windows."[25]

Others on the campus sought a resolution. Some faculty joined the
Ad Hoc Faculty Group, patrolling the campus in an attempt to keep
things peaceful and seeking to negotiate with the occupiers. But the resolution they presented was unacceptable to both sides, especially the call
for amnesty for most of the strike leaders—leading to Kirk's previously
mentioned statement on no amnesty.

On Friday April 26, Columbia officials announced that work on the
gym was suspended and that the police would not be called. In the early

morning of April 30, however, they did just that. Busloads of Tactical Police Force (TPF) members swarmed the campus. A thousand New York City policeman spread out, targeting all five buildings. To the surprise of many, the Black students in Hamilton peacefully left the building, avoiding a confrontation with the police, and were led off in paddy wagons. This would not be the case in the other four. Low occupiers came to a collective decision to resist "civil-rights-movement style," to go limp and have the police carry them out. They barricaded the door with furniture, but also cleaned up the occupied rooms and waited. "Soon axes were crashing through the door, the barricade was breached, and an army of TPF piled in, first prying apart the singing clump of us, then forming a gauntlet to pass our limp bodies down the corridors, whacking our heads with flashlights along the way, and dragging us by the feet down the marble steps so our heads bounced."[26]

Several faculty trying to insinuate themselves between the students and the police ended up in the hospital. One recalls, "I ran back to campus and saw dozens of plainclothes police pouring out of Low Library, wearing Delphi, N.Y.U., and Stony Brook college sweatshirts, and they started beating the shit out of people. No one was resisting. I was standing next to the 64-year-old English professor Fred Dupee when he was punched in the face."[27] Things seemed to get worse, once the buildings had been cleared. George Pataki recalled, "from around the back of Low Library comes this wave of TPF guys just clubbing everybody in sight. I guess their orders were to clear the campus, which was incredibly stupid and counterproductive because many of the people outside the buildings were the anti-radicals—the pro-cop people." "I saw the university rabbi being beaten by police," one student remembered, "and I saw random students who were beaten for just being outside on campus."[28] One young professor remembers putting on a coat and tie and venturing to one of the campus gates. "I then joined the cop assigned to the gate who was entirely sympathetic to the students and we watched with horror as the cops beat up kids that had come out of their dorms to find out what all the ruckus was about...I will never forget one small sized student being chased by a group of cops with clubs intent on beating him up—

he finally took refuge on top of a car where he tried to avoid their swings. They finally knocked him off and pounced with their clubs."[29] "I remember running up the steps of Mathematics Hall," recalled Pataki, "and there were TPF guys on horses coming toward me, and I jumped off the steps and ran out onto Broadway. I was getting chased by a guy on a horse up Broadway. What are you going to do? The horse is faster than you are and the guy's got a club, so I dove under a car."[30]

Later analysis suggested that it had been a serious error to keep the TPF officers on buses for days. "It was a mistake to keep us sitting on buses for four days waiting to go in," said one TPF officer. "Nobody on TPF joined the police department to sit on buses. We were workers. We thought the students were a bunch of spoiled kids complaining about whatever they were complaining about, who needed a good spanking." Said another, "When the green light finally came for the police to go in and restore order, they were pretty eager to do it."[31]

Firsthand accounts suggest that something more than "a spanking" was administered. "I remember vividly a cop with a frozen grin on his face going up to a girl, a Barnard student. He lifted up his very long utility flashlight and slammed it on her head. And it wasn't just once—it was again, and again, and again." There were numerous equivalent descriptions. The actions of the police had an unexpected impact. "Virtually all my friends who'd been in the Majority Coalition switched sides," George Pataki noted, "just because the cops were nuts. Those who had been supportive of the administration and the police were completely demoralized." Another Majority Coalition member recalls, "A few days after the bust there was a real sense of despair and unhappiness on campus as a result of the police action. It just seemed that this was a family matter and that we should have been left to settle this amongst ourselves. It felt like an invasion, a violation."[32]

The news stories the following day angered the students. "The *Times* ran a front-page story with a photo of... the President's Office, which was a total wreck (mean-spirited graffiti sprayed on the walls, bookshelves toppled, etc)... it was not us who made the mess and sprayed the graffiti!"[33] Reaction was strong against another story in the *Times* written by editor

"A.M. ['Abe'] Rosenthal...in which he said that we students were bar-
barians." Stephan Salisbury, son of *Times'* assistant managing editor,
Harrison Salisbury, went straight from jail to his parents' home, where a
cocktail party was underway. "When we walked into the living room I
made a beeline for Abe. I couldn't take my eyes off that motherfucker,
and I said to him, 'The story that you wrote in today's paper was one of
the most, if not the most, dishonest pieces of journalism I have ever seen
in any publication. You should be ashamed.' He said, 'I described a situation exactly as it appeared.' The room was quiet and our voices were
raised. He left the party soon after."[34]

In the end, 705 arrests were made, 120 complaints of police brutality
were filed. That fall, a commission created by the university and headed
by Harvard Law professor and future Watergate special counsel Archibald
Cox, concluded that the police had used "excessive force" and "engaged
in acts of individual and group brutality" that "caused violence on a harrowing scale." Student behavior "was in no way commensurate with the
brutality." The commission further added that "too often [Columbia]
conveyed an attitude of authoritarianism, and invited mistrust," as well
as creating "unhealthy relations with her neighbors." It was likely, they
concluded, that "the grievances felt by the occupiers and their supporters
were shared by 'a majority' of the students."[35]

The building occupation was over but the campus was still consumed
by the events. A student strike was almost total. A faculty meeting
devolved into a conflict between factions, with one group demanding
the resignation of Kirk and his key aides. When summonses for student
discipline went out to some of the strike leaders, tempers flared again.
Vindictiveness seemed to fuel the anger. The registrar's office contacted
local draft boards, telling them that suspended male students were no
longer enrolled and therefore eligible to be drafted—and likely to go
to Vietnam.

The TPF returned to campus a second time. Demonstrators had
begun at a sit-in in a Columbia–owned apartment building in Harlem,
which led to the police response. This then led to a move back into

Hamilton Hall and another wave of mass arrests. These led to further campus confrontations.

A counterculture air reigned on campus. The Grateful Dead came to perform. Poet Alan Ginsberg read his poetry to a large outdoor audience. No official classes had been held since April 23, replaced by "Liberation classes" held on the lawns. On May 1, the university announced it was suspending final examinations and instructed professors to give only grades of Pass or Fail. Commencement was moved from its usual location, the plaza in front of Low Library, to the Cathedral of St. John the Divine. History professor Richard Hofstadter replaced Kirk as the main speaker. As Hofstadter stepped to podium, 300 students and a number of faculty members stood. There had been a prearranged signal. Students carried radios under their gowns and when WKCR, the Columbia station, played "The Times They Are A Changin'" they walked out.[36]

School may have been done for the year, but the issues still burned in Morningside Heights and beyond. The irony is that in the end, most of what the students desired came to be. The gym was never built in Morningside Park. A smaller alternative was built on campus a few years later. Columbia severed its ties with IDA. That summer, Grayson Kirk resigned, but his handpicked successor (and aide throughout the turmoil) did not get the post. The university dropped most of the trespassing charges. Various reforms, in governance, academic rules, and social life were introduced.

The impact of what happened at Columbia resonated across the country and around the world. Echoing Che Guevara's famous, "Create two, three...many Vietnams," Tom Hayden wrote, in his review of the Columbia events, "The goal written on the university walls was 'Create two, three, many Columbias.'" For Hayden, "It meant expand the strike so the U.S. must either change or send its troops to occupy American universities." Students had too long been told, Hayden concluded, that "barricades are part of the romantic past... But the students at Colombia discovered that barricades are only the beginning of what they call 'bringing the war home.'"[37]

15

The Paris Student Strike

Tom Hayden's wish for "two, three, many Columbias" was already well underway to being fulfilled across Europe and around the globe by the time the Columbia strike came to an end in May 1968. Regardless of the political ideology of their nation—communist, fascist, social democratic—student rebellions erupted globally throughout the first half of the year. Each was tailored to the political realities of its situation, but each also echoed sentiments shared by all. By 1968, students everywhere had come to embrace the idea that they represented a unique and vital force in society, not merely engaged in a kind of professional apprenticeship program, but whose identity and purpose were central to social transformation.

In January, a production of a classic nineteenth-century Polish play, *Dziady*, by the National Theatre in Warsaw, ran afoul of the authorities. Announcing that it was closing down the production led to a demonstration by several hundred students, who chanted, "Free Art, Free Theatre." At a February meeting of the Warsaw Writers' Association, members criticized the shutdown of the play. One speaker slammed the administration of Polish culture as a "dictatorship of the dumb." "We thought a Czech-style evolution was possible," recalled one student leader. A peaceful march by students in March was met by club-wielding police and hostile workers trucked in by the government. "They smashed faces with their fists, massacred girls with police batons," one observer reported. "They randomly hit defenseless, innocent passersby…It was truly a Bloody Sunday."[1] Forty to fifty students were arrested. None of this was reported in the Polish press, but Polish dissidents had come to the realization that reporting stories to the Western press would lead to their being broadcast on Radio Free Europe, which would then lead to their being heard by Polish citizens.[2]

Soon students were marching to the offices of university officials, demanding reforms and the freeing of the arrested students. Ultimately all of Poland's universities went on strike, with students battling police in the streets. Well aware of what was going on elsewhere in the Soviet sphere, chants of "Long Live Czechoslovakia" rang through the streets.

That same month, the fascist government of Francisco Franco closed Madrid University and expelled students in other universities around the country. These prompted demonstrations and school shutdowns across Spain. Spanish universities had been in a tumultuous state for the past year, with frequent confrontations, police actions, and campus arrests lasting throughout the spring. In January, the government had stationed a permanent police force on the Madrid campus, including 35 jeeps, two cavalry platoons, and a water cannon. Despite this show of force, campus riots continued to erupt, one ending with students throwing bottles, bricks, and furniture from campus windows. A bus was set afire and traffic was blocked. In response, the university was closed on March 1, with its students forced to reapply for admission, thus forfeiting their enrollment fees.

When the university reopened in May, posters plastered the campus, students clashed again with police, and the rioting spread across the city. The government's announcement of modest reforms did little to quiet the students. The trials of arrested student leaders only spawned more demonstrations.[3]

Also in March, clashes in Rome between police and students led to hundreds of arrests and injuries. The academic year of 1967–68 had witnessed student tumult throughout Italy. Nineteen of Italy's 33 state universities experienced some unrest—building occupations, marches, and mass gatherings in the largest cities. In Turin, Milan, Pisa, Venice,

Naples, Palermo, and elsewhere across the nation, students took to the streets, often with the support of Italian workers and left-leaning politicians. By March, there had been demonstrations at 26 universities and it was estimated that half a million students were on strike.

Outside issues compounded internal questions. Five thousand Romans, including many students, attempted to march on the American Embassy to protest the Vietnam War. Neo-fascists, carrying banners proclaiming "Duce" and other slogans associated with Mussolini, clashed with the marchers. Again, hundreds were hurt, and many required hospitalization. Attempting to defuse the university situation by offering alternatives to the traditional end-of-year examinations did little to reduce tensions. Four thousand students gathered in Piazza di Spagna only to be attacked by police. This event was repeated several days later in Piazza Cavour, site of the Palace of Justice. Confrontations continued throughout the Italian spring and into the early summer.[4]

Italy was not the only centrist social democratic European nation to experience this kind of unrest that spring. On April 11, six days after the assassination of Martin Luther King, a 23-year-old, small-time criminal and unemployed worker, Joseph Bachman, approached German student radical leader Rudi Dutschke on the streets of West Berlin. Shouting "you dirty communist pig," he fired three shots at Dutschke, hitting him in the chest, face, and brain. "I heard of the death of Martin Luther King," Bachman later explained, "and since I hate communists I felt I must kill Dutschke."[5]

The Free University of Berlin had emerged as the center of German student radicalism. Some of the student complaints took aim at typical student issues—such as overcrowded classes and an antiquated curriculum—but there began to be a growing critique of the prevailing social structure, with discussions of materialism and bourgeois democracy joining issues of free expression and student autonomy. In addition, the right-wing newspaper chain of Axel Springer became a central target. These newspapers were often racist, decidedly pro-American, and extremely critical of the German students and left-leaning intellectuals.

It encouraged individual attacks—"DON'T LEAVE ALL THE DIRTY WORK TO THE COPS!," read one headline. "If you ask me," Springer commented, "there are more genuine communists in West Berlin than in the whole of East Germany."[6] Joseph Bachman was a devoted reader of one of Springer's tabloids, *Bild Zeitung*.

Dutschke survived the attack, but he was left with aphasia and brain damage, leading to his early death in 1979 at the age of 39. (Bachman committed suicide in prison in 1970.) News of Dutschke's shooting spurred demonstrations and rallies all over West Germany and beyond. Demonstrations erupted in New York, Berkeley, Toronto, London, Paris, Rome, Milan, Belgrade, Prague, and other cities. "It was the first time that an event affecting a student movement in one country led to student protests internationally," observed historian Ronald Fraser.[7] In West Germany, club-wielding students battled police water cannons. It was the worst German street rioting since before Hitler came to power in the early 1930s. An Easter peace march of 4,000 resulted in 350 arrests. While the majority of West Germans remained critical of the students, the generation gap so typical of the period was clearly visible. Among the arrested was Peter Brandt. His father, former West Berlin mayor Willy Brandt (now a cabinet minister in Bonn and soon to be West German chancellor), had been both a hero in the U.S. for his stand against communism and also a socialist with a long anti-fascist record. Regardless, Peter became openly critical of his father. He had moved to the center, his son argued. "We don't agree anymore."[8]

Listing the many places where these kinds of confrontations took place could go on and on. One edited work contains essays about events in 39 countries around the globe in 1968, virtually all generated by students and other young people. Among the places discussed:

Greece: The year 1968 was the second year of the junta—the so-called regime of the Colonels of 1967–1974—and it was a dark year...The only cultural activity [was] a radio culture focused on two foreign broadcasts...The programs first informed us about the events of May 1968 in France and about the student movement in Germany and other European countries. Here, we first heard the names of student leaders Rudi Dutschke and Daniel Cohn-Bendit. With our ear stuck to the radio, we found out about occupied universities and various states' inability to deal effectively with these revolts.[9]

Venezuela: In 1968, student protests helped bring about changes in participatory procedures in the university community, in the decision-making process, in student co-administration, and in the relationship between university and society... The university increasingly became the principal agent spurring social changes. The students' activities produced unusual forms of protest as teachers, workers, and [university] officials joined in. People in Venezuela took note of the protests and actions of the youth movements in other countries of the world. From the United States came rock music and the hippie movement, from France and Germany radical philosophies and the vehemence of the student revolts, and from London psychedelic drugs. Prague gave us a spring that held out the prospect of socialism with a human face.[10]

Senegal: On May 27, 1968 the Association of Senegalese Students and the Dakar Association of Students in the nation's capital called for a strike of indefinite length and for a boycott of examinations. Police quashed riots on campus, and foreign students were expelled from the country by armed force. In the street fighting that followed, one student was killed and over 900 were arrested. Student demonstrations developed into an opposition against the ideology of the ruling-class monopoly of power, and the regime's submission to the former French colonial power when the trade unions went on strike to support the students.[11]

Yugoslavia: The Yugoslavian "1968" began on the night of June 2–3 in that year with a clash between students and police in...a student district in the capital of Belgrade. Hundreds of young people wanted to go to a concert for which there were not enough tickets. When they began to riot at the door, the police intervened with guns, and the situation escalated into a street battle. Students began to chant, "Down with the red bourgeoisie." "We're sons of working people." Students and professors "occupied" the university and declared an all-out strike...The Student Assembly decided to rename the Belgrade University "the Red University of Karl Marx." The events in Belgrade immediately prompted similar actions in Zagreb, Ljubljana, and Sarajevo. The biggest protest movement since World War II rocked the political system. It took a week of striking for [Josip Broz] Tito, the head of state and party leader, to publicly praise the young people's commitment...and agree to meet the students halfway."[12]

Across the world, students proved the vanguard core of reactions and uprisings against the established order, be it right, left, or center. And word of one moment inspired others, one city and university after another becoming the latest site in this uncoordinated but connected global rebellion.

* * *

"American educators are fond of telling their students that barricades are part of the romantic past," Tom Hayden had concluded his 1968 assessment of the Columbia strike. But "the students [have] discovered that barricades are only the beginning of what they call 'bringing the war home.'" Those "romantic" barricades had mostly been associated with nineteenth-century street clashes in Paris, including the Revolutions of 1830 and 1848 and the Paris Commune of 1871. It is hardly surprising that Paris would again figure prominently in the events of 1968. Yet, amid everything that was happening in the first months of the year, it is also unsurprising that the first rumblings from France would go largely unnoticed elsewhere.

In the postwar years, France had its own baby boom. By 1963, a third of its population was under the age of 20, which meant they had no memory of the World War II. A youth culture emerged—in fashion, music, films—creating a youth-oriented popular culture. Deemed rebellious and insufficiently respectful of traditional French culture, this clashed with the vision of French President Charles de Gaulle. The embodiment of French national pride during World War II and the postwar years, de Gaulle had returned to power in 1958 when the country was wracked by debates over France's troubles with the rebellion in its

Algerian colony. With the support of the military, de Gaulle came out of retirement to oversee the formation of the Fifth Republic and then served as its president. His attempts to build an independent France, coupled with his appeals to the French cultural heritage and its "historic *grandeur*," might have found approval with a population that recalled the battle against Hitler. But the "baby boom" generation looked to a "'glorious revolutionary tradition' that harkened back to public protests and radicalism well before the formation of the Fifth Republic."[13] As with many Western societies, France found itself divided more by age than by party.

De Gaulle had tried to steer French foreign policy in a new direction. The Algerian war had ripped apart French society, radicalizing many of its youth. But when de Gaulle finally ended the war in 1963, public life calmed. In fact, despite French involvement in Algeria and Indochina, de Gaulle seemed to take great pleasure in criticizing American policy in Vietnam. And with the advent of television, French citizens could now see images of the American war in Southeast Asia as well as footage of the civil rights movement and anti-war activities in the U.S.

The growing youth culture began to exhibit its modern manifestations, including France's first public rock concerts. In France, unlike much of the rest of the Western world, American and British rock "n" roll found its way into the national culture via the unique French approach of "adaptation." These were not direct cover versions, but songs reworked to maintain their melody and rhythm, but with original lyrics. While this practice had begun in the 1950s, with adaptations of songs by Buddy Holly and Paul Anka, among others, as one contemporary cultural analyst has put it, "The explosion of rock and twist music, coincident with the discovery of a vast and relatively prosperous cohort of young consumers" rose to "unprecedented levels" in the 1960s.[14] Maintenance of a unique French culture seemed embedded in de Gaulle's vision of modern France. But young people could not resist an international cultural force. Adaptations allowed French kids to participate in it without abandoning the nationalistic imperative.

Meanwhile, the economy settled into a period of steady growth, with consumer products available as never before. While the economy grew, however, the working class fell behind, their wages not keeping pace with inflation. On May Day 1967, for the first time in years, the French Communist Party sponsored public demonstrations.[15]

This modernization would also have an impact on the French university system. Like many countries in the West, France's universities had undergone massive expansion in the postwar years, as more and more students clamored for public education. Looking for guidance on how to develop this newly massive university system, both in terms of creating many new campuses and reforming the curriculum to make it more professional and responsive to French economic needs, the government turned to the U.S. model for guidance. One adviser to the Minister of Education argued that "after World War II, the North American model of the multiversity tended to be recognized as the system that was best suited to industrially developed countries."[16]

There is a certain irony that in the period when American students began to express their criticism and discontent with the current form of postwar universities, the French and many other European governments chose to shape their education reforms along this very American model. And just as American students had begun to express discontent with their educational system, so too did French students.

In the decade before 1968, France's student population had exploded from 175,000 to 530,000. The professoriate had grown from 2,000 at the end of World War II to 22,000 in 1967. Additionally, the French student population had become increasingly female and working class. Yet three-quarters of these students never earned a degree, often failing their end-of-year exams.

By the middle of the decade, French students were voicing the same kind of critiques heard throughout the Western educational world. As mentioned above, students at the University of Strasbourg (France) published a pamphlet in 1966, *On the Misery of Student Life*. It became one of the most widely read tracts of the decade. By 1969, approximately 300,000 copies had been printed.[17]

"The student is the most universally despised creature in France, apart from the priest and the policeman," the tract began. A student lives "a double life, poised between his present status and his future role." The educational critique was coupled with a general critique of the modern French economy. "Modern capitalism and its spectacle allot everyone a specific role in a general passivity. The student is no exception." The older notion of the university had vanished. "A mechanically produced specialist is now the goal...The university has become a society for the propagation of ignorance; 'high culture' has taken on the rhythm of the production line...Art is dead, but the student is a necrophiliac."

French students were aware of what had happened in the U.S. Events at UC Berkeley confirmed some of their own critique. American students, such as those at Berkeley, "have seen their revolt against the university hierarchy as a revolt against *their whole hierarchical system*, the dictatorship of the economy and the State." American students had discovered a crucial truth, "that a coherent revolutionary alternative can and must be found *within* the affluent society."[18]

It should not, then, have surprised authorities that French students, like their counterparts in the U.S., would come to criticize the new educational system, which as noted had been developed along lines taken by American universities, and to which American students had grown increasingly critical of throughout the decade.

As part of the expansion of the French university system, a new term for France, "campus," entered the discussion. Older universities wound through the city center, while these new "campuses" were located outside the main cities. The vibrant life of the Latin Quarter, for example, could compensate for the alienating aspects of university life, like large, impersonal lecture classes and little interaction with faculty. The new French campuses, built to absorb the huge increase in students, were situated in very different environments, such as Nanterre, in suburban Paris. Every depiction of this campus shares the same imagery—a depressingly impersonal and ugly structure of concrete, glass, and steel, set amid slums and low-cost housing for the poor, including many Algerian immigrants. To one instructor, Henri Lefebvre, Nanterre "contains misery, shantytowns, excavations for an express subway line, low-income housing projects for workers, and industrial employees. This is a desolate and strange landscape." The lack of a completed subway line only added to the students' sense of isolation. But all this, Lefebvre continued, had ideological underpinnings. "The university was conceived in terms of the concepts of industrial production and productivity of an advanced capitalist society." It was designed, he concluded, "to produce mediocre intellectuals and junior executives for the management of society. [In this suburb] unhappiness becomes concrete."[19]

Ten to twelve thousand students lived in sterile dormitories, in which male students were not allowed to visit women's rooms, and only women over 21 or with parental permission could visit a man's room. (This issue had been a source of contention on many American campuses, as well.) As with students in many Western countries, grievances about their educational system and about their social life first stirred campus actions, including a 1967 sit-in at Nanterre by a group of male students in the entrance hall of a women's dormitory, as well as a boycott of classes to protest the alienating educational structure. In January 1968, a small confrontation occurred at Nanterre, which, though little known at the time, would become a symbolic moment in the history of subsequent events. The French Minister of Youth and Sport came to the campus to celebrate the opening of a campus swimming pool. A Nanterre student, Daniel Cohn-Bendit, confronted him. "Monsieur le Ministre, you've drawn up a report on French youth three hundred pages long. But there isn't a word in it about our sexual problems. Why not?" The minister tried to brush off Cohn-Bendit, who stood his ground. The minister ultimately insulted him. "No wonder, with a face like yours, you have these problems. I suggest you take a dip in the pool." Cohn-Bendit shot back, "Now there's an answer worthy of Hitler's youth minster."[20]

Cohn-Bendit was among the most radical of the Nanterre students, the *enragés*. He would emerge as the most prominent face of the French student strike of 1968. The son of leftist Germans who had fled the Nazis, Cohn-Bendit had been born in France. At 13, he returned to Germany to attend secondary school, then came back to France in 1966 to study at Nanterre. He had traveled to the U.S. in 1964. While in New York, he went to a memorial for the three SNCC workers killed in Mississippi. He later recounted being "impressed by the atmosphere," as well as that two of the victims were "white Jewish guys who went to Mississippi. How dangerous. That was something different than what I was prepared to do."[21]

Students at Nanterre soon began a series of demonstrations, aimed at everything from campus concerns, including the plainclothes policemen who had been assigned to monitor student activities, to the war in Vietnam. When several Nanterre students were among those arrested in an anti-Vietnam demonstration in central Paris, students on campus moved to occupy the campus administration building. Responding like their peers at Berkeley and Columbia, on March 22, 1968, they seized the eighth floor of the administration building including the office of the Dean. The "March 22 Movement" was born. The leaders of student movements around the globe did not know one another personally, but as Cohn-Bendit later put it, "We met through television, through seeing pictures of each other. We were the first television generation...we had a relationship with what our imagination produced from seeing pictures of each other on television."[22]

Across Europe and around the world, as university administrators confronted these student uprisings, they often made two common mistakes. The first, as at Columbia, was to wait too long to announce minor educational reforms. By the time they began to begrudgingly address the initial student concerns, the protesting students had moved well beyond the point where minor tinkering would satisfy their demands. Second, in numerous places officials decided that the best way to defuse the explosive situation was to discipline and, often, expel the student leaders. This always resulted in the opposite effect, as we have seen, again, at Columbia. Paris was no different.

When students returned from the Easter recess, they discovered that Cohn-Bendit and seven others had been ordered to appear before a disciplinary board at the Sorbonne on Friday, May 3. That day Cohn-Bendit and the others met with students at the Sorbonne to discuss their upcoming hearing as well as the closing of Nanterre the previous day. Rumors begin to circulate that a group of neo-fascist, right-wing students was heading to the Sorbonne, intent on forcibly deporting the German-born

Cohn-Bendit and ending the strident agitation.[23] The elderly rector of the Sorbonne, Jean Roche, grew increasingly nervous as crowds begin to gather and, according to some, began to lose his nerve. He turned to the young, conservative education minister, Alain Peyrefitte, who had few qualms about how to act. He instructed Roche to call in the police.

By late afternoon, police filled the Sorbonne courtyard, arresting many of the student leaders. News of this clash ignited the Latin Quarter, with other students pouring in to confront the police. The crowd attacked the police with rocks and, in French tradition, overturned cars to create barricades. They were met with tear gas and truncheons. Rector Roche decided to close the Sorbonne for only the second time in its centuries-long history. The first was when the Nazis had invaded Paris in 1940.

Two British journalists covering these events would conclude, "The immediate effect of the authorities' crude display of strength was to unite the mass of uncommitted students—and their teachers—behind the enragés. In a few minutes a mass movement was created."[24] The following Monday, this mass movement was on full display. Student leaders had called for a national strike and 5,000 students gathered in the Latin Quarter and began to march toward the Sorbonne. As they neared the university, police charged the crowd. The clash would go on all afternoon and into the night. Again, tear gas and truncheons versus paving stones and overturned cars. By day's end, over 400 had been arrested and numerous injuries had occurred on both sides.

Like so much in 1968, the news from Paris competed with that of simultaneous other events. Paris, itself, was the scene of another important moment, as preparations were underway for Vietnam peace talks to be held there, the ones initiated by Johnson's withdrawal speech. Fighting in Vietnam itself continued to be front-page news, as did the events at Columbia and in Prague, the Kennedy-McCarthy primary battles, and the beginnings of the Poor People's March. Friday's Paris events garnered only a small front-page article in the *New York Times*. Monday's street battles, on the other hand, earned a front-page photo to go with the story of the battle between police and students. By Wednesday, the *Times* reported that de Gaulle had warned French students about repercussions, but that the marches continued. This reporting did note that students had maintained a sense of order. It also noted, in this and several other dispatches, that most French students seemed apolitical and that the organizers and marchers represented a minority of French students.

By week's end, the demonstrations mounted again. On Friday evening, May 10th, 15,000 demonstrators gathered to march, their numbers growing to 50,000 as the evening wore on. Groups throughout the city begin to construct more barricades. "Singing the *Internationale*," recalled one observer, "paving stones formed the foundation of every barricade. On top of these were piled cars, gas-soaked wooden branches of trees...and as much wire as could be found."[25] In the middle of the night, police received orders to clear the barricades. Firing tear gas grenades, they stormed into the Latin Quarter. One participant later argued, "I must insist that the general mood was defense, *not* offensive; we just wanted to hold the place like an entrenched sit-down strike."[26] But the police charged, battering hospital orderlies who tried to retrieve the wounded, assaulting those already assaulted, sometimes dragging them from stretchers. They raided private homes to find refugees. By night's end, 367 people had been injured, 460 arrested, and 180 cars damaged.[27]

Something else was emerging with the students' protests—a sense of liberation and enthusiasm. While the clashes and the violence garnered the headlines, Parisians seemed to be reveling in the new spirit. "Paris was wonderful then," a student from Nanterre remembered. "Everyone was talking." Sometimes at the barricades, sometimes on the Métro. Some discussions involved sweeping analyses of the nature of revolution. Some focused on more mundane topics. Students spoke with their professors (something not usual in the French system), students began to talk to workers. "The real sense of '68," recalled Radith Geismar, wife of one of the student leaders, "was a tremendous sense of liberation, of freedom, of people talking, talking on the street, in the universities, in theaters. It was much more than throwing stones...a whole system of order and authority and tradition was swept aside."[28]

When it came to using modern media, the students always seemed to have the upper hand. Invited to appear on French television before a panel of television journalists, three student leaders, including Cohn-Bendit, carried the day. This debate was preceded by a prerecorded message from aging Prime Minister Georges Pompidou, who negatively depicted the students as dangerous radicals. When the debate began, the journalists seemed uptight and confrontational, the students amiable and relaxed. "We destroyed them," Cohn-Bendit later stated, understanding that "I had a special relation with the media. I am a media product...For a long time I was the media's darling."[29]

A student in her last year at a Catholic high school, Lily Métreaux, remembers going to the demonstration instead of going to school one morning. "How can I describe it? A fabulous happening, a tremendous joy!" People were "holding hands...shouting, laughing." High school students joined their university counterparts. Métreaux and her brother helped lead their school out on strike, "going from classroom to classroom. All the kids ran into the streets...I felt our time had come at last," Métreaux recalls. "There was sort of a magic island coming out of nowhere, and it was us, the young ones, who were pulling it out." "May was like living on a constant high," a university student, Henri Weber, remembers. "Life was beautiful, the weather was lovely, the men were handsome, and the women superb. Everything we did immediately belonged to History. All the hierarchies had suddenly dissolved."[30]

The spirit of the counterculture infused the political activities. "Romance, sex seemed part of the air: students with rooms in the center of towns left doors unlocked to give overnight shelter, and teenagers no longer went home to sleep." One young Parisian woman recalled, "I remember after a euphoric night of fighting the police...I crashed at a friend's in the Latin Quarter...I woke to find an unknown mustached face looking down at me. He asked me to have coffee and we became lovers."[31]

The violence, especially on the part of the police, and the general enthusiasm had begun, it appeared, to move public opinion in France. One poll reported that 80 percent of the French population supported the students.[32] Public buildings were left open for everyone, "park keepers no longer chased off young lovers lying on the grass in public gardens." Despite the street battles and the underlying critique of capitalism, "there was virtually no vandalism; very few shop windows were broken, and the crime rate dropped to an all-time low."[33] One large march took a route that led them by a prison. "The demonstrators cheered," one marcher recalls, "when the inmates waved handkerchiefs through the barred windows." Local residents "were at their windows, offering us food and milk...People were releasing all their repressed feelings, expressing them in a festive spirit."[34]

The walls of the city became the palette for slogans and posters, capturing the political as well as the cultural moment. An estimated 2,000 slogans decorated the walls around the Sorbonne and other parts of the city.

- THE IMAGINATION TAKES POWER
- THE WALLS ARE EARS, YOUR EARS ARE WALLS
- DREAMS ARE REALITY
- BE REALISTIC, DEMAND THE IMPOSSIBLE
- IT IS FORBIDDEN TO FORBID
- A BARRICADE CLOSES THE STREET BUT OPENS A PATH
- THE AGGRESSOR IS NOT THE PERSON WHO REVOLTS BUT THE ONE WHO CONFORMS
- EVERYTHING IS POSSIBLE
- CONSUME MORE, YOU'LL LIVE LESS
- ALCOHOL KILLS, TRY LSD
- IF WE DON'T FUCK, THEY'LL FUCK US
- I AM A MARXIST OF THE GROUCHO FACTION
- THE MORE I MAKE LOVE, THE MORE I FEEL LIKE MAKING A REVOLUTION;
  THE MORE I MAKE THE REVOLUTION, THE MORE I FEEL LIKE MAKING LOVE.[35]

The art schools became poster factories, producing hundreds of silk-screen posters day after day, often reproduced in quantities of 2,000–3,000 prints. They were never signed and distributed without charge. The themes ran from support for the students to harsh depictions of the authorities. Cohn-Bendit was depicted in one of the most famous posters, with the words "We are all undesirables [aliens]," responding to the attacks on him as German and Jewish. Other posters equated the police with the German SS, or the Fifth Republic with the fascist governments of Franco's Spain or Salazar's Portugal. One referenced the French tradition of erecting street barricades. Another was a drawing of a paving stone. "Under 21 years old, here is your ballot," the poster proclaimed. In August, President de Gaulle actually had all the cobblestones in the Latin Quarter paved over with asphalt. The General himself came in for harsh depictions in many posters, some making him appear ridiculous. He had used the phrase *chienlit* ["shit in the bed"] in one of his speeches against the students—"Reform yes, *Chie-en-lit* no!" The poster in response depicted De Galle's easily recognizable silhouette with the words, "*La Chienlit C'est Lui*!" ["He is the Shit in the Bed!"]

Members of the art world joined in the proliferation of public art. Support for it and the students, in general, came from a number of prominent artists, including Picasso, Alexander Calder, and Max Ernst. A group of 25 French art dealers signed a petition in support of the students and promised to distribute the posters without personal profit. Some of the most prestigious galleries and architectural firms in France made donations to the students.[36]

Theater students also chose to act. On the night of May 15, as an audience was leaving the Odéon National Theater, young people flocked in. By midnight there were 4,000 inside, hanging a banner that announced, "The Odéon is Closed to a Bourgeois Audience." A new theatrical plan was launched. "The Odéon has stopped being a theater. It has become a meeting place for workers," they announced. "The only theater was guerilla."[37]

Across Europe and around the world, students from Warsaw to Rome and Columbia to Berkeley began to demonstrate and otherwise cheer on their French counterparts. Just as Cohn-Bendit had learned about the others through media, they too had learned about him. "The first television generation" appeared to be engaged in an uncoordinated but remarkably similar assault on the political and social structures around them.

That May, as well, something extraordinary happened within France. In nearly all of the many conflicts in Europe and the U.S. between students and authorities, workers and workers' organizations had remained on the sidelines, if not in active support of the government. The most notable example of this was the support of Johnson and the Vietnam War by the major U.S. labor organization, the AFL-CIO. In France, it was not as though the workers initially moved *en masse* to share the student's agenda, but they soon seemed swept up in the currents of the day. Back in March, the French Communist Party had dismissed the student movement—"False Revolutionaries," their leader had called them, "some of the *bourgeoisie* contemptuous toward students of working class origins."[38]

By May, their tune was changing. Some leaders began to call for an alliance with the students. The brutality of May 10 seemed to have been the last straw. Well before their leadership moved to support the students, French workers and common people joined in. A march by a few hundred students in Lyons suddenly swelled, according to one participant. "People from every walk of life joining in, people who had nothing to do with students…It was as if the whole city had been waiting for it."[39]

On May 13, the 10th anniversary of the coup that had brought De Gaulle to power, the Communist Party and all the major trade unions called for a one-day strike. It was not, as many in the West felt, that the workers and the students had finally joined in a single movement with a shared agenda. It is more likely that the student challenges had sparked feelings among workers, especially those who felt that their situation had deteriorated and had been ignored by the de Gaulle government. This seemed especially true among many young workers, who had a generational connection to the students that their older leaders lacked. But from the outset, it was also clear that the workers—young and old—saw this moment as an opportunity. Workers' wages had stagnated, not keeping pace with inflation, and the workweek had grown incrementally. At the same time, they had been drawn into the consumptive trends of postwar life, buying more on credit and desiring the conveniences of modern life. Over the course of the decade, more and more workers bought household appliances: refrigerator ownership rising from 22 percent of working-class homes in 1958 to 91 percent by the end of the 60s, for example; homes with televisions growing from 12 percent to 77 percent, and automobiles 23 percent to 75 percent. Workers' credit indebtedness added to their economic anxieties.[40]

A series of wildcat strikes erupted across France. A sit-in strike by 200 workers at a Renault plant in Cleon seemed to mirror the student sit-ins, including locking the plant manager in his office. The next day several thousand students joined the 35,000 workers who had stopped working. A wave of sit-in strikes spread among coal miners, utilities workers, and postal workers. By week's end, two million workers were on strike, and 120 factories were occupied. Mail delivery stopped. Banks limited cash withdrawals. Gasoline stations began to run out of fuel. The cross-channel ferries suspended operations. Garbage piled up on street corners. In the next week professionals joined—air traffic controllers, state television workers, teachers, government workers. By May 22, the number of strikers had risen to nine million.

Actions against the government began to spread across the country and across class lines, merging into something akin to an unplanned general strike. To many of the student leaders and other radicals, these all signaled the beginnings of a revolution, some urging "wage earners to destroy the power of the bourgeoisie by taking over the organization of production and distribution." Radical intellectuals and writers, including Jean-Paul Sartre, Simone de Beauvoir, and Marguerite Duras, joined in support of this general approach.[41] It was never clear, however, that workers' organizations or even the French Communist Party saw this as their objective. The largest trade union federation, the CGT, continued to argue for bread-and-butter issues—wages, hours, and job security.

Just as the strikes began, de Gaulle surprisingly left for a four-day trip to Romania. When he returned on Friday May 17, the situation had escalated to a point where he had no choice but to respond, going on television on Friday, May 24 to promise change and to propose a nationwide referendum to give him a mandate to institute reforms—though what such reforms were was not spelled out in his speech. The 77-year-olf General seemed hesitant, his voice sounding its age. As the speech ended, one Paris demonstrator waved a handkerchief over his head, shouting, "Adieu de Gaulle!" Thousands of others repeated this gesture.

Too little, too late, the student demonstrations continued. Weekend negotiations with employer associations and union leadership led to an agreement for large wage increases, added fringe benefits, and half pay for strike days. When the union leaders met with their workers across the nation, they were often booed. At one factory after another, workers voted no. De Gaulle seemed to be losing his base of support. Left-wing politicians demanded his resignation. Francois Mitterrand, leader of the opposition, called for a "provisional government."

But the government was not the passive agent that the pubic often perceived. Under the general supervision of Prime Minister Georges Pompidou, it began a series of moves to discredit the students and striking workers, as well as rally the largely conservative base of French voters. In some cases inaction by the government, initially perceived as passivity, was actually intentional. The government failed to clean up some areas of Paris and other cities, where street conflicts had left visual symbols of destruction. Abandoned barricades and burned-out vehicles dotted the landscape, reminding citizens of what the students had done. The piles of garbage became another reminder. At other points, the government employed the military to break strikes or brutally smash student demonstrations.

Gasoline proved a significant component in the French struggles, and not as the fuel for Molotov cocktails and other incendiary devices. The inability to procure gasoline meant it became increasingly difficult to get consumer goods, especially food, to market. Prices rose, as did public resentment. The lack of gasoline led to serious frustration among many of the French, the government directed the public ire toward the students and the striking workers. Despite the strikes, certain gas stations were reopened for the exclusive use of truckers, manned by the military and other government employees. "The thousands of small groceries of Paris and its suburbs," the government declared, "must be able to get whatever they need to satisfy housewives."[42] As gasoline started to become increasingly available to the French public, they once again took to the roads. Over one long holiday weekend, Parisians left town for a traditional weekend away. When they returned to the city, the roads were jammed. With other forms of transport still on strike everyone had taken their car and now they all tried to return home, creating the worst traffic jam in French history.[43] Traffic accidents that weekend accounted for 68 deaths. To many, the government had restored the means, gasoline, by which they could enjoy their holiday weekend, but the strikers had created an atmosphere in which their joy turned to frustration, anger, and death. As Alain Geismar, one the of the student leaders, later put it, "gas killed the Revolution."[44]

And then on Wednesday, May 29, de Gaulle abandoned Paris. Purportedly going to his country retreat, instead de Gaulle secretly went to French military headquarters in eastern France and then onto the headquarters of French troops in West Germany, where 70,000 French troops were stationed, commanded by Jacques Massu, who had been central to de Gaulle's taking power in 1958. While his exact plans were never known, it is clear that when de Gaulle returned to Paris on May 30, he was confident in the support of the French military for whatever was to come.

This time he spoke over the radio, evoking his World War II broadcasts from London to occupied France. De Gaulle's tone had changed dramatically from his previous televised address. He called off the referendum and called for new national elections. The National Assembly was dissolved. At the same time, he also identified whom he felt responsible for France's calamity, "totalitarian Communists and their allies." They had used "intimidation, intoxication, and tyranny" to coerce students, teachers, and workers. These were not Soviet agents or outside agitators, as older Cold War propaganda might have once suggested. They were homegrown French Communists. The government began to court right-wing forces for support, including granting amnesty and pardons to members of the OAS, the right-wing terrorist organization of the Algerian War era. One freed prisoner had been serving a life sentence for planning the assassination of De Gaulle, himself.[45]

Patriotic demonstrations were organized, including a huge march of perhaps one million up the Champs-Elysees, with car horns sounding and chants that ranged from "France Back to Work!" and "Clean out the Sorbonne" to "Cohn-Bendit to Dachau." (This led to the student reply, "We Are All German Jews.") British poet Stephen Spender characterized this march as "the triumphant bacchanal of the Social World of Conspicuous Consumption, shameless, crowing, and more vulgar than any crowd I have ever seen on Broadway or in Chicago."[46]

At the same time, new contracts were negotiated with many of the striking unions. They offered significant wage increases, reductions in the workweek, and additional days of paid vacation. The disparities between male and female, as well as older and younger workers, were addressed, as were the differences between wages in Paris and elsewhere in the nation. Some contracts offered partial pay for the days workers had been on strike. Others included improved benefits, including health benefits and full paid leave for pregnant women and new mothers. This time, workers approved these contract offers.

The first round of voting on June 23 resulted in a huge victory for de Gaulle. After the runoffs a week later, his party came out with an absolute majority, rare in a multi-party state. The revolutionary zeal had been defused. Cohn-Bendit was deported and remained outside of France for 10 years, his critics not only among those on the right. After De Gaulle's sweeping victory, the head of the French Communist Party declared, "It's all Cohn-Bendit's fault."[47]

Still, in those momentous months, France had not only teetered on the brink of massive social upheaval but also the dreamed-of coalition between workers and students, while never as solid as perceived, appeared closer than it ever had been. France, especially Paris, felt vital and alive, youthful enthusiasm and working-class desires appeared to mesh. And students around the world looked on in wonder. The lore of "the barricades" now had its twentieth-century chapter.

16

Robert Kennedy—The Road to Los Angeles

At a New York dinner party, Jacqueline Kennedy took me aside and said, "Do you know what I think will happen to Bobby?...The same thing that happened to Jack... There is so much hatred in this country, and more people hate Bobby than hated Jack...I've told Bobby this, but he isn't fatalistic, like me."

—Arthur Schlesinger, Jr.[1]

Knowing the end of a story can color the entire narrative. Any history of the days and weeks that remained of the Democratic primaries after Lyndon Johnson's withdrawal, and especially the history of the candidacy of Robert Kennedy, always contains the knowledge of where things will end, the tragedy at the end of the tale. But that should not undermine the importance of what happened between that Sunday night at the end of March when LBJ dropped out and that Tuesday night in early June when Kennedy was shot. During those ten weeks, American politics reset itself.

Both Eugene McCarthy and Robert Kennedy had staked their political insurgencies on targeting Lyndon Johnson and the war in Vietnam. Defeating the president had been the objective, and their competition involved who was best suited to challenge him. Then suddenly he was out of the game. "I feel as if I've been tracking a tiger through the jungle grass," McCarthy said, "and all of a sudden he rolls over and he's stuffed."[2]

Before they could confront the new reality of the '68 presidential campaign, they had to deal with the assassination of Martin Luther King. King's death put the entire nation on hold, especially its political actors. Kennedy was campaigning in Indiana, the first major primary in which he would be on the ballot, when he heard the news about King. In what would become a signature moment not only of the campaign but of his life, Kennedy decided to continue with a planned campaign event in the heart of the Black community of Indianapolis that night. Against the advice of the Indianapolis police chief and without police protection, he took the rally stage, the back of a flatbed truck. "Ladies and gentleman, I have some very bad news for all of you," he began. Speaking extemporaneously, he continued. "Martin Luther King was shot and killed tonight in Memphis." As the crowd reacted in anger and pain, Kennedy continued, praising King and allowing that Black people might be "filled with bitterness, and with hatred, and a desire for revenge...I would only say that I can also feel in my own heart the same kind of feeling. I had a member of my family killed, but he was also killed by a white man." Calling for "love and wisdom" instead of "violence and lawlessness," Kennedy asked people "to return home, to say a prayer for the family of Martin Luther King...and more importantly to say a prayer for our own country." He quietly concluded, "Let us dedicate ourselves to what the Greeks wrote so many years ago: to tame the savageness of man and make gentle the life of this world."[3] That night and in the next days, riots, as we have seen, broke out all over the U.S. None were reported in Indianapolis.

No one in American politics desired to be president more than Vice President Hubert Humphrey. Yet when his opportunity arrived, he was in several awkward positions. On the morning of Johnson's televised withdrawal, Humphrey was readying himself to leave on an official trip to Mexico City, when Johnson and Lady Bird came to his residence. Informing Humphrey of his plans, Johnson told his vice president, "If you're going to run you'd better get ready damn quick."[4] That was easier said than done. He needed to wait an appropriate amount of time after LBJ's announcement, so as not to seem overly eager. Yet he also feared that delay would allow Kennedy to secure the support of party leaders. When he returned from Mexico, his aides reported that most party leaders had held off, pending his decision. Then came the King assassination. It would appear unseemly to make an enthusiastic political announcement—Humphrey's trademark style—amid the national mourning for the fallen civil rights leader, especially someone who had been closely connected with the civil rights movement.

There was a positive side to a delay, however. McCarthy and Kennedy had harnessed the enthusiasm of those opposed to the war, of the young, and probably much to Humphrey's frustration, Kennedy had great support among minority voters. Filing deadlines for primary elections had passed in many states, so only a few remained for which Humphrey could qualify. McCarthy had just soundly defeated Johnson in Wisconsin. Humphrey's chances against either McCarthy or Kennedy would be even worse than LBJ's. So in the first weeks after Johnson withdrew, Humphrey initiated his strategy of lining up support from party leaders and state caucuses and conventions rather than entering primaries. It was a strategy that would ultimately prove successful, though as one campaign reporter put it, "from the start, the Humphrey campaign had about it an aura of staleness."[5]

Finally on April 27, four weeks after Johnson's speech, Humphrey announced he was running. "Here we are," he proclaimed, "the way politics ought to be in America: the politics of happiness, the politics of purpose and the politics of joy!" This struck many as weirdly tone deaf to the contemporary political realities—stretching from Tet to King. Reacting to Humphrey's speech, Kennedy told his next audience, "If you want to be filled with Pablum and tranquilizers, then you should vote for some other candidate," clearly referring to the vice president. "If you see a small black child starving to death in Mississippi, as I have, it is not the politics of joy."[6]

Humphrey suffered other handicaps, not the least of which was the public perception that he had evolved from a fiery liberal into Johnson's unquestioning yes-man. Twenty years earlier he had championed civil rights on the floor of the Democratic Convention, leading to the

Dixiecrat walkout of 1948. Now he seemed to merely be Johnson's toady. A joke at the time imagined him walking with LBJ. "Hubert, did you fart?," the president asks. "No," replies his VP, "was I supposed to?" Publicly he remained a staunch supporter of LBJ's Vietnam policy, though privately he had always had some misgivings. Three years earlier, he had sent Johnson a long memo warning him about deepening Vietnam involvement, fearing the negative impact on the Great Society programs that were Johnson's pride. Instead of heeding his advice, Johnson excluded Humphrey from his inner circle of policymakers.[7] Humphrey understood the rock and hard place he was in on Vietnam. Early in the campaign he went to see Johnson, his aide Ted Van Dyk later told reporter Jules Witcover, to suggest that he might support a conciliatory Vietnam plank at the convention. "What happened?" Van Dyk had asked Humphrey. "He said if I issued it he would denounce me. Then he said I would have the blood of his sons-in-law on my hands." After a pause, Van Dyk recalled Humphrey adding, "I've eaten so much shit in the last two years, I've almost gotten to like the taste of it."[8]

So Humphrey continued to publicly support Johnson, on literally everything but especially on Vietnam. It was his only choice if he hoped to gain the White House. Nineteen seventy-two had been his target. Now, instead, he was thrust into the cauldron of 1968, forced to become the public symbol of an administration and a war that were increasingly being rejected by the American people.

The withdrawal of Lyndon Johnson from the campaign seemed to take some of the air out of the sails of the McCarthy campaign, robbing him of his target and instead making the primary races merely a competition between Kennedy and himself. The initial kinetic energy of his candidacy—the kids pouring into New Hampshire and Wisconsin, the added impetus of Tet, the realization of LBJ's vulnerabilities—had run its course. There was disappointment when some of his youthful cadre began to abandon his camp for that of Robert Kennedy. The campaign awaited fresh injections of energy. While McCarthy still maintained the loyalty and enthusiasm of many supporters, especially those who championed him because he had been first, reporters, analysts, and even some volunteers developed doubts about his campaign.

Now that Johnson was out, some people began to feel that for McCarthy the primary battle was turning into a personal feud. "It's narrowed down to Bobby and me," he told two campaign aides. "So far he's run with the ghost of his brother. Now we're going to make him run against it. It's purely Greek: He either has to kill him or be killed by him. We'll make him run against Jack."[9] Richard Goodwin said McCarthy told him that the Kennedys never "appreciated" him.[10] McCarthy campaign aide Ben Stavis, in his campaign memoir *We Were The Campaign,* talks about growing concerns among some of the staff. McCarthy "seemed to pay no attention at all to his campaign. He viewed it as a spontaneous happening…He would arbitrarily cancel events, permitted confusion at the top of his staff to demoralize the entire campaign."[11]

Still, he had been there first and maintained the strong loyalty of his supporters, especially the students. "When it mattered," campaign staffer Jeremy Larner noted, "Gene had gone into New Hampshire. Bobby, hung up, had refrained." The proudest button in the campaign, Larner believed, read "FMBNH: For McCarthy Before New Hampshire."[12]

For Bobby Kennedy it became about Indiana. Here, the first direct confrontation with McCarthy would occur. There were, however, complexities and complications. First, it was not a clear one-on-one battle. Indiana Governor Roger Branigan was running as a favorite son, explicitly as a stand-in for Humphrey. Branigan had wide support in the state, from the business community, the unions, the state party, and the conservative *Indianapolis Star,* the state's leading newspaper. The *Star* had called Kennedy "Unfit, Unshorn, Unwanted."[13] McCarthy had strong support in university towns, among students, and in the suburbs. Branigan was strong in the rural areas and small towns, and among Indiana's largely conservative blue-collar whites, many of whom, while still Democrats, had begun to voice support for third-party candidate George Wallace.

In addition, two personal issues about Kennedy worried the campaign, his money and his religion. In the 1920s, Indiana had been the non-Southern state where the Ku Klux Klan was most powerful. And anti-Catholic sentiments still ran deep in some areas where Kennedy set out to contest Branigan. He tried to make his religion appear more humanistic. He frequently joked about a nun, who wished him well, and told him she was praying to St. Jude for him. "I learned," he would tell the crowd, that St. Jude was "the patron saint of lost causes." He would get a laugh and in the process help defuse some of the Catholic issue.[14]

His wealth was something about which everyone knew, just as they knew it about Republican candidate Nelson Rockefeller. That money was in clear evidence in Indiana. As one analyst recently put it, "The state had never seen anything like it—a modern major-league presidential campaign devoted entirely to Indiana voters, complete with chartered planes, motorcades, TV ads, paid telephone canvasses, huge crowds, and Kennedys. Kennedys everywhere."[15] But it didn't seem to people that Robert Kennedy was merely out to buy the election. He was everywhere across the state, from small towns to larger cities, in ghettos and on college campuses. He met voters head on, answered their questions—whether they liked his answers or not. "Robert Kennedy raced across the face of Indiana," Jules Witcover commented, "like a political pied piper." He would stand in the back of an open convertible, with one of his entourage kneeling with his arms around the candidate's legs, as RFK leaned out to touch the crowds. They grabbed at him, for a handshake, to grab a cuff link, his shirt cuff, even his shoes.

During one motorcade, Kennedy noticed a small boy who had stopped running alongside his car to help his fallen little sister back to her feet. He instructed that his car stop, lifted the kids into the convertible, and continued. After a number of blocks, Kennedy had his car exit the motorcade and drove the kids home. His mother greeted them with lemonade, and Kennedy sat on her steps and talked with her for a few minutes, while the motorcade waited. The press reported it all. The campaign may have been spending money hand over fist, but Kennedy's personal interactions with Indiana voters added poignant moments that under-cut any sense that he was "buying" the election.[16]

"For all the talk about New Politics, for all the hippie beads and quota-tions from Camus, Robert Kennedy could play the ethnic-politics game with considerable professionalism," wrote three British reporters follow-ing the campaign. He'd show up at ethnic festivals, eat ethnic foods, and utter a few words of greeting to ethnic voters in their own language.[17] To win some of the more moderate and conservative voters, Kennedy began to talk more about "law and order," a topic that had emerged in the cam-paigns of George Wallace and Richard Nixon, who would both run on it through November. Kennedy talked about wasteful federal programs but made his priorities clear. Asked if a federal rat-control program was waste-ful, he countered, "Do you know there are more rats in New York than people, and there are nine million people there?" His audience thought he was joking and laughed. "Don't Laugh!," he admonished them. When addressing medical students at the University of Indiana, he faced a hos-tile crowd. One student criticized his call for neighborhood clinics. "Where's the money gonna come from?" he asked. Kennedy pointed his finger at the questioner and barked, "From you!" And then went around the hall, pointing and repeating, "From you!...You!...You!." He also told the students that he did not see many Black faces in the audience or among other groups of medical students. And tying this issue to the central ele-ment of his candidacy, he observed, "as white students sit here in medical school...it's the black people who carry the major burden of the struggle in Vietnam."[18]

Kennedy ended the campaign with a motorcade across northern Indiana. Large crowds slowed the motorcade. The final speech, sched-uled for five o'clock, was not given until ten. The next day, Indiana gave Robert Kennedy a solid win, 42 percent to Branigan's 31 percent and McCarthy's 27 percent. Significantly, voter analysis showed strong sup-port in both blue-collar neighborhoods and the Black community.

The Indiana experience was largely replicated in Nebraska. While the Kennedy campaign swung into high gear, the McCarthy campaign was slowed by disorganization and dwindling funds. McCarthy shocked voters and the press by skipping the annual Jefferson-Jackson dinner in Omaha, the Democrats' major event of each year, at which both Kennedy and Humphrey appeared. The most compelling moment of the primary came when Kennedy spoke at Creighton University. When asked by one student, "Isn't the Army one way of getting young people out of the ghetto?" Kennedy shot back. "Here at a Catholic university, how can you say that we deal with the problems of the poor by sending them to Vietnam?" He went on. "Look around you. How many black faces do you see here? How many American Indians? How many Mexican Americans?...You're the most exclusive minority in the world. Are you going to sit on your duffs and do nothing?"[19]

Kennedy won the primary with 52 percent, McCarthy garnering 31 percent. Humphrey write-ins came in at 8 percent. Kennedy hoped that McCarthy would drop out after successive losses in Indiana and Nebraska, but McCarthy pressed on. He wanted a clear one-on-one with Kennedy and argued he would get it in Oregon and then California.

Oregon was a state tailor-made for Gene McCarthy. Probably no state in the nation had as public a reputation of opposition to Vietnam. Its Democratic senator, Wayne Morse, had been one of the two senators who had voted against the Tonkin Gulf Resolution back in 1964. Republican senator Mark Hatfield had been one of the first major GOP national figures to come out against the war. To many Oregonians, McCarthy seemed to be a third anti-war pioneer, the first to challenge LBJ.

Additionally, the make-up of the Oregon electorate was not suited to Kennedy's appeals. When one Kennedy strategist arrived, he asked Congresswoman Edith Green, the state chair of the Kennedy campaign, "Have we got the ghettoes organized?" Green replied, "There are no ghettoes in Oregon."[20] In addition, Green was not popular among the state's Young Democrats, who called her "The Madame Nhu of

Oregon."* The minority population was small, ethnic resentments minimal. "This state is like one giant suburb," Kennedy observed.[21] From the outset, the Kennedy people knew it was going to be tough sledding. Another whistle-stop campaign trip brought out good crowds, but they were not the hysterical, rock star-like carnivals of past weeks.

As the California primary would occur only a week after Oregon, the candidates shuttled between the states. By this point, one reporter recalled, "their vague contempt for each other had metastasized into a bitter loathing. Kennedy had come to see McCarthy as lazy, arrogant, and dishonest, and McCarthy viewed Kennedy as a spoiled rich boy."[22] In a major speech at the Cow Palace in San Francisco, McCarthy launched his most direct attack on Kennedy and Humphrey. While the speech had been billed as being about Vietnam, McCarthy expanded it to a critique of postwar American foreign policy, including criticism of John Kennedy, something no major Democrat had done since 1963. Calling out JFK's Vietnam policymakers by name, he implicitly rolled RFK into the mix. And then he added, "I am not convinced that the Senator from New York has entirety renounced those misconceptions." And "at the very time when American policy grew most disastrous, Vice President Hubert Humphrey became its most ardent supporter."[23] McCarthy gave virtually the same speech in Portland a few nights later.

When Oregonians went to the polls they did something that no electorate had ever done before. They handed a defeat to a Kennedy, 45 percent to 39 percent. McCarthy appeared before a jubilant crowd of supporters. They were back in the game, counterculture enthusiasm mixing with the mechanics of political organizing. "The President said we will have riots in the streets this summer," McCarthy declared. "Instead of riots, we'll have singing and dancing in the streets...We'll

---

* Madame Nhu was the sister-in-law of Ngo Dinh Diem and was First Lady of South Vietnam. Ultimately depicted in the foreign press as the "Dragon Lady," she became a symbol of the repressive nature of the Diem regime, instituting a very strict code of morality on the South Vietnamese. Further, her sharp tongue only added to negative appraisals of her and of the regime. For example, after the Buddhist monk set himself on fire in protest, she referred to it as a "barbeque." She added, "Let them burn and we shall clap our hands."

take the fence down around the White House and have a picnic on the lawn." Looking ahead, he added, "The next test is California. . . . California, here we come!"[24]

The morning after the Oregon primary, Robert Kennedy flew to Los Angeles, clearly aware of the meaning of what had transpired. "I'm not the same candidate I was before Oregon and I can't claim that I am," he told reporters at an airport press conference.[25] And for the first time, he said he was ready to debate Gene McCarthy.

Leaving the airport, he headed straight into another of his motorcades, plunging into Chicano and African American neighborhoods. The crowds poured out, the exuberance returned. "These are my people!" he yelled. One woman raced after his car shouting, "Piss on Oregon! Piss on Oregon!" Chicanos chanted "Viva Kennedy." Office workers showered him with confetti made from newspapers and phone books. Back at his hotel, he told campaign workers, "If I died in Oregon, I hope Los Angeles is Resurrection City." But it was clear to one reporter, who had covered him throughout the campaign, that he seemed a touch less confident than before, a bit more nervous. "Oregon had shaken Kennedy," he observed.[26]

The next day, Kennedy set out across the Central Valley, where he had built strong support among Chicano farm workers. United Farm Worker leader Cesar Chavez, often thought of as the Hispanic Martin Luther King, had agreed to be listed as a Kennedy delegate. Chavez later estimated that for every Chicano that worked for JFK in 1960, 50 worked for RFK in 1968.[27] Exuberant crowds again poured out, two to three thousand at each stop. Kennedy asked for their votes, and they screamed he had them. These last days of campaigning were not to win converts, but to solidify his support and to restore energy to the campaign.

In a Friday night speech in San Francisco, Kennedy accused McCarthy of distorting his record, including accusing Kennedy of being part of the decision to invade the Dominican Republic, something that had occurred months after Kennedy had left the Johnson administration. But Kennedy also pushed his own Vietnam critique. "We still seem to

hold a naïve faith in our military power," he observed. "We must abandon the futile dream of crushing the enemy's forces or his will to continue the struggle." That night Kennedy spoke to a gathering of
thousands in Oakland. The night before, Black Panthers had given him
a hard time when he appeared at a forum hosted by the Northern
California Black Caucus. But on this night, the Panthers responded to
the enthusiasm of the people, clearing a path for him to move through
the crowd. To one Oakland community activist, Kennedy was not
"the last of the great liberals" but "the last of the great believeables."[28]

McCarthy too was reaffirming his left credentials. Tom Wicker, writing in the *New York Times*, argued that McCarthy possessed "the most
radical theme of any man in the race." It was not just the war that he was
challenging but "the whole basis for that policy," critiquing the idea that
America should assume "the role of the world's judge and the world's
policeman." Among the "faulty assumptions" McCarthy sought to
counter were "America's moral mission in the world; the great threat
of China; the theory of monolithic Communist conspiracy" and,
most strikingly, "the duty to impose American idealism upon foreign
cultures."[29]

McCarthy also maintained the most star-studded entourage, cultural
figures like playwrights Arthur Miller and Neil Simon, novelist William
Styron, and poet Robert Lowell; movie stars, like Paul Newman and
Dustin Hoffman; and singers Paul Simon and Art Garfunkel. Kennedy
had his share, but football player-turned-actor Roosevelt Grier or singers
Andy Williams and Bobby Darrin hardly possessed the same cache.
Kennedy sometimes complained that McCarthy got the "A students."
He also got the "A celebrities."

On Saturday June 1, just three days before the primary, Kennedy and
McCarthy finally met at their long-anticipated debate. Like most debates
between political candidates, the experience never matched the expectations. Their positions on many crucial issues were similar. They mostly
set out to establish their credentials. Kennedy reiterated his past positions, reminding voters he had been a member of the National Security
Council, the Attorney General, and sat in the Cabinet. McCarthy could

only talk about his work on various congressional committees. Their differences on Vietnam were minor, as compared with Humphrey's or Nixon's. The one dramatic moment came in a discussion of improving economic opportunities and low-income housing. Kennedy pushed for federal programs for improved housing, along with getting the private sector to contribute. McCarthy agreed but also argued that low-income housing for ghetto residents should be built in rural areas and suburbs. Kennedy replied with a comment that some identified as demagoguery. "You say you are going to take ten thousand black people and move them into Orange County." Orange County was at that point among the most conservative counties in the nation, and Kennedy's charge distorted McCarthy's position. Most importantly, it sounded to people like he was playing to the white resentment festering in the country and buoying the third-party candidacy of George Wallace. For someone who had spent so much time cultivating the Black vote, this assertion was jolting.[30]

Not jolting enough. Most commentators saw the debate as a draw. By this point, voters had pretty much made up their minds. Tuesday evening began well for Kennedy with the news that the South Dakota primary had gone to him. The conservative *Rapid City Journal* called Kennedy's win "a smashing victory," noting that turnout was the largest in the state's history. Kennedy appeared pleased that he had done well in both blue-collar precincts and among American Indians. "In one county there were 858 Indian votes," he told reporters. "I got 856, Humphrey got two." And then to twist the knife just a bit, he smiled and said, "McCarthy got none."[31]

Of course, California was the crucial contest. The early returns looked positive for Kennedy, and nothing happened that evening to change things. By 10:30 p.m., sufficient voters had been tabulated for CBS to declare him the winner. Black and Chicano voters had come out in large numbers and their vote overcame McCarthy's suburban strength.

As Kennedy headed to the Ambassador Hotel, it was clear the victory had shifted his perspective. McCarthy was beaten and now the foe was Humphrey. "I've got to spend time going to the states," he told Richard Goodwin, "talking to delegates before it's too late. My only chance is to chase Hubert's ass all over the country. Maybe he'll fold." He even hinted, Goodwin later claimed, that they might quietly offer McCarthy the position of secretary of state in exchange for his withdrawal from the race.[32]

Kennedy called an old JFK hand Kenneth O'Donnell, who was watching the returns in Washington with Illinois congressman Dan Rostenkowski, a close ally of Chicago Mayor Richard Daley. He asked for Rostenkowski's support. The congressman replied, "Daley is my guy... You win California, you get Daley, we all come along." O'Donnell also believed that if he won California, Daley would back him. The pieces appeared to be dropping into place. When O'Donnell said that Kennedy now seemed "poised to win the nomination," he replied, "I think I may." Then, in a telling aside, he told JFK's old aide, "I feel now for the first time that I've shaken off the shadow of my brother. I feel I made it on my own."[33]

The day before, while campaigning in San Francisco's Chinatown, Robert and Ethel Kennedy were standing on the back seat of a convertible, waving to the crowds. They had been warned about the possibility of fireworks being set off, but when a string exploded near their car, people gasped. Ethel collapsed onto the floor of the car. Bobby seemed to momentarily twitch but then continued to wave. It seemed to unsettle the crowd and the reporters more than the candidate.[34]

The idea of an attempt on Kennedy's life had been present from the outset of the campaign. Sometimes it was addressed with dark humor, sometimes with grim determination. In Michigan, police spotted a man with a rifle on the roof across from Kennedy's hotel. When one of his aides went to draw the curtains, Kennedy responded. "Don't close them. If they're going to shoot, they'll shoot." Leaving the hotel by the basement garage, rather than main lobby, Kennedy rebuked his handlers. "We always get into the car in public. We're not going to start ducking now."[35] There had been threats throughout the campaign. "Why don't you all get out of Indiana before it's too late!" read one message sent to Ethel. Every week, the FBI provided press secretary Frank Mankiewicz with photos of potential assassins. Mankiewicz scanned the faces at airports and rallies. Asked by a reporter if he ever worried about being assassinated, Kennedy replied, "There's just no sense in worrying about those things. If they want to, they can get you."[36]

Normally Kennedy concluded his victory speeches by walking through the crowd to an exit and shaking hands with supporters. In fact, at the Ambassador, some of his people had begun to clear a path for him to do just this. They turned and saw that the candidate had instead headed in a different direction, through the kitchen. In the kitchen waited Sirhan Sirhan, a Palestinian immigrant who worked there, holding a small .22 caliber revolver. He reached out from the crowd and fired, hitting Kennedy in the head and wounding five others, all of whom survived. He was wrestled to the ground.

Rushed to the hospital, Kennedy clung to life for the next 24 hours. Ethel was able to listen to his heartbeat. "If he survives this, we'll make him president," promised civil rights leaders Walter Fauntroy and Hosea Williams. But he didn't. Twenty-six hours after he was shot, Frank Mankiewicz read the brief statement that "Robert Francis Kennedy died at 1:44 am...He was 42 years old."[37]

From the moment of the shooting, the reaction was clear and deeply felt. Roosevelt Grier, a giant of a man, put his head down on a table and cried. Reporters who had covered the campaign did the same. In the Kennedy suite in the hotel, civil rights leader John Lewis was awaiting Kennedy's return. When he saw the events on television, he remembered, "We all dropped to the floor, crying." He said that all he wanted to do was get out of Los Angeles. He took the first flight to Atlanta he could get, "and I think I cried all the way back."[38]

Kennedy's body was flown to New York on a plane dispatched by the White House. In a scene eerily reminiscent of the flight that brought JFK's body back from Dallas, Ted Kennedy sat with Ethel by the casket, just as Bobby had sat with Jackie.

The funeral was held at St. Patrick's Cathedral. Jackie Kennedy had arranged for Leonard Bernstein to choose and provide the music.

Lyndon Johnson, Hubert Humphrey, Eugene McCarthy, Richard Nixon, and Nelson Rockefeller all attended. So did conservative Barry Goldwater and socialist Michael Harrington, civil rights icon Julian Bond and segregationist senator James Eastland of Mississippi, poet Robert Lowell and conservative economist Milton Friedman, comedian Tommy Smothers and Cesar Chavez, and many others. Among those who had asked to be invited but had been denied were Los Angeles Mayor Sam Yorty, George Wallace, and the Rev. Billy Graham.[39] Ted Kennedy delivered the eulogy, stirring and substantive. "My brother need not be idealized...beyond what he was in life...to be remembered simply as a good and decent man...who saw wrong and tried to right it, saw suffering and tried to heal it, saw war and tried to stop it." He ended by quoting a line that RFK himself had used often during the campaign. "Some men see things as they are and say why. I dream things that never were, and say why not."[40]

A funeral train was to take the body to Arlington National Cemetery. Seven hundred guests were invited to join the ride. Kennedy's casket was placed in a picture-windowed car, propped up on chairs so it could be seen. Perhaps as many as two million people lined the tracks.[41] The outpouring of grief was palpable. The trip had been scheduled for four and a half hours. It took over eight. A brief candlelight service took place at Arlington, and then Robert Kennedy was buried next to his brother.

Tom Hayden was likely the New Left leader most sympathetic to Robert Kennedy. Friendly with journalist Jack Newfield, Hayden listened when Newfield told him about Kennedy's desire to reconcile hostility between African Americans and blue-collar whites. Hayden recalls Newfield telling him that Kennedy "agreed with you, but because of who he is, he can be elected president."[42] Just a month after being arrested among the Columbia demonstrators, Hayden was in California for the last days of the primary. When the shooting occurred, on what he called "another haunted night," he recounted that he "watched the constant reruns...I listened without hope to the periodic hospital reports...Jerry Rubin called in hysteria...I called a few close friends as if I might never talk to them again...I was behaving, without quite recognizing it, as one does before one's own death."[43]

Flying back to New York the next day, Hayden met up with Newfield and a few friends from the McCarthy campaign. Arriving very late at St. Patrick's Cathedral, where the public would be able to view the casket the next morning, they found hundreds of people already queuing up. A Kennedy aide recognized someone in their party and invited them in. "I sat down in a pew toward the back...It was a while before I noticed the coffin containing all that remained of last night's hopes of the poor." Tom Hayden—author of the Port Huron Statement, the essential founding document of the New Left; the veteran of numerous civil rights campaigns; who had traveled to Hanoi with anti-war compatriots; had joined the commune at Mathematics Hall as part of the Columbia strike only weeks before; and who was busy organizing the demonstrations that were being planned for the Democratic Convention later that summer—sat quietly in the church pew, broke down, and cried.[44]

Thinking about the losses of Kennedy and King, Hayden later observed, "I think Jack Newfield said it best when he said, 'after that, we became a generation of might-have-beens.'"[45]

17

Washington

The Poor People's Campaign

On May 2, 1968 the Rev. Ralph Abernathy, who had taken over as leader of the Southern Christian Leadership Conference after the death of Martin Luther King, conducted a memorial service at Memphis' Lorraine Motel, on the balcony where King had been murdered a month before. Coretta Scott King laid a wreath and Abernathy unveiled a marble marker on the spot where King fell. Along with a gold star and a large, engraved cross was the Biblical inscription: "They said one to another, behold, here cometh the dreamer. Let us slay him and we shall see what becomes of his dreams."

Abernathy then led a group of nearly 1,500 marchers for three miles through some of the African American neighborhoods of Memphis. At the end, buses waited to carry 500 of the marchers to Marks, Mississippi, the first stop on their journey to Washington, DC.

Four days later, Abernathy led 1,000 marchers across the famed Edmund Pettis Bridge in Selma, Alabama, scene of the brutal assault by police on civil rights marchers in 1965, which Abernathy called "a sacred spot."

The caravan then moved on to Montgomery, site of the 1956 bus boycott that first brought King to national attention, laying a wreath at the Dexter Avenue Baptist Church, King's congregation in the mid-1950s. It then traveled to Birmingham, where several major civil rights confrontations had occurred and where four teenage girls had been killed in 1963 in a tragic church bombing.

In a matter of days, these marchers of the Poor People's Campaign had touched several of the most sacred and symbolic places of the civil rights movement, linking their current effort to the most evocative sites of this history. In Atlanta, Mayor Ivan Allen warmly welcomed the marchers. That night SCLC put on a benefit concert—featuring Harry Belafonte, The Temptations, and The Supremes—that drew 13,000 people.

The Poor People's Campaign was off to a conspicuous and positive start. In a month filled with headline-grabbing political and social events, the campaign that King and others had begun envisioning in 1967, seemed to be taking shape, garnering positive press, numerous volunteers, and general public approval. King's dream appeared to be alive. Over the next weeks, the nation would come to see, after he had been slain, "what became of his dreams."[1]

> *The Poor People's March on Washington went ahead. Resurrection City was setup on 13 May and dismantled by the police in late June—with 1600 regular troops on standby. Protesting on the steps of the capitol, the Revd Ralph Abernathy and 343 of his followers were arrested. Some of the refugees from Resurrection City merged into the ghetto and another bout of rioting began.*
>
> *The Poor People's Campaign was a resounding flop.*[2]

Most of the goals of the Poor People's Campaign never came to fruition, often beset by both personnel and logistical problems. What is striking, however, is the way it has been erased or minimized in the history of these years. The first paragraph quoted above, for example, is the only mention of the PPC in a 797-page tome on the decade. Another comprehensive work on the Sixties devotes significantly more time to discussing Sharon Tate and the Charles Manson murders than the PPC.[3] The second characterization above begins the single paragraph on the PPC in a third history of the 1960s. The entire campaign is dismissed with brief comments, such as Abernathy "lacked charisma" and the campaign "lacked drama." A gathering of some 75,000 at the Lincoln Memorial is mentioned in passing mainly noting the booing of Hubert Humphrey and the cheers for Eugene McCarthy. "Then most went home," it concludes.[4] In other histories of the 1960s, and even in some specifically focused on 1968, the campaign is often ignored altogether.[*]

Nonetheless, there is an important story here that deserves significantly more attention than it has been given.[5] Throughout May and June there were many dramatic and compelling moments in the campaign, across the nation and especially in Washington, following the paths that had been laid out in the planning for the PPC. And these moments demonstrated many of the interconnected political and cultural themes that epitomized events of 1968. Mule-drawn wagons carried poor people across the nation, creating poignant images of the impoverished slowly heading to the nation's capital. Numerous multiracial and multicultural bus caravans departed from cities all cross the country. In addition to the gathering at the Lincoln Memorial, there was a Mothers' Day March in DC that drew several thousand. Coretta King, joined by Ethel Kennedy and Betty Friedan, led the march through the areas damaged by the riots that erupted after Martin Luther King's death.[6]

And then there was Resurrection City, an encampment erected in a grassy area that stretched from the Lincoln Memorial toward the Washington Monument along the side of the National Mall. Several thousand people settled into plywood A-frame huts, intending to live there as they lobbied Congress.

While the plans for the Poor People's Campaign had been developing since King's declarations of 1967, support for the PPC exploded in the wake of his assassination. "The phone started ringing off the hook," recalled on SCLC staff member. "The black community started calling and saying, 'We want to help, we want to help,'" recalled another. Black activists from the NAACP to the Black Panthers reconsidered their initial hesitations. Funds began to pour in, including from a number of celebrities. The Hollywood Support Committee sponsored a fundraiser

---

* I am not guiltless in this area either. I am embarrassed to note that while there are over 200 documents in the reader I coedited of primary sources from the 1960s, there is not one on the Poor People's Campaign.

at the Hollywood Bowl, putting on a sold-out concert featuring Barbra Streisand, Harry Belafonte, Bill Cosby, and Herb Alpert and the Tijuana Brass.[7] Cosby, Sidney Poitier, and others joined with the SCLC staff to create a committee that would provide entertainment in Resurrection City. Marlon Brando, TV host Merv Griffin, and comedian Steve Allen were among those who did TV and radio spots in support of the campaign.

King's death also spurred the connections that were being developed between the Black activists and other activists of color. This had always been part of King's vision. Chicano leader Reies Tijerina declared, "We're going to strengthen our ties, our unity. We have no other choice."[8]

King's vision found audiences across the landscape. *Look* magazine had planned to publish an essay by King, "Showdown for Nonviolence," before his death. Its publication went ahead, appearing two weeks after King's murder. In it, he argued that the PPC would restore nonviolence as the crucial tactic of the movement, though this time its "economic problems—the right to live, to have a job and income"—would be central. It is also clear that King was well aware of the growing militancy within the movement for racial justice and that he needed to connect his message to it. The "Washington demonstration" would need to be "militant, massive nonviolence," he wrote, as "the discontent is so deep, the anger so ingrained, the despair, the restlessness so wide" that something is needed "to serve as a channel through which these deep emotional feelings, these deep angry feelings, can be funneled."[9]

For King, this action would mean moving into new areas and employing new tactics. There would still be nonviolent disruptions of government operations leading to arrests, with the hope that the publicity and indignation would bring out large numbers of new volunteers. This had been a tactic of the civil rights movement for years. Images of Southern sheriffs beating and arresting demonstrators would now be replaced with Washington police jailing poor people, which would generate attention and sympathy.

In addition, new strategies emerged. A national boycott of specific industries or shopping areas was planned, aiming to coerce business leaders into pressuring Congress. The coalitions that were to be created with other non-white movements also brought new questions into the discussion. Tijerina and other Chicano leaders had argued that the 1848 Treaty of Guadalupe-Hidalgo, which ended the Mexican War and ceded vast acreage to the U.S., had promised land grants for people living in the newly ceded area. These had never been granted. Further, they claimed that the Treaty had also promised support for maintenance of both the language and culture of the Southwestern population, again something never pursued by the U.S. Government. By 1968, language and culture had become key elements in the growing movement for Hispanic rights and identity.[10]

As the planning proceeded, Abernathy and SCLC decided against King's idea of mass arrests, likely fearing they might fail to gather significant sympathy and backfire into accusations of lawlessness. "Law and Order" had become a slogan of the candidacies of both Richard Nixon and third-party candidate George Wallace—a coded appeal more about race than about crime in the streets. Instead, SCLC opted for the creation of a tent city, "a model for the rest of the nation to emulate," Abernathy would later write. People of all "races, ethnic backgrounds, and religious beliefs" living together in "peace and mutual respect." Using this city as a base, they would then "go from government agency to government agency, representing the poor" by asking for "concrete things from our government, the richest in the world."[11] At the end of April, even before the ceremony at the Lorraine Motel that had initiated the caravans heading to Washington, lobbying in Washington had begun. The plan had been to create a multiracial movement of the poor. Yet, it was also to be a movement led by the poor, themselves. This had begun at meetings King had held in spring. As they organized for coming to DC, a "Committee of 100" was created, the "advance lobby caravan" of the PPC. It was essential that this committee be made up of representatives from various ethnic and racial groups, all from low-income backgrounds.[12]

The Committee of 100 issued its own Declaration, first listing grievances against the government and then followed by a set of demands.

"Affluent Americans are locked into suburbs of physical comfort and mental insecurity" the Declaration noted, "poor Americans are locked inside ghettos of material privation and spiritual debilitation."[13] There followed a list of five demands:

1. A meaningful job at a living wage for every employable citizen.
2. A secure and adequate income for all who cannot find jobs or for whom employment is inappropriate.
3. Access to land as a means to income and livelihood.
4. Access to capital as a means of full participation in the economic life of America.
5. Recognition by law of the right of people affected by government programs to play a truly significant role in determining how they are designed and carried out.[14]

The Committee then began targeted lobbying efforts aimed at a number of the offices in the executive branch. At the Justice Department on April 29, Abernathy argued that the department had failed to enforce existing laws and blamed that failure for a lack of respect for justice, which led to a citizens' willingness to engage in riotous behavior. The particular needs of the Latino poor led to concerns about "'green-card' strikebreakers" being used against the United Farm Workers' grape strike in California as well as concerns about "illegal jailings" and "brutal beatings of Mexican-Americans," throughout the Southwest. Concern was also expressed for the rights of Indians, including protection from police violence and a protection of their hunting and fishing rights.[15]

After presenting their arguments, the Committee of 100 initiated a tactic it would employ throughout the campaign, having individual poor participants recount personal experiences to reinforce the general points. One poor Black woman demanded that the Fair Housing Act be enforced, while a migrant farm worker described his living conditions as "legitimate murder."[16] Of all the executive offices that the PPC would visit, the most receptive audience was at Justice. One scholar has summarized the role of Attorney General Ramsey Clark in the entire campaign as doing "more than any other prominent official in the executive branch to see that the poor people's movement not be turned away from the nation's capital without some victories."[17] Justice's Community Relations Service division (CRS) was headed by Roger Wilkins, nephew of NAACP head Roy Wilkins and a central Justice Department advocate for civil rights since arriving in Washington in the early1960s. The CRS would be crucial in aiding the caravans that moved across the country and made various attempts to alleviate problems that developed in Resurrection City.

The FBI also falls technically under the aegis of the Justice Department, and the antipathy that FBI Director J. Edgar Hoover felt for Martin Luther King has been well documented. Plans for the PPC only intensified Hoover's hostility to King and led to his directing FBI agents to move to limit or suppress the movement. These efforts included disinformation campaigns as well as attempts to disrupt and undermine its actions. It would later become clear that FBI undercover agents infiltrated Resurrection City, to serve as informants, at the least, if not *agent provocateurs*.[18]

The other executive departments the PPC targeted reflected many of the issues crucial to poor people. Following Justice, Abernathy led a group to the Department of Labor. Arguing strongly for jobs programs—which every public and private analysis of U.S. racial problems cited as a key to their solution—the PPC representatives advocated for job bills, fair employment regulations, and on-the-job training programs. Again, movement leaders like Denver's Corky Gonzalez joined representatives of the poor from across the nation— from New York's Puerto Rican community to Eastern Kentucky to Mississippi to Oklahoma Indians—in telling their personal stories and denouncing government inaction. Secretary of Labor Willard Wirtz echoed Ramsey Clark's support for the aims of the PPC and promised "actions—not words."[19]

The issue of hunger fell under the aegis of the Department of Agriculture, which became the scene of many demonstrations during these weeks. Several proposals to combat hunger had failed to move forward, though the department had issued several reports that had cited serious concerns about "chronic hunger and malnutrition." The PPC asked for expanded food stamp programs, school lunches, and aid to small farmers. In addition to hunger, the regulation of agribusiness fell to this department, and this was of crucial concern to farm workers, for example, attempting to organize, as with the United Farm Workers. Personal testimonies of hunger, of trouble with federal programs like food stamps, and the obvious relationship between unemployment and poor housing and diet, buttressed the call for government action with personal stories.[20]

Unlike his colleagues at Justice and Labor, Agriculture Secretary Orville Freeman, was resistant to the Committee's demands, citing how much he thought his department had already done. He later declared that he thought PPC demands were really a "publicity stunt," that "they didn't want anything done, they wanted attention." He also claimed that free food stamps was a bad idea, fearing the poor would use the stamps for things other than food and they would still go hungry. Freeman also would not listen to any suggestions about the impact of government subsidies on the business of agriculture as well as about the rights of those who worked to produce the nation's food.[21]

Similar actions were taken at other departments whose functions involved issues affecting the poor. At the Department of Health, Education, and Welfare (HEW), SCLC's Bernard Lafayette read a statement about the problem of health care for the poor.

> We come to ask why the American know-how that can move a wounded Marine from the jungles of Vietnam to the finest medical care in minutes cannot and does not do the same for a sick child in the Mississippi delta or on an Indian reservation...
>
> We come to tell you that there are children in this country who have never been examined by a doctor or a dentist...
>
> We come to tell you that the poor live in open contact with serious health hazards—rats and vermin; accumulation of waste and garbage; sewage lines and water lines so dangerously close that the contents sometimes mingle.

This was followed by a long list of demands to improve the health of the nation's poor, from health care programs to Medicare expansions to include the poor of all ages, to sanitation programs, and more.

HEW also dealt with educational issues, another area frequently cited as closely related to poverty. The Committee called for programs that would lead to massive increases in educational spending as well as those that would "permit black, brown, and white children to express their own worth and dignity as human beings."

At the Department of Housing and Urban Development, Bernard Lafayette declared that the time had come to listen to the poor about what they needed, rather than "the builder, the banker, and the bureaucrat." The Committee called for more low-income housing, but also to involve those below the poverty line in a number of ways, from planning new developments to employing poor people to work in the construction and rehabilitation of low-income housing.

At the State Department, the issue of the Treaty of Guadalupe-Hidalgo was the topic of debate. The Department of the Interior contained the Bureau of Indian affairs. Indian activist Melvin Tom identified issues crucial to American Indians and declared that the government "operated under a racist and immoral and paternalistic colonialist system...The Indian system is sick, paternalism is the virus, and the Secretary of the Interior is the carrier."[22]

Some of this received coverage in the press; some went completely ignored. And the tone of the reporting ranged from sympathetic to severely critical. For anyone paying attention, however, the declarations and demands of the Committee of 100 vividly sketched out the problems facing the multiracial world of America's poor.

As representatives of the Committee of 100 marched from one executive branch office to another, thousands of other marchers left for Washington in the caravans that would come from all parts of the country, intending to converge on the nation's capital, populate the tent city under construction and, through their presence and persistence, start America down the road to eliminating poverty.

The Mule Caravan that had left Memphis after the King ceremony proved extremely popular. The national press and network news programs offered frequent stories about it. The "mule skinners" who drove the caravan became objects of interest for both reporters and onlookers. Two of the mules were named "Stennis" and "Eastland," after Mississippi's two segregationist senators, something the crowds that came out to view the caravan found hilarious. There was actually no possibility that the Mule Caravan could walk to Washington in time to join the planned actions, but their presence on the road kept the PPC in the news. But as this caravan was essentially all Black, it partly concealed how multiracial and multi-ethnic the overall endeavor was.[23]

The caravans organized in other parts of the country, planning to come to Washington by bus, were much more diverse than the Mule Caravan and did make it across the country in plenty of time. These caravans were sometimes identified by the departure points—the Eastern, Midwestern, Southern, and Western Caravans—or by names that that signaled their identity, such as the Indian Trails Caravan or the Freedom Train. The Western Caravan may have evidenced the PPC's greatest initial success in creating a multiracial cohort. On the bus 47 Mexican-Americans, including leaders and members of the militant Brown Berets of East Los Angeles, joined the predominantly African American bus riders, joking they would "ride in the back." Brown Beret leader Carlos Montes came to believe the trip was a "good experience," one that lessened some of the prejudice he felt some Chicanos held for Black people. For them, the "caravan was eye-opening."[24]

Leaving Los Angeles on May 15, the Western Caravan moved through the Southwest, in some places holding significant rallies, while in others, like El Paso, running into the Texas Rangers, who ushered them into the El Paso Coliseum, ostensibly for their own protection but likely to contain them in a closed area where authorities could maintain surveillance and control. In Albuquerque, Ralph Abernathy joined Tijerina in leading a procession that included a number of religious leaders, ending with a rally that featured speeches by Marlon Brando, Abernathy, Tijerina, and several Indian leaders. At each stop, new people joined the caravan.[25]

In Denver, the Western Caravan linked up with the San Francisco Caravan, and together they moved on to Washington. The joint caravan now contained 18 buses as well as various cars and trucks. The people on the buses became a new community. "We sing, hold philosophical discussions…play checkers and learned Spanish," one rider recalled. They sang old labor songs, civil rights anthems, and renditions of Spanish songs like "La Cucaracha," but with new lyrics reflecting the present moment and endeavor. After eight days on the road, they reached Washington.[26] Meanwhile, the Indian Trails Caravan had departed from Seattle, taking a route that wound through northern reservations before arriving in DC.

On Monday, May 13, a day after Coretta King had led the Mothers' Day March through Washington, Ralph Abernathy stood on the National Mall, in the shadow of the Lincoln Memorial. He turned to a young American Indian girl and asked for her permission to use the land, despite already having a permit from the federal government. When she granted permission, Abernathy proceeded to pound the first stake into the ground of what would become Resurrection City.

For several months, as other elements of the PPC were being organized, a small group of architects and urban planners had been planning for the tent city. They ultimately settled on a plan for small individual units, built of plywood and 2x4s. Prefabricated parts were created so that when construction began on site, homes could be built quickly, and individuals could construct their own houses.

The initial enthusiasm of the project paralleled that of the other early aspects of the campaign. Volunteers included "suburban housewives and do-it-yourself husbands, Washington high school students, college students from Berkeley, Michigan and Harvard, a carpenter from New Hampshire and a minister from New York, and a number of Catholic brothers," recalled the chief architect. In addition to the individual houses, there would be a dining hall, a cultural center, and a daycare center. The optimism of the venture buoyed the leaders. People came "from all of the poor areas of the country…all races, and creeds, and colors," one PPC coordinator noted. "If you can gather these folks together, and harness their energies, that is seeds for revolution right there."[27]

This all evoked the Bonus Marchers who had journeyed to Washington in the late spring and early summer of 1932 to inhabit a tent city and lobby the government to pass the Bonus Bill, which would have immediately granted to World War I veterans a bonus planned for 1945. The Hoover Administration ultimately called out federal troops to drive the Bonus Marchers out and burn down their tent city, for which it was severely criticized. Keen to avoid this kind of criticism, the government negotiated with the PPC, agreeing to a permit to run from May 11 to June 16, with a maximum population of 3,000. Firearms, liquor, and open fires were prohibited. SCLC was to provide sanitation, garbage collection, and bathrooms. Park Police were not allowed to enter the city without permission from the PPC.

A short ceremony followed Abernathy's driving of the first stake. The newly trained "foremen" helped individual participants gather their pre-fab materials and build their homes. While individuals built their own homes, community buildings and spaces were constructed. "Main Street" was the site of the telephone and mail services, as well as the Dining Hall, where residents would receive three meals a day. Only one meal was hot and it had to be cooked offsite and trucked in; but for many of the poor, consistently available food was a new experience. The Coretta Scott King Day Care Center housed a Head Start Program for the children of the city. Volunteer doctors, nurses, dentists, and public health experts provided health care. Resurrection City even had its own zip code.

An Entertainment Committee was established with the help of Bill Cosby and Sidney Poitier. A stage was built and top-flight entertainers agreed to pay their own way to Washington to perform. One resident recalls seeing both Harry Bellefonte and Cosby; another remembers seeing James Brown, Little Richard, Mahalia Jackson, and Ray Charles.[28] At the Many Races Soul Center, people from the Highlander Folk School and the Smithsonian created programs to offer cultural understandings across races. Some featured well-known performers like folk singer Pete Seeger or civil rights icon Bernice Reagon, founder of the Freedom Singers. There were discussions or informal sing-a-longs featuring artists from different racial and cultural backgrounds.[29]

The Poor People's University offered lectures and workshops at a downtown college campus. Speakers included socialist Michael Harrington, radical journalist I.F. Stone, anti-war activist David Dellinger, author Alex Haley, and Chicano leader Corky Gonzalez. Workshop topics ranged from "English as a Racist Language" and "The Negro in American Literature." to "The History of Violent and Non-Violent Protest" and "How to Talk to Your Congressman and Get Results."[30]

Some structural problems inevitably emerged. The original plans had called for tapping into existent water and drainage systems, but this never worked. The population swelled beyond the 3,000 person limit, reaching nearly 7,000 by June. Despite personal discomfort, many residents found the experience positive. "It was really like camping out," one young man remembered. "They provided running water. We were able to brush our teeth and wash our face. They provided food." But for many, the problems began to multiply too quickly. The city became "almost a microcosm of an over-crowded big-city ghetto," recalled Andrew Young—civil rights activist and future Ambassador to the United Nations. Still most of the residents knew why they were there and understood that the hardships were just a circumstance of their political effort. "It ain't no picnic living here," Chicagoan Mary Hyde recalled. "We've lived with trouble all of our lives and we're here to stop trouble." For Dempsey Price, "I'm here because I'm 59 years old and there are people who still call me boy."[31]

And then there were the marshals. Not wishing to ask the Washington police to provide security, the PPC decided to have round-the-clock patrols to keep out nonresidents, prevent vandalism, and keep trouble in check. And unlike the police that most non-whites had dealt with for their entire lives, these security forces would come from the populace and have their support and respect.

Many of the marshals had been recruited among the young men coming to Resurrection City, including some from the street gangs the PPC had hoped to draw into the movement. They had all signed pledges "to safeguard lives and property, maintain order and discipline; to inspire strength and confidence in peaceful non-violent action against oppression and intimidation." But there had been no time for training, no possibility of drawing them into the idea of nonviolence. PPC officials and coordinators now faced the additional task of marshalling the marshals. "I bought many bus tickets and shipped people out," one recounted, for "insubordination...getting drunk and messing with women or for stealing."[32]

Stories of the internal problems began to seep into press coverage, those of violence naturally garnering the most attention. Some felt the reporting was exaggerated, and some believed violent encounters had been fomented by outside agitators who had insinuated themselves into the city. Still, there is ample evidence that a number of marshals instigated violence and harassment. These reports began to diminish the public support for the campaign. Inside the city, they became one of the factors that began to dispirit the residents. Overall, *Newsweek* depicted "true-to-life squalor, an ill-housed, ill-fed, self-segregated, absentee-run slum afflicted with low morale, deepening restiveness, and free-floating violence."[33]

Other dispiriting elements followed. Many accused Abernathy and other SCLC leaders of choosing to live in a more comfortable place, the Black-owned Pitts Motel, where SCLC held press conferences and the leaders took rooms. And then the rains came. It began raining on May 23 and rained, sometimes torrentially, for 11 of the next 14 days. Resurrection City turned into a waterlogged bog, with deep puddles throughout. The roof of the Dining Hall tent came down in one downpour. The sanitation facilities became sufficiently compromised, leading Roger Wilkins to send in a team from the Public Health Service who found the potential for serious disease "very high." One SCLC board member who came to visit in June bitterly complained, "The staff of the SCLC is living at the Pitts Motel while the poor people are up to their ass in mud."[34]

The residents continued their daily lobbying, arriving at one department after another, meeting with members of the House and Senate, but making little apparent progress. Some actions took the form of public protests sure to elicit press coverage. Twenty-five American Indian men,

dressed in their tribal costumes, including face paint, carrying toma-
hawks, and peace pipes, marched to the Supreme Court, looking to one
observer like "a war party on patrol." In the lobby of the Supreme Court
building, they lit a peace pipe and, after waiting for an hour, began to
drum and chant. The justices never appeared.[35]

At the Agriculture Department, Jesse Jackson led a group focusing on
hunger into the department cafeteria. They filled their trays. Jackson
then announced, "the government owes us a lot and they just began to
pay a little bit of it with this lunch." SCLC did pay for the lunches later,
but the meaning behind the protest was clear.[36]

Despite the initial national enthusiasm for the campaign, many
Congressional leaders had been cool about it from the start. This
included powerful Southern Democratic senators who characterized the
coming campaign in starkly negative terms, citing their fears of violence
and of pandering to the poor. Majority Whip Russell Long of Louisiana
threatened to censure or expel any senator who supported "bending the
knee to the lawbreakers." West Virginia's Robert Byrd pushed for a DC-
wide ban on the PPC. Arkansas' John McClellan took to the Senate
floor to accuse Abernathy of trying to create violent incidents, attacked
"permissive liberal" judges, and claimed that "recruits for the march are
being told to go to Washington one night and get on welfare the next
day." He concluded with a harrowing picture of Black militants infiltrat-
ing the movement to foment rioting, looting, and armed insurrection.[37]

So, despite some sympathetic responses from a few of the executive
department heads and the initial public support of the campaign, the
lobbying efforts showed little progress. Congress seemed unmoved by
the arguments being made or the mere presence of Resurrection City.
Hope began to focus on Solidarity Day, initially planned for May 30, as
the last chance to ignite the movement and move official Washington
into action. The date had to be postponed until mid-June, as SCLC
leaders realized how overextended they had become with the other
aspects of the PPC. Long-time civil rights activist Bayard Rustin, the
prime coordinator of the 1963 Mach on Washington, was brought in to
coordinate the Day. Attempting to streamline the call of the event,

Rustin issued a revised list of demands, which some applauded but many found lacking. The Vietnam War was no longer discussed, as were the land issues so crucial to Chicano participants. King's radical vision seemed to have faded from these new demands. In addition, Rustin had issued the demands without gaining the approval of Abernathy or the SCLC, in general. After several days of argument and internal squabbling, Rustin quit on June 7. This only fueled more press coverage of the tumult within the PPC.[38]

The task of pulling off the daylong event, scheduled for June 19 ("Juneteenth"), fell to Sterling Tucker, the DC Urban League Director. As SCLC planned, so did the DC authorities. Eleven hundred National Guardsmen and 500 police reserves were ready to aid the regular DC police force. This was not going to be 1963 all over again.

Regardless of the short time available, the differing objectives of the campaigners, and the fears of local officials, Tucker and his staff were able to pull off a remarkable achievement. They made it clear that this was to be a one-day demonstration and that all visitors should arrive and depart on that day, and that they were to bring their own food. Children under the age of 14 were discouraged. They planned a three-part event: entertainment from 10 to noon, hosted by actor Ossie Davis; a march; and then speeches at the Lincoln Memorial. While police and press estimated the crowd at around 75,000, Tucker thought it was larger. The actual number is less relevant than the mere fact of a large, midweek turnout for a campaign that seemed to have declining public support. Press reports noted that half of the crowd was white.[39] All the presidential candidates were invited, but only Eugene McCarthy and Hubert Humphrey made a brief appearance, and neither spoke.

James Bevel, whose civil rights activism stretched back to the Nashville Sit-Ins of 1960, began the speeches. He was followed by representatives of most of the groups who made up the PPC coalition, as well as United Auto Workers president Walter Reuther and representatives of the major civil rights organizations. Songs from well-known artists broke the litany of the speeches. Coretta Scott King read a telegram of greeting from Ethel Kennedy. She then went on to condemn poverty as "producing a most deadly kind of violence...Starving a child is violence...discrimination against a workingman is violence...contempt for equality is violence." She ended her speech evoking King's "I Have a Dream Speech," the crowd taking up the chant of the last line, "Free at last, thank God a'mighty I'm free at last." Gospel singer Mahalia Jackson followed Mrs. King.[40]

Ralph Abernathy spoke next. Never as great an orator as his friend Martin Luther King, Abernathy nonetheless gave a powerful speech, one the *New York Tines* described as "militant."[41] He attacked the "unjust, immoral, and tragic escalation" of Vietnam, noting that the "premise of the Great Society was burned to ashes by the napalm in Vietnam." He criticized the failure of the various executive departments and Congressional committees. Drawing on his political and religious focus, he declared, "I see nothing in my Bible about the riches of the world or this nation belonging to [Rep.] Wilbur Mills or [Sen.] Russell Long; nor do they belong to General Motors, the grape growers in California, the cotton kings in Mississippi, and the oil baron in Texas." He proudly declared, "There is no need of God's children going hungry in 1968."[42] After Abernathy, Aretha Franklin led the singing of a hymn.

Jesse Jackson then spoke briefly, and the day ended with a mass singing of "We Shall Overcome" and a final benediction. And the participants, many of whom had already been slowly dispersing for a few hours, headed home—to Resurrection City or back to the places from which they had journeyed to the nation's capital. The organizers always knew that Solidarity Day could never match the sacred place of the 1963 March on Washington, but it did demonstrate that, amid all the negative press and all the competing events of the day, people could still be drawn to the cause.

The leaders had assumed that they would be given a grace period once their permit for Resurrection City had expired, but it wasn't to be. On Monday morning, June 24, 1,500 police surrounded the site. "The permit on this property has expired" a police loudspeaker boomed. "You must leave here within the next 56 minutes to avoid arrest and prosecution."

By this point most of the residents had already departed. Only about 150 remained. Yet fully armed police—with riot helmets and flak jackets, brandishing shotguns, tear gas, and billy clubs—moved onto the grounds. It took about 90 minutes to clear the site and level the A-frames. "The jerry-built town came apart as easily as a frontier set on a studio backlot," *Newsweek* reported, "exposing the encampment's seamy artifacts— rag-bag blankets, game-legged army cots, ranks of road-worn shoes."[43] As a reporter for the *Wall Street Journal* concluded, "the villains in the public's view have turned out to be the demonstrators themselves." They were no longer "the sympathy-deserving downtrodden, but rather a bunch of unruly, undeserving riffraff."[44]

Two months after the murder of Martin Luther King, all the enthusiasm and commitment that had been poured into what turned out to be the last campaign of his life, evaporated on the streets of Washington and in the mud of Resurrection City. Government harassment, political resistance, poor planning, a nation distracted by war, and a year with more political turmoil than any in memory contributed to the decline, fall, and dismissal of the Poor Peoples' Campaign. Its story was moved to the sidelines by all the other events of the day.

A rich history remains, however, one too often neglected, part of which is an answer to the question etched into the marble marker at the Lorraine Motel: "Let us slay him and we shall see what becomes of his dreams." What America came to see was far from what King and his legions had dreamt. And far from what future generations might have wished.

18

Prague Summer

At the 1967 Czechoslovak Writers Congress, Ludvik Vaculik's condemnation of the Communist Party, as we have seen, had led to his expulsion from the Party. In April 1968, as part of the thaw in press censorship and the encouragement of free speech, Alexander Dubček had annulled the punishments against Vaculik and the other writers who expressed critical remarks in 1967. Two months later, Vaculik issued what David Caute called "the most eloquent and famous challenge to the Dubček regime's half-cocked liberalization."[1] Vaculik's manifesto, "Two Thousand Words to Workers, Farmers, Scientists, Artists, and Everyone," took direct aim at the Party and its detrimental effect on Czech society.

Speaking as a communist—again in direct contrast to the Western notion of the political ideology of the Czech dissidents—Vaculik reaffirmed the role of the communists in the emerging reforms ("we oppose the view…that a democratic revival can be achieved without the communists, or even in opposition to them.") but chastised the Party leadership. They had "transformed a political party and an alliance based on ideas into an organization for exerting power, one that proved highly attractive to individuals eager to wield authority, to cowards who took the safe and easy route and to people with a bad conscience…We all bear responsibility," he admitted, "for the present state of affairs. But those among us who are communists bear more than others." Cosigned by 70 leading Czech writers and intellectuals and appearing in four Czech publications, "Two Thousand Words" was a warning to Czechs to avoid letting the reins of reform slip from their hands and back into those of self-aggrandizing bureaucrats. "We all know, and every worker knows especially, that they had virtually no say in deciding anything." It was clear that some party leaders had recognized the error of their ways and "they are redressing old wrongs, rectifying mistakes, handing back powers of decision-making to rank-and-file party members and members of the public." Everyone felt the strong sense of "experiencing a regenerative process of democratization." They also knew, however, that in the summer "we are inclined to let everything slip." However, "we can safely say that our dear adversaries will not give themselves a summer break."

The reformers had called for the election of a new Party Congress, which would elect a new Central Committee. "Let us demand the departure of people who abused their power, damaged public property, and acted dishonorably or brutally," Vaculik declared. "Let us form committees for the defense of free speech...Let us give support to the police when they are prosecuting genuine wrongdoers, for it is not our aim to create anarchy or a state of general uncertainty." Prague Spring was the first step, "a great opportunity...as it was after the end of the war." Now the Czech people needed to seize the day. "We have the chance to take into our own hands our common cause that, for working purposes, we call socialism, and give it a form more appropriate to our once-good reputation and to the fairly good opinion we used to have of ourselves." Vaculik concluded with a realistic view of what was to come. "The spring is over and will never return. By winter we will know all."[2]

Vaculik's manifesto put Dubček in an extremely difficult position. The Soviets had always raised the specter of having to put down "counter-revolutionary" forces in Czechoslovakia. In 1956, they had made this charge the rationale for their invasion of Hungary. Evidently Brezhnev called Dubček the day of the publication of the manifesto, citing the document as evidence of just such a plot. The manifesto also emboldened conservatives within the Czech government. Even some of the moderates were worried. A meeting of the Presidium was called for that night. One member warned Dubček, "If we do not put a stop to this now, the tanks will solve it."[3]

Beginning in the late spring, Brezhnev held a series of meetings, as well as phone conversations, with Dubček. The Soviet leader's tone ranged from anger to paternal familiarity. He fluctuated between the familiar and formal verb forms and often called Dubček "Sasha." One letter was addressed "Dear Aleksandr Stepanovich." Slovaks do not employ patronymics—using one's family name in greetings—but Russians do. This greeting suggested Dubček was one of the family.

For Brezhnev, the scope of the problems led far beyond the Czechoslovakian borders. A number of Eastern bloc countries, including East Germany and Poland, remained solidly aligned with the Soviets and their leader. Yet Polish students had taken heart from the events in Prague. "Long live Czechoslovakia," they had chanted as they battled police in March. Other bloc countries were showing independent streaks, some more clearly than others. Tito's Yugoslavia had always walked an independent line, and now Rumania and Hungary were agitating for increased autonomy. The French and Italian Communist Parties, the two largest in Western Europe, both called on the Soviets to abandon any plans to invade. To the Soviet leadership, advances in Czechoslovakia threatened further changes in the Soviet bloc. Based on a prior agreement, Warsaw Pact military exercises began in Czechoslovakia in late June. Though concluded in early July, the Soviet troops did not immediately leave the country.

Despite the presence of the troops and the growing worries about Soviet countermeasures, the streets of Prague continued to exhibit the same spirit as in the spring, especially among the young. In early August, a *New York Times* story concluded, "If you are under 30, Prague seems to be the place to be this summer." Prague was "thronged" with "young sympathizers from the West." "The Czechs are the good guys this year," an American expatriate observed. "To give a human face to socialism," a young French woman declared. "How beautiful this is to us… That is exactly what we wanted to do in Paris this spring." The young debated openly all over the city. "To them, the atmosphere is electrifying." Young Czechs and young foreigners "drink beer together," "they go to the movies," and "hold joint dance and folksong sessions." "With their long hair,

beards, turtleneck sweaters, levis and their relaxed bearing," it was difficult to tell whether a young person was Czech or foreign, the *Times*
reporter observed. Graffiti decorated the walls of the city—some in
Czech, some in English. "Viva Dubček and his boys!" "Kennedy
Everywhere!—Johnson Never!"[4]

Over the course of July and into early August, Brezhnev and Dubček
continued their careful ritual dance—Dubček trying to mollify the
Soviet leader while maintaining the path the Czech reformers had laid
out, Brezhnev trying to cajole Dubček back into line. At one meeting,
Soviet Premier Alexei Kosygin was more blunt. "We can assure you," he
told Dubček, "that if we wanted to, we could occupy your entire country
in the course of twenty-four hours." Reminding the Czech leader that
his country was part of the Soviet bloc, Kosygin reiterated long-standing
Soviet policy. "We have only one border, the border of the West…It is
the border of the Second World War, it is a border from which we shall
never retreat."[5]

In the face of ongoing Soviet pressure, Dubček began to promise concessions about reining in free speech and limiting the reform. Still, he
remained vague about his plans for its implementation. In one speech,
he denounced all "anti-Soviet" and "anti-socialist obscenities," but proclaimed that the Czechs would alone control their own affairs.[6] *Pravda*,
the official newspaper of the Soviet Communist Party, began to argue
that the ultimate goal of the Czech revolutionaries was the reestablishment of "a bourgeois regime." At a small meeting on the Czech–Soviet
border, Brezhnev blasted the crimes of the Czech "counter-
revolutionaries" and the publication of articles by "bourgeois revision-
ists." Dubček was encouraged to postpone the upcoming Party Congress.
He continued to pay lip service to this suggestion, but never actually
delayed the planned start of the meeting.[7]

On August 20, the Czech Presidium met for what they assumed would
be the last time before the convening of the Party Congress three weeks
later. At 11:40 p.m., the prime minister announced that their nation had
been invaded. Troops from five Soviet bloc countries joined the invasion,
the largest number, of course, coming from the Soviet Union. In all,

165,000 troops and 4,600 tanks crossed the border that night, the largest coordinated Soviet force since World War II. One Soviet assumption had been that once the invasion began, pro-Soviet elements would assume control of the government as well as take over the television stations. These never occurred. The Presidium drafted a formal proclamation denouncing the invasion though decided that armed resistance would be futile and counterproductive.

For the Soviets, the armed invasion was the easy part. Each additional step proved increasingly difficult. Unable to gain full control of the state media, the Soviets were also unable to prevent the broadcast of the Presidium's denunciation of the invasion, contradicting the Soviet declarations of having responded to an invitation from the Presidium, including from Dubček.[8] Crowds had gathered in front of the State Radio building and it was not until the morning of the 21st that troops had secured the radio headquarters. Still, for several hours, they failed to realize that broadcasts were still being transmitted from the upper floors of the building. Once these were halted, anti-Soviet broadcasts resumed from auxiliary studios. The radio system had been so antiquated and unreliable that these smaller transmitters had been built in the previous few years as patches for the weak system. None of this was known to Soviet officials. As a result, a network of underground transmissions quickly developed, never fully silenced by the invaders. These underground stations countered Soviet announcements and broadcast Soviet troop movements.[9] Czechoslovakian television had been suspended. Nonetheless, members managed to smuggle out as much film footage as they could. The Vienna branch of the European Broadcast Union recorded all it could from Bratislava (located just across the Danube) as well as anything else it could pick up. All this visual evidence rebutted Soviet claims of having been welcomed as liberators by the Czechs.[10]

Meanwhile, Czechs, especially the young, poured into the streets. At various points the crowds, like those in Paris a few months earlier, attempted to construct barricades across the streets. The tanks easily smashed the first makeshift barriers. Later ones included cars and overturned buses. The Russian language had been a compulsory subject for students in Eastern European countries. Even when not fully fluent, the

Czech young knew enough to converse with the Soviet tank crews, questioning them about why they were there and what they believed they were doing. This was often accompanied by the throwing of Molotov cocktails. At some points, young Czech girls flirted with Russian tank drivers while their male colleagues smashed headlights and tried to set the tanks on fire. Occasionally, the invaders fired into the crowds, killing some of the demonstrators, but the conflict persisted.

As in Paris, graffiti and posters festooned walls all over the country, this time the slogans often written in Russian.

- IVAN GO HOME!
- SOCIALISM, YES; OCCUPATION, NO
- THE RUSSIAN NATIONAL CIRCUS HAS ARRIVED,
  DO NOT FEED THE ANIMALS
- THIS IS NOT VIETNAM!
- HITLER: 1938; BREZHNEV: 1968
- LENIN AWAKE! BREZHNEV HAS GONE MAD!

Two of the wall slogans suggested that the Czech students saw themselves as part of the international movements of 1968.

- MAKE LOVE, NOT WAR
- WE SHALL OVERCOME

Both walls and the tanks themselves were often decorated with the initials of the USSR written so the two S's were made to look like the lightning bolts in the insignia of the German SS.[11] Czechs painted over many of the directional signs throughout the country, adding to the confusion among Soviet forces, who were ill-prepared for finding their way in a foreign territory.

The leadership of the artistic unions met and proposed a two-minute protest strike to be held at noon on August 21. The call was broadcast over Radio Prague. At 12:00 all work stopped, and the city stood still. "Not a drop of water for the invaders," the radio advised. "Show the invaders your scorn in silence."[12]

Facing a response that they little expected, Soviet officials had to decide what to do. Yugoslavia, Romania, and China denounced the invasion, as did the French and Italian Communist Parties. Protestors took to the streets of Belgrade and Bucharest. There were even small protests in Moscow itself. Dubček and the Czech reformers were still in their offices on the morning of the 21st, waiting for a Soviet official to arrive to negotiate with them. Instead, sometime after 9 a.m., Soviet troops entered his office. Dubček and some of the other Czech leaders were arrested, handcuffed, and flown by a circuitous route, that included East Germany and Poland, to the Ukraine.

The Soviets now turned to Ludwig Svoboda. The aging general was a hero of the Czech resistance to the Nazis in World War II as well as having remained in good stead with the Soviet leadership. In the spring, Dubček had supported the choice of Svoboda as president. This seemed a shrewd political choice for Dubček, hoping to reassure the Soviets. In the days before the invasion, Soviet officials had convinced Svoboda that they were being invited in. When he arrived at the post-invasion Presidium meeting, he understood that this had not been true. His only immediate public statements were that Czech citizens should remain calm and display dignity and discipline.[13] Believing that they could convince Svoboda to become the center of a newly formed government, the Soviets flew him to Moscow on August 23. Though he had been staunchly pro-Soviet since World War II, he resisted the plan. When the Soviets tried to increase the pressure on him, Svoboda countered, even threatening suicide. He insisted that he would do nothing until the arrested Czech leadership, stashed away in Ukraine, joined him. Late that night, he was able to speak with the pale and weakened Czechs who had been brought to Moscow.

In the following days, the two sides sat down for negotiations, though it was clear that the Soviets held the advantage. Brezhnev again returned to calling Dubček "our Sasha" and using the familiar verb form. Dubček maintained the formal form. In this voice, he continued to bring up his disagreements with Brezhnev. Ultimately, he knew he had few bargaining positions. Svoboda pushed hard for a settlement, one that would end the killing and hostilities back in Czechoslovakia. By this point, there were 500,000 foreign troops and 6,000 tanks in the country. Moscow's goals appeared uncertain, seemingly more intent on canceling the upcoming Party Congress than removing the current leadership. Full government control over the media would be restored, and many of the independent vehicles for free speech and artistic expression would be eliminated. They promised that the troops would not interfere in internal affairs and would also be gradually withdrawn, "once the threat to socialism had been dispelled." All of these changes would be bundled under the name "The Moscow Protocol," which claimed it had "normalization" as its ultimate objective.[14]

Dubček therefore returned to Prague and remained the nation's titular leader, but his ability to function independently was in doubt. He would stand firm against the Soviets on some occasions and capitulate on others. His hope to continue with even modest reforms proved a pipe dream. Eventually he gave up entirely, resigning in April 1969. Later that year, he was removed from the Central Committee and, in May 1970, expelled from the Communist Party and assigned to a clerical job in a Slovak factory.

While Czechoslovakia returned to its place in the Soviet sphere, vestiges of the Prague Spring remained, connected both to the upsurge of enthusiasm in Prague as well as the swirl of world events. In January 1969 the Central Committee met with Dubček still its leader. Toeing the Soviet line, he stressed the need for unity and denounced "petit-bourgeois radicalism" and "anarchistic" tendencies among the young.[15]

That afternoon, with the plenum still in session, word arrived that a young man had set himself on fire in Wenceslas Square, in the center of Prague, an act reminiscent of other similar actions of recent years. In 1963, a Buddhist monk had set himself on fire in the center of Saigon, sparking international awareness of the oppressive nature of the Diem regime. In 1965, a Quaker pacifist had set himself on fire in a plaza of the Pentagon, in full view of Robert McNamara's office, in protest over the Vietnam War. Now Prague became the setting for this extremely powerful type of protest.

Jan Palach, the young man, had left a note describing a group of volunteers "who are resolved to let themselves be burnt alive for our cause.

I have the honor to draw the first lot...and become our first torch." He promised that unless reforms were reinstated, "further torches will burst into flames." He ended with the declaration, "Remember August!" Palach died three days after the incident. Thousands of students rallied at the university where he studied. Speakers denounced Dubček, and a makeshift sign renamed the university's main square after Palach. Demonstrations erupted across the country. One estimate suggested 120,000 people came to Prague for his funeral. Another claimed that 350,000 lined up to pass by his coffin as it lay in an open-air university courtyard. It was estimated that 800,000 joined the funeral procession.[16]

Anti-Soviet sentiments erupted two months later when the Czech national hockey team beat the Soviets twice during the world championships. After watching the second game on television, people poured into Wenceslas Square as soon as it ended, armed with firecrackers and noisemakers. The crowds chanted, "Russians go home!" and "Today Tarasov [the Soviet hockey coach], tomorrow Brezhnev." Some added, "Long live Mao!" Eventually some demonstrators broke into the offices of Aeroflot, the Soviet airline. Windows were smashed. Russian travel posters, model planes, and pictures of Lenin were all either trampled or tossed into a bonfire.[17] The "hockey riots" are often seen as one of the factors leading to Dubček's removal or resignation.

The new Czech leader, Gustáv Husák, oversaw the expulsion of many pro-Dubček members from the Communist Party. Once an ally of Dubček, Husák had changed course and initiated the repeal of many of the reforms of Prague Spring. Czechoslovakia began to resemble, on the surface, the grey political landscape of the Novotny era. A generally positive economic environment, coupled with Soviet subsidies during the world energy crisis of the early 1970s, helped to keep down overt antagonism to the government among Czech citizens. But as two Eastern European historians suggest, there existed under the surface, "a vast submerged iceberg of popular frustration and disaffection."[18] Just a tip of that iceberg emerged on January 1, 1977, less than a decade after the

Prague Spring, when a group of artists and political dissidents issued a declaration, Charter 77, which called for the government to respect the basic rights and freedoms guaranteed in two international covenants it had signed but never followed. "Basic human rights in our country exist, regrettably, on paper only," the Charter declared. The statement went on to list all the rights that remained circumscribed in Czechoslovakia, in violation of the international covenants—freedom of speech, education, religion, travel, and more. It made it clear that "Charter 77 is not an organization; it has no rules, permanent bodies or formal member." Instead, "Like many similar citizen initiatives in various countries, West and East, it seeks to promote the general public interest."[19] However its roots were clear, if never explicitly stated at the time. As one activist would later put it, "My signature was an act of dissent against a regime whose legitimacy I had denied since the suppression of the Prague Spring in 1968."[20] Among the signers were a number of literary and intellectual voices of 1968—including Ludvik Vaculik and Václav Havel—as well as hundreds of newer voices. Many of the signatories also went on to form the Committee for the Defense of the Unjustly Prosecuted (known as VONS, an acronym of its name in Czech) that sought to publicize the plight of dissidents and create connections with international human rights organizations, such as Amnesty International and Helsinki Watch.

After the Soviet invasion, Václav Havel had his works banned in Czechoslovakia. At one point, he took a job in a Czech brewery, an experience he wrote about in a play, "Audience," that became well known in the Czech underground, as did other of his works. He also became increasingly more engaged in direct political activism. Soon after the creation of VONS, he was arrested and imprisoned for nearly four years, his prison letters to his wife becoming another popular underground document.

The coming to power of Mikhail Gorbachev in the Soviet Union in the late 1980s instigated massive changes both at home and throughout Eastern Europe. Gustáv Husák was ill-suited to initiate the kinds of reforms in Czechoslovakia that Gorbachev was pursing. Havel helped found the Civic Forum, aiming to unify dissident forces. As change swept across Eastern Europe, Czechs once again took to the streets. A Prague demonstration in November 1989 brought out 750,000. Two days later, the Civic Forum called for a two-hour general strike. Within days, the Czech leadership resigned. On December 29 the Federal Assembly unanimously chose Václav Havel as the new president. Among those enthusiastically endorsing what had become known as the Velvet Revolution was Alexander Dubček.

It may be the cultural legacy of 1968 that actually had the longest and strongest impact on Czech society. Youth culture had exploded in Czechoslovakia in the Sixties, with nothing more powerful than rock 'n' roll. In September 1968, only a month after the Soviet invasion, the rock band The Plastic People of the Universe was formed, taking its name from a 1967 song by Frank Zappa and the Mothers of Invention, "Plastic People." The Czech band was also heavily influenced by the Velvet Underground, which was a part of Andy Warhol's Exploding Plastic Inevitable. While in New York in the spring of 1968, as we have seen, Václav Havel saw a performance by the "Mothers" at the Fillmore East and had smuggled home a copy of the Velvets' first album. The Plastic People, and other less well-known bands, seemed to embody the spirit of Prague Spring, even as government repression and censorship limited its expression elsewhere. The band was initially given a music performance license, which was revoked two years later by the government. Still they staged underground concerts and became part of the growing cultural resistance movement growing in Czechoslovakia. Havel, who felt that "the whole spirit of the 60s affected significantly the spiritual life of my generation and of the younger people," believed that suppressing the music of the Plastic People and jailing some of its members had been a major factor inspiring the Charter 77 manifesto. Over subsequent years, Václav Havel never denied the connections between the Prague counter-culture, including the influence of the Velvet Underground, and the Velvet Revolution.[21]

19

All Roads Lead to Chicago

During the week that preceded the opening of the Democratic National in Chicago in August, all the groups assembling for the event—party officials, the media, the police, those organizing protests—were busy in various forms of preparation. On Tuesday, August 20, news that Soviet forces had rolled across the Czechoslovak border and occupied Prague stunned the city and the world. With barely a moment's hesitation, the two arenas of conflict were fused in the minds of many of those gathering in Chicago. Abbie Hoffman started calling the city "Czechago." Others began to refer to Chicago as "Prague West." A joke began to make its way around the city, suggesting that Leonid Brezhnev had called Chicago Mayor Richard Daley and asked for 2,000 of his finest.[1]

Virtually all the various tensions and struggles of 1968 ultimately ended up in Chicago that August. Of course, the Democratic convention had a significant story of its own to unfold, and it did. Still, it is striking how much of what had gone on in the previous eight months seemed to converge, with gale force, on the streets of the Windy City. All the roads of 1968 led to Chicago.

By the time they had played out, the events of August had transformed the image of the city and the connotation of its name. Vietnam is a Southeast Asian nation with thousands of years of history, but in the minds of many, especially in the United States, Vietnam is not a place. It is an experience. "Vietnam" means one thing, the failed military experience in which the U.S. was engaged from 1945 to 1976. So too Tet, no longer just the name of the Vietnamese Lunar New Year, but now the North Vietnamese and Viet Cong assault of January 1968. By the end of August, "Chicago" was no longer the "Hog Butcher for the World" or the "City of Big Shoulders," as poet Carl Sandberg had once put it. It was not the "Toddlin' Town" that Frank Sinatra sang about. It became synonymous with the clash that took place within and around the 1968 Democratic National Convention. One only had to speak the name "Chicago" to conjure an array of images and violent confrontations that marked where the nation—and likely the world—had arrived by that August.

The elements that combined to create "Chicago" were multiple and complicated. In recent decades, the presidential nominee of each party has been long settled by the time of its national convention. The week's televised festivities have become a kind of four-night infomercial for the campaign. This had not always been the case. While there had not been anything other than a first-ballot victory at any U.S. political convention since 1952, parties often went to their convention with the nomination still in doubt, as in the 1960 nomination of John Kennedy.

Chicago upended all the anticipated scenarios. It seemed obvious in 1967 that Lyndon Johnson would be renominated. By early March 1968 he had dropped out. The primary struggles between Eugene McCarthy and Robert Kennedy seemed to have been settled in California in June, with RFK's victory. Then he was murdered. Meanwhile, Vice President Hubert Humphrey, who had not entered a single primary, had emerged as the frontrunner, piling up delegate votes from party leaders and state caucuses and conventions. The Democratic convention was shaping up to be a unique and tumultuous gathering, not merely because of the personalities involved or that the outcome of the Democratic primaries was going to be entirely ignored, but because of Vietnam. The war had come home, not only to the streets of America, but to the floor of the convention of one of its political parties.

In the wake of the assassination of Robert Kennedy, each of the political campaigns within the Democratic Party attempted to reboot and move forward, adjusting to the changed landscape. Eugene McCarthy's enthusiasm had seemed to rise and fall all spring after Johnson withdrew, and that pattern continued into the early summer. "I think Gene was rather schizophrenic," one of his advisers later reported. "A lot of the things that needed to be done were distasteful to him, and a lot of it was plain laziness." One young New Jersey delegate who felt he might "have been swayed by McCarthy," ended up disappointed. "He was just so lifeless—we felt he didn't even like talking to people," as three British journalists, Lewis Chester, Godfrey Hodgson, and Bruce Page quoted in their comprehensive post-election analysis of the campaign.[2]

Someone who loved to talk to people was Hubert Humphrey. His major problem was what to say. He remained the victim of his own making, tied in the public imagination to LBJ's failing Vietnam policies yet unable to abandon the president and the party leadership, despite his personal inclinations. Humphrey tried to talk about everything else. Harkening back to his liberal beginnings and his domestic agenda, he pushed for government poverty programs, calling for a "Marshall Plan for America's Cities," and promising an "open presidency." He reminded audiences of his civil rights record and trumpeted the endorsements of African American entertainers like James Brown and Diana Ross. It all felt old and stale that summer. Even Lyndon Johnson told friends, "Humphrey was too old fashioned for 1968."[3] One of the British reporters covering the campaign reprinted his notes from Humphrey's Fourth of July speech at Independence Hall. "There is an unmistakable whiff of mediocrity about the Humphrey operation these days…Humphrey's speech worked in almost every cliché known to politics, 'One nation indivisible, under God'…'I have a dream'…and even 'Let's get this country moving again!'" Meanwhile, at every stop, Humphrey was greeted with chants and placards, reminding him of his woes.

"DUMP THE HUMP"

"WE WANT GENE"

"ALL JOHNSON'S FORCES AND ALL JOHNSON'S MEN COULDN'T GET HUBERT ELECTED AGAIN!"

And perhaps the harshest,

"HITLER, HUBERT AND HIROHITO"[4]

No matter how hard Humphrey tried to change the subject, it always came back to Vietnam. While Kennedy and McCarthy had offered moderate suggestions for spurring the peace process along—most notably a unilateral halt to American bombing—Johnson held fast to his plan for continued war and the Paris negotiations. And he held Humphrey fast to his plan. Humphrey's advisers were always pushing for him to develop his own position on Vietnam. A speech would be drafted that Humphrey would accept. He'd show it to LBJ and the president would say, "Hubert, if you do this I'll have to be opposed to it, and say so."[5] Humphrey kept telling voters and delegates that he was "his own man," when it came to Vietnam policy. And yet, as Lawrence O'Donnell has recently written, "it never occurred to him to actually be his own man."[6]

The central issue that had led to the major fissure within the party and that had brought Johnson's downfall earlier in the year still plagued the Democrats as they headed to their nominating convention. And it spurred hundreds of others to head to that same convention, intending to have their voices heard concerning Vietnam policy and to demonstrate their disapproval of all that the Democratic leadership stood for and promised. David Dellinger, who had been at the front of numerous peace and pacifist movements since World War II, former SDS leader Rennie Davis, and Tom Hayden emerged as the central spokespeople for The National Mobilization to End the War in Vietnam, or as it was always known, the Mobe.

After the success of Stop The Draft Week and the March on the Pentagon in October 1967, the Mobe joined with other groups within the antiwar movement to choose as their next major arena of action, the Chicago Convention. As plans emerged in early 1968, while Lyndon Jonson was still a candidate, the focus was threefold: the immoral and unjust war, the undemocratic electoral politics, and American racism. Their plan was for "a week of demonstrations, disruptions, and marches... clogging the streets of Chicago." The culmination would be a march on the convention center on the night Johnson was renominated. Even with LBJ out of the race, they continued planning for August. Contacting a variety of organizations across the country, they announced a planning meeting at Lake Villa, just outside Chicago for late March. While a number of groups, including The Resistance, agreed to come, the Mobe had less success with those committed to African American issues. A representative of CORE told them, "we are working from separate concerns...Blacks are focusing on Black Liberation."[7]

Abbie Hoffman and Jerry Rubin fronted one significant contingent at Lake Villa. At a 1967 New Year's Eve party at Hoffman's Greenwich Village apartment, they had been, according to Hoffman, "stoned [on LSD], rolling around on the floor." They had spoken generally about what things they would plan for Chicago, which *The Realist*'s Paul Krasner called a "convention of death." Rubin suggested they offer the opposite, a "Festival of Life"—an outdoor celebration full of music and dance, flowers and drugs. Krasner, responding to the image of this giant youth festival, began to utter the phrase "Yippie." It sounded like the perfect name—it contained the essence of hippie, but suggested something more, something celebratory. Anita Hoffman, Abbie's wife, argued that while the kids would understand what "Yippie" meant, they needed a formal name for the media and the larger audience. She suggested that Yippie could stand for "Youth International Party." This might have been the only time an organization's acronym preceded its full name. But it worked.[8]

"Join us in Chicago in August for an international festival of youth music and theater," began the first "Yippie Manifesto," published in January. "Rise up and abandon the creeping meatball!" The call went out to "rebels, youth spirits, rock minstrels, truth seekers, peacock freaks, poets, barricade jumpers, dancers, lovers and artists." Planned for the week when the "NATIONAL DEATH PARTY meets to bless Johnson," there would be "500,000 of us dancing in the streets, throbbing with amplifiers and harmony. We are making love in the parks...We are coming from all over the world!...We demand the politics of ecstasy...We will create our own reality, we are Free America."[9] The counterculture was heading to Chicago.

Jerry Rubin expanded on the call in the pages of the underground newspaper *The Berkeley Barb*, with a more serious argument. Rubin echoed the 1963 "Port Huron Statement," only now in an updated rhetorical style. The U.S. was in a state of transformation, and the young would lead it. "History has chosen us, born white in middle class America—to reverse centuries of America…to vomit up our inheritance…Ours will be a revolution against privilege and a revolution against the boredom of steel-concrete plastic…Chicago is LBJ's stage and we are going to steal it."[10]

And the Yippies began to gather converts from more traditional radical movements. Julius Lester, the Black activist and academic, saw their roots not in "Mao or Che but in the Provos [Dutch counterculture radicals], rock and Lenny Bruce. They ignore what a man thinks and grab him by the balls to communicate their message…The Yippies are a hard slap, a kick in the crotch, a bunch of snipers pinning the enemy down and making him afraid to move." Or as historian David Farber was to conclude years later in his history of the Chicago convention, "the real joke the Yippies played on a fascinated society was that they meant not what they said but what they did."[11]

At the Lake Villa conference, the Yippies fluctuated between traditional left activities and their counterculture style of politics. Rubin gave a relatively serious talk. Hoffman suggested politics was "the way you lead your life, not who you supported." They also often argued for their typical guerilla theater style, ultimately suggesting that the Mobe's plans were not the "particular format" they were drawn to. They did promise, however, to see the others in Chicago.[12]

Over the course of the spring, the Yippies continued to depict the various tactics they claimed they would employ to disrupt the convention. They painted images of 10,000 naked protestors floating in Lake Michigan. Female Yippee "nookers" would seduce delegates and slip LSD into their drinks. Male hippies would seduce delegates' wives and daughters. Greased pigs would be released into the Loop, the center of Chicago, causing massive traffic jams. And maybe most frightening of all, LSD would be dumped into the city's water supply.[13] Very few of these had any realistic chance of occurring. Yet every one added to the anxiety of the city officials planning for the convention. And no one was more anxious about any trouble occurring in Chicago that August than the city's mayor, Richard Daley.

Richard Daley was the last in a long line of big city bosses, a line that had stretched across the nation and back nearly a hundred years. These bosses had built their base of support with strong ground-level precinct organizations and constituent services that earned them the loyalty of the citizenry. Daley had risen through the Chicago Democratic machine, eventually becoming mayor in 1955. In exchange for reelection, he provided jobs, hospitals, schools, mass transit. In 1960 he may have provided the Democrats with enough votes to gain the presidency and, as we have seen, he was still considered a crucial endorsement for Robert Kennedy and Hubert Humphrey in 1968.

By 1968, however, the negatives were beginning to overwhelm the positives; none more so than his response to the riots that followed the murder of Martin Luther King. Daley sent 10,000 police into the streets, bolstered by 12,000 National Guardsmen and Army regulars. And he gave the order "to shoot to kill any arsonist or anyone with a Molotov cocktail" and "to maim or cripple anyone looting any stores in our city." Jesse Jackson called this order "a fascist response." Some progressive Democrats suggested moving their convention to Miami, where the Republican convention was going to be held that summer, but Daley stood firm. "Nobody is going to take over this city."[14]

Just as the Mobe and the Yippies had begun to plan for Chicago early in the year, so too did Daley begin to plan for their arrival. Chicago updated its tear gas weaponry, looked to buy equipment that would analyze LSD, ordered new vehicles equipped with barbed wire battering rams, and made sure all Chicago police officers were trained in crowd control techniques. In addition, the police department's Red Squad— whose activities stretched back to anti-union investigations in the 1920s and anti-communist ones in the postwar years, and which by the mid-sixties had turned its attention to Black Nationalist movements—now added the coming demonstrators to its focus. Following the example of the FBI and its COINTELPRO program, the Chicago police infiltrated the organizations planning for the convention. And they passed the information they gathered to the FBI. J. Edgar Hoover thought this information was sufficient to ask Attorney General Ramsey Clark for authorization to wiretap a number of the leaders, including Hayden, Davis, and Dellinger. Clark refused. Still, the FBI continued to pass what information it obtained back to the Chicago police, who also had reciprocal relationships with the intelligence units of a number of other urban police forces.[15] In the aftermath of Chicago, the antiwar leadership was shocked at how many of their close associates—from body guards to organization officers—proved to be agents of one police force or another, from the FBI and the CIA on down. By the time the convention opened, one estimate put the number of federal agents in Chicago at 1,000. Meanwhile, the leaders of the Mobe and the Yippies were well aware of the plainclothes police tails who followed them day and night. As Charles Kaiser put it 20 years later, "America in 1968 was more like the 'police state' radicals had alleged than most people suspected."[16]

Other events of the spring added to the enthusiasm for what lay ahead in Chicago. The Columbia student strike energized Hoffman and Rubin, both of whom were arrested during the demonstrations there. They applauded the radical theater aspects of some of the confrontations and how so much of what happened at the Morningside Heights campus appeared every night on television. Tom Hayden delayed coming to Chicago to join the Columbia occupation, as we have seen. His assessment of Columbia, argued that it "opened a new tactical stage in the resistance," one sure to find its place in Chicago.[17]

Beginning in the spring, the Mobe had filed permit requests for a variety of activities during convention week. They were either rejected or stalled. By June, Rennie Davis began to call the mayor's office repeatedly. He never got through. One of the Mobe assistants called the Deputy Mayor every day, without success. Sometimes they thought that the permits would be granted close to the events, as they had been for the DC marches in the fall of 1967. Other times they understood that they were being stonewalled. Davis met with Roger Wilkins, the director of the Justice Department's Community Relations Service, who had assisted organizers in the Poor People's Campaign. With Davis promising that all their actions would be within the law, Wilkins agreed to try to contact the Chicago authorities. He did secure a meeting with the mayor, but was cut off almost immediately, Daley telling him that Chicago would take care of itself, ending the discussion in less than 15 minutes.[18]

The International Amphitheater, where the convention was to be held, was in a working-class section of the city, near the famed stockyards. An electrical workers' strike had stalled installation of the cables and other equipment that were needed for televised coverage. By the opening gavel the city had managed to get a few lines installed for feeds from inside the arena, though nothing could be relayed instantly from the outside or from the hotels and city parks in the Loop, where much of the action would take place. These could only be shown on videotape or film, which took hours to process and relay to the stations. NBC news anchor David Brinkley felt Daley had intended to "greatly curtail" coverage of the convention.[19]

Nothing stood in the way, however, of the measures taken to protect the building. A barbed wire fence, over 2,000 feet long, was installed around the parking lot. Every manhole was tarred shut. Roadblocks limited street access. An elaborate security system was created to screen delegates as they entered the arena, requiring them to show credentials multiple times. And nothing would stand in the way of measures to protect the city, as a whole. The week before the convention, under the rationale that "an ounce of prevention is worth a pound of cure," Daley announced that all of Chicago's 12,000 police would be on active duty, working twelve-hour shifts, supplemented by nearly 6,000 National Guardsmen and over 7,000 regular Army troops.[20]

Still despite these preparations, by late summer the Chicago authorities remained on high alert and their own surveillance systems only added to their fears, though these reports contained many unfounded and false reports. One report from police intelligence claimed that the Black

Panthers were planning a series of "incidents in the Negro area," and that they were going to use "incendiary devices" and "employ prostitutes to solicit delegates." The police believed Tom Hayden was directly involved in these plans. Another report claimed that members of the Blackstone Rangers, Chicago's most notorious street gang, had been hired to assassinate the presidential candidates and Mayor Daley. While all these proved to be false, they only added to the anxieties of the already nervous authorities. On August 13th, the president of Chicago's Patrolman's Association declared, "We feel that the insane tactics shown by some groups are getting out of hand."[21]

The final Mobe permit requests asked for picketing at the delegates' hotels, gatherings in three urban parks—Lincoln, Grant, and Hyde—and for a march to the Amphitheater, among others. The requests also asked for permission for overnight camping in the parks. All that the city ultimately approved was for a rally in Grant Park on nomination night. Grant Park is located along Lake Michigan, across from the Hilton Hotel where many delegates were staying. It was, however, 10 miles from the Amphitheater. The Mobe went to court to secure a permit for a march to the Amphitheater, but was denied.

Within the convention structure, the anti-Humphrey forces began their counteroffensive. This involved filing challenges with all three of the convention's main committees—Rules, Credentials, and Platform. Before the Rules Committee, the argument was to contest the "unit rule," which was used in some states to require delegates to vote as a block, enhancing the power of the state's leadership. While Humphrey had for years been opposed to the unit rule, he had begun to waffle a bit, needing the support of powerful state leaders like Texas governor John Connelly. The Rules Committee decided to leave it to the convention as a whole to decide the question.

The debates before the Credentials Committee harkened back to the 1964 convention and the challenge by the Mississippi Freedom Democrats and the emotional and stirring testimony of Fannie Lou Hamer. The compromise solution had been the promise that by 1968 the undemocratic nature of delegations would have been resolved. At the 1964 convention, lawyer Joseph Rauh had led fight before the credentials committee. He was back in 1968, arguing that the Mississippi delegation was again undemocratically chosen, and the committee agreed. Also appearing before the committee was Julian Bond, the former SNCC leader and now a state senator from Georgia. Bond had put together an alternative slate of Georgia delegates, half Black and half white, challenging the slate headed by segregationist governor Lester Maddox, who was certain to endorse George Wallace's candidacy that fall. As Maddox ranted, Bond appeared cool and compelling. The committee chair, the governor of New Jersey, declared, "That man [Bond] is a symbol, we have to have him." The committee compromised, seating half of Maddox's delegation and half of Bond's. The committee also recommended that the delegate selection process be reviewed for 1972, making it unlikely that a candidate who had not entered any primaries, like Humphrey, could ever again secure the nomination.[22]

The Platform Committee emerged as the hot center of the intra-party warfare. The McCarthy and Kennedy people wanted a "peace plank" to replace the one the committee had proposed, which supported LBJ's Vietnam policy. Anti-war senators met with McCarthy and Kennedy staffers, developing a plank that would move Humphrey away from the president, but not too far. No one wanted to alienate organized labor, an important group within the Democratic base, whose leadership strongly favored the war. After much internal wrangling, they finally approved an alternative Vietnam plank that walked many fine lines, but included a call for an unconditional bombing halt and the implicit understanding that the South Vietnamese government would recognize the Viet Cong. Johnson responded to a delegation of pro-war party leaders telling them that a bombing halt could cost American lives and stoked fears that the Viet Cong might be planning another offensive like Tet. He would not accept the peace plank. And neither, then, could Hubert Humphrey. On the day before the formal opening of the convention, the platform committee approved the pro-war plank, 65 to 35. The peace plank did receive enough votes, however, to guarantee it would be brought to the convention floor the following week.[23]

The Soviet invasion of Czechoslovakia only added to the frustrations developing around Eugene McCarthy. While the peace movement roundly condemned the invasion, notably Benjamin Spock's picketing of the Soviet mission at the United Nations, McCarthy observed, "I do not see this as a major world crisis." He thought it would be a bigger problem for the Russians than the Czechs. McCarthy received so much pushback from friends and delegates that he issued a second statement, saying "of course I condemn this cruel and violent action." Still the damage had been done. All summer he had been trying to woo uncommitted and Kennedy delegates, with limited success. Remarks like this did not help.[24] In fact, back on August 10, South Dakota Senator George McGovern had declared his candidacy, from the same Senate Caucus Room where RFK had done so five months before, promising to carry on "the goals for which Robert Kennedy gave his life," including that the "war must be ended now."[25]

By the middle of the week before the convention was to open, opposition groups had begun to move into place. Both the Yippies and the Mobe set up headquarters in Lincoln Park, four miles from the Hilton and eight from the Amphitheater. "Headquarters" actually meant a few folding tables and a place for marshals to train for upcoming protests. The police put up signs reminding everyone that the park would close each night at 11.00.[26] Parks had often been a place of refuge for Chicagoans looking for a cool place to sleep on hot summer nights. This was not going to be allowed in 1968.

Sometime after midnight on Thursday the 22nd, police stopped two long-haired young men near the park. They claimed that one of them, a 17-year-old Native American named Dean Johnson, had drawn a gun. Police asserted that he pulled the trigger but that his gun misfired. They responded by firing three times, killing him. That night, at a quickly organized service for Johnson, one SDS leader declared he had "died of pig poisoning" and questioned the police version of events.[27]

The Yippies planned on holding their own nominating convention on Sunday, the 25th. With typical Yippie style and humor, the idea was to nominate an actual pig as their candidate. Friday morning, at the Civic

Center, Jerry Rubin, folksinger Phil Ochs, and several other Yippies led a 150-pound pig, who they named Pigasus, out of a truck. Rubin called for Pigasus to be given secret service protection and to be invited to the White House for the foreign policy briefing afforded all candidates. As Rubin spoke, the police moved in and arrested him and six others for disturbing the peace. The pig was taken to the Humane Society. Rubin was quickly released on $25 bail. The story ran in newspapers and on television news across the country. A perfect Yippie political moment.[28]

By Saturday the 24th, things had begun to coalesce in Lincoln Park, although they remained relatively peaceful. A crowd of 2,000 had gathered, many from the neighborhood, dancing, playing guitars, sharing food and drugs. At the same time Women for Peace, a group of 60 or so middle-class women, picketed the Hilton Hotel, where many delegates were staying and where Humphrey and McCarthy both had their headquarters. Allen Ginsberg had arrived in Chicago and came to the park. As the curfew hour approached, Ginsberg and Ed Sanders of the Fugs began to chant, "Ommm" to keep the atmosphere calm. At 11:00, as police bullhorns announced that the curfew had begun, most protestors left the park.[29]

The intensity began to ramp up the next day. A crowd of 500–800 hundred picketed the Hilton from across the street in Grant Park. Police lined the sidewalk blocking the hotel. Others marched through the Loop, chanting anti-war slogans. Before events escalated there, the protesters ceased marching and headed to Lincoln Park where the Yippie Festival of Life was scheduled to begin. Instead of the grandiose plans of the spring, the Festival attracted a smaller crowd, estimated at about 2,000, and only one well-known band, the Detroit political rockers MC-5. The plan had been to use a flatbed truck as a stage, but police had refused to allow it. The band had to play standing on the grass, out of sight from many in the crowd, who pushed forward to get a better view. Even when the music ended, people stayed in the park, lighting bonfires and smoking dope. All night groups shouted at the police, "Oink Oink," "Motherfuckers," "Pigs eat shit." Police announced that anyone remaining in the park after 11:00 would be arrested, including journalists. At the stroke of 11:00 they moved in, pushing the crowd toward one of the streets that bordered the park. At one moment, the police moved forward, shouting, "Kill the Commies" and "Let's get these bastards." Police began to beat people with their clubs. News photographers attempting to photograph the scene were also clubbed, their cameras destroyed. A *Newsweek* photographer identified himself to police. "*Newsweek* fuckers," a cop yelled and clubbed him mercilessly. An assistant U.S. attorney in a suit and tie was beaten. Medics, dressed in white, attempted to provide first aid. They too were clubbed. Mace was sprayed. Tear gas canisters tossed. Demonstrations erupted at other points in the city, some overturning garbage cans or blocking intersections. All were met by police. It wasn't until around 2 a.m. that the streets were cleared and calm restored.[30]

On the eve of the opening of the convention, Chicago had turned into a war zone.

Meanwhile, inside the Democratic Party, a different form of warfare threatened. A number of party officials remained worried about a Humphrey candidacy, including Richard Daley, whose Illinois delegation had not yet chosen a candidate. Pressure began to build for a draft of Ted Kennedy. Kennedy brother-in-law Stephen Smith had flown to Chicago to assess the situation. Smith found that even in Humphrey delegations, there was strong support for a Kennedy draft, enough to stop Humphrey. Beyond that, with Kennedy running, crucial states would fall into the Democratic column in November, including New York, California, and Illinois. Enthusiasts envisioned a chain reaction—Humphrey would be stopped, the peace plank approved, Nixon defeated, and the war ended.

Michael DiSalle, former governor of Ohio and longtime Kennedy family supporter, planned to place Ted's name in nomination. And finally, Kennedy people approached Eugene McCarthy. On Tuesday afternoon, August 27th, Smith met with McCarthy. McCarthy evidently admitted that he thought he could not make it, but wanted to have his name placed in nomination, even if it was just symbolic. He'd publicly withdraw and throw his support to Kennedy. And then McCarthy may have added (there is some dispute about this), "While I'm doing this for Teddy, I never could have done it for Bobby." Ted Kennedy himself remained ambivalent, and certainly did not want anything other than a real draft from the delegates. He refused to let any of the Kennedy loyalists, like DiSalle, nominate him. When a leak of the McCarthy–Smith meeting hit the news, suggesting there were backroom negotiations in all this, Kennedy shutdown any idea of a draft. And with it another 1968 optimistic vision evaporated.[31]

Monday evening, August 26, Speaker of the House Carl Albert gaveled the 1968 Democratic National Convention to order. From his vantage point at the podium it would be clear to anyone surveying the convention floor as to who held the reigns of control in the Amphitheater. The anti-war delegations, including New York and California, had been assigned seats in the outer reaches of the hall. Front and center was the Illinois delegation, with the Mayor at its head. During the convention the microphones used by delegations like Illinois and Texas were set at full volume, while those of the anti-war ones were muted. After Aretha Franklin led the singing of the national anthem, Daley welcomed the delegates, pointedly excluding "extremists who would make a mockery of our institutions" and promising there would be "law and order in Chicago."[32]

Almost immediately tumult erupted on the floor. Southern delegations believed that Humphrey had agreed not to challenge the unit rule, but the Rules Committee had decided to put the issue to a voice vote of the entire convention, which chose to abolish the rule, leading some Southerners to accuse the Vice President of being a "sellout." The Credentials Committee's plan to split the Georgia delegation between Lester Maddox's and Julian Bond's slates led to further high-volume antagonism, especially from Southerners. This only spurred catcalls and booing from all sides on a variety of issues. The poorly functioning air conditioning intensified the conflicts. The air inside the Amphitheater was stifling. Delegates wrestled for microphones. Carl Albert refused to recognize some delegates wishing to speak. All of this went out on national television. No one had ever seen anything like it before.

At 3 a.m., without having resolved all the credentials fights, Albert gaveled the first day to a close.

Amid the coverage of chaos on the convention floor, networks cut to Lincoln Park where the previous night's battle was repeated. Several thousand had gathered in the park. While Abbie Hoffman and SDS leaders had quietly counseled groups to leave the park at 11:00, some began to build barricades. Announcing they had evidence that demonstrators possessed weapons, the police moved in. One police car attempted to breach a barricade, but was met by a barrage of rocks, smashing its windows. A force of 300 gas-masked police responded, launching tear gas and smoke grenades and driving out the protestors. Again, people took to the streets, throwing rocks and bottles at police. Observers thought the police were even more brutal than the night before. When one hippie girl proclaimed that she had a right to be on the sidewalk, a policeman screamed, "You hippies are all alike. All you want is free love." He then clubbed her to the ground, yelling, "Free love, free love, I can give you some free love." When a Black reporter waived his press credentials at the police, after being knocked to the ground, an officer responded, "that don't mean nothing to me nigger!" and beat him again. Police fractured the skull of a minster wearing a clerical collar. After clearing Lincoln Park, police vandalized cars left in the parking lot, many with McCarthy bumper stickers, slashing tires, breaking car windows, snapping off antennas."[33]

The convention reconvened on Tuesday, the delegates knowing that they would have to face the debate and the vote on the Vietnam War plank. First, though, the credentials challenges had to be resolved. Party officials had come up with the plan for a voice vote on the Georgia compromise, awarding half to the Maddox slate and half to the Bond slate. When it passed, anti-war delegates began to chant Julian Bond's name, while Southerners, especially Georgians, booed. Attempting to interview some of the angry Georgia delegates, CBS reporter Dan Rather was blocked by security guards. As viewers watched, Rather confronted the guards, "Take your hands off me unless you intend to arrest me!" While CBS anchor Walter Cronkite spoke to him and still on camera,

Rather was shoved to the ground and later said he had been punched in the stomach. "I think we've got a bunch of thugs here," Cronkite observed.[34]

Other credentials challenges took time, and it was not until after midnight that the Vietnam debate began. As the platform committee chair began to read the plank, delegates shouted for recognition, asking for the convention to adjourn until the next day. Perhaps hoping to keep this debate confined to hours when the television audience would be small, the chair ruled against the motion. Boos cascaded from the balconies, as delegates yelled, "Let's go home! Let's go home!" As the booing grew, party officials decided to get this off of national television. Daley finally signaled Albert, who in turn recognized Daley, who moved to adjourn, which they did at 1:15 a.m.[35]

Tuesday night's gathering in Lincoln Park involved a special guest. Despite initial hesitations in the spring, Black Nationalist and Black Power organizations and individuals had begun to join the larger crusade and became part of the week's events. Tom Hayden had invited Black Panther leader Bobby Seale to come to Chicago. Flying in from Oakland on Tuesday, Seale headed straight to Lincoln Park. His talk mixed his political arguments with the rhetoric of the times, all in the context of what the demonstrators were facing each night. "If a pig comes up to us and starts swingin' a billy club…and you got your piece—you gotta down that pig in defense of yourself." Seale went on to add, "The strongest weapon we each individually have is all of us united in revolutionary principles."[36] Although Seale left Chicago the next day, it was clear that his presence and his message sent shockwaves through the ranks of the authorities. This one speech led to his indictment, seven months later, as one of the Chicago 8, charged with crossing interstate lines with intent to incite a riot.

The other movement event of Tuesday night was the anti-birthday party for LBJ, held at the Chicago Coliseum, an older indoor arena. Bands played, people chanted "Fuck You, LBJ," draft cards were burned. Leaders announced that the next day there would be a march to the Amphitheater. As the night's curfew approached the audience was advised to gather in Grant Park, across from the Hilton, to greet the delegates as they returned from the convention. For a third consecutive night, police clashed with demonstrators in Lincoln Park, again spraying tear gas and clubbing fleeing protestors.

A crowd of 4,000 gathered in Grant Park, listening to speeches and talking about the planned Amphitheater march for the following day. At about 3 a.m. a significant change occurred, the National Guard began to replace the Chicago police. Arriving in jeeps with barbed wire grills and in army transports, they appeared in full battle attire, brandishing bayonets. Using their bayonets they began to push the crowd back, away from the hotel. Shouting at the delegates in the hotel, the crowd chanted, "Flash your lights if you're with us." Lights on the floors occupied by the McCarthy staff blinked on and off. The National Guard commander finally ordered the bayonets removed and that the guardsmen's rifles not be loaded. Slowly the crowd began to drift off, readying themselves for Wednesday the 29th, which would include the most important events of the convention—the vote on the Vietnam War plank, the nomination of the candidate, and the planned march on the Amphitheater.[37]

At one o'clock Wednesday afternoon, the convention reconvened to debate and vote on the Vietnam War plank. Among those arguing for the substitute anti-war amendment were Senators Wayne Morse of Oregon and Albert Gore of Tennessee, as well as old Kennedy hands, Theodore Sorenson and Pierre Salinger, who evoked Robert Kennedy's name. Maine Senator Edmund Muskie led off for those behind the pro-war plank. Congressman Wayne Hayes of Ohio tied his opposition to the anti-war plank to the demonstrators in Chicago's streets, suggesting that a vote for the majority plank was a vote against the foolishness of the counterculture. "They would substitute beards for brains, license for liberty. They want pot instead of patriotism, sideburns instead solutions…riots for reason." Finally, Platform Committee chair and Louisiana congressman Hale Boggs directly linked the anti-war plank to the Soviet invasion of Prague. America's resolve in Vietnam was part of the effort to maintain world peace, he argued. He also claimed he was granted permission by LBJ to publicly read a secret intelligence report that argued that a bombing halt would increase enemy strength by 500 percent.[38]

After three hours of debate, the convention voted for the pro-war plank, 1,567 to 1,041. Later analysis suggested that a number of Humphrey delegates had voted for the anti-war choice. Immediately, members of several delegations donned black armbands and pinned black crepe to their badges. The New York delegation began to sing "We Shall Overcome," soon joined by many other delegates. "STOP THE WAR" posters appeared. A few anti-war delegates suggested that they should nominate Johnson later that night instead of Humphrey. "Why take the dummy when you can have the ventriloquist himself?," one argued.[39]

That afternoon the protestors began the one rally for which they had been granted a permit, a gathering in Grant Park across from the Hilton. Somewhere between ten and fifteen thousand people showed up. Police ringed the area, warning those in attendance not to begin any marches. About 30 minutes into the program, a young man started to climb the flagpole, intending to either lower the flag or to rehang it upside down, the international symbol of distress. Before he could climb to the top, police dragged him back down, clubbing him before his arrest. The crowd pelted the police with rocks and other objects. Rennie Davis ran to the flagpole and attempted to position a row of marshals between the police and the crowd to defuse the confrontation. Instead, the police charged the marshals. Five policemen headed straight for Davis. He was clubbed to the ground and beaten to unconsciousness. Rushed to a local hospital, it took 13 stitches to close his head wound. Police came to the hospital to arrest him, but, according to Tom Hayden in his 1988 memoir, "hospital staff hid him under a sheet, rolled him on a gurney through police lines, and placed him in a cab."[40]

When Hayden stood to address the rally, the personal impact of Davis's beating was clear. "Rennie has been taken to the hospital, and we have to avenge him," Hayden declared. At this point there were thousands of police, Army troops, and National Guardsmen on the scene. "We must move out of this park in groups," he said, "and turn this excited, overheated military machine against itself. Let us make sure that if blood is going to flow let it flow all over the city."[41] The plan was to march from Grant Park to the Amphitheater, where the convention would soon begin the nomination process. While David Dellinger repeated over and over that the march must remain nonviolent, National Guardsmen moved into position armed with M-1 rifles, grenade launchers, gas dispensers, bayonets, and .30 caliber machine guns.[42]

As the marchers began to assemble on Michigan Avenue, there appeared, like an apparition, a contingent from another of the struggles of 1968, the Mule Caravan of the Poor People's Campaign, led by Ralph Abernathy. After the end of the PPC campaign in Washington, SCLC had decided that they would appear at both the Republican and Democratic conventions, to further demonstrate for their agenda of economic justice. They had been granted a permit to march. The Grant Park protestors filed in behind the Mule Caravan, intending to share in their permitted status. Police stalled the entire group, and then allowed the wagons through their line, but closed it off again once they had passed. Thousands of people were trapped in the street in front of the Hilton. Police ordered the protestors to clear the streets. While some police exercised restraint, others ploughed straight into the crowd. Some in the crowd resisted, which intensified the situation. Using Mace, tear gas, and clubs they attacked in all directions. People watching from the sidewalk were clubbed. Fleeing marchers were chased for blocks. As police trucks pulled up they were filled with beaten and arrested protestors. One group of police reinforcements charged out of their bus chanting "Kill!, Kill!, Kill!"[43]

The first floor of the Hilton boasted a lobby bar, The Haymarket Lounge, with a huge plate-glass picture window looking onto Michigan Avenue. Those sitting at the cocktail tables had a first-hand view of the action. Soon they became part of it. One protestor recalled seeing a young girl beaten to unconsciousness on the sidewalk, "I ran to pick her up." As he did, "three policemen came and pushed us." The window shattered. Glass flooded the cocktail lounge, followed by the police. Tom Hayden was also pushed through the shattered window. "The police leaped through the windows," he recalled, "Turning over tables in the swank lounge, scattering the drinkers, breaking glasses and tables."[44]

The battle had now moved inside the Hilton. Bloody demonstrators filled the lobby, some trying to sit inconspicuously in the lobby chairs.

The smell of tear gas wafted through the hotel, including to the upper floors, irritating Humphrey's eyes and skin. McCarthy, looking down on the scene from his twenty-third-floor suite, said it looked "like a Breughel." His staff turned their fifteenth-floor headquarters into an impromptu first aid center. Bed sheets were torn to make bandages. McCarthy came down to this refuge to help.

As the protestors began to regroup with the intention of continuing their attempt to march to the Amphitheater, a chant went up that would become symbolic of the entire Chicago experience. "The whole world is watching," they shouted. "The whole world is watching!"

And it became a prophetic declaration. Given the inability to provide a live feed, it took the networks until 9:30 p.m. to begin broadcasting footage of the horrific scene. The impact was overwhelming, across the country and at the convention, where people crowded around television sets to see it all. The footage was the first that many delegates knew of what was unfolding. Just as the convention had reconvened, some began to shout for an adjournment, based on the carnage in front of the Hilton. Carl Albert dismissed them, and the roll call for the nomination of the candidates began. A ruckus in the New York delegation led security guards to try to remove one delegate. Others responded to protect him. When CBS News' Mike Wallace attempted to find out what was occurring, a guard punched him in the face.[45]

The vote on the Vietnam plank had demonstrated that the night's outcome was a foregone conclusion. But that did not stop the nominating process from having its own indelible moment. San Francisco mayor Joseph Alito's nominating speech for Humphrey was dull political boilerplate. As Cleveland's African American mayor Carl Stokes began his seconding speech, the networks switched to first available footage of the police brutality. After the scene at the Hilton, McCarthy asked that his name not be placed in nomination but was told it was too late. It was the nomination of George McGovern, however, that ignited another seminal moment. Connecticut Senator Abraham Ribicoff, an old Kennedy hand and former cabinet officer in the JFK administration, gave the nominating speech. His prepared remarks praised McGovern and talked about Vietnam, poverty, and ending hunger. Then he departed from his text.

He noted that both Jack and Bobby Kennedy had rallied America's youth to their standards. "And with George McGovern," he declared, "we wouldn't have to have Gestapo tactics in the streets of Chicago." Cheers erupted from anti-war delegates, boos from the Daley and Humphrey people in the hall. Daley, seated right in front of the podium, jumped to his feet. His enraged image picked up by the television cameras, he glared at Ribicoff and shouted, "Fuck you, you Jew son of a bitch! You lousy motherfucker, go home!" Ribicoff looked down on Daley and coolly replied, "How hard it is to accept the truth. How hard it is."[46]

The rest of the night was decidedly anticlimactic. At nearly midnight, Pennsylvania's vote put Humphrey over the top. Evidently Humphrey had been near tears earlier in the evening. Now, sitting in his hotel suite surrounded by reporters, he was all smiles. He jumped to his feet and whooped. From the visitor's gallery, his wife's face appeared on the TV. Humphrey ran to the television and kissed the glass screen. "Mom, I wish you were here." When an Illinois delegate moved to ask that the nomination be made unanimous—a traditional convention gesture—delegates shouted no. Without talking any vote, Carl Albert declared the motion had passed. Dissenting delegates were handed candles and they left the convention in what looked like a funeral procession.[47]

A very different kind of confrontation also occurred that evening, one that proved a harbinger of changes coming to the American cultural landscape. In these years, the ABC television network ran decidedly behind its competitors CBS and NBC. They could not even fund full coverage of the convention. Instead, they opted for an hour-long recap nightly, highlighted by an impromptu debate between conservative editor and television personality William F. Buckley and novelist and liberal social critic Gore Vidal. There was little love lost between the two and their nightly jabs at one another proved compelling television. On Wednesday night, their sparring turned ugly. Defending the protestors, Vidal claimed, "They came here for free assembly. They came here to demonstrate against the Vietnam War, which you," he told Buckley, "happen to love." When Buckley claimed that some of the demonstrators were "pro-Nazi," Vidal shot back. "The only pro- or crypto-Nazi

I can think of is yourself." Buckley lost control. "Now listen, you queer," he yelled at Vidal, "stop calling me a crypto-Nazi or I'll sock you in your goddamn face and you'll stay plastered."

Vidal had never hidden his homosexuality, though he did not talk about it publicly. Buckley's tirade had outed Vidal, something that was even more harmful in 1968 than it would be in subsequent years. The full emergence of the gay rights movement was still several years away, as was the common appearance of antagonistic commentators on television news panels. The term "gay bashing" had not become a phrase of common usage, but few could mistake the sentiment, even if it did not yet have a label, in Buckley's attack. Buckley regretted his outburst for the rest of his life.[48]

There was not much left to do on Thursday, the final night of the convention, save the nomination of the vice-presidential candidate and the showing of a Robert Kennedy tribute film. Humphrey had selected Senator Edmund Muskie of Maine as his running mate, though Kennedy and McCarthy delegates had offered the name of Julian Bond as their choice. While Bond had emerged as a popular and charismatic figure at the convention, this would give them an opportunity for a series of platform speeches to continue their critique of what had been happening all week. The problem was that Bond was only 28 and the Constitution required that the vice-president be 35. The nomination went to Muskie.[49]

Reminiscent of the 1964 convention tribute film about JFK, the 1968 film on RFK had been scheduled for the last night, so the emotions it was sure to stir up would not provoke anti-Humphrey or anti-LBJ eruptions. Regardless, the final image of Bobby Kennedy walking on a beach led to a standing ovation that would not end. Carl Albert tried to gavel the convention back to order, but delegates, many in tears, began to sing the "Battle Hymn of the Republic." Daley backers who filled the gallery began to chant, "We love Daley!" This was met with chants of "We want Teddy!" Finally, a Black Congressman associated with the Daley machine appeared on the platform to offer an unscheduled tribute to Martin Luther King and asked for a moment of silence. With that, the demonstration ended.

Protestors rallied again in Grant Perk on Thursday. Echoing his spring call for "two, three, many Columbias," Tom Hayden now called for

"One, two, three hundred Chicagos." After another permit to march had been denied, comedian Dick Gregory, who lived in Chicago, invited the crowd to a party at his house, on the South Side in the vicinity of the Amphitheater. The police allowed a ten-block march, but then barricaded the street, arresting those who wished to go further, including delegates wearing their convention badges and journalists. Among those taken to jail was Harris Wofford, veteran of the JFK administration and later Senator from Pennsylvania. He later wrote in his 1992 memoir, "spending the night in a Chicago jail was hardly the way I expected to mark the nomination of Hubert Humphrey. It may have been as good a way as any, however, to celebrate the end of an era."[50] If there was a single moment that gathered up the various threads that were twisted together to make up the Chicago Democratic Convention of 1968, this may have been it.

There was one final, brutal clash. At about 4 a.m. Friday morning, police raided the fifteenth-floor ballroom of the Hilton, the space the McCarthy people had used as a first aid refuge and where many had slept in sleeping bags all week. Claiming that objects were being thrown at them from that floor, police moved in. One McCarthy staffer said he heard police in the lobby deciding to "drag them all in and give them a beating. Teach them a lesson." Given passkeys by the hotel, they entered individual rooms, as well, dragging the sleeping McCarthy workers from their beds, beating them, and taking them downstairs. McCarthy came down to the lobby, asking to speak to someone in authority, but no one stepped forward. Most of the McCarthy kids were allowed to head back upstairs, save for the four who were sent to the hospital with head injuries.[51]

There was no post-convention bounce for Hubert Humphrey, no energy generated by the adoration of his party's delegates that would spring him forward into the fall campaign. Richard Nixon, the Republican nominee, led Humphrey by 15 points in the immediate post-convention polling. The Democrats, who had won one of the greatest election landslides only four years before, now looked like a shattered party, their candidate reviled by a significant portion of its members and blamed for the national discord over a war that left the civic fabric in tatters. All this spelled gloom and defeat.

As for the city, Chicago emerged from these terrible weeks as the new symbol of police brutality and anti-democratic politics, with Richard Daley as its arch villain. His post-convention justifications were filled with accusations of Communist infiltration and claims of intelligence reports showing plans to assassinate party leaders. Hubert Humphrey joined in this vision. "It is time to quit pretending that Mayor Daley did anything wrong."[52] On December 1, Daniel Walker, director of the Chicago Study Team of the National Commission on the Causes and Prevention of Violence, issued a report, "Rights in Conflict," that contradicted the Mayor and the Vice President. Calling the conflict a "police riot," the Walker Report went on to say, "the nature of the response was unrestrained and indiscriminate police violence...made all the more shocking by the fact that it was often inflicted upon persons who had broken no law, disobeyed no order, made no threat." "In Chicago, for the first time in my life," *Newsweek* columnist Stewart Alsop concluded, "it began to seem to me possible that some form of American fascism may really happen here."[53] It would take years for Chicago to move beyond the taint of the convention.

What had begun with enthusiasm, optimism, and a vision of an electoral victory that would lead to the end of the Vietnam War, concluded with the forces of reform rejected, a reaffirmation of the U.S. government's Vietnam policy, and with those who sought change brutally beaten and bloodied in the streets. This pattern of violent responses was repeated across the nation and around the globe. Sometimes, as in Memphis or Los Angeles, a movement was stalled by an assassin's bullet. Sometimes, as at Columbia, in Washington's Resurrection City, or on the streets of Chicago, it was by local police forces. And sometimes, as in Prague, by an invading army. In all these cases, the Establishment, as those in power were often called in the 1960s, employed brute force to crush movements that looked as though they were about to bring about significant change.

After his supporters had been routed from their sleep at the Hilton, Eugene McCarthy delayed his departure from Chicago until Friday afternoon. When his chartered plane was finally airborne, the pilot came on over the intercom. He announced dryly, "We are leaving Prague."[54]

Atlantic City

"No More Miss America!"

In December 1962, *The Saturday Evening Post* devoted most of one issue to "The American Woman." For this issue, the magazine had commissioned a Gallup Poll to survey attitudes among American women. George Gallup, the head of the polling organization, was one of the coauthors of the article summarizing the findings. The poll included women "of high and low income," those with PhDs as well as "less than four years of grade school." It included single, married, divorced, and separated women. There was no discussion of the racial breakdown of the interviewees. Gallup, however, was convinced that "this sample of American womanhood not only is statistically sound but also accurately reflects the activities and attitudes of the American woman." One of the photographs accompanying the article showed a Black woman school-teacher, though all the family images were of whites. Generally the survey found a strong reiteration of the basic presumptions of postwar America. Married women decisively felt, 60 percent to 36 percent, that they were "happier than their mother was." Single women were split 49 percent to 51 percent on the same question. Ninety-six percent of married women thought that mothers were happier than single women and 77 percent of single women agreed. A hint of the desire for some autonomy came in responses like the one from a Texas mother. "I'm my own boss. If I don't want to do the dishes or the laundry right now, I can do them later. My only deadline is when my husband comes home.

I'm much more free than when I was single."[1] Her expression of independence was framed by the prevailing male/female standard.

Also in 1962, a newspaper survey of newly married Detroit women (again with no racial distinctions noted) found that two-thirds of them believed that "most of the important decisions in the life of the family should be made by the man of the house." Just over half of these women did not think their husband needed "to help around the house after coming home from a hard day's work." And 45 percent believed "there is some work that is men's and some that is women's, and they shouldn't be doing each other's." One respondent in the initial Gallup survey, who previously had a career before she married, felt that "a woman needs a master–slave relationship whether it's husband and wife, or boss–secretary. This shows she's needed and useful. Women who ask for equality with men are fighting nature; they wouldn't be happy if they had it. It's simply biological."[2]

When turning to the public arena—especially the political one—opinions, as expressed in surveys, continued to reflect the norms of the past. Asked if they approved of having a woman as president, only 28 percent of the women surveyed by Gallup responded positively, 62 percent disapproving. Only 19 percent of married women and 29 percent of single women thought women were discriminated against in the professions. One woman justified any discrimination. "A male doesn't want to be completely in the hands of any woman, and must be, with a female doctor or lawyer." Finally, the Gallup Poll revealed that two-thirds of American women did not believe that any real discrimination existed against American women.[3]

By 1962, America had been discussing civil rights issues for over a decade, and struggles for equality and justice had been front-page news for years. Even before the emergence of civil rights as the central domestic political issue of the day, a number of Black women, as we have seen, had begun to understand and respond to the issues that confronted them as women as well as African Americans. And yet, for the majority of white women (and certainly many Black women), the seemingly logical connections between the discussions emerging from the civil rights movement and the situation of American women were not yet being made. While a great many Americans had come to understand the need for rectifying racial injustice, they had yet to see the need for addressing injustices based on gender.

Despite the emphasis during the postwar years on a woman's place being in the home, women's participation in public sector activities, most notably employment, rose steadily over the 1950s. As shown earlier, the number of working women grew between 1950 and 1960, with working wives accounting for much of the increase. And this growth would continue through the 1960s. It was not only the number of women working that changed but also the kind of work they did. In 1960, clerks, salespeople, secretaries, and domestics were the four largest categories of women's employment. By 1970, while secretaries and clerks remained the first and third most popular categories, teachers, bookkeepers, and nurses completed the top five. Domestic work had fallen to the tenth most numerous category. Women had begun to move increasingly, if slowly and modestly, into the professions.[4]

Racial differences complicate this overall conclusion. Before 1960, 33 percent of all Black women worked as domestic servants. Black women did gain some new access to other occupations and the percentage of Black women who worked as domestics declined steadily over the following years. A small number were able to find modest professional jobs. However, never to the extent of white women.[5]

It was among these professional women that the newly organized National Organization of Women (NOW), founded in 1966, gained its early adherents. Among the first members were lawyers, educators, and academics. "These women wanted economic and legal equality in professional life," feminist Ann Popkin would write a few years later.[6] Their focus remained on women's public roles. The NOW Bill of Rights dealt mostly with employment and public sector issues—passing the Equal Rights Amendment, banning sex discrimination in employment, maternity leave, tax deductions for home and childcare expenses, child daycare centers, and equal job training. Only its last demand, "the right of woman to control their own reproductive lives" and "repealing penal laws governing abortion," while still having public-sector implications, crossed into private-sector concerns.[7]

Leaders like Betty Friedan and organizations like NOW had to steer a very tricky course in the political and social waters of the time. Even while committed to economic justice, some women found the inclusion of abortion rights too much. The head of another new organization, the Women's Equity Action League (WEAL), felt it was best to avoid "issues that polarize people—like The Pill or abortion or husbands washing dishes."[8] Some women in the labor movement feared that absolute economic equality and passage of the ERA would dismantle the laws that had been passed to protect working women. On the other hand, some younger and more radical women began to see NOW as the "women's NAACP," equating it with the most mild and mainstream of the civil rights organizations. For her part, NOW leader Betty Friedan "referred to women who pandered to male sexism as Aunt Toms."[9]

NOW achieved some major victories, including pressuring Lyndon Johnson to issue an executive order banning sexual discrimination in the awarding of federal contracts and challenging the ruling of the Equal Employment Opportunity Commission (EEOC) that allowed for gender-segregated want ads.[10] Individual women moved into positions never before occupied by a female before—from a seat on the New York Stock Exchange to serving on juries in states that had banned their inclusion in jury pools. When airline stewardesses moved to challenge their particular working conditions, however, the line between public and private sector issues began to blur. Airlines insisted on hiring only young, attractive, single white women as stewardesses.* They had to maintain a slim figure (and could be fined if they gained weight), to retire when they married, and to expect to lose their job once they reached the age of thirty-two. They were told how to wear their hair and makeup, how to

---

* In 1958, the small Mohawk Airlines hired the first African American woman as a flight attendant, but the larger airlines were slower to employ Black women—Delta's first Black stewardess was hired in 1966, Pan Am's in 1969.

dress, and to wear girdles. When challenged, the airlines labeled these as the "requirements" of the job.[11]

Younger women in the various movements of the 1960s discovered that, as the decade progressed, their position within the movements or the way they were viewed by their male counterparts had not evolved much at all. It remained, as writer David Caute later put it, a world of "male captains and female corporals."[12] In fact, some elements of other Sixties' movements often added to the challenges women faced. For some women, Ann Popkin recalls, "the advent of the birth control pill and the counterculture brought expectations of more equality in social relationships." So, too did a counterculture that emphasized, "gentleness, love, personal relationships, cooperation, and the rejection of the striving competitiveness of U.S. life." However, "we were still the movement secretaries and the shit workers," three SDS women later wrote, "We served food, prepared the mailings, and made the best posters." They were also often expected to adopt the new sexual attitudes of the era. "Women who did not want sex on (some man's) demand were called 'uptight chicks,'" Popkin argued. "We were earth mothers and the sex-objects of movement men," the SDS women complained. "We were the free movement 'chicks'—free to screw any man who demanded it, or if we chose not to—free to be called hung-up, middle class and uptight."[13]

On the other hand, however, participation in the various social movements proved crucial to the creation of the women's liberation movement, even beyond the obvious connections women felt to civil rights. Many women were deeply involved in the antiwar movement as well. The increasing militancy among those opposed to the Vietnam War only added to the growing general critique of American life, as well as influencing the tactics women employed. As historian Linda Gordon would put it, the war "turned 'peaceniks' into critics of American economic and military imperialism."[14]

The rise of Black Nationalism and the movement for Black Power proved complicated for many women, especially Black women, again trying to both find their place within the movement as well as understanding what would apply to their own situations. This was especially true within the women's movement. Florynce Kennedy found that what she referred to as her "black feminism," her biographer notes, was "profoundly shaped by her relationship to Black Power." She pushed NOW to create strong ties with the Black Power and antiwar movements, often in the face of opposition from Betty Friedan and other more moderate NOW leaders. On the other hand, Kennedy faced strong opposition when she tried to include younger white feminists in gatherings focused on Black Power. At one workshop on Black Artists and the Media, Kennedy's talk was interrupted by one delegate declaring, "these white women have to get out! This meeting is for blacks only!" Kennedy had invited Ti-Grace Atkinson and Peg Brennan of NOW's New York City chapter. "These are my guests," Kennedy responded. "I don't invite people some place then tell them to leave!"[15]

Tensions were not only across racial lines. Within Black nationalist movements, gender issues would sometimes confound racial ones. The women of the Mt. Vernon/New Rochelle women's group, who were working on developing a sense of solidarity among Black women of all ages around issues that included birth control and control over their own bodies, found that these positions sometimes ran up against other emerging positions. They had to confront the argument made by some Black Nationalist men that birth control was part of a genocidal conspiracy by whites to eliminate Black people. The women responded that while they were strong supporters of nation building among Black people, they had to be allowed to "decide for themselves whether to have a baby or not to have a baby. Poor black women would be fools to sit up in the house with a whole lot of children and eventually go crazy... Middle-class white men have always done this to their women."[16]

The unequivocal reverence shown for Black Panther Eldridge Cleaver, despite his history as a rapist and his tortured justification of his actions in his book of essays, *Soul on Ice*, made some women feel that too often the issues they were raising were viewed as secondary. Cleaver had begun writing the essays while still in Folsom Prison. They eventually appeared in the New Left magazine *Ramparts* and were published by McGraw-Hill in 1968, with an introduction by the literary citric and biographer Maxwell Geismer. The book went on to sell over 2 million copies in the next few years. Although Cleaver qualified his views about rape in his introduction, in one essay he recalled once believing that his rape of white women was "an insurrectionist act." He stated he began "practicing" on Black women, before becoming a serial rapist of white women, feeling he "was trampling upon the white man's law...and I was defiling his women."

In forty-two of the first published reviews of *Soul on Ice*—from *The New York Times Book Review* and the *Saturday Review* to local daily newspapers from Wichita to Santa Monica, and written by men and women, white and Black—there seems to have been no discussion of how women were treated and objectified in Cleaver's view. Instead, one reviewer thought Cleaver was the one recent writer worthy of comparison to Jean Genet, especially his "candor in handling sexuality" and "his ability to infuse a significant philosophical stance into his sexual symbols." Another praised "Cleaver's moral energy." A third, by a young Black woman in *The New York Times*, believed the book "is about the imprisonment of men's souls by society." To still another critic, "*Soul on Ice* is what Hemingway might have called a true book...Here is not only experience, but the soul of experience." Finally, "Cleaver speaks for the black man and the black revolution, but he also speaks for and to all men."[17] The absence of judgment about the symbolic role that women play in both his life and in his revolutionary mentality as it evolved during his prison years remains striking. Cleaver was not alone in these perceptions. One British Panther wrote, "When a Black man is in bed with a white woman, he is not looking for pleasure. He is seeking revenge. As a symbol of European motherhood, she deserves to be raped."[18]

These statements represented some of the conflicting currents that emerged within the 60s movements, especially when race and gender were added to the mix. Clearly the Panthers' appeal was built on what one critic called "a masculinist rhetoric and bravado, most recognizable in the group's imagery of Black men dressed in leather jackets, wearing black berets, and holding weaponry." At the same time, recent scholarship has suggested that Panther leaders Huey Newton and Bobby Seale "promoted the idea of a gender-inclusive activist community." They "theorized about the need for a strong manhood but didn't counter that with descriptions of submissive womanhood." Newton would, within a few years, openly argue that they should "express explicit support for the goals of the women's liberation movement," as well as "show tolerance to the gay liberation movement."[19] Panther women not only proved crucial to the various community projects that the Panthers initiated—from schools to breakfast programs, and more—but also held significant positions of leadership.

Puerto Rican women in the Young Lords Party sought to counter what they saw as its masculinization. They decided they would hold a "sex strike"—refusing to have sex with their male partners until women were added to the party's leadership and until there was a reduction in what they identified as "revolutionary machismo."[20]

The first task of any reform or revolutionary movement is to persuade its audience that a real problem exists and that the current situation demands action. Once that awareness is achieved, the next step involves the tactics to confront the issues and move toward their resolution. Few industrial workers in the late nineteenth century were unaware that their wages were shameful and their working conditions abysmal. There were likely a very small number of African Americans who did not feel the abuses of racism or sought to deny its impact on their lives. It did not take much to persuade the vast majority that their lives were determined and structured by racist attitudes and limitations. By the mid-sixties, however, though a growing number of women saw clear parallels with African Americans in the obvious discriminatory patterns practiced against women, they still needed to develop strategies to raise the awareness of the majority of women, especially white women (and men), that these problems even existed. Numerous surveys, like the ones noted at the beginning of this chapter, suggested that there was much work to be done.

A crucial tactic involved forming and participating in consciousness-raising groups. Building on the strategies of a number of political discussion groups, from "rap sessions" in SNCC and SDS, the "speaking bitterness" sessions of the Chinese Revolution, and the multi-generational discussions among Black women in the Mt. Vernon/New Rochelle women's group, many women began to gather in small groups. "We told each other our life stories," Ann Popkin recalls of her group in Boston. Sometimes it was asking simple questions. "Doesn't my boss know how to make a cup of coffee?" Or making simple statements. "I can't stand walking down the street by the construction workers on their lunch hour." The discussions often moved from describing problematic situations to understanding women's roles in their perpetuation. "I began to get sick at the thought of these liberal men 'helping' their wives with the housework," Barbara Susan observed. "Every time I'd say 'thank you,' I was reinforcing the idea that it was my job!" As San Francisco feminist Pam Allen later summarized, there seemed to be "four processes in consciousness raising—opening up, sharing, analyzing, and abstracting." Slowly, as Charlotte Bunch would write, "women began to discover ourselves as an oppressed people and struggle against the effects of male supremacy on us."[21]

These were not therapy groups aimed at curing an individual woman's personal issues. Quite the contrary. Certainly sitting and talking with other women helped individuals see clearly how discrimination influenced their lives, but it also helped develop strategies and mentalities for dealing with that discrimination. Barbara Susan found the absence of men "pleasantly surprising." Harkening back to the problems Betty Freidan had first written about, Susan discovered that "the relief at finding I was not alone was incredible."[22] And these epiphanies pushed thinking and understanding even deeper. Here, finally, appeared the explicit articulation of what had been evolving within so many of the movements of the Sixties, stretching back as far as The Port Huron Statement of 1962—the most concrete example that the personal *was* political.

The electricity this generated among women was palpable. As civil rights veteran Carol Hanish put it, "This whole movement is the most exhilarating thing of my life. [It has] been a personal revolution." "I was shot into this movement," wrote activist Kathie Sarachild, who coined the phrase "Sisterhood is Powerful," "and they are going to have to shoot me to get me out of it." Women's groups sprang up all over the country. "I had never known anything as easy as organizing women's groups," recalled one woman, "as easy and as exciting and as dramatic."[23]

It proved a small step from the revelations of a consciousness-raising group to developing organizations whose aim was to bring the questions and awareness to the political struggle of women. Groups sprang up in New York and Chicago, Boston and San Francisco, Gainesville and Toronto, and more. Women began to plan conferences, marches, and demonstrations—to bring the issues of private life into the public sphere. For many women, the desire was to move beyond the economic agenda of groups like NOW. As historian Sara Evans was later to conclude, "only a movement that addressed the oppressions at the core of their identity could have generated the massive response that in fact occurred."[24]

Political realities reinforced personal motivations. The National Conference for a New Politics, a coalition organization of radicals and liberals, gathered in the late summer of 1967 in Chicago. The conference chair blocked a proposal from the women's caucus. "We don't have time for a resolution about women," he said. When several women attempted to seize the microphone to protest, the chair patted one of them on the head. "Cool down, little girl," he suggested, "we have more important things to talk about than women's problems."[25] Instead of cooling down, that "little girl," Shulamith Firestone, joined with several other enraged women delegates to organize a radical women's group in Chicago. Later that fall, Firestone joined Robin Morgan, Carol Hanish, Kathie Sarachild, Pam Allen, and Elizabeth Martinez Sutherland to launch a group they called New York Radical Women (NYRW). They were ready to take their message to the streets.

A women's anti-war march by the "Jeannette Rankin Brigade" in Washington in January 1968 demonstrated to many young women how marginalized women were. There had been women's marches through-out the Sixties, as we have seen, from the Poor People's March to Women's Strike for Peace. Jeanette Rankin, the first woman member of the House and the only member of Congress to vote against both the war declarations in 1917 and 1941, was, at eighty-seven, still active in 1968. Leading a biracial group of 5,000 women, including notable individuals like Coretta Scott King and singer Judy Collins, the group was blocked from entering the capitol and left to stand in the snow as only Rankin and King were allowed to enter and speak with a few of the Congressional leaders. And despite the large turnout and the high profile leadership, the march received very little coverage in the press. The *New York Times* ran a short article about the march on page three. The *Times'* managing editor, Clifton Daniel, later admitted that the lack of coverage was due to the fact that "violence seemed unlikely."[26]

The younger women decided the time had come to take things a step further. Frustrated with the reception of the Rankin Brigade, the New York Radical Women (NYRW) proposed a "funeral procession" to mark the death of "Traditional Womanhood." As one handout declared,

TRADITIONAL WOMANHOOD IS DEAD.
TRADITIONAL WOMEN WERE BEAUTIFUL...BUT REALLY POWERLESS.
UPPITY WOMEN WERE EVEN MORE BEAUTIFUL...
    BUT STILL POWERLESS.
SISTERHOOD IS POWERFUL!
HUMANHOOD THE ULTIMATE!

Kathie Sarachild, who wrote the leaflet, later recalled that the phrase "sisterhood is powerful" was a combination of "black power and union organizing." Little did the NYRW know how resonant that phrase would become. The funeral procession included a coffin and an effigy of a blonde woman. The dummy was carried like a funeral bier, strewn with items denoting women's situation—curlers, garters, hairspray, and more. Echoing tactics that were emerging in other political actions, like those of the Yippies, Sarachild recalls that the idea was to create "a guerrilla theater action to try to get anti-war women to start addressing actual women's rights issues rather than being stereotypical 'women for peace.'"[27]

When the marchers assembled in an auditorium, Sarachild gave the "Funeral Oration for the Burial of Traditional Womanhood."

She directly addressed the idea that other current issues—the war in Vietnam, Civil Rights—trumped those of women. "Now some sisters here are probably wondering why we should bother with such an unimportant matter at a time like this…while hundreds of thousands of human beings are being brutally slaughtered [in Vietnam] in our name." But she countered, "Sisters who ask a question like this are failing to see that they really do have a problem as women in America—that their problem is social, not merely personal—and that their problem is so closely related and interlocked with the other problems in our country, the very problem of war itself—that we cannot hope to move toward a better world or even a truly democratic society at home until we begin to solve our own problems." "Yes, sisters," she concluded, "we have a problem as women all right, a problem which renders us powerless and ineffective over the issues of war and peace, as well as over our own lives."[28]

Slowly, mainstream America and its press corps began to take notice of the growing feminist movement. Unsurprisingly, only as white women began to speak out more and more on women's issues did news organizations began to write about it. In March 1968, the *New York Times Magazine* published "The Second Feminist Wave," by Martha Wienman Lear, to introduce this new wave of feminism, the first having been the one that led to women's suffrage early in the century. After mentioning a few of the events that had occurred in recent years, Lear announced that, "feminism, which one might have supposed as dead…is again an issue." She went on to note that one of the main burdens feminists face is that "theirs is the only civil rights movement in history which has been put down, consistently, by the cruelest weapon of them all—ridicule."[29] Lear's account could not, however, escape the sexist mentality and vocabulary of the age. A good portion of her article focused on Ti-Grace Atkinson, head of the New York chapter of NOW. While Lear noted that Atkinson was an "analytic philosopher working on her doctorate at Columbia," she was also described as "29, unmarried, good-looking," and "in *The Times* she has been described as 'softly sexy.'" The positions Atkinson herself articulated pushed beyond the conventional NOW perspective. "Most women don't really see themselves as human beings with potential," she argued. "They live through their husbands and children, the institution of marriage has the same effect the institution of slavery had...To say that a woman is really 'happy' with her home and kids is as irrelevant as saying that the blacks were 'happy' being taken care of by Ol' Massa."[30]

In the same issue of the *Times Magazine* in which the article appeared, many of the advertisements either reinforced traditional gender roles or sought to minimally adapt them to the changing reality. Right in the middle of Lear's piece one advertisement for women's lingerie declared, "My wife and my wallet are in great shape—Thanks to Soft Skin—America's greatest girdle value, still only $2." Earlier in the magazine another advertisement showed minimal awareness that young women's roles were beginning to evolve. The ad employs an only slightly adjusted perspective and attempted to use what it thought was hip lingo to convince young women to buy stereo consoles. "Some bachelor girls will [use the stereo] when they furnish their pads. But all single girls have good reason to know about stereo consoles. After all, single girls get married every day."[31]

On June 3, elements of the various political and social movements of the era converged when a young woman entered Andy Warhol's Factory, both a movie studio and a counterculture hangout for his coterie, random visitors like Robert Kennedy and Truman Capote, as well as various hangers on. Valerie Solanas had lived on the streets of Greenwich Village and had insinuated herself into the Warhol scene, getting small parts in a few of his films. Her childhood in New Jersey had been extremely difficult. She claimed she had been a victim of family sexual abuse, which led to a period of homelessness in her teens. She managed to graduate with honors from the University of Maryland and begin graduate work at the University of Minnesota. By this point—in the mid-1960s—she was an out lesbian and had moved to New York. She had also authored the "SCUM Manifesto," which she sold on the streets of New York. While denying that SCUM was an acronym for "Society for Cutting Up Men," as the press often suggested, it was nonetheless a harsh critique of patriarchy.* "Life in this 'society' being, at best, an utter bore and no aspect of 'society' being at all relevant to women, there remains to civic-minded, responsible, thrill-seeking females only to overthrow the government, eliminate the money system, institute complete automation and eliminate the male sex." Olympia Press eventually agreed to publish her manifesto. It appeared later that year, with an introductory essay by Yippie Paul Krasner. In the book, Solanas envisioned a vanguard party of women, SCUM. "If SCUM ever marches, it will be over the President's stupid, sickening face; if SCUM ever strikes, it will be in the dark with a six-inch blade."[32] Walking into Warhol's Factory that June, Solanas drew a gun and fired three times at the artist, hitting him once. She also shot a visiting art citric, and took aim at a third man, before her gun jammed.

In the tumultuous aftermath, so many contemporary themes converged in this one episode—feminism, lesbianism, the counterculture, political assassination, and more, including the SCUM Manifesto, which now was seen by some as one of the major texts of radical feminism. Solanas became a disputed figure in feminist circles. Ti-Grace Atkinson called her "the first outstanding champion of women's rights" and "a heroine of the feminist movement." Flo Kennedy was hired to defend Solanas.[33] Meanwhile, Betty Friedan tried to persuade Kennedy to "desist immediately from linking NOW in any way with Valerie Solanas," arguing that she contradicted "NOW's goals of full equality for women in truly equal partnership with men."[34] Solanos ultimately served a three-year prison sentence, some of it in a psychiatric hospital.

Much of what was developing within feminist circles still remained obscured from public awareness, in part because so many social and political moments—from the Prague to Columbia to Paris and more—dominated the front pages. But that would change by summer's end. Following the example of The Mobe and the Yippies who planed major public events at the 1968 Democratic Convention in August,

---

* When first printed, Solanas used "SCUM." The Olympia Press edition used "S.C.U.M.," which reinforced the belief that it was an acronym for "Society for Cutting Up Men."

the New York Radical Women began to make plans for a demonstration at that September's Miss America Pageant in Atlantic City. Carol Hanisch, who first thought up the idea, saw this moment as a perfect opportunity to further the awareness of the movement. "Up to this time we hadn't done a lot of actions." The pageant seemed perfect. It was a "gutsy thing to do," Hanisch recalled.[35]

The Miss America Pageant had always been driven by commercial motives, coupled with a very narrow vision of what the ideal American woman should look like. Founded in 1919, the pageant initially judged the winner only on appearance. In the 1930s, a talent component was added to suggest that the competitors were more, but only slightly more, than just a pretty face. But which pretty faces could compete suggested which women fit the ideal. Contestants were limited to single, white women between the ages of 18 and 28. (The "whites only" language disappeared in the 1950s, though African American women were excluded until 1970.) All contestants were to abstain from alcohol, cigarettes, and premarital sex, facing disqualification for any transgressions. The winner would spend her year's "reign" performing community service appearances, helping to market the pageant sponsors' products, and entertaining U.S. troops.[36]

The extremely narrow vision of the ideal of Miss America had been exposed in 1945, when, only months after the German surrender and days after Japan's, a young Jewish woman, Bess Meyerson, won the Miss America competition. Meyerson would ultimately end up as television personality in the fifties and sixties and the first Commissioner of the New York City Department of Consumer Affairs in 1969. The initial reaction to her pageant participation and victory proved telling. One of the pageant organizers suggested that she change her last name to something less ethnic sounding, by which he meant "less Jewish." She refused. Judges received anonymous hostile phone calls. Sponsors received threats of boycotts. After she'd been chosen, several of the sponsoring companies withdrew their support for her post-pageant tour. One country club where she was scheduled to speak revoked its invitation because she was Jewish. Meyerson encountered anti-Semitism throughout the year.

By 1968, there was much to object to about the Miss America Pageant, and the New York Radical Women protest organizers knew it. The call that went out to announce the Atlantic City action, "No More Miss America!," touched on most of them. Instead of recognizing the "ideal" American woman, the plan was to "liberate the contest auction-block," spearheaded by "de-plasticized, breathing women." The liberators would come from "Women's Liberation Groups, black women, high-school and college women, women's peace groups, women's welfare and social-work groups, women's job-equality groups, pro-birth control and pro-abortion groups—women of every political persuasion." Echoing the initial vision of "The Festival of Life" the Yippies had planned for Chicago, the organizers envisioned a "day-long boardwalk-theater event...We will protest the image of Miss America, an image that oppresses women in every area in which it purports to represent us." There would be picket lines, guerilla theater; leafleting, lobbying, and "a huge Freedom Trash Can...into which we will throw bras, girdles, curlers, false eyelashes, wigs, and representative issues of *Cosmopolitan*, *Ladies Home Journal*, *Family Circle*, etc." Women were encouraged to bring "any such woman-garbage you have around the house...It should be a groovy day on the Boardwalk in the sun with our sisters."

"No More Miss America!," written by poet, activist, and former child actor Robin Morgan, went on to list ten major points of protest, a number of which moved beyond issues specific to women and touched on concerns swirling in the air in 1968. Certainly, several spoke directly to the sexist nature of the competition and its role in perpetuating women's situation.

> *The Degrading Mindless-Boob-Girlie Symbol.* The Pageant contestants epitomize the roles we are all forced to play as women...forced daily to compete for male approval, enslaved by ludicrous "beauty" standards.

> *The Unbeatable Madonna–Whore Combination.* Miss America and Playboy's centerfold are sisters over the skin.

> *The Irrelevant Crown on the Throne of Mediocrity.* Miss America represents what women are supposed to be: inoffensive, bland, apolitical.

Miss America as Dream Equivalent To—? Every little boy supposedly can grow up to be President, what can every little girl hope to grow to be? Miss America. Real power to control our own lives is restricted to men.

Miss America as Big Sister Watching You. The pageant exercises Thought Control to enslave us all the more in high-heeled, low-status roles.

But other points clearly connected with other issues of the time.

Racism with Roses. Since its inception in 1921, the Pageant has not had one Black finalist...never a Puerto Rican, Alaskan, Hawaiian, or Mexican-American winner. Nor has there ever been a true Miss America—an American Indian.

Miss America as Military Death Mascot. The highlight of her reign each year is a cheerleader-tour of American troops abroad—last year she went to Vietnam...We refuse to be used as Mascots for Murder.

The Consumer Con-Game. Miss America is a walking commercial for the Pageant's sponsors. Wind her up and she plugs your product.[37]

Flo Kennedy was central in recruiting Black feminists to participate as well as building on her connections with Atlantic City's Black community. She located a small locally owned Black resort that demonstrators could use as a base.[38]

Over the course of the summer, a second counter-event to the Miss American Pageant was also taking shape. Purportedly, the daughters of a Philadelphia African American businessman, J. Morris Anderson, answered "Miss America," when he asked them what they wanted to be when they grew up. Anderson knew the reality his daughters—and all Black women—faced with regard to the pageant. While some in the NAACP had tried to work with pageant organizers to integrate the contest, Anderson joined Phillip Savage, a local NAACP official, to organize a separate event, the Miss Black America Pageant. We have already seen the reticence of the national NAACP to become involved in what it considered issues tangential to its mission, such as Vietnam War critiques like those expressed by Martin Luther King in 1967 or the Poor People's March. Here again, attitudes within the Black community confronted those held by the NAACP leadership. Echoing the treatment of women's issues within New Left circles, one NAACP official wrote to NAACP chair Roy Wilkins. "We do not regard the 'Miss America stunt,'" as he called the proposal for the Miss Black America Pageant, "as an important issue." It was "trivial" compared to "more serious politics."[39]

Others disagreed. Attitudes about integration and Black history and culture had certainly evolved over the previous few years, including embracing new ideas about African American culture, personal styles, and physical appearance encapsulated in the phrase "Black is Beautiful." Phillip Savage, who was Tri-State Secretary of the NAACP, announced, "we want to be in Atlantic City at the same time the hypocritical Miss America contest is being held. Theirs will be lily white and ours will be black."[40] Savage's central role led to the impression that the Miss Black America Pageant had NAACP sponsorship. In fact, Salvage was acting on his own. He and Anderson had to scramble to pull their event together, able to gather only a dozen contestants by the time of their pageant. Still, they believed it was the public perception of the event rather than the specifics of the competition that would garner attention and help realize their intentions.

On Saturday, September 7, just a week after the tumultuous end of the Chicago Democratic Convention, several hundred marchers gathered on the Atlantic City Boardwalk to protest the Miss America Pageant. The pageant was to take place that night at the Convention Hall, where it had been held since 1940. They walked a picket line carrying posters with statements like: "Can Make-Up Cover the Wounds of Our Oppression," and "Uppity Women Unite." In keeping with the times, some of the posters pushed cultural boundaries. One poster copied the image employed by butchers and cattle farmers that showed where various cuts of meat came from on a steer. Titled "Break the Dull Steak Habit," it used the image of a nude woman, shown from the back and wearing a cowboy hat, with lines and words on her body identifying the sections—"Chuck," "Rib," "Rump," and more. Posters using this image read, "Welcome to the Miss America Cattle Auction," and "If You Want Meat—Go to a Butcher."

As in Chicago and elsewhere, guerilla theater moments captured public attention. A sheep was crowned "Miss America," just as a pig had been nominated for president the week before. A larger-than-life effigy of Miss America appeared—a very tall, blonde woman in an American flag bathing suit with long eyelashes. A number of protestors, including Flo Kennedy and Bonnie Allen, a Black housewife from the Bronx, chained themselves to the doll to suggest the parallels between slavery and women's enslaved situation. Peggy Dobbins dressed as an auctioneer in a long black coat and striped pants. "Step right up!," she shouted, "How much am I offered for this number one piece of prime American property?! She sings in the kitchen, hums at the typewriter, purrs in bed!"[41]

What garnered the most public attention, however, and would forever remain associated with the Miss America demonstration was the Freedom Trash Can. All sorts of items had been collected—bras, girdles, hair curlers, false eyelashes, high heels, dish detergent, floor wax, *Playboy*, women's magazines, and more. The initial plan had been to set the accumulated "women-garbage" aflame. Atlantic City officials would only issue a permit to march, however, if the organizers promised not to light the trash can on fire, fearing the potential of setting flame to the wooden boardwalk. Despite the lack of a conflagration, media reports had picked up the initial plan and fastened onto the inclusion of one item. The protestors were labeled "bra-burners" and the image stuck. "All the dumb male media monkeys could talk about," Flo Kennedy later wrote, "were the bra burners." But Kennedy admitted that she kind of liked the label, because it made the women "seem tougher than we really were."[42]

An article in the *New York Post* several days before the demonstration opened with the provocative line, "Lighting a match to a draft card or a flag has been a standard gambit of protest groups in recent years, but something new is due to go up in flames this Saturday. Would you believe a bra burning?" The woman reporter assigned to the story, Lindsy Van Gelder, felt her editors wanted a puff piece. She wanted something more serious, especially after interviewing Robin Morgan—"the more she talked, the more my mind was going *click, click, click*."[43] Van Gelder wrote the opening lede to satisfy both her editors and herself. The article ran under the editor-chosen headline, "Bra Burners Plan Miss America Protest." The image was cemented in public consciousness when nationally syndicated humor columnist Art Buchwald wrote about the event a few days later. After describing the boardwalk demonstration and the Freedom Trash Can, Buchwald added, "The final and most tragic part of the protest took place when several of the women publicly burned their brassieres," something that never happened. Regardless, he continued, "as one who has always been on the side of protestors, I regret to say this demonstration in Atlantic City has gone too far...By demanding that women do away with all beauty aids...so they will be on an equal footing with men, these well-meaning but misled females were trying to destroy everything this country holds dear."

Once again, ridicule and patronization became the tools undermining women's efforts. The American woman, Buchwald continued, "beautiful though she is, needs all the help she can get...If the average American female gave up all her beauty products she would look like [the oddly dressed, eccentric counterculture singer] Tiny Tim, and there would be no reason for the American male to have anything to do with her at all." Buchwald even tried to tie Chicago and Atlantic City. "As we saw in Chicago, there are still many men who would like to club women over the head, if they're given the slightest excuse, and there is no better excuse for hitting a woman than the fact that she looks like a man." He concluded by saying it is legitimate to object to the Miss America Pageant being "lily white" or even that it is "a bore," but burning bras suggests "dissent in this country has gone too far."[44] Because of Buchwald's wide readership, the name "bra burners" took hold. Even a sympathetic treatment of the demonstrations by Shana Alexander in *Life* continually referred to the women on the boardwalk as "bra burners."[45]

By the time the Pageant finally began that night, 15 to 20 activists, who had used the nearby Black resort secured by Flo Kennedy to change into traditional women's clothes and put on make-up, had insinuated themselves into the audience in the hall, planning several actions. Peggy Dobbins remembered that as a girl, "my mother used to hold my head down in the sink and pour on this stinking stuff [Toni home permanent] to make my hair curl. So when we found out that Toni home permanent was the sponsor of the Miss America pageant we decided to sprinkle [it] along the aisles." They filled small atomizers with the liquid and began to spray it on the carpet. "I got caught!," Dobbins recalls. "I watched the end of the pageant in jail with women who were arrested for prostitution, and I wrote on the wall of my little bunk, 'Prostitutes of the world unite, we have nothing to lose but our pimps!' "[46] Flo Kennedy arrived to post Dobbins' bail and later was able to persuade the court to drop all charges.[47]

Four other women had secured seats in the front row of the balcony. On cue, they stood and unfurled a banner that read "WOMEN'S LIBERATION," as well as shouting that phrase and "No More Miss America!" Kathie Sarachild, one of the four, recalled looking down, seeing Peggy Dobbins' arrest, and fearing the same would happen to her. Police were in the balcony within minutes, the banner removed, and the women hustled out the door. They were not arrested. "We pulled it off," Sarachild shouted, as they all laughed sighs of relief.[48]

When Judith Ann Ford of Illinois was declared Miss America that night, it appeared to television audiences as though the demonstrations had been merely a minor sideshow to a typical pageant. Yet, even here, small elements of the changing landscape crept in. Ford was a college gymnastics athlete, specializing in the trampoline. She was the only woman on her university's gymnastics team and the first woman to win any varsity letter at her school. When Illinois officials enrolled her in a program to improve her beauty contest presence, one of the instructors chided her, "You walk like an athlete." "Thank you," she replied. When she chose a trampoline routine for the talent competition, she was told that it was inappropriate, as Miss America contestants did not sweat. She rejected the advice. During the afternoon, she was one of several of the contestants who ventured out to the boardwalk to take in the demonstrations. When asked a question, as part of the competition, about how she could make America a better place, she replied, "I think that a person has to learn that he is no better than his neighbor, and that all people are equal and should be given equal opportunity for all things." This was considered a "political" answer in 1968.[49]

The organizers of the Miss Black America Pageant had decided they would begin their program at midnight, in the hope that the reporters who were covering the main pageant would wander over to the hotel where the dozen or so Black contestants gathered. Earlier, they held a parade on the same boardwalk as that day's demonstrators. The contestants rode in a motorcade through the Black sections of town, led by a band of "Bongo players in African garb," as one newspaper put it. When the competition got underway at the Ritz Carleton Hotel, it still contained the typical competitions in talent, bathing suits, and evening gowns. It was clear, however, that some of the content was radically different. The ultimate winner, Saundra Williams of Philadelphia, performed a traditional African dance as part of the talent portion. She wrote a poem, "Awareness," which was set to music and told of the shame young Black girls felt about their appearance. Her poem concludes, "For Black, Black is my color / And my hair is kinky and brown / My nose is wide and my lips are thick / but never again will I hold my head down." While Williams appeared in a traditional evening gown and bathing suit, she wore her hair naturally curly, in a style that was just coming to be called an "Afro." During the question-and-answer period, she said she believed husbands and wives should perform the same amount of housework, "I think the male is getting awfully lazy." This elicited boos from some of the men in the audience.[50]

Coming so quickly after Chicago, it is unsurprising that the Miss America demonstrations would get somewhat lost in the shuffle of national attention. The forms of protest were so different, as well. Flo Kennedy later compared the two. Chicago was like "throwing a brick through a window," where Atlantic City "is comparable to peeing on an expensive rug at a polite cocktail party." That kind of protest still could have a strong impact. "The Man never expects the second kind of protest," Kennedy observed, "and very often that's the one that really gets him uptight."[51] Chicago also loomed large in some of the protesters early assessments of Atlantic City. Judith Ford representing Illinois was not ignored. A month after the event, Robin Morgan would write of "the crowning of Miss Illinois as the 'real' Miss America, her smile still blood-flecked from Mayor Daley's kiss."[52]

And the ridicule and disdain persisted. In the *New York Post*, syndicated columnist Harriet Van Horne dismissed the demonstrators as "those sturdy lasses in her sensible shoes." Quoting her father, she declared, "If they can't be pretty, dammit, they can at least be quiet!!" "This lady of the press," she said of herself, "has something better to do on a Saturday night than burn her undergarments on the boardwalk of Atlantic City. And I suspect that the deep-down aching trouble with these lassies is that they haven't." Reacting to the critique of the "degrading, mindless boob-girl symbolism" that the feminists decried, Van Horne also believed, "most of us would rather be some dear man's boob-girl than nobody's cum laude scholar." In fact, she believed feminist women had just been consorting with the wrong men, the "New Male" who "wears ruffled shirts, Edwardian frockcoats, and a chain around his neck like a wine steward." Women needed men who understood that what a woman wanted was to "feel utterly feminine, desirable, and almost too delicate for this hard world." In one sweeping set of false generalizations, Van Horne dismissed feminism, the counterculture, and the modern reality.[53]

It took time for people to come to understand the impact of the Miss America demonstrations. "The pageant has been called the birth of the women's movement," Robin Morgan recalled. That assessment "is a) totally untrue, and b) deeply satisfying." She noted that much work had gone on with groups like NOW for several years. She and other New York Radical Women also remembered how women poured into the movement after Atlantic City. "Our meetings exploded," Kathie Sarachild remembers.[54]

Maintaining the guerilla theater style of the era, actions continued around the nation. New York women created the WITCH Halloween demonstrations. Like the Yippies, whose political style they emulated, WITCH was an acronym before it had a full title. For the Halloween demonstrators, they declared the name stood for Women's International Terrorist Conspiracy from Hell. (For a subsequent demonstration against the Bell Telephone Company, they became "Women Incensed at Telephone Company Harassment.") On Halloween, members dressed as witches entered the New York Stock Exchange, as the Yippies had done in 1967, and formed a "sacred circle," intending to put a hex on the exchange. They handed out leaflets that described their group. "WITCH is an all-woman Everything. It's theater, revolution, magic, terror, joy, garlic, flowers, spells. It's an awareness that witches and gypsies were the original guerillas and resistance fighters to oppression—particularly the oppression of women…WITCH lives and laughs in every woman." When the Dow Jones Industrial average dropped sharply the following day, some members took credit, often facetiously.[55]

New York was not the only site of women's collective action. Across the country and around the globe, moved by a variety of issues and in variety of forms, women's groups took their complaints to conferences, to legislative hearings, and to the streets. By 1969, women's liberation, as it was now publicly identified, had come out of the shadows of other movements. No longer dismissed as frivolous or secondary, women's issues and the women's movement emerged as a dynamic and central political force of the era.

The boardwalk demonstrations in Atlantic City represent not the beginnings or even the coalescing of the women's movement. Rather, they proved a huge step in its growing public awareness. As historian Estelle Freedman was to conclude years later, with the Miss American demonstration women's liberation "scored [it's] first publicity coup." Some elements of the women's movement stretched back to the postwar years and on into the 1930s. Other elements connected to various Sixties movements. The energy and cross-pollination with other movements of 1968 helped solidify the idea of a women's movement. "Why not us ?," became an obvious question. Atlantic City proved crucial in the emergence of one of the central movements created in the later years of the decade, a political, social, and cultural force that would only gain strength—and significant achievements—in the coming years.[56]

21

Mexico City

Machine Guns and Raised Fists

Throughout 1968 powerful currents of unrest and change swirled around the nation and the globe—an event in one part of the world would have an impact on another event half a world away—Saigon to New Hampshire, New York to Paris. And as we have seen, these currents converged and collided in August on the streets of Chicago. In Mexico City that summer and autumn two independent streams seemed to coincide, if never fully converging—one deriving from tensions within Mexican society, the other representing a new arena in the quest for racial justice. The later would lead to international headlines. The first to an event of staggering proportion and horror.

Nineteenth-century Mexico was marked by political instability and military coups. Beginning in 1876, Porfirio Diaz, who had come to power in one of the coups, brought about some sense of stability but with no movement toward anything that might be considered democratic. Though he was elected eight times over 31 years, there was little doubt that his was an authoritarian regime—election results were manipulated, voter interest remained low. By the early twentieth century, unrest boiled over, leading to the Revolution of 1917. Various factions emerged throughout the country, including those following popular figures such as Emilio Zapata and Pancho Villa, leading to another era of frequent elections, coups, and U.S. military intervention. This instability was finally overcome with the creation of the Institutional Revolutionary Party, in Spanish the Partido Revolucionario Institucional or the PRI. The PRI ruled Mexico for 71 years, from 1929–2000. A veneer of democracy was maintained by having presidents serve only a single, six-year term. In all, there were 16 consecutive presidents from one party. Every six years the PRI chose its next leader. In 1963, they announced that its candidate in 1964 would be Gustavo Díaz Ordaz. Facing only token opposition, Díaz Ordaz was elected with nearly 90 percent of the vote.

One of Díaz Ordaz's ambitions as president was to advance the image of Mexico in the eyes of the world, to raise it out of the category of "banana republics" and Latin American dictatorships. It would no longer be seen as an underdeveloped nation, but a rapidly developing and modernizing one. Part of that effort was Mexico's successful application to host the 1968 Olympic games, winning out over Detroit, Lyons, and Buenos Aires. This would be the first time that the Olympics would be held in Latin America. "All the eyes of the world will be on Mexico," Díaz Ordaz announced.[1]

Among Díaz Ordaz's deepest concerns, one he shared with the U.S. government, was the appeal of Fidel Castro and the Cuban Revolution among the young. Castro's 1959 victory had been an inspiration for many, not only in Latin American but also in the U.S. Before Castro's regime came to be viewed as just another Soviet satellite—albeit one only "90 miles from home," as anti-Castro elements in the U.S. use to declare—many saw the utopian promise emanating from Havana. Castro was often portrayed as the "Robin Hood of the Caribbean," a dashing figure whose charismatic persona was positively depicted in the pages of mainstream American newspapers and periodicals. He appeared on *Meet The Press* and, amazingly, *The Ed Sullivan Show*. And even after Castro's mystique began to dim, there was the figure of Che Guevera, who remains a romantic figure for many to this day.

Among those most interested in Cuba was C. Wright Mills, whose work, as we have seen, was essential to the emerging New Left. In the last years of his life, Mills visited and wrote about Cuba. His 1961 book *Listen, Yankee* became one of the first major works on the new Cuban regime. Cuba's appeal appeared in many sectors of the emerging 1960s landscape. Allen Ginsberg and other members of the Beats, including poet Lawrence Ferlinghetti and playwright LeRoi Jones (later Amiri Baraka), became "enamored with the Cuban revolution," wrote one Cuban historian.[2] Invited to Cuba in 1965, Ginsberg ran afoul of Cuban authorities both for his support of Cuban dissident poets and some homoerotic comments, and was expelled. A number of individuals connected with Black Nationalism and Black Power were also attracted to the Cuban experiment. When Castro came to the U.S. in 1960, he met with Malcolm X in Harlem. By the mid-1960s, just as someone like Ginsberg was getting off the Cuban express, Huey Newton, Eldridge Cleaver, Stokely Carmichael, Baraka, and Rap Brown were getting on. For some, such as Carmichael, the Cuban Revolution linked to the work of writers like Frantz Fanon, whose *Wretched of the Earth* was critical to discussions of decolonization.

Young Mexicans, like young people around the world, "lived in the thrall of the Cuban Revolution and the Vietnamese resistance," wrote Mexican writer and activist Paco Ignacio Taibo.[3] The growing criticism of what the PRI called their "Mexican Revolution" contrasted with the allure of the actual revolution in Cuba. During the 1950s, Fidel and Raul Castro had fled Cuba, spending time in New York and then in Mexico, where they met Guevara, who was Argentinean and had witnessed the 1954 CIA-orchestrated counterrevolution in Guatemala. Along with 80 others, the three landed in Cuba on July 26, 1956. By 1959, they had toppled the U.S.-backed dictatorship of Fulgencio Battista. The Cuban Revolution became the model for many young Mexicans, as well as others around the world, and "the icon of Che," historian Elaine Carey notes, became the "conception of the New Man...the revolutionary who was not tied to the constraints of modern society...anti-imperialist and anti-capitalist."[4] After he was gunned down in Bolivia in 1967, "El Che...was our number-one ghost," wrote Taibo. "He was no more, yet he was still with us—the voice, the personality, the rousing injunction to throw everything aside and go on the road...Che was the guy who was everywhere even though he was dead. He was dead—but he belonged to us."[5] This kind of attitude worried Díaz Ordaz, and it worried the American government as well.

Despite initial enthusiasm for Castro among Americans, the U.S. government was suspicious from the outset. The plan for the Bay of Pigs invasion, intended to set off a counterrevolution, was hatched during the waning years of the Eisenhower administration, soon after Castro had come to power. It's spectacular failure in the early months of John Kennedy's presidency only intensified the animosity. Self-preservation sent Castro into a defensive alliance with the Soviet Union, which would ultimately lead to the Cuban Missile Crisis. Throughout the decade, worries about "Communist subversion" in the Western hemisphere always put Havana at their center. Mexico's Ministry of the Interior, headed by Díaz Ordaz before he became president, was as vigilant as J. Edgar Hoover's FBI in keeping track of suspected Communists, including anyone who sang Cuban songs at rallies or visited Havana. During his tenure at the Interior department, Díaz Ordaz cultivated relationships with the FBI and the CIA. Throughout the decade, the CIA kept close watch on activities in Mexico.[6]

A second concern for Díaz Ordaz and the PRI was the influence of the French. The long-term mystique of Paris, especially among the young, persisted. Jean-Paul Sartre remained the Mexican ideal of an intellectual: A degree from a French university remained the most prestigious. French Marxist intellectual Regis DeBray became a philosophy professor at the University of Havana. With his imprisonment in Bolivia in 1967 (for working with Che), Debray's case became an international cause célèbre. As one Mexican activist recalled, "We all read Debray's *Revolution in the Revolution*," which focused on the role of guerilla warfare in anti-colonial struggles. The May 1968 demonstrations in Paris intensified the connections between Mexican and French students, as well as Díaz Ordaz's obsession and fear. Radical parties called for repeating the French experience in Mexico. During the summer, several French students from Nanterre—where the French student movement first erupted—came to Mexico City to meet with student activists.[7]

Both the students and the government watched what was happening in Paris, Prague, and on the streets of the U.S. The Mexican government closely monitored American students who came to visit Mexico and Mexican students who studied in the U.S. Mexico was one of the few nations that did not condemn the Soviet invasion of Czechoslovakia. As historian Mark Kurlansky concluded in his history of 1968, "The Institutional Revolutionary Party did not like revolutions anymore."[8]

The PRI perpetuated a vision of a stable Mexico resisting subversive political trends and fostering a sense of what domestic life should be like. Their ideal of the Revolutionary Family offered an image of home life that mirrored their political vision. Mexican author Octavio Paz observed, "Behind the respect for Señor Presidente there is the traditional image of the Father."[9] The idealized Mexican family was not very different from the idealized American model, with the father at the center, the mother as child bearer and homemaker, the children obediently loyal. What added emphasis was the articulated connection between the family and political stability.

Mexico's proximity to the United States and the global pull of American culture created tensions. American cultural penetration of Mexican society increased throughout the 1950s. Supermarket shelves offered Rice Krispies, Campbell's soup, Coca-Cola, and Heinz Ketchup. Mexicans could watch American television shows like "Leave it to Beaver" and "The Lone Ranger." Mexican Christmases began to look like those in the U.S.—with Santa Claus, stockings, and gifts under decorated trees. Some Mexicans were highly critical of these cultural intrusions; others welcomed them. This was what it was like to be modern, contemporary, middle class, they believed. If Mexico was rising out of the "underdeveloped" category, it was appropriate that it begin to evidence these signs of modernity.[10]

Into this mix came rock 'n' roll. At its core, rock 'n' roll was a call to the young to resist parental authority, to develop an independent youth culture, and to begin to entertain, if only tentatively, youthful sexuality. All this flew in the face of the role ascribed for the young in the image of the Revolutionary Family. Again, though, rock 'n' roll meant what it was to be modern, to connect with the prevailing cultural zeitgeist. It was nearly impossible for Mexican youth, or young people anywhere in the world, to resist American culture. In part, this was driven by economic pressures. American record companies began to develop Latin American divisions, for example, to produce and distribute their music. As in the U.S., youth culture now became a marketable entity, in music and movies.

Mexican youth were drawn to the same heroes of youth culture as Americans and other young people all over the world—especially Elvis Presley, Marlon Brando, and James Dean. Some of the heroes of the Mexican Revolution, like Villa or Zapata, presented rebellious images within the PRI mythology. But now they were being replaced by these modern icons, rebels disconnected from Mexican history.* One of the first Mexican rock singers recalled how Brando's *The Wild One* influenced everyone around him. "We rode around on motorcycles...rock 'n' roll was this wild thing...Our parents didn't even have time to tell us not to do it; it hit like an avalanche."[11] There was also a backlash against these modern icons, parallel to the one developing in the U.S. The title of James Dean's movie *Rebel Without a Cause* offered a phrase with which to disparage much of this youthful phenomenon—in Spanish *"rebeldismo sin causal."* As in the U.S., talk of juvenile delinquency filled the air. The new American role models seemed to embody it. In addition, a fabricated story claimed that Elvis Presley was prejudiced against Mexicans. "I would rather kiss three black girls than a Mexican," Presley was falsely reported to have said. Radio stations boycotted his records.

The stakes were greater, authorities argued, than one singer or even one music form. "If this amoral condition continues to penetrate our society," one newspaper editorialized, "it is no exaggeration to say the collapse of the family will lead to the collapse of society, the state, and the

---

* The irony here is that in 1952, Marlon Brando starred in Elia Kazan's motion picture, *Viva Zapata!*, which had a screenplay by John Steinbeck. While well received at the time, including several Academy Award nominations, it was later criticized for minimizing both the left-wing aspects of Zapata's struggle as well as the brownface makeup Brando wore in the film. While Brando became an icon for Mexican youth, his role as Zapata was rarely mentioned.

nation."[12] The solution was a reassertion of Mexican culture and of Mexican artists. Radio stations were coerced into playing more music made by Mexicans. One Mexican legislator accused the radio and television industry of negative programming affecting "the morality of our homes." The government needed to prohibit "transmission of programs which damage children and contribute to juvenile delinquency," as well as leaving "men and women without moral scruples and lacking respect for society." A bill aimed at addressing this issue passed unanimously. Some believed the effect of the legislation to be a great success. "Young People Have Forgotten Rock 'n' Roll and Prefer Oldies," one newspaper declared. Claims were made that the kids had rejected "rabid" rock music in favor of "sentimental melodies." Or so the authorities thought—or, perhaps only hoped.[13]

After the initial explosion of rock 'n' roll in America in the mid-fifties, by the late 1950s and early 1960s this first flush quieted, with the music becoming more programmed and the record companies exercising more control. Mexican popular culture evidenced a similar calming. As in France, the idea of "adaptation" developed, as we have seen, rewriting the lyrics of popular songs in French—keeping the melodies but changing the lyrics. Mexican bands with names that clearly represented a cultural amalgam were everywhere—Los Loud Jets, Los Teen Tops, Los Black Jeans, Los Hooligans, and more. Their songs, known as *refritos*, were all over the radio. They satisfied both young people's desire for a driving beat and the government's desire for music made by Mexicans, as well as toning down some of the more provocative lyrics of the English-language original. Los Teen Tops' cover of Little Richard's "Good Golly Miss Molly," for example, changed "Good Golly, Miss Molly, sure likes to ball" to "Here comes the gal, she sure likes to dance." The lyric "When she's rocking' and a-rollin', can't hear her mama call," became "When she's rocking' and a-rollin', she's the queen of this place."[14]

Then, as Mexican cultural historian Eric Zolov put it, "the Beatles arrived and changed everything...The British invasion of Mexico signaled a definitive shift in the musical direction of rock 'n' roll toward what increasingly became known simply as *rock*." Bands from along the

Rio Grande and in Tijuana, adept at English-language cover versions of the British hits, became the rage in Mexico City. Radio programming began to play the "authentic" originals, rather than the rewritten Spanish substitutes. The counterculture now began to flower.[15] And it was more than just the rockers. "We listened to Joan Baez and Bob Dylan, Pete Seeger and Peter, Paul, and Mary," remembered Paco Ignacio Taibo, "the music of the anti-Vietnam War generation."[16] "We loved Eldridge Cleaver, Muhammad Ali, and Angela Davis," recalled another student leader. They sang "We Shall Overcome," read Norman Mailer, and praised the Black Panthers. "We were more interested in American culture than our parents. In the fifties, students wore shirts and ties. We wore jeans and indigenous-style shirts."[17] Along with counterculture styles—long hair on men, young women in miniskirts, psychedelic imagery—came a rise in marijuana and other drug use. The image of the hippie now entered the Mexican cultural debate, with derogatory depictions in mainstream media equivalent to those heard in the U.S., but with the added element that this social phenomenon was being perpetuated by "dirty, long-haired North American youth."[18]

By 1967, all these trends in youth culture, from the personal to the political, merged into something the Mexican young called "La Onda," which translated as "the wave." Descriptions of the meaning of La Onda echoed thinking similar to that in the U.S. and across Europe, akin to the use of "The Movement" in the U.S. "A new spirit, the repudiation of convention and prejudice, the creation of a new morality...the expansion of consciousness," wrote one young Mexican. It was a new era and a new consciousness connected to "Che Guevara, Malcolm X, Allen Ginsberg, Fidel Castro, and Mick Jagger."[19] The full meaning and impact of the youth rebellion of the Sixties had reached Mexico.

It is therefore not surprising that things would erupt in Mexico. And again, as elsewhere, it began among college and university students. Reports of minor skirmishes among students and between students and police began to be reported in the summer of 1968. The government employed the *granaderos*, their feared riot police, to quell the troubles, revealing just how important it was for the state to keep civic order in the run-up to the Olympic Games, scheduled for that October. This also added to the notoriety of these incidents and attracted new participants. Press coverage justified the beating of the students and depicted the demonstrators as a radical minority. A march was organized for July 26 to protest the police brutality, coinciding with a planned protest against the American war in Vietnam, and to commemorate the fifteenth anniversary of Castro's first revolutionary action. While the sponsoring organizations had obtained the necessary permits, when 5,000 demonstrators went into the streets, they were met with a violent police response. The next day, the students moved to shut down their schools and, like the Parisian students, used buses to barricade the streets. "From that day forward," wrote historian Elaine Carey, "the movement coalesced."[20]

Government propaganda continued to blame communists and outside agitators. Students had carried banners proclaiming, "Che is not dead, he lives in us." This may have been in keeping with the ethos of the protests of '68, but it provided an easy target for the government. Communist Party offices were ransacked, student members of communist groups detained. Blame was placed on foreign agitators, followers of "Fidel, Che, and Mao, apostles of hate and anarchy," one newspaper declared.[21]

The American government took special interest in all this, as declassified documents later revealed. In mid-July, a CIA assessment warned of Cuban influence among Mexican students, seeking to disrupt the Olympics. Without having any hard evidence to support the government's claims that the Mexican Communist Party was responsible for the riots, the U.S. Embassy in Mexico City suggested that Moscow may have ordered them "to counteract the impact of events in Czechoslovakia."[22]

Over the next week, more and more schools became involved in the street activity, from the prestigious National Autonomous University of Mexico (UNAM) to the National Polytechnic Institute (Poli), the largest technical school. Students from secondary and vocational schools also began to take part. The following week, the demonstrations led to the government's decision to clear the streets, using light tanks and armored vehicles. When students took shelter in a preparatory school, the military fired a bazooka at its ancient baroque door, destroying it. While the government claimed only arrests and minor injuries, the demonstrators claimed both students and bystanders had been killed. The military actions only further angered the students and led more of them to join the movement.

In an attempt to calm the situation, the rector of UNAM, Javier Barros Sierra, a distinguished scholar and once considered a possible PRI presidential candidate, led a march of Poli and UNAM students in support of students' political and civil rights. Barros Sierra's participation helped undermine the government's continuing depiction of the students as "thugs" or "overindulged brats." Marches and demonstrations continued for most of August, as public support grew. The foreign journalists arriving for the upcoming Olympics added to the positive appraisal of the students. "The organized cleptocracy of Mexico," one British newspaper observed, "is seriously threatened. Finally the citizens have awakened from their lethargy."[23]

Protests continued for the next month and a half, the movement grew daily, and the government waxed between conciliatory gestures and hard-line responses. The number of schools joining the strike rose to 70 by mid-August, with artists, workers, and opposition parties also voicing their support. Groups of students and others organized "lightening brigades" to protect demonstrators and keep the public informed. These brigades organized meetings in public spaces—factories, supermarkets, cinemas, bus stations—to spark impromptu public discussions. Mexican students began to produce posters and flyers. As in Paris, these appeared all over the city, and like the French ones that caricatured the leaders, many in Mexico used the easily recognized face of Díaz Ordaz, well-known for his unattractive looks. Others turned to guerilla theater, again in public spaces. In one example, an older actor, usually a woman, would buy a newspaper, scan the front page, and then loudly castigate students as "troublemakers" and "Communists." A younger actor, also female, would respond. Their voices would escalate, with the onlookers always coming to side with the younger woman's viewpoint.[24]

American counterculture sensibilities penetrated the movement. Jamie Pantones remembers that as a young teen he did not really understand the political realities, "but I supported...the students. This was because Díaz Ordaz was a shithead" and "they persecuted people with long hair; they repressed those who smoked pot [and] they didn't allow rock."[25] It is also clear that ideas about gender restrictions and possibilities found their way into the movement. Women's roles in many public actions challenged long-held ideas about their engaging in public sector activities. As in the U.S. and elsewhere, women encountered sexist attitudes within the movements. One woman recalled that mostly we were "maids and secretaries"; another that the male activists "wanted to send us to the kitchen."[26] Paco Ignacio Taibo recalls, "there was always some dope who wanted the women to run the kitchen but there would always be someone slightly less dopey to say that that was everybody's job." Taibo describes how young Mexican women in the sixties developed their own public identity, a combination of miniskirts, Simone de Beauvoir, fishnet stockings, and velvet hair bands. "For thousands of sisters the times offered a chance to be equal...the stereotypical Mexican 'little mother' was on her way out."[27]

While Díaz Ordaz had made some gestures toward public dialogue and potential conciliation, the tone of his annual address to the nation on September 1 was hard line. "We defend as men that which we must defend: our home, integrity, life, and liberty," he declared, asserting the right of the government under the Mexican Constitution to use "military force for the security of the country." With more and more international journalists arriving for the Olympics, plans were announced for a silent march on September 13. To counter the government's depiction of the students as Communist sympathizers, the organizing committee, the Comité Coordinator de Huelga de UNAM (CNH), asked that images of Che and Ho Chi Minh be replaced by those of Mexican heroes. The silence of the marchers would guarantee no chanting or singing that could be misrepresented. "Our silence must be interpreted as unanimous repudiation of the injustice and violence unleashed by the government," the CNH declared. In mid-afternoon, students gathered in a park in the center of the city, some putting white tape across their mouths, and began a march to the Zócalo, the main square in the center of the city. It was an "immense river of people," one marcher recalls. Even when passing the U.S. Embassy, they remained silent. "The silence was the most impressive thing about the crowd," remembered another participant. The Zócalo eventually filled with thousands of demonstrators, some holding large images of Pancho Villa and Emilio Zapata. Although there were speeches, the crowd remained silent until the event ended with a singing of the National Anthem.[28]

The great success of the Silent March won many new supporters to the student cause. It also intensified the government's resistance. They felt they were losing control, with the Olympics only weeks away. The media continued to fan the flames of antagonism, depicting the students as radicals out to humiliate Mexico in the eyes of the world. Two thousand people in a small mountain village attacked and murdered five young men, outsiders stranded in the town because of a severe storm. Without any real connection to the students in Mexico City and not involved in the protests, to the townspeople they nonetheless represented the threat about which the government and their priests had warned them.[29]

On the morning of September 18, the streets surrounding the grounds of UNAM, the national university, were crowded with military transports, tanks, and thousands of soldiers. Blocking the main access to the campus, the army, dressed in full riot gear, invaded the campus. Some students fled, others, along with innocent bystanders, were arrested and imprisoned. The government claimed the students had been spending their time drinking and reading communist propaganda, turning the empty liquor bottles into Molotov cocktails. While the government justified its actions in the sympathetic press, the invasion of the university added additional voices to the chorus of criticism, including professional groups and women's organizations. Even some right-wing groups voiced their opposition.[30]

Protests, strikes, and other political actions continued around the country. On October 1, the CNH announced a meeting for the following day, in the Plaza de las Tres Culturas, in the heart of the Nonoallco-Tlatelolco housing complex. The plaza, which contained the remains of an Aztec temple and cathedral dating from the Spanish occupation, sat in the center of several apartment buildings. It was only accessible on foot. The CNH chose a third floor balcony of one apartment building as their platform. By 5:00 p.m., the designated starting time, ten to twenty thousand demonstrators had gathered. The army filled the side streets. The first speeches began about 5:30 p.m. At around 6:00 p.m. helicopters, which had been hovering overhead, shot brilliant military flares over the crowd. This was a "prearranged signal" for the army, one captain recalled. "We were to seal off…the two entrances and prevent anyone from entering or leaving."[31] Some demonstrators remembered noticing that some in the crowd in civilian dress had put a white glove on one hand, which was later revealed to have been a sign to other members of the army that they were themselves members of the military or the police. Some of the white-gloved plainclothes police drew pistols and began to fire at the crowd. Army battalions entered the square and also began to fire. Tanks followed the soldiers, shooting at the crowd. As many as 5,000 troops and police may have been involved.[32] When those on the speakers' platform on the third-floor balcony turned to escape they were confronted by machine guns carried by police wearing one white glove.

Foreign journalists had come to the plaza, including the famed Italian reporter Oriana Fallaci. Invited to the third-floor balcony, when the helicopters began to hover she warned some of the CNH leaders that this was not a good sign. "Come on," they replied, "you are not in Vietnam."[33] She was subsequently shot by the police, pulled by the hair, thrown to the ground, and beaten, ending up in a hospital. She later argued that of all the war zones she had covered, this was the only one where there had been no warning signal before shooting began, the only one where she had seen soldiers shoot at civilians at point-blank range.[34]

Some thought the shooting lasted for nearly a half an hour. Others longer. "Sixty-two minutes of round after round," wrote one journalist, "until the soldiers' weapons were so red-hot they could no longer hold them." The plaza became a scene of horror. "There was lots of blood underfoot, lots of blood smeared on the walls." "The very first thing I noticed was all the people lying on the ground; the entire Plaza was covered with the bodies," Diana Salmerón de Contreras remembered. "The second thing I noticed was that my kid brother had been riddled with bullets...Soldier, please have somebody bring a stretcher," she pleaded. "Shut up and stop pestering me," the soldier replied, "or you'll be needing two of them!" It was "a scene straight out of hell," one reporter observed. "The gunfire was deafening. The bullets were shattering the windows of the apartment and shards of glass were flying all over, and the terror-stricken families inside were desperately trying to protect their youngest children."[35]

The first headlines in the Mexican press claimed the military had only been responding to shots fired by radical sharpshooters.

SHOTS EXCHANGED BY SHARPSHOOTERS AND THE ARMY IN CIUDAD TLATELOLCO

TLATELOLCO A BATTLEFIELD: SERIOUS FIGHTING FOR HOURS BETWEEN TERRORISTS AND SOLDIERS

FOREIGN INTERLOPERS ATTEMPT TO DAMAGE MEXICO'S NATIONAL IMAGE

ARMY FORCED TO ROUT SHARPSHOOTERS[36]

Recent investigations have concluded that the snipers were, in fact, also working for the government.

Initial reports identified seven dead. Then the number was revised to 29 dead and 80 injured. To eyewitnesses, these numbers seemed staggeringly low. Eventually the government settled on 49 as the number of deaths. Most agree that the number was much higher, but no one knows the exact count. Some have argued for 300 to 400, others for even greater than that. Several thousand attendees were held overnight in a convent next to the cathedral. The Mexican government admitted that over 1,300 people had been arrested.

The U.S. government initially endorsed the interpretation offered by the Mexican regime, that anti-government snipers had initiated the action. By late in the week, the FBI was privately suggesting that "confusion between the army and other security agents" might have been to blame, though this was never announced publicly. Declassified documents later showed that by the end of the month, doubt about all the Mexican government's conclusions had grown substantially. Nevertheless, the Johnson administration reaffirmed support for Díaz Ordaz, including suggesting that further economic aid might be necessary should the student movement continue to grow.[37]

The American press followed its government's lead. A front-page story about the massacre, in the *New York Times* of October 3, suggested, "the events cast into serious question the prospects for the Olympic Games, which are scheduled to begin here on October 12." By the next day, however, the *Times* reported that, "sadly but proudly, riot-plagued Mexico plunged ahead today with preparations for the Olympics." Stories began to appear that were typical of days immediately preceding the opening of an Olympics, about hotel and ticket availability, what visitors should eat, covering the arrival of the U.S. team, and a story about how disinterested Soviet athletes were in watching the baseball World Series on television.[38]

"The massacre of October 2 crushed the [student] movement," Elaine Carey declares. Student leaders were murdered or arrested, many went underground, some just retired after the trauma of Tlatelolco. The Olympics, as we shall see, went on as planned, though not without their own controversy. "In memory," Paco Ignacio Taibo concluded, "the second of October has replaced the hundred days of the strike. The black magic of the cult of defeat and of the dead has reduced '68 to Tlatelolco alone." Still, the impact and meaning of the movement persisted, from the political to the cultural to the personal. "After Tlatelolco I changed a lot," observed one student. "Whatever sort of person I [became]...that's the way I'm going to be til I die." For some older Mexicans, it was the cultural challenge that was at fault. "It's the miniskirt that's to blame," one man argued. For a younger activist, "it was the history of how a son rebelled against his government because he could not confront his father, while a president who felt impotent against his own son's rocker lifestyle* took revenge against hundreds of students."[39]

---

* Diaz Ordaz's son Alfredo was a rock musician, later becoming a music producer.

Many believe that the seeds of the end of the PRI's single-party dominance, which finally came about in 2000, were sowed in 1968. "All of us were reborn on October 2," Raul Palavers Garín, a CNH leader, concluded. "And on that day we also decided how we are all going to die: fighting for genuine justice and democracy."[40]

The second stream that began to flow toward Mexico City in 1968 had its headwaters in the fight for racial justice in the U.S. The situation of Black athletes within the larger society—adulation on the field and continued racist hostility off of it—became a focus. So too the special role that successful athletes could take in assisting Black communities and underprivileged youth. Finally, questions emerged about what role Black athletes played in perpetuating racist institutions by being on teams that represented one city, one university, or a national team of the United States. In 1964, the activist-comedian Dick Gregory and former Olympic track-and-field gold medalist Mal Whitfield had proposed a boycott of the Tokyo Olympics. Cleveland Browns running back Jim Brown had, while still playing in the NFL, helped found the Black Economic Union (BEU), which employed Black athletes in helping create Black-run enterprises, as well as developing inner city athletic facilities and programs for the young. In 1967, as we have seen, Brown had brought Black athletes together in support of Muhammad Ali's refusal to be drafted into the Army.

So, it was no surprise when a Black sociologist from San Jose State named Harry Edwards began to talk in 1967 about organizing a boycott by African American athletes of the 1968 Olympics. Edwards, himself, had been raised in poverty in East St. Louis. A multisport athlete, he spent one semester at a California junior college, before being recruited by San Jose State, where he played football and basketball and ran track. His athletic successes and campus prominence did not make his daily life any easier. There were only 72 Black students at San Jose, out of a student body of thousands, almost all of them athletes. Edwards could not join any fraternity or many campus clubs and had to wait to be assigned to a dorm room until they found another Black student to be his roommate. Though his academic work would ultimately win him a scholarship for graduate study in sociology at Cornell, at San Jose he had to have his professors sign a weekly report for the athletic department to attest that he was keeping up with his studies, something white athletes were not required to do. When he graduated in 1964, Edwards turned down an offer from the NFL in order to pursue his graduate studies. While at Cornell, he would frequently travel to New York to hear Malcolm X speak.[41]

When Edwards returned to San Jose in 1966 to join the sociology department, he found things had changed very little. "I knocked on door after door bearing 'vacancy' signs, but Mr. Charley was so sorry—the rental room suddenly wasn't available." Edwards soon came to know Tommie Smith, a sprinter on the school's track team and the world-record holder in the 220, who told him, "I have you beat...My wife's pregnant. So far 13 lovely people have turned me down."[42] Edwards and a colleague developed a list of demands to improve the situation of Black athletes on campus. Their demands were summarily rejected. In response they proposed cancellation of that fall's opening football game. Failing that, they said they would lead a group onto the field to disrupt the game itself. As word leaked about these plans, the Hell's Angels motorcycle gang announced it would come to San Jose to protect the game. The Black Panthers then announced they would come to respond to the Hell's Angels. California Governor Ronald Reagan said he would send the National Guard, if necessary. As the rhetoric escalated it became clear that the game had to be cancelled. San Jose's president agreed to improve the situation for Black athletes on campus. And Harry Edwards became a national figure at the intersection of education, athletics, and African Americans.[43]

During the 1967 Thanksgiving weekend Edwards held a meeting in Los Angeles with 60 Black athletes, including sprinters Tommie Smith, John Carlos, and Lee Evans, as well as UCLA basketball phenom Lew Alcindor, to talk about the Olympics. After two hours of discussion, Edwards called for a voice vote. "Boycott" was the overwhelming response. Employing the heightened rhetoric of the era, Edwards declared,

"It's time for the black people to stand up as men and women and refuse to be utilized as performing animals for a little extra dog food." The next day he announced the Olympic boycott. By December, the project, now titled the Olympic Project for Human Rights (OPHR) and with the public support of Martin Luther King, expanded to include the exclusion of South Africa and Southern Rhodesia from the Olympics because of their racist regimes, the integration of the all-white U.S. Olympic Committee, and the reinstallation of Muhammad Ali as heavyweight champion. One special target was American Avery Brundage, head of the International Olympic Committee. Brundage had held the position for decades, stretching back to his toleration and support of Adolf Hitler and the 1936 Berlin Olympic Games, which was a propaganda spectacle put on by the Nazis. Brundage was well known as anti-Semitic and racist.[44]

Immediately, the call for an Olympic boycott elicited emotional responses from all sides. The United States Olympic Committee (USOC) brought out Jesse Owens, the African American who had won four gold medals at those Berlin Olympics, to argue, "there was no place in the athletic world for politics."[45] Owens was joined by other former Black Olympians, including Rafer Johnson, who would become deeply involved in Robert Kennedy's '68 campaign, and Ralph Boston, a former gold medal-winning long jumper expected to medal again in Mexico City. Muhammad Ali was solidly behind the boycott, while former heavyweight champion Joe Louis was not. The assassination of Martin Luther King in April 1968 sent a jolt of electricity into the boycott movement. Some athletes, like Ralph Boston, began to rethink their position. Others began to think about the overall meaning of what underlay the boycott in their regular athletic activities. The University of Texas at El Paso, another predominantly white school with a heavily African American track team, insisted its Black athletes compete in a track meet the weekend after King's murder. After participating, the athletes developed second thoughts. Their next meet was to be against Brigham Young University, which had discriminated against Black students for years. They asked out. When eight of them refused to compete, the school suspended their scholarships. One of them, long jumper Bob Beamon, who would set a world record in Mexico City, received a call from a bank the next day, asking for payment of his bills.[46]

Basketball players had an easier time joining the boycott. The Olympics was not the pinnacle of their sport, as it was for track and field athletes. For them, an NBA championship was the ultimate goal. As a result, 20 or so players had declined invitations to attend the Olympic Trials.* One of them, Lew Alcindor (later Kareem Abdul-Jabbar), went on the *Today* show. The interviewer was the usually jovial Joe Garagiola, a former major-league catcher who had used his homespun wit and baseball insight to develop a post-baseball career as a television personality and announcer. Yet, when Alcindor stated, "Yeah, I live here, but it's not really my country," Garagiola's demeanor turned. "Well, then, there's only one solution. Maybe you should move."[47]

Meanwhile, the initial calls for a boycott itself and revelations of racism within sports had begun to prompt small changes and a new awareness. National magazines ran stories like *Newsweek*'s "The Angry Black Athlete." *Life* magazine ran an article in March titled "The Olympic Jolt." It sent reporters around the country to test Edwards' accusations and assess their impact. Reporters visited seven campuses in various parts of the country and found that at every one Black athletes considered themselves "in a second class position compared to whites." *Life* also found that "the word being passed" among Black athletes was, "hell no, don't go."[48]

Surprise supporters of the Olympic Project for Human Rights popped up around the athletic universe, none more seemingly incongruous than Harvard's crew team, an all-white, Ivy League contingent, who won their Olympic trial and would represent the U.S. in Mexico City. After their victory, two members stayed in California to go to San Jose and meet with Edwards. Long jumper Phil Shinnick became another white

---

* Until 1992, the U.S. Olympic basketball team was made up of amateurs, mostly college basketball players plus an occasional member of a team from the Amateur Athletic Union (the AAU). The 1992 "Dream Team" was the first to feature professional players from the NBA. Regardless, by 1968, the U.S. had won every gold medal since the introduction of basketball as an Olympic sport in 1936.

supporter. While a student at the University of Washington, he had become involved in various Sixties issues, including racism on his campus and in Seattle. He participated in demonstrations and stood on street corners passing out leaflets. By 1968, he was a captain in the Air Force. When he was interviewed by ABC at the Olympic Trials, Shinnick voiced his support for the Black athletes. The following day, an Air Force general warned him that his remarks might lead to a court martial or his being transferred to Vietnam.[49]

Still, as the Olympic Trials and then the Games themselves grew closer, some of the resolve of 1967 began to wane. The athletes had spent too much time and had worked too hard to let it go completely. Edwards began to understand that the boycott would never materialize fully. Instead, he still hoped they would create some actions to publicize their cause. It was also clear that the movement had led to some small changes. Black assistant coaches, for example, had been added to Olympic teams. At the end of the summer of 1968, Edwards announced there would be no boycott. Regardless, he continued to receive death threats. His apartment was ransacked, his dogs murdered, and he was tailed by the FBI. Edwards and the San Jose athletes began to share some of their hate mail with one another.[50]

Press reporting on the Olympic trials was not restricted to the issues involving Black athletes. What coverage there was of the women's team evidenced the same chauvinistic and patronizing attitude that had marked it for decades. The message of Atlantic City had certainly not penetrated the minds of male sportswriters. *Sports Illustrated*'s story about the women's team was titled, "Dolls on the Move to Mexico." It noted how there had occurred "an influx of pretty young things" into the sport, the writer observing how wonderful they looked in their warm-up suits. He did conclude that the United States had "put together the best women's track and field team it has ever had." Regardless of how many medals the women's team would earn, "these pussycats are ready to call the future theirs." One team official was quoted in the *SI* story. "The girls are finding there can be a certain glamour in all this. For one thing, running does great things for the legs. It makes them shapelier... And they get to meet a lot of boys."[51]

As the Games opened in Mexico City, the press was full of the kind of praise Díaz Ordaz had dreamed about. "It is not true that Mexicans are lazy," one article proclaimed. The new hotels, highways, and Olympic venues presented a modern image. The Tlatelolco massacre was reported in the international press, though never in a manner commensurate with the severity and horror of the actual event. It seemed like just another 1968 confrontation with rebellious students. "I was at the ballet last night," Avery Brundage told reporters, "and we heard nothing of the riots."[52]

With the failure of the boycott, the OPHR organizers decided that individual athletes could demonstrate or protest as they wished. Early in the first week, when the track events were held, the 200-meter final contained both Tommie Smith and John Carlos, two San Jose State runners who had been central to the initial boycott plan. They were also the favorites. Smith blazed to victory in world record time. An Australian sprinter, Peter Norman, finished a fraction ahead of Carlos, who took the bronze.

On his way to the medals ceremony, Norman had asked one of the Harvard crew members for an OPHR button to pin to his uniform. As the ceremony approached, Smith and Carlos took off their running shoes. When the Star-Spangled Banner began to play, they each bowed their heads and held one black-gloved fist aloft. "I wore a black right-hand glove and Carlos wore the left-hand of the same pair," Smith explained. "My raised right hand stood for the power in black America. Carlos' raised left hand stood for the unity of black America... The black scarf around my neck stood for black pride. The black socks with no shoes stood for black poverty in racist America. The totality of our effort was the regaining of black dignity." He later added that their bowed heads were a remembrance for those who died in the struggle for "black liberation... Malcolm X, Martin Luther King, and others." Carlos later explained that the beads he wore represented the lynchings of southern Black people and that his unzipped warm up jacket was a salute to the working man.[53]

Peter Norman, who had talked with Smith and Carlos on their way to the podium, stood quietly during the anthem wearing his OPHR button.

For this alone, he became a pariah within the Australian track world, kept off the 1972 team, and not even invited to be celebrated among the past Australian medalists at the 2000 Sydney Olympics. In 2012, the Australian House of Representatives passed a posthumous resolution apologizing to Norman for the treatment he received upon returning from Mexico City.*

Press reaction in the United States was mixed, tending more heavily toward condemnation than approval or even understanding. The *Los Angeles Times* called it "a Nazi-like salute," while the *Chicago Tribune* described it as "an embarrassment...contemptuous of the United States." A *Time* magazine illustration replaced the Olympic motto "Faster, Higher, Stronger" with "Angrier, Nastier, Uglier." Brent Musburger, then a young reporter and later a well-known television sportscaster, complained, "One gets a little tired of having the United States run down by athletes who are enjoying themselves at the expense of their country." He labeled Smith and Carlos as "juvenile" and "a pair of black-skinned Stormtroopers." The *Los Angeles Times* commented that the crowd greeted the moment with "boos and catcalls," with some making the "thumbs-down gesture as they would a Mexican matador preparing for the kill." Not all the reporting was critical. Robert Lipsythe, in the *New York Times*, noted, "After all we'd come through this year and this is it? This is the mildest, most civil demonstration of the year."[54]

Under pressure from the IOC, the United States Olympic Commission (USOC) kicked Smith and Carlos off the Olympic team and ordered them to vacate the Olympic Village. When Jesse Owens was dispatched to deliver the news to Smith and Carlos and warn other athletes about further demonstrations, he met hostility from both Black and white athletes. The USOC sanctions seemed to many to be overkill. The *New York Times*' highly regarded columnist Red Smith felt that "by throwing a fit over the incident, the badgers multiplied the impact a hundredfold." Black athletes began lining up behind Smith and Carlos, joined by more and more white ones. Asked about whether they had discredited the flag,

---

* At Norman's funeral in 2006, Smith and Carlos gave eulogies and served as pallbearers.

Tom Waddell, a white decathlete, countered, "I think they have been discredited by the flag more often than they have discredited it."[55]

Two days after the 200-meter event, the long jump produced what was likely the most amazing performance of the games, Bob Beacon's staggering jump that bettered the world record by nearly two feet. The medal ceremony became the next moment of personal demonstrations. Ralph Boston, who took second, had been initially opposed to the boycott and other actions. Over the course of 1968, he had been moved by events to more active participation. He had taken particular umbrage at Joe Garagiola's harsh retort to Lew Alcindor. When he approached the podium, he was barefoot. "Send me home too," he declared. Bob Beamon, who had lost his scholarship at UTEP for boycotting the Brigham Young track meet, mounted the podium with his black sweat pants rolled up his shins, displaying long black socks in support of Smith and Carlos. When the national anthem ended, he turned toward the crowd and raised his right fist.[56] The U.S. team contained so many talented runners that even the loss of Smith and Carlos did not affect the results in the 400-meter relay, which they won easily, setting a world record. As the relay team mounted the medals platform, they donned black berets and waved their fist. But they smiled all the while. "It was harder to shoot a guy who's smiling," Lee Evans noted later. When the national anthem began, Evans raised his fist again, yet continued to smile.[57]

When George Foreman won the gold medal in the heavyweight boxing division the next week and ran around the ring waving a small American flag, journalists and commentators seized on the moment to laud him for seeking to counter the demonstrations of the track athletes. The truth was more complicated. Foreman, at that point, was not the jovial pitchman who regained the heavyweight title at age 45 and went on to advertise his eponymous counter-top grills. He was a recalcitrant, troubled youth, who in fact resented that the athletes contemplating a boycott and podium demonstrations had not even contacted him. At one pre-Olympic event, he was approached by a political operative and asked if he went on to win the gold medal would he support the operative's candidate, Richard Nixon. Without really knowing anything about Nixon or the campaign, Foreman agreed, just happy to have been asked. During the boxing competition, when one of his teammates was unjustly disqualified, Foreman grew furious. When he won his event, he pulled his lucky flag out of his robe and began to wave it in support of his teammate, he later claimed. "I was thinking, *Gotcha*, to those judges. That's all. The international rules of boxing were, cheat America." To an interviewer in 2018, he suggested that when he first met athletes of color from other countries, "I realized that the only thing that could identify us was our nation's colors. I thought that, after I win my last fight, when I bow to the judges, I am going to carry our flag. [Everyone] is going to know where I am from. I sincerely didn't think they would. I waved the flag so they knew I was American...That is the only reason I had that flag."

His explanations didn't matter. In Mexico City the IOC and USOC cheered. Avery Brundage attended his first podium event involving a Black athlete. Many in the white American press made Foreman the heroic counterweight to Smith, Carlos, and the others. Back home, he was asked by an old friend, "How could you do what you did? How could you wave that flag when our brothers were protesting?" "It broke my heart," Foreman later confessed. As he began to understand what his gesture had come to mean, he put his gold medal away, not looking at it again for many years.[58]

There were other small moments, some public and some private, in which the political events and the athletic competition intersected. One sprinter, Mel Pender, had medaled in 1964 and then spent a tour of duty in Vietnam, earning a Bronze Star. He came back to qualify for the '68 team. While deeply patriotic he was also sympathetic to the issues raised by the boycott discussion. As a member of the military, he was barred from public protests. He thought he was headed to helicopter school after the Olympics, as he had been promised. Instead, he found the promise discarded and was ordered back to Vietnam, where he remained until 1970.

Vera Castalia, a Czech gymnast had publicly joined the anti-Soviet movement of Prague Spring but then fled the capital when Soviet troops invaded. She was ultimately invited back to the national team. When she shared the gold medal in one event with a Russian gymnast, she had to stand on the podium as the Soviet national anthem was played. She bowed her head in protest, a gesture she repeated a second time when she again stood on the platform listening to the Soviet anthem.

As the moments of 1968 accumulated, they colored those that followed in sequence. After all that had happened in the spring and summer it would have been naïve to expect that something would not develop in Mexico City that October. As in so many places, conflict between the students and the authorities turned tragic in Mexico that summer. Gustavo Díaz Ordaz knew the eyes of the world would be on his capital and what they would see would mean so much in the way Mexico was viewed by the outside world. He could not let the image of his country be one of demonstrations and disorder. Given all that was developing in the U.S. regarding the movement for equality and racial identity, including the ambivalent place of Black athletes within American society, it was no surprise that race leaders would use the Olympic games to highlight their cause and further their efforts.

And in keeping with other events of the year, it is equally unsurprising that the authorities, when pressed, would rely on brute force—or that these efforts would end in tragedy.

22

The Ebb Tide

There's battle lines being drawn
Nobody's right if everybody's wrong
Young people speaking their minds
Getting so much resistance from behind
　　　　　　　—*Buffalo Springfield,*
　　　　"*For What It's Worth,*" *1966*

The signs had begun to emerge well before 1966. There had always been opposition and resistance to many of the decade's movements and ideas. Segregationists had violently resisted desegregation, with white nationalist groups frequently visible. Cold warriors and those steeped in the anti-communism of the postwar years had questioned the patriotism of the growing chorus of anti-Vietnam War voices. Chauvinist voices belittled early feminists. Older Americans scoffed at counterculture styles, branding long-haired men as effeminate or women in miniskirts as tramps or sluts.

These attitudes seemed to be overwhelmed by the sheer kinetic energy of the times. The trend appeared to be with those within the movements. White Southern racists became the villains of the race question. The antiwar movement gained more and more adherents as the decade progressed, including older and more establishment types, including elected officials. Counterculture styles began to appear within the mainstream. When Robert Kennedy ran for president in 1968, his hair was longer than the Beatles' hair had been when they first appeared on

The Ed Sullivan Show. The fashion industry started to incorporate counterculture styles into their clothes.

Along with the counterculture, however, there was another counter-current that slowly began to develop in the early 1960s, not merely a critique of an individual aspect of the movements but of the kind of society that would result from the combined successes of all these efforts. This critique slowly took on an identifiable coherence as the decade progressed.

Colleges and universities had grown dramatically in the postwar years, with ever-increasing numbers of young people now able to attend. These universities had long prided themselves as bastions of open thought and intellectual and political discussion. Student organizations took this notion to heart, especially as these organizations began to receive greater funding from their colleges. As a result, both the institutions, them-selves, and their student organizations started to invite controversial speakers to campus, ranging across the political spectrum.

In his inaugural address in January 1963, Alabama Governor George Wallace proclaimed, "I draw the line in the dust and toss the gauntlet before the feet of tyranny, and I say segregation now, segregation tomor-row, segregation forever." That June he had stood in a doorway at the University of Alabama, in a failed attempt to block its integration. Yet Wallace had also proven to be a curiously attractive spokesperson for his position. Organizing a speaking tour of the north, Wallace proved addi-tionally appealing to colleges, as he asked for no honorarium or reimburse-ment for his expenses. On November 4, 1963, he stepped onto the stage at Harvard's Sanders Theater. He had edited the speech written for him to eliminate any crude racist statements and mostly argued the unconstitu-tionality of recent Supreme Court decisions on segregation. He also proved to be funny and engaging, willing to joust with audience members without rancor or accusation. One observer recalled that students would pose a question they were sure was a "stumper...but would walk away chagrined." From Harvard he pressed on to Dartmouth, Smith, and Brown, as well as doing radio and television interviews. As Wallace biogra-pher Dan Carter put it, the speaking tour "gave him status and legitimacy."[1]

In early 1964, Wallace ventured onto the campus of one of the schools where the left was most prominent, the University of Wisconsin. Wallace had honed his approach when facing hostile student audiences. He "oozed Southern charm," one student recalled. He joked with them about being glad to check out the "newest beard styles" and was more a "hillbilly humorist" than a "race-baiting demagogue," one historian observed. The state of Wisconsin had also been the home of Joseph McCarthy, the most visible anti-communist figure of the 1950s, and his views still held sway with many residents. While still in the state after his talk, the Wallace team was contacted by a conservative organizer who argued that Wallace should enter their presidential primary in part based how easy it was to get on the Wisconsin ballot. There was a wellspring of opposition waiting to be tapped, he told them. In fact, Wallace had been thinking of entering some of the Democratic presidential primaries.

When Wallace returned to Wisconsin to formally declare his candidacy in March, the exterior of his private plane had been redecorated, replacing the Confederate flag with an American one and changing the campaign slogan from "Stand Up for Alabama" to "Stand Up for America." Still, Wallace's announcement stirred little response nationally. None of the television networks mentioned it. The *New York Times* buried the story on page 76 of a Sunday edition. Wisconsin governor John Reynolds, who was on the ballot as a favorite-son stand-in for Lyndon Johnson, claimed to be "shocked and appalled" that Wallace thought, "he could make some kind of mark" in Wisconsin.[2]

As he had with the student audiences, Wallace had modified his general message. When he ventured into his critique of the civil rights bill being debated in Congress, he avoided racist assertions. Instead, he talked about "property rights" and the threats of an "all powerful central bureaucracy." Blue-collar workers should fear for the loss of seniority rights, he argued, while suburbanites needed to worry about open-housing legislation. At one telling rally in an ethnic neighborhood of Milwaukee populated by many Eastern European families, the local organizer stirred the crowd with racist accusations. They "rape our womenfolk. They mug people. They won't work," he declared. When Wallace took the stage, he tried to calm the crowd. "I want us all to be in good humor tonight." His stump speech was a harangue, though one whose targets were a State Department that had abandoned Eastern Europe, a Supreme Court that outlawed Bible reading in schools, and a civil rights bill that would "destroy the union seniority system and impose racial quotas." People would not be able to sell their homes to whomever they chose and neighborhood schools would be a thing of the past. All this was greeted with cheers and standing ovations.[3]

In early March, polls had shown Wallace getting 5 percent of the Wisconsin Democratic vote. But in the April primary, against the liberal LBJ stand-in, Wallace polled nearly 34 percent. While liberals tried to put as good a face on the result as they could—"two thirds of the Democratic voters…rejected an appeal to fear, prejudice, and hatred," one newspaper editorialized—it was clear, as one political analyst concluded, that "few, if any [liberals] have not been astonished and dismayed."[4]

The Indiana primary followed Wisconsin's in early May, and Wallace again shocked prognosticators. Despite a much more coordinated effort by Democrats to stand against him, he polled 30 percent. "If any responsible official had suggested six months ago that a segregationist from the Deep South could poll such a vote in Indiana," editorialized the *Indianapolis Star*, "he would have been hooted into silence."[5]

Maryland was next in mid-May. Again, Wallace created euphemisms to mask the real meaning of his arguments. Claiming the civil rights bill would tell employers whom they had to employ, he chose as an example: "If a man's got 100 Japanese-Lutherans working for him and there's 100 Chinese-Baptists unemployed, he's got to let some of the Japanese-Lutherans go so he can make room for some of the Chinese-Baptists." No one missed the point. Maryland's racial history, urban issues, and class divisions augmented Wallace's appeal. When the vote was cast, some estimates suggested turnout went up 40 percent. Wallace won 43 percent of total vote and carried the white vote. He carried some of the white ethnic neighborhoods of Baltimore, which had gone two-to one for John Kennedy in 1960. Having avoided public racial epithets throughout the campaign, he was less guarded when he privately assessed the result. "If it hadn't been for the nigger bloc, we'd have won it all."[6] On Maryland's Eastern Shore, an overwhelmingly white area with strong anti-Black feelings, Wallace took 90 percent of the vote. One local newspaper reported that voters, "went to the polls with big grins on their faces... They were going to show Uncle Sam they had had it."[7]

In 1963, the California state legislature had passed a fair housing act, known as the Rumford Act after its sponsor Byron Rumford. While it was seen as one of the strongest state measures battling housing discrimination directed at minorities, it was still limited to public housing and residential properties with five or more units. Single-family homes were not covered. Still, in 1964 an organization of real estate agents secured enough signatures to put an initiative on the November ballot to amend the state constitution to prohibit any law or regulation which would "deny, limit or abridge, directly or indirectly, the right of any person," to sell or rent their property to whomever they chose. Conservatives, as well as hate groups, like the American Nazi Party and the White Citizen's Councils, endorsed the measure, known as Proposition 14. The AFL-CIO, California's Democratic governor, and other state officials joined in opposition. So did many others, including Martin Luther King, who came to the state several times to campaign against it. Significantly, the *Los Angeles Times*, the state's most influential newspaper—but in these years staunchly right wing—endorsed Proposition 14. "One of man's most ancient rights in a free society is the privilege of using and disposing of his private property in whatever manner he deems appropriate," the *Times* declared. "Housing equality cannot safely be achieved at the expense of still another basic right."[8]

That November, Lyndon Johnson carried the state of California with 60 percent of the vote. Yet Proposition 14 passed with 65 percent. It won in every country in the state, save for a tiny rural county in its northeast corner, where it failed by only 19 votes. It prevailed in liberal counties like Alameda, which included Oakland and Berkeley, with 60 percent; in San Francisco with 53 percent; and in Los Angeles with a two-thirds majority. Despite being declared unconstitutional in 1966 by the California State

Supreme Court—a decision affirmed by the U.S. Supreme Court in 1967—the success of Proposition 14 proved a harbinger of a growing conservative undercurrent in a year usually identified as a liberal pinnacle.

Lyndon Johnson stood atop that Democratic pinnacle in November 1964, victor in a landslide election over conservative Republican Barry Goldwater. LBJ won 61 percent of the popular vote nationally and carried every state except Goldwater's home state of Arizona and five states in the Deep South. The Democrats also picked up 37 seats in the House of Representatives and two in the Senate, leaving them with majorities of 284:140 and 68:32, respectively. Lost in the post-election analysis that depicted the seeming destruction of the Republican Party was the impact of one moment during the Goldwater campaign. At the end of October, the campaign presented a half-hour commercial, the entirety of which was a speech by actor and television personality Ronald Reagan. In fact, it became known as "The Speech," the one that took a man whose acting career had been declining for several years and catapulted him into national political prominence.

Ronald Reagan had spent much of the 1950s hosting the weekly *General Electric Theater*, a Sunday night dramatic series that had the good fortune of following the popular *Ed Sullivan Show*. He also served as a corporate spokesman (called a "corporate ambassador") for GE. Over these years, in a series of speeches he made to GE executives and employees and for the company to other groups around the country, he had honed his ideas about individual rights and government intrusion into people's lives. These speeches taught Reagan the art of giving a campaign speech, how to use humor and statistics, how to handle questions, as well as how to conserve his voice.[9] Slowly themes began to emerge in his GE talks, such as "encroaching control" or "our eroding freedoms." The speech he gave for Goldwater that October might have been called, as his biographer Lou Cannon put it, "The Collected Speeches of Ronald Reagan." It was actually titled, "A Time for Choosing." It laid out a vision very different from the one being offered by LBJ, he claimed.

We're at war with the most dangerous enemy that has ever faced mankind in his long climb from the swamp to the stars.

If we lose freedom here, there's no place to escape to. This is the last stand on earth.

We have so many people who can't see a fat man standing beside a thin one without coming to the conclusion the fat man got that way by taking advantage of the thin one.

The trouble with our liberal friends is not that they're ignorant; it's just that they know so much that isn't so.

No government ever voluntarily reduces itself in size...a government bureau is the nearest thing to eternal life we'll ever see on this earth.

We believe in our capacity for self-government or...confess that a little intellectual elite in a far-distant capitol can plan our lives for us better than we can plan them ourselves.

Reagan ended his speech with a phrase from Franklin Roosevelt, "You and I have a rendezvous with destiny," and an apocalyptic vision. "We'll preserve for our children this, the last best hope of man on earth, or we'll sentence them to take the last step into a thousand years of darkness."[10]

Though "The Speech" did little to help Barry Goldwater, it did offer Republicans a small light in the darkness of the crushing political disaster. Conservative America now had a new spokesman and a charismatic new political figure.

Two years earlier, in 1962, California's popular Democratic governor, Edmund G. (Pat) Brown had run for reelection, soundly defeating Richard Nixon. Nixon was seeking a political comeback after his slim 1960 presidential loss. He had narrowly carried California in 1960, while losing the national popular vote to JFK by 118,000 votes. In 1962, he lost to Brown by nearly 400,000 in California alone. Prognosticators saw this as the end of Nixon's political career. By 1966, when he announced his intention of running for a third term, Brown's reputation had taken something of a beating. The Watts Riots and the student uprising at Berkeley both took their toll. So too did his continued support of Johnson's Vietnam policy. For Pat Brown, 1966 proved very different from 1962, and Ronald Reagan proved a very different opponent from Richard Nixon.

The success of "The Speech" in 1964 prompted a group of wealthy Southern California Republicans to see Reagan as a strong candidate for governor in 1966. When he declared his candidacy, one major criticism of Reagan was his lack of political experience. His reply, made in numerous speeches, shifted the focus away from him and toward what many Americans had come to distrust. "I am not a politician. I am an ordinary citizen with a deep-seated belief that much of what troubles us has been brought about by politicians." Ordinary citizens could add some "fresh-air common sense thinking" to the political arena.[11] It is clear that Regan's political views echoed the anti-government attitudes of Goldwater and his supporters. They were simply packaged in a much more likable way.

Reagan did not, like George Wallace, need to hide past racist statements. However, it was also clear, as it was to Wallace, that there was a growing opposition among many whites to the course that the movement for racial equality had taken. Reagan began to talk about states' rights, which in the postwar years was code for opposition to integrationist measures. And, like Wallace, he also began to talk about law and order, again seen as way to appeal to white voters fearful of urban minorities. "Our city streets are jungle paths after dark," Reagan declared when he announced his candidacy. California, he claimed, had "more crimes of violence than New York, Massachusetts, and Pennsylvania combined."[12]

Reagan also began to tap into white working-class hostility to programs they perceived as benefiting minorities at their expense, and to the activities and the indulgences allowed to privileged college students. One way of talking about this—and about race without sounding racist— was to attack the welfare system. We can't make "welfare a way of life," Reagan declared, "freeloading at the expense of more conscientious citizens." Welfare recipients were stereotyped as indolent Blacks, despite evidence to the contrary. Welfare fraud was also minimal, as a *Los Angele Times* investigation had revealed. But Reagan falsely claimed that anyone coming to California could begin receiving welfare payments in just three weeks. He was tapping into growing resentments and drawing alienated voters. "Everything he says is America," one young woman supporter proclaimed.[13]

The University of California was a place with special significance for many during the 1960s. The system had been one of the great educational success stories of postwar America. By 1966, its eight campuses represented an inexpensive opportunity for California's young to gain an education on par with any university in the nation. This included many of the children of a working class whose sons and daughters were the first in their family to go to college. Reagan claimed he had found a great deal of pride among Californians for their state university system. But he also found great concern, especially because of the student movement. He later recounted that very early in his campaign he discovered that no matter where he was in the state, "the first question is: 'What are you going to do about Berkeley?'"[14] In his campaign announcement he declared, "Will we allow a great university to be brought to its knees by a noisy, dissident minority?" Or, he asked, should we demand that university leaders "enforce a code based on decency, common sense, and dedication to the high and noble purpose of the University." He would not allow, he declared in one speech, "malcontents, beatniks, and filthy speech advocates to disrupt the academic community and interfere with the university's purposes." Reagan put it even more firmly on the campaign trail, "No one is compelled to attend the university. Those who do attend should accept and obey the prescribed rules or get out."[15]

It was not only student political actions that Reagan challenged. It was the entire notion of the counterculture, again something that older Californians (and many other Americans) had trouble comprehending. At numerous campaign stops, he luridly recounted the story of a dance held at Berkeley that spring. "The hall was entirely dark except for two movie screens. On these screens the nude torsos of men and women were portrayed...Three rock bands played simultaneously." And, of course, there were drugs. "The smell of marijuana was thick throughout the hall...There were indications of other happenings which cannot be mentioned."[16] Anyone who had been to rock performances across the Bay at the Fillmore or Avalon in San Francisco or in many other venues around the country would have found this to be a typical night. To the "straight" world, however, which was Reagan's prime audience, these were unfathomable images.

Reagan also belittled counterculture youth, tapping into a growing bewilderment of and hostility to the young. He often did it with his trademark humor, as in one campaign stop. He said he had seen protestors carrying "MAKE LOVE, NOT WAR" signs. "The only trouble was they didn't look like they were capable of doing either." About one he joked, "his hair was like Tarzan, and he acted like Jane, and he smelled like Cheetah."[17]

It was not just the kids who were at fault. It was the adults who led them, particularly professors. Echoing a growing anti-intellectualism, he claimed that too many college professors "use their classrooms to indoctrinate and propagandize," undermining "the traditional values of a free society." This was, Reagan argued, especially appalling to an "ordinary citizen who may have not had the benefit of a college education, but who is sharing a very heavy tax burden, some of which goes to pay the cost of professors' salaries."[18]

In the McCarthy era of the 1950s, college campuses had been branded as hotbeds of Communism, and these notions persisted. Communists were using the student movement for their own purposes, Reagan claimed. Berkeley had become, "a rallying point for Communists and a center of sexual misconduct." He promised that, if elected, he would appoint a former director of the CIA to investigate how this had come to be and what could be done about it. (Once elected, Reagan never implemented this plan.) Part of the solution would be a "code of conduct" for faculty and the expectation that campus administrators would either enforce it or lose their jobs.[19] (Once elected, Reagan never implemented either of these plans.) Despite rational voices in the media who argued how exaggerated were all these accusations, these lurid scenarios stuck in the imaginations of many.

A month before the 1966 election, events at Berkeley added to the imagery Reagan was painting and seemed to firmly tie together a number of the issues that were motivating the growing backlash. Following the common pattern of inviting controversial speakers to campus, a Berkeley student organization invited SNCC chair and Black Power advocate Stokely Carmichael to campus. On October 30, a crowd of 10,000 turned out to hear his castigation of the Vietnam War and overall U.S. foreign policy and his claim that U.S. domestic policy was racist, as well as calling on students to resist the draft. Reagan had asked Carmichael to cancel his appearance, yet it was clear that his appearance only helped Reagan's campaign. As one newspaper summarized, there was "a major, but usually unspoken, issue of the campaign—the possibility of a white backlash against talk of 'black power.' "[20]

When California voters went to the polls that November, they gave Reagan a landslide victory of nearly a million votes over Pat Brown. He carried traditional Democratic working-class districts as well as some in suburban and rural areas. The year 1966 was a strong comeback year for Republicans across the country. It was also clear, however, that Reagan's victory was built on a cluster of issues that spoke to the frustrations growing among many Americans, from high taxes to failing wars to a belief that government policies were favoring minorities over whites. Reagan was able to cobble together antagonisms to a number of elements that the mainstream public perceived as representing the 1960s—and to forge out of these resentments a political posture that many Americans found appealing.

The champions of these frustrated and "forgotten" Americans were not only politicians with national audiences. At the local level, individuals and groups sprang up, tapping into the same resentments and fears and much more willing to say exactly what they meant. In Newark, for example, Tony Imperiale became the savior of one group of white New Jerseyans. "I didn't see any flags in the city of Newark lowered to half mast when Gov. Lureen Wallace [George's wife] died…Why not, when they could do it for that Martin Luther Coon?"[21] To Imperiale, the problems in his neighborhood were the result of "communist-inspired racial pressures." He and his supporters owned guns, trained in karate, and set out at night in teams to patrol their neighborhood, warding off intruders from neighboring Black communities. "The colored just come looking for trouble." The police needed to be supported, not criticized. "They ought to register Communists, not guns, " he declared.

The neighborhoods of Newark's North Ward, where Imperiale lived, had declined from solidly middle class to "shabby," as one journalist put it. The Black population of the North Ward continued to grow, as many whites moved out. Owner-occupied houses declined. Single-family homes had been broken up into several apartments. "There is a crowded ticky-tack feeling about it all." Yet, Imperiale proclaimed, "the Negros get all the antipoverty money." Life was growing more difficult for his white neighbors. "You know how many come to me night after night, because they can't get a job? They've been told, 'We have to hire Negroes first.'" As *New York Times* critic Paul Goldberger concluded, "The people sense that their backs are to the wall...and no help is on the way."[22]

Imperiale was hardly alone. In Detroit, Donald Lobsinger, who worked for the city's parks department, led a group called Breakthrough. Lobsinger became the "official voice of angry white Detroiters," as one historian put it, standing against any integration of white neighborhoods. Communists, Breakthrough argued, were behind Black Power and anti-Vietnam War organizations.[23] In Oakland, California, one group called the Home Defense Association published a guide for its followers that suggested tactics for "Neighborhood Perimeter Defense," which employed firearms and ammunition.[24]

Local political leaders began to emerge, offering less violent paths of opposition within the electoral system, but seeking the same ends. Boston School Committeewoman Louise Day Hicks, once thought to be a reformer, became the most prominent voice opposed to the integration of Boston's schools, which studies showed evidenced severe *de facto* segregation. While Democratic and Republican state and local politicians began to seek ways to overcome this segregation, opposition exploded. To Hicks, the Black children were merely "pawns." "Boston schools are a scapegoat for those who have failed to solve the housing, economic, and social problems of the black citizen," she said. Hicks asserted that while 13 Boston schools were at least 90 percent Black students, Chinatown schools were 100 percent Chinese students, the North End had schools that were 100 percent Italian American students, and South Boston contained schools that were mostly Irish American students. These arguments led CORE's James Farmer to brand her "The Bull Connor of Boston." In 1967, running for mayor under the slogan, "You Know Where I Stand," Hicks finished first in the multi-candidate primary. She went on to lose the general election by only 12,000 votes.[25, 26]

Philadelphia's Frank Rizzo made headlines as the hardline police commissioner who "got tough" with his city's African American population, arresting Black Panthers and slowing the integration of the city's police force and allowing its community relations programs to decline. He also had gay bars raided and hippies arrested for sleeping in the city's parks. Rizzo's department ultimately boasted 7,000 riot-trained police, including 125 sharpshooters. They rode in vehicles with so many weapons—rifles, submachine guns, tear-gas, and grenades—that one analyst thought they "carried enough weaponry to equip a combat vehicle in Vietnam." His tough stances won support in Philadelphia's white ethnic enclaves, large enough to elect him mayor a few years later.[27]

It was not only national or local politicians who tapped into white working-class frustrations. Groups began to emerge challenging progressive and counterculture elements they believed were seeping into the culture. One group in California favored an initiative that would forbid any judge from dismissing any pornography charge. Pornographers were deemed responsible for an "epidemic of rape, perversion, and venereal disease." Another group sought to ban the use of an American history textbook by the African American historian, John Hope Franklin, on the grounds that it "destroys pride in America's past...mocks American justice, indoctrinates toward Communism, [and] emphasizes Negro participation in American history." White House press secretary Bill Moyers, a Baptist pastor, came under fire from one Oklahoma minister, for "conduct that brings dishonor to the work and name of our Lord Jesus Christ." Moyers transgression: dancing the Watusi at a White House function.[28]

Mainstream voices also began to express derogatory attitudes about young people and their cultural movements, perpetuating the kind of sarcastic reactions heard when the Beatles first appeared on the *Ed Sullivan Show*. The kids may have loved it, but the older generation remained perplexed. When demonstrators started coming to Washington to protest the Vietnam War, liberal humor columnist Art Buchwald found his "real objection" to these demonstrators was not their ideas or intentions, "but the fact that many of the demonstrators are unwashed and uncombed." He quoted one onlooker as stating, "If they really believed in America they'd shave." Former President Dwight Eisenhower told a *Boston Globe* reporter that "all this long hair" evidenced a "lack of decorum...I've always thought that sloppy dress was indicative of sloppy thinking." Ike also disliked the way young women were wearing their hair. It was "all over their faces so they look like baboons."[29]

The music blaring out over the radio was not only loud and incomprehensible to older listeners. They thought it was filled with sexual innuendo and drug references. In 1965, *Newsweek* described the song "Satisfaction" as being "panted rather than sung by a leering quintet called the Rolling Stones." Sexual innuendo may have always been a part of sophisticated music, but "Cole Porter and Lorenz Hart did it with such class and taste that it sounded mature," observed one New York disc jockey. "The average 14-year-old," suggested an Atlanta DJ, "digs all the dirt." The once-criticized Beatles now seemed innocent. "I Want to Hold Your Hand" was replaced by the Stones' "King Bee...buzzing around your hive" or the suggestive "Let's Spend the Night Together." Drug references also troubled some older folks. "Puff the Magic Dragon," Peter, Paul, and Mary's seemingly "whimsical fairy tale...sounded to some like a narcotics cryptogram."[30]

In 1966, Christian evangelist David Noebel declared that rock music was "riot causing," creating many detrimental side effects. The "noise...is basically sexual, un-Christian, mentally unsettling and riot-producing." The explanation for all this came from the work of Ivan Pavlov, the Russian physiologist. He had been "invited to Moscow as the personal house guest of Nikolai Lenin," Noebel continued. "One is immediately impressed with the almost perfect analogy between what our youngsters experience under Beatlemania and the technique inflicted on Pavlov's dogs to develop 'artificial neurosis.'" Rock music "dulls the capacity for attention and creates a kind of hypnotic monotony which lures and makes unreal the external world." Inhibitions against "committing sexual acts and other delinquency" evaporated. In this state, "young people can be told to do practically anything—and they will." Commenting on one Beatles concert, Noebel quoted a Seattle radio announcer. "That entire evening seemed *designed* to arouse every animal and sex instinct in the audience up to an uncontrollable pitch." The kids would "scream, faint, gyrate…It was an orgy for teenagers." This was not merely a replication of Pavlov's experiments. This was the intent of the communists, an "ingeniously conceived master music plan" aimed at America's teenagers, "preparing them for riot and ultimately revolution to destroy our American government and the basic Christian principles governing our way of life."[31]

As 1968 approached, these growing frustrations and resentments fueled the campaigns of three politicians seeking to ride them to national office. Richard Nixon joined George Wallace and Ronald Reagan as the champions of those Americans who felt forgotten and overlooked.

Wallace had maintained his national prominence after 1964, continuing to speak around the country. Term limits made it impossible for him to run again for Governor in 1966, but it did not prohibit his wife, Lurleen, from seeking the office. Campaigning for her around the state, Wallace was able to reinforce his message, as well as championing women's rights, when her opponent suggested she wasn't qualified because of her gender—"we don't want no skirt for governor," he had said. Wallace's defense of his wife was no feminist response. When one of Lurleen's opponents pointed out that she was a high-school dropout, he was criticized for a lack of chivalry, and his support collapsed. Wallace also reiterated the anti-intellectualism erupting on the right. One of his critics was a Southern-born local newspaper editor, Ray Jenkins, who had spent a year as a Niemen Fellow at Harvard, "You know, he's one of them

Hahhh-verd-educated intellectuals that sticks his little finger in the air when he sips tea," Wallace had mocked, "and looks down his long nose at ordinary Alabamans."[32] With voters knowing that she would function as a stand-in for her husband, Lurleen Wallace won by a nearly two-to-one majority. Virginia Durr, a white liberal who had been involved in politics since the New Deal era and had been a steadfast champion of civil rights, wrote to a friend. "I know you think I am crazy when I say [George Wallace] expects to be President." He had convinced whites, she told her brother-in-law, Supreme Court Justice Hugo Black, "that everything they believed in was being swept away by an overbearing and oppressive federal government." These whites believed it was them, and not African Americans, who "were the victims of oppression."[33]

During the first months of 1968, Wallace faced two challenges as far removed from one another as might be possible. He had chosen to run for president as an independent and needed to get on the ballot of all 50 states. Most states had varying requirements—the number of petition signatures required, different filing dates, and more. It was a measure of both the enthusiasm of the Wallace volunteers and the amount of money he had been able to raise that led to these hurdles being surmounted. The second challenge was his wife's health. Lurleen Wallace had been diagnosed with cancer in 1967, her strength waxing and waning throughout the year. By early 1968, her condition worsened. Her illness limited Wallace's campaign swings, which he still undertook but with a restricted schedule. On May 7, at the age of 41, she passed away. Three weeks later, George Wallace was back on the campaign trail.

Wallace's '68 campaign brought together a great many of the feelings that numerous Americans felt about what they perceived as the problems of contemporary life. His platform harangues would touch on an array of topics as he paced the stage, pointed his finger, and berated a wide cast of characters. The U.S. should have never gone into Vietnam alone. Either our European allies and other non-communist nations should have joined the U.S., or it should have "cut off every dime of foreign aid and make them pay back every cent they owe us datin' back to World War One." As president, he would ask the Joint Chiefs,

"Can we win" and if the answer were yes, "I would make full use of the country's conventional weapons to quickly end the war and bring our boys home."[34] Wallace would then tie this argument to antagonism toward the antiwar movement. He had earlier claimed that much of the discord in the U.S. had been instigated by a "conference of world guerilla chieftains in Havana," which aimed to create "revolutionary guerilla war in American cities." This continued with the anti-war activities. "I am sick and tired of American servicemen being killed by the Communists," he said, while pro-Communist professors raised money for the enemy and called for a Communist victory.[35] "There's a big difference between dissent and treason!," he would declare to thunderous applause. "If anyone waves a Viet Cong flag...we're gonna throw him under a good jail someplace!" The time had come to stop indulging the radical youth. "The first time they lay down in front of my limousine, it'll be the last one they'll ever lay down in front of."[36]

Young people, in general, earned Wallace's scorn. The phrase "dirty hippies" was a constant in his speeches. "The only four letter words that hippies don't know are 'w-o-r-k' and 's-o-a-p.'" Beards became a symbol of what was wrong, an easy way to identify those to despise, from counterculture youth to "bearded Washington bureaucrats." A large dose of anti-intellectualism suffused the critique. America was being led by "pointy-headed intellectuals who couldn't park a tricycle straight." These "bleeding hearts" would defend a criminal by "saying that the killer didn't get any watermelon when he was 10 years old...People are fed up with the sissy attitude...of the intellectual morons" who surrounded Lyndon Johnson and set public policy.[37]

And, of course, there was always the racial component that sat at the base of his critique. Even as Wallace continued to use euphemisms and code words, the message was clear. Urban riots, welfare programs, antipoverty legislation, local schools, law and order, even the criminal who did not get watermelon as a child—all these suggested racialized images in the minds of his followers. Wallace campaigned in Cicero, Illinois, an all-white town with a well-known racist history that bordered Chicago. In 1966, Martin Luther King had led open housing marches into Cicero where he was met with racist chants and hurled bricks and rocks. At the Wallace event, members of the crowd assailed an anti-Wallace protester. "Shoot 'em, kill 'em," one woman yelled. "You nigger-loving homosexual," screamed another. One crowd member called a reporter "a Jew bastard."[38]

Douglas Kiker, a highly respected national reporter for NBC and a Southerner by birth, came to a shocking conclusion covering the Wallace campaign. "It was as if somewhere, sometime a while back, George Wallace had been awakened by a white, blinding vision: they all hate black people, all of them. They're all afraid, all of them. Great God! That's it! They're all Southern! The whole United States is *Southern*."[39]

When journalist Pete Hamill interviewed Wallace supporters, he found people like Jim Lewis, a carpenter. "Get these long-haired scum in the colleges straightened out. Stop the gah-dam kneegroes from riotin' an' lootin'. Stop taxin' us to pay for people not workin'. Let our boys win that war in Viet-Nam. Hell, any plain fool knows what we gotta change." Or as one woman told Hamill, "Kids today got too much. They don't do anything for themselves. And ever since this civil rights business started people have been unhappy."[40]

Back in November 1962, just five days after Richard Nixon had lost the California gubernatorial election to Pat Brown, ABC News presented a prime time special, "The Political Obituary of Richard Nixon." Among the guests whose comments were interspersed with footage of Nixon were former president Gerald Ford and Alger Hiss, whose spy case had catapulted Nixon to public prominence in the late 1940s. Americans may have come to believe that Nixon's public career was done. No one disagreed with that assessment more than Richard Nixon himself. In his infamous "Last Press Conference," days after the election defeat, he announced he was moving to New York to join a law firm and bitterly attacked the press—"just think, you won't have Dick Nixon to kick around anymore." He had no intention of moving to the sidelines, however. As he later told one staffer, "If I had to practice law and nothing else, I would be mentally dead in two years and physically dead in four."[41]

As the Republicans party split apart over the nomination of Barry Goldwater in 1964, Nixon became Goldwater's best-known supporter. He made 150 speeches for Goldwater and other Republican candidates during the campaign. When Goldwater went down to defeat, Nixon stood in the center of the badly divided party. The conservative wing hated Nelson Rockefeller and other GOP moderates for their failure to back Goldwater. They also fell in love with their new champion, Ronald Reagan. The liberal wing of the party, for their part, hated how Rockefeller had been booed at the 1964 convention and the policies the conservatives were espousing. Assessing the dilemma of his party for the *New York Times*, Nixon felt there was room in the party for both camps, but "the center must lead." The problem, as Lawrence O'Donnell would later put it, was "no one was left in the center. Except Nixon."[42]

As Nixon charted his path toward being nominated again in 1968, he was well aware of the forces that were propelling Wallace and Reagan. His task was to hew just close enough to the right to join those tumultuous political currents, without appearing demagogic or reactionary. In 1966, he wrote an article in *U.S. News and World Report* in which he acknowledged that in traveling around the country he had found "public concern increasingly focusing upon the issues of disrespect for law and race turmoil." He dismissed the solutions of "extremists" on both sides. One group wants "the ruthless application of truncheons and an earlier call to the National Guard." The other is "more articulate, but their position is equally simplistic. To them, the riots are to be excused upon the grounds that the participants have legitimate social grievances or seek justifiable social goals." It was a mistake to see rioting as caused by "unredressed Negro grievances alone." The prime reason was "the deterioration of respect for the rule of law all across America."[43]

In addition to African Americans, young people were infected with this "contagious national disease." They exhibited "contempt" for the police. "We see them in the public burning of draft cards and the blocking of troop trains." And it was not just the kids or Black people who were to blame. "It is my belief that the seeds of civil anarchy [have] been nurtured by scores of respected Americans: public officials, educators, clergymen, and civil rights leaders as well." Even as he paid lip service to the idea of rejecting the "extremist" ideas of someone like Wallace, Nixon clearly cleaved to that side. He moved beyond a critique of the ideas of the more radical voices on race issues like Malcolm X or Stokely Carmichael. "I think it is time the doctrine of civil disobedience was analyzed and rejected." His fear was that "the rule of law would be replaced by the rule of the mob." Civil disobedience "creates a climate of disrespect for law." In fact, if "the rule of law goes, the civil rights laws of recent vintage will be the first casualties." By criticizing both the current ideas for racial juristic and even the sanctified approach of someone like Martin Luther King, Nixon was presenting himself not as a critic of civil rights and racial justice, but as its defender, appropriating the vocabulary and imagery of the right to suggest it was the way to protect the achievements of the left. And then, he concluded with an analogy that connected it all to a basic postwar mentality. "Civil disobedience and racial disorders are building a wall of hate between the races which, while less visible, is no less real than the wall that divides freedom and slavery in the city of Berlin."[44]

From 1966 through 1968, Nixon's task was to appear to represent the center of his party, while at the same time courting those drawn to the backlash. As ever, Nixon was dogged in this endeavor.

In 1968, it was the story in the Democratic Party that garnered the biggest headlines—the McCarthy campaign, LBJ's withdrawal, Robert Kennedy's victories and his assassination. There was a compelling and telling tale on the Republican side, as well. The conservative wing of the party desperately wanted Ronald Reagan to run. The California governor demurred, however, never announcing while keeping his options open. Richard Nixon had established a solid position within the party and among GOP voters in the primaries, a position bolstered when early front-runner, Michigan Governor George Romney blundered. After visiting Vietnam, Romney complained that he had been "brainwashed" by American military and civilian officials who had repeated the government's optimistic but inaccurate assessments of the war. The hostile reaction was mostly due to Romney's use of the phrase "brainwashed," which echoed anti-communist rhetoric from the 1950s. The backlash was enormous, and Romney's campaign never recovered. Days before the New Hampshire primary, he withdrew from the race. Nixon began to easily win a string of early primaries.

In an effort to stop Nixon, New York governor Nelson Rockefeller, the titular leader of the liberal wing of the party, made a late entrance into the race. The Nixon camp also knew the threat that Reagan presented. Many Southern Republicans, newly emboldened after Goldwater had carried five states in 1964, saw Reagan as their new savior. To blunt this enthusiasm, the Nixon campaign secured the support of South Carolina Senator and former Dixiecrat candidate Strom Thurmond, who in 1964 had left the Democratic Party for the Republicans. When asked if he was embarrassed by his alliance with one of the nation's most famous segregationists, Nixon had replied, "Strom is no racist. Strom is a man of courage and integrity."[45] Nixon also had the support of Barry Goldwater himself, happy to return the favor Nixon had done him in 1964. Nixon and his advisers were always aware of the threat of George Wallace to their electoral strategy. Nixon and Wallace, as well as Reagan, campaigned hard to be the champion of the frustrated and disenchanted.

Nixon could see how much Vietnam mattered to voters, especially after the successes of the McCarthy and Kennedy campaigns, and how much of the critique focused on Lyndon Johnson. Some advisers suggested he needed to articulate a position that clearly separated him from the current administration and its policies. At the beginning of March, before LBJ's departure from the race, Nixon declared, "If in November this war was not over, I say that the American people will be justified in electing new leadership. And I pledge to you the new leadership will end the war and win the peace." When pressed for how he would accomplish this, Nixon resisted specifics. It would be inappropriate to "give away bargaining positions in advance." Reporters began to refer to Nixon's "secret plan" to end the war, a phrase that stuck. Pat Buchanan, a Nixon staffer, later admitted there had never been any specific plan.[46]

In other areas, especially those appealing to the "forgotten Americans," Nixon was often much more detailed. He was quick to respond to the Kerner Commission report that identified the United States as being two societies, "one black, one white, separate and unequal." "Segregation and poverty," the commissioners argued, threatened "the future of every American." The report "in effect blames everybody for the riots except the perpetrators of the riots," Nixon asserted. Repeating the common theme frequently heard on the right, he argued, "Until we have order, we can have no progress." It was necessary to make it clear that "the law will move in with adequate force to put down rioting and looting at the first signs of it." Nixon tempered this threat with his "conviction to bring the America dream to the ghetto." Again, he was painting himself as the compassionate George Wallace.[47]

After the destruction of Resurrection City and the end of the Poor People's Campaign in Washington that June, the PPC's leadership decided to make their presence known at both the Republican and, as we have seen, Democratic conventions. As the Republicans gathered in Miami, Ralph Abernathy led the marchers. The mule caravan appeared again, representing, Abernathy said, "the 51st state—that of poverty." He saw Rockefeller as the only hope of Republicans winning any significant Black votes. When the convention was gaveled to order, Senator Everett Dirksen, the Republican leader in the Senate and the chair of the convention, used his opening remarks to address the issues Abernathy raised. The Republicans would stand against "the tyranny of the rioter, the blackmailer, the arsonist." They would stand with "law-abiding citizens" who had to "don bulletproof vests to safely take an evening stroll." America's "great cities," Dirksen declared, had become like the "hamlets, guerilla-infested, in Vietnam."[48]

The nomination ultimately came down to which way the Southern delegates would swing. Reagan knew this and his hope rested on Nixon being unable to win on the first ballot. After that, sentiment might overwhelm initial commitments and votes might move his way. Reagan spent the pre-convention days giving speeches and talking to Southern delegates. He told one television interviewer, "It's very difficult to disagree with most of the things Mr. Wallace is saying." Although he always claimed he was no more than California's favorite son, when his delegation declared him "a leading and bona fide candidate," he was able to argue that he was only responding to their draft. "In keeping with the delegation's resolution," he explained, "as of this moment I am a candidate." "Gosh, I was surprised," he told reporters. "It all came out of the clear blue sky."[49]

Nixon needed to counter this. And he did. He met with a series of Southern delegations. To one group he said, "I don't believe you should use the South as a whipping boy." He repeated his opposition to the busing of school children for desegregation purposes. Of the Supreme Court he said, "It is the job of the courts to interpret law and not make law."[50] And the Nixon people sent in Strom Thurmond to follow up. Despite Thurmond's belief that Reagan was the future of the party, Nixon was the Republican of the moment, and he impressed that on his fellow Southerners. His last argument to them was that they would heartily approve of Nixon's vice-presidential nominee. He hinted, stretching the truth a bit, that he had veto power over Nixon's choice.[51]

When the roll call began, well after midnight, the hopes of both Ronald Reagan and Nelson Rockefeller began to evaporate, as defections were few and far between. Wisconsin put Nixon over the top. He ended with a slim 26-vote victory.

When it came time to choose a vice-presidential candidate,* Nixon went through a pro-forma process of consulting various party leaders, but it was evident that he had someone in mind, someone who met his own requirements. Internal polling showed that almost any of the better-known prospects, like Reagan or New York mayor John Lindsay, would hurt Nixon, driving either liberals or conservatives away. Also, Nixon did not want a charismatic star in the #2 slot, drawing attention from the duller #1. Among a second-tier group of prospects, Nixon continued to push one name that other advisers had never even considered. "How

---

* Unlike today, in these years the presidential nominees waited until after formal nomination before announcing their vice-presidential choice.

about Agnew?," he kept saying. Maryland governor Spiro Agnew had initially been a strong Rockefeller supporter but had moved to Nixon in the spring. He was, as Nixon understood, not a Southerner but acceptable to the South. Maryland was, in fact, below the Mason-Dixon Line and had had its own racial issues over the years. Agnew had first run as a liberal Republican, but had proven, as we have seen, a harsh critic of both the Black Power and student movements in his state. When Nixon and Agnew met in the late spring, historian Rick Pearlstein later observed, "They hit it off. They shared the same resentments. They shared the same enemy... There was something *culturally* conservative about Agnew."[52]

Agnew was so little known that when TV interviewers asked people on the street about "Spiro Agnew," one thought it was a "kind of disease," another a "kind of egg."[53] This mattered little to Nixon. Having lost the presidency by the slimmest of margins, Nixon was not going to choose a running mate who would drive liberals to the Democrats or Southerners to Wallace. There was a short-lived rebellion in the ranks of some of the more liberal GOP delegates, hoping to nominate Lindsay, but by the evening it had fizzled, and Spiro Agnew joined the ticket. Lindsay, in fact, was persuaded to second Agnew's nomination. He was, as Lawrence O'Donnell would later write, "the last liberal to stand at a Republican convention podium. When John Lindsay finished speaking that night, liberalism in the Republican Party died."[54]

In his acceptance speech, Nixon touched all the bases. He reiterated the nation's problems. "We see cities enveloped in smoke and flame. We hear sirens in the night. We see Americans dying on distant battlefields abroad... millions of Americans cry out in anguish." There was one group that who possessed the values that could save the nation. "It is the voice of the great majority of Americans, the forgotten Americans—the non-shouters; the non-demonstrators." These "forgotten" Americans "work in America's factories. They run America's businesses... They provide most of the soldiers who died to keep us free... They give lift to the American Dream." The backbone of America, "they are decent people; they work, and they save, and they pay their taxes, and they care."

And then Richard Nixon, who rarely engaged in sweeping rhetoric, promised, "the long dark night for America is about to end." Americans were about "to leave the valley of despair and climb the mountain so that we may see the glory of the dawn—a new day for America, and a new dawn for peace and freedom in the world."[55]

When the Democrats left their convention in Chicago three weeks later, as we have seen, they looked like a broken party. Nixon's lead in the polls continued to widen, and Wallace's numbers improved dramatically. By the end of September, a Gallup poll gave Nixon a 15 percent lead over Humphrey (43 percent to 28 percent) with Wallace climbing to 21 percent. Nixon's fear—and Wallace's dream—was that Wallace would carry enough states to deny Nixon an Electoral College majority, which would leave the final decision to the House of Representatives, where Wallace would exercise tremendous power as the states (each given one vote) would decide the outcome.

Two events and one old political reputation began to readjust these numbers. Wallace had not yet named a running mate. In October, he chose former Air Force General Curtis LeMay, head of the Strategic Air Command under Eisenhower and someone who always favored bombing. During the Cuban Missile Crisis LeMay had counseled Kennedy to bomb the Soviet missile sites in Cuba, earning the nickname "Bombs Away LeMay." When Wallace introduced LeMay to the press as his running mate, one of the first questions was about using nuclear weapons to end the war in Vietnam. "We seem to have a phobia about nuclear weapons," LeMay responded. "I think there are many times when it would be the most efficient to use nuclear weapons." As Wallace squirmed, LeMay went on to describe how after 20 nuclear tests on one Pacific island, the animals and vegetation had returned to their lush state. "The rats are bigger, fatter, and healthier than they ever were." Finally, Wallace edged LeMay away from the podium, trying to defuse the situation, but the damage was done. Opponents began to refer to the "Wallace-LeMay ticket." Humphrey called them the "Bombsy Twins." Wallace's poll numbers began to decline, the gap between his support among white men and women grew larger. In one week, his overall poll numbers dropped by five percent.[56]

The Humphrey team decided it was finally time for their candidate to put some space between Lyndon Johnson's Vietnam policies and his own, even if the space was really small. In a televised speech at the end of September, Humphrey announced that as president he would "stop the bombing of North Vietnam as an acceptable risk for peace," promising that should the enemy show bad faith, "I would reserve the right to resume the bombing." Immediately the cash-strapped Humphrey campaign began to receive increased contributions. Vietnam critics like Allard Lowenstein and Abraham Ribicoff—who had been the target of Richard Daley's anti-Semitic attack at the Chicago convention—endorsed Humphrey. Even Eugene McCarthy eventually threw his support to him. Anti-Vietnam protests at campaign events quieted a bit. And Humphrey's poll numbers began to slowly climb.

The campaign also began to tap into the underlying ambivalence that many voters had always felt about Richard Nixon, trying to revive the image of "Tricky Dick," as Nixon had often been called. "Would you buy a used car from this man?," had been an old taunt. "Trust Humphrey" became one of the campaign's slogans.

By the end of October, Humphrey was only five percent behind, and the numbers continued to move slowly in his direction. But time ran out. When Americans went to the polls on November 5, they gave Richard Nixon an extremely narrow victory, seven-tenths of one percent in the popular vote, 301:191 in the Electoral College. George Wallace gathered an impressive 13.5 percent of the popular vote and carried five states in the Deep South with 46 electoral votes. They were insufficient, however, to keep Richard Nixon from becoming the next President of the United States.

And so, at the end of a year that had witnessed so much in the way of hopeful thinking and so many movements dedicated to the progressive transformation of various aspects of everyday life, from Eastern Europe to the West Coast of the United States, a year when the internal challenges within the Democratic Party over its failing Vietnam policies had forced a sitting president to drop out of his race for reelection, when young people and women and people of color had organized and demonstrated in numerous locales around the globe to improve their condition and raise their status, a year when change seemed to be the word on the tongue of nearly everyone, in this most extraordinary of years, the American people went to the polls and elected Richard Nixon.

Nixon represented not the urges or mentality of the 1960s, but of the decade that preceded it. He was the epitome of *square*, not a *cool* politician like one of the Kennedys or John Lindsay or, even, Gene McCarthy. He was a man of the Fifties—World War II veteran, suburban father, notorious anti-communist, Eisenhower's vice president, the candidate who had saved his political career by tearing up when talking about his daughters' cocker spaniel, who had bragged in an impromptu face-to-face debate with the leader of the Soviet Union about the wonder of American color television as an example of its technological greatness. And he had become the leading spokesperson of the backlash that had developed among many Americans to all the achievements and intentions of the decade—a backlash against the young, the poor, women, and especially those of different races.

The election was close, the victory razor thin. The shouts of resistance and frustration had not completely overwhelmed the voices of hope and change. It was rather evidence of a bitterly divided nation, one camp looking forward toward a society that rectified inequities and continued to promote social justice for all, the other believing that what little they had was slipping away and that it was those arguing for further progress who were threatening their insecure existences. This was certainly not the legacy of this tumultuous year that the people of the movements had envisioned. And yet it was not that their dreams had turned to ashes, either. Rather they had awakened to a sobering dawn.

Epilogue

The Sobering Dawn

The kinetic energy released in 1968 carried through to the end of the decade and beyond. Vaclav Havel recalled the crucial role that the Prague Spring had on subsequent events in Czechoslovakia. It carried the spirit of resistance, especially among those in the artistic underground, through the 1970s and helped reignite the anti-government actions that led to the Velvet Revolution of 1989. "All of us were reborn on October 2," the day of the Tlatelolco Massacre in Mexico City, observed one Mexican student leader. "And on that day we also decided how we are all going to die: fighting for genuine justice and democracy."[1] This spirit would contribute to the end of the one-party rule of the PRI at the turn of the twenty-first century. In France, the spirit of '68 did not change the government, but it deeply affected many of its citizens. "Everyone had started to believe in a violent future," wrote Nobel Prize-winning novelist Annie Ernaux some years later. People "hoped and worked toward 'May Redux' and a new society." And even if this future did not come to be, Ernaux believed, "we felt we had nothing left to lose by trying everything. 1968 was the first year of the world."[2]

In the United States, the post-'68 years fueled both the movements aimed at social transformation and those resisting the change. The presidency of Richard Nixon proved an amalgam of the two, which was

surprising given Nixon's life-long political positions and his exploitation of the resentments of the backlash in the 1968 campaign. Many
programs later associated with the 1960s and with Lyndon Johnson's
Great Society were actually enacted under Nixon, including Affirmative
Action, the creation of the Environmental Protection Agency (EPA),
the Occupational Safety and Health Administration (OSHA), and congressional passage of the Equal Rights Amendment. Nixon did not
resist increased spending for social welfare programs like food stamps,
Social Security, or Aid to Families with Dependent Children (AFDC).
As Pat Buchanan, Nixon's very conservative speechwriter and later one
of the most extreme right-wing cultural critics, put it, "Vigorously did
we inveigh against the Great Society," but "enthusiastically did we
fund it."[3]

Of course, the Vietnam War, so crucial to most of the movements of
1968, continued through the years of Nixon's presidency. Rather than
ending the war, Nixon tried to shift the burden of the fighting back to
the South Vietnamese army—"Vietnamization" he called it—hoping to
lessen domestic opposition by reducing the number of American troops.
However, he also escalated the bombing campaign against North
Vietnam dramatically, trying to force the enemy into a negotiated peace.
In another attempt to pacify home front antagonism, Nixon introduced
a draft lottery in 1969 to eliminate the Selective Service system of deferments, as well as reduce the number of years that young men would
remain available to the draft from seven to one. In 1973, he ended conscription entirely by creating an all-volunteer military.

Despite his career-long vehement opposition to communism and his
commitment to the Cold War, in early 1972, Nixon made an historic visit
to China. This began the reestablishment of relations between the
Americans and the Chinese, ending twenty-five years of no communica-
tion or diplomatic ties between the two nations. Nixon's visit was carried
live on American television, including dinners with premier Zhou Enlai
and cordial meetings—bewildering to many, especially those on the
right—with Mao Zedong. The trip proved both a diplomatic coup and
a major public relations achievement.

Nixon's moves did little to defuse the anti-war sentiment at home. Opposition to Vietnam remained constant during Nixon's time in the White House. The National Moratorium of October 1969 included a rally of 250,000 in Washington, with major rallies in a number of American cities, including the 100,000 that turned out in Boston. A young American Rhodes Scholar at Oxford, Bill Clinton, helped organize the demonstration in England that day. A second march in the nation's capital in November drew over 500,000 people. In the spring of 1970, Nixon approved an invasion of Cambodia aiming to destroy North Vietnamese supply lines and command centers. His televised announcement of this "incursion," as he called it—thinking it sounded better than "invasion"—led to an enormous national reaction. Demonstrations occurred on over 700 college campuses, a number of which had never held an anti-Vietnam demonstration before. A hundred thousand marchers descended on Washington. Four days after Nixon's announcement, national guardsmen at Kent State University in Ohio opened fired on campus demonstrators, killing four and wounding nine. Ten days later at Jackson State College, a predominantly Black school in Mississippi, police fired on a group of students, leaving two dead and eleven injured. The May Day demonstrations of 1971 were less peaceful than previous ones had been, including a week-long series of acts of civil disobedience in Washington, leading to 12,000 arrests. The spirit of rebellion persisted well into the post-1968 days but became more confrontational and, often, violent.

Freed of their ties to Lyndon Johnson, the majority of Democrats could fully embrace the anti-war position in the 1972 election. George McGovern, who had stepped in as the stand-in candidate for the Robert Kennedy delegates at the Chicago convention, now ran on his own. He was able to mobilize many of the same anti-war forces and emerged from the primaries as the Democratic nominee. McGovern's primary campaign ran exceptionally smoothly, but the general election campaign proved disastrous, disrupted by internal mistakes and external attacks. Major segments of the Democratic coalition abandoned their candidate, including many in organized labor and elected Democratic officials. The Republican campaign fastened onto a number of the perceived 1960s' attributes of McGovern's campaign, ones that conservative voters would find objectionable. In one jibe, McGovern was depicted as the candidate of "Acid, Amnesty, and Abortion," the "Amnesty" label attacking those who proposed amnesty for the young men who had fled to Canada to avoid the draft. In addition, people later learned of all the dirty tricks and illegal activities that comprised what became known as Watergate, the actions of the Nixon campaign to undermine the opposition and unlawfully influence the election outcome. Nixon won a landslide victory, carrying 60.7 percent of the popular vote and forty-nine states. McGovern carried only Massachusetts and the District of Columbia. For many, the defeat felt like the death of one important aspect of 1960s life.

Race relations, one of the prime inspirations for Sixties activism and often at the root of the backlash against it, continued to agitate American society. The Republicans had been the minority party since the days of Franklin Roosevelt in the 1930s, and Nixon aimed to end it. He saw the white South that had been attracted to George Wallace as an area of potential Republican growth, along with the disenchanted white working class Nixon had courted in 1968. A so-called "Southern Strategy" emerged, aimed at bringing these two groups into the GOP. Central to this effort was a scaling back of efforts to end racial injustice and rectify inequities. Nixon did not, however, want to appear as racist. Instead, he took the advice of his urban affairs adviser, Daniel Patrick Moynihan, later the Democratic senator from New York. Moynihan argued to Nixon that Black people had been "too much talked about." What was needed, he felt, was "a period of 'benign neglect.'"[4] Nixon was in full agreement. He opposed court-ordered busing, tried to keep Congress from renewing the Voting Rights Act of 1965, and nominated a white Southerner to the Supreme Court. In fact, he nominated two. When the Senate rejected his first Southern nominee, Clement Haynsworth, he chose another, G. Harrold Carswell. Both were cited for having previously uttered racist, sexist, and anti-Semitic statements as well as their perceived judicial "mediocrity." In defense of one of these nominees, a Republican Senate supporter argued that there were many "mediocre" people in the U.S. and "they are entitled to a little representation...We can't have all Brandeises, Frankfurters and Cardozos," naming three distinguished Jewish justices.[5]

A number of Republican Senators broke ranks and joined with Democrats to reject the two appointees on all these substantive grounds. Yet, Nixon called it "regional discrimination." When he nominated a qualified Republican judge from Minnesota, Harry Blackmun, he was confirmed unanimously.

Many Americans, especially the young, were not ready to give up on the values of the 1960s, especially the cultural ones. Counterculture ideals and aspirations persisted. The Woodstock Music and Art Fair took place in August 1969. Initially depicted in the media as a rain-soaked disaster, instead the three-day music festival became an icon of counterculture celebration. Half a million people had gathered and, despite the pouring rain and fields of mud, shared in a peaceful, communal experience. The phrase "Woodstock Nation," coined by Abbie Hoffman, suggested that the values and sense of community exhibited by the thousands who attended might be translated into a movement to create a society based on the communal counterculture values engaged in by the concertgoers. The spirit of the counterculture seemed to be alive.

Four months later, though, the Rolling Stones put on a free concert at the Altamont raceway in Northern California. The scene turned ugly. The motorcycle gang Hell's Angeles had been hired to provide security— the same group that had help lost children find their parents at the first Human Be-In in San Francisco in 1967. At Altamont, they attacked members of the audience, beating many and kicking and stabbing one young Black man to death right in front of the stage while the Stones were playing. Mick Jagger looked on, helpless and horrified. Again, for many, this proved another end to the spirit of 1968.

A driving force of 1968, the women's movement, had just been coming into its own. The Miss America demonstrations in Atlantic City became the moment when what had been slowly growing for years gained wide national attention. The momentum continued on into the coming

decade. In fact, if anything, the great successes of the women's movement occurred in the 1970s. Once it began to question the situation of
women within it, there was hardly an area in American society that
remained unaffected. From politics to health care, the place of women in
the military to their roles in the home, personal rights over one's own
finances to proper recognition of women in athletics; one area after
another witnessed massive changes. Feminist books became bestsellers,
national magazines like *Ms.* found wide audiences, and sexist language
was called out and reduced, from television programs to the floor of
Congress. In 1973, the Supreme Court ruled, in the case of *Roe v. Wade*,
that women had the right to have legal, safe abortions.

The time seemed right to bring back the Equal Rights Amendment to
the Constitution, which stated "equality of rights under the law shall not
be denied or abridged by the United States or by any State on account of
sex." It had been first proposed in the 1920s following the passage of the
suffrage amendment, but it made little progress in Congress over the
ensuing decades. Reintroduced in 1971, it passed the House 354 to 23.
The next year, the Senate passed it eighty-four to eight. With the backing
of leaders in both political parties, it was ratified by thirty-five of the
thirty-eight states necessary for it to be added to the Constitution. Then
the opposition set in. Fueled by many of the same arguments that had
arisen with the backlash, including a reassertion of traditional gender
roles—"I am for Mom and apple pie" was one anti-ERA slogan—
ratification stalled, ultimately failing to reach the required number.
Several states, in fact, voted to revoke their ratification.

Like the Miss America demonstrations nine months earlier, the June
1969 riots at the Stonewall Inn, a gay bar in Greenwich Village, announced
the emergence of another movement to address discrimination, the Gay
Liberation Movement, which drew both gay men and lesbians. Gay
rights organizations, like the Daughters of Bilitis and the Mattachine
Society, had quietly grown in the 1960s. Anti-gay discrimination was
compounded by regular police harassment, including raids on gay bars.
At Stonewall, the resistance to a police raid boiled over. "When did you

ever see a fag fight back?," one participant recalled. "Now, times were a-changin'... this shit has got to stop!"[6] The riots went on for four nights.

Echoing the sentiments and often the vocabulary of radical feminism and black nationalism, the movement for gay rights included efforts to have gays come out publicly, as well as seeking to end the discrimination of gays in numerous areas of American life. Public events, such as the emergence of Gay Pride parades, raised public awareness. And vehement opposition. Anita Bryant, a popular singer who had joined Bob Hope's tours of Vietnam to entertain the troops and was the television spokesperson for Florida orange juice, became the leading voice of an anti-gay rights coalition, Save Our Children. She fanned fears that gay teachers would "recruit" children to become gay. Once a benign smiling entertainer, Bryant became the major public symbol of the opposition to gay rights.

San Francisco grew to be the most commonly identified gay city in the U.S. and in 1977 elected Harvey Milk, the first openly gay man elected to public office in the country, to the Board of Supervisors. Milk sponsored, among other measures, a bill banning discrimination based on sexual orientation in public accommodations, housing, and employment. It passed the Board by an overwhelming eleven to one vote. Tragically, in 1978, Dan White, a former supervisor who represented a white working-class district hostile to gays and who had been the single board vote against Milk's bill, shot and killed both Milk and Mayor George Moscone.

Since the nineteenth century, writers like John Muir and Aldo Leopold and public figures like Theodore Roosevelt and Gifford Pinchot had been arguing that Americans were not taking sufficient care of the environment. Over the course of the 1960s, a series of books exposing important environmental issues captured American public attention, including Rachel Carson's *The Silent Spring* (1962), which exposed the dangers of pesticides, and Paul Ehrlich's *The Population Bomb* (1968), which voiced serious concerns about the rate of population growth.

These books and others helped trigger an environmental movement. A wide array of issues, from air pollution caused by automobiles to declining fish populations in the Great Lakes to the harm caused by oil spills from damaged tankers, attracted attention. This led to the coalescing of an identifiable environmental crusade. Its major public activity was the creation of the Earth Day celebrations, beginning in 1971. Congress responded, again under Nixon, with a series of bills, including the Clean Air Act (1970), the Clean Water Act (1972) and the Endangered Species Act (1973). Some in the movement pushed for more direct and, sometimes, militant approaches, including Greenpeace, which favored nonviolent direct action. This was cheered by some, opposed by others. Resistance to environmentalism also came from groups in the private sector that saw the proposed regulations and programs as expensive and limiting profits. Some began to argue that the environmental movement cared more about saving some obscure species of lizard than people's jobs. Environmentalists were often dismissed as "tree huggers," "granola heads," or simply and disparagingly as "hippies." This all served to delegitimize the movement in the eyes of many. Again, an effort that initially appealed to a wide majority ended with two divided constituencies, one favoring action, the other resisting change.

Even within the progressive political movements, the unanimity that had developed in the second half of the 1960s began to fray. Frustrated by many of the failures of their efforts and growing increasingly angry at the "Establishment," political groups around the globe broke into rival factions. Some of these factions began to pursue a violent approach. In Germany, the Red Army Faction, often called the Baader-Meinhof Gang, engaged in a series of bank robberies, bombings, and assassinations. The Red Brigades, formed in Italy in 1970, committed kidnappings, sabotage, and bank robberies. Most famously, they kidnapped and later executed Italian Prime Minister Aldo Moro.

At the 1969 SDS national convention, the organization splintered. One faction, the Weathermen, declared that new tactics and a new perspective were needed. "After years of peace marches, petitions, and the gradual realization that [Vietnam] was no 'mistake,'" they argued, the reality was that they were in a "war in which there are only two sides." Their side stood "for liberation and the unchaining of human freedom."

And unlike the earlier tactic of the anti-Vietnam war effort, "this is a war in which we cannot 'resist'; it is a war in which we must fight."[7] Intending to "bring the war home," they organized the "Days of Rage," a series of actions in Chicago that October, including smashing windows, blowing up park statues, and numerous confrontations with police. A number of the leaders then went underground, continuing to engage in a series of bombings. These were intended to destroy property—usually associated with the war effort—and not human lives. In fact, the only people killed by Weathermen bombs were three of their own, who died when the bombs they were building in a Greenwich Village townhouse detonated.

This new approach proved attractive to some, impossible to others. As Tom Hayden later put it, "They had started, characteristically, as idealistic and benign people. And then something happened. Some of it was a response to events, in which moral suasion of the power structure seemed to be an obsolete idea." Hayden understood what had led the Weathermen and others to the place to which they had come. "I didn't want to cross that line," he later observed. He harkened back to the optimism and idealism of the early days of the New Left, the promise of participatory democracy, and the belief that people were, as the Port Huron Statement put it, "infinitely precious and possessed of unfulfilled capacities for reason, freedom, and love." "It was the political side," Hayden believed, "the Port Huron side, that saved me."[8]

While the spirit the 1960s, in general, and of 1968, in particular, would continue into the new decade, many felt that the context had changed. The hopes and utopian visions seemed tainted, adulterated—if not destroyed outright. Individual moments might make people feel passionate again. These enthusiasms, however, often turned wary and uneasy.

Bob Dylan had moved to upstate New York in 1966 after being injured in a motorcycle accident. He was joined by the musicians who would later become The Band, one of the most important musical groups of the 1970s. Moving back to Greenwich Village in 1969, Dylan later told author and journalist Charles Kaiser, "the spirit that had been there in the sixties wasn't there anymore." Kaiser asked if the events of 1968 were responsible. "All those blows to your hope will make you deader and deader and deader," Dylan observed.[9] More and more it seemed that the people of the movements were coming to understand both the achievements and the limits of their actions. Once feeling they were a part of a social transformation that would radically change the world, they still took pride in what they had done, still believed they could enact further change. Yet, consciously or unconsciously, they also came to be haunted by what Jack Newfield felt after the assassination of Robert Kennedy—the fear that they had become "a generation of might-have-beens."[10]

Endnotes

INTRODUCTION

1. Letter to Karl Jaspers, cited in *AHR Reflections, American Historical Review*, v. 123, no. XX (June 2018), 706.

2. See Rafael Rojas, *Fighting Over Fidel: The New York Intellectuals and the Cuban Revolution* (Princeton: Princeton University Press, 2116), 31–41.

3. David Scott Robarge, "CIA's Covert Operations in the Congo, 1960–1968: Insights from Newly Declassified Documents," Homeland Security Digital Library, September 2014, https://www.hsdl.org/c/abstract/?docid=759725.

4. Stephen R. Weissman, "What Really Happened in Congo: The CIA, the Murder of Lumumba, and the Rise of Mobutu," Foreign Affairs, June 16, 2014, https://www.foreignaffairs.com/democratic-republic-congo/what-really-happened-congo; Stephen R. Weismann, "Review of *Death in the Congo: Murdering Patrice Lumumba*," *Intelligence in Public Media* v. 59, no. 4 (December 2015), 53–54.

5. Douglas Kellner, *Ernesto Che Guevara* (New York: Chelsea House, 1988), 60.

6. Che Guevara, "Colonialism Is Doomed" (speech, December 11, 1964), Che Guevara Internet Archive, https://www.marxists.org/archive/guevara/1964/12/11-alt.

7. Che Guevara, "Create Two, Three, Many Vietnams: Message to the Tricontinental," https://www.historyisaweapon.com/defcon1/cheus.htm

8. Martin Luther King, Jr., "The Rising Tide of Racial Consciousness," in *The Global Revolutions of 1968*, ed. Jeremi Suri (New York: Norton, 2007), 11–12.

9. Quoted in Mark Kurlansky, *1968: The Year That Rocked the World* (New York: Random House, 2004), 224.

10. Langdon Winner, quoted in Charles Kaiser, *1968 in America* (New York: Grove Press, 1988), xxii.

11. Barry Melton, "Everything Seemed Beautiful: A Life in the Counterculture," in *Long Time Gone: Sixties America Then and Now*, ed. Alexander Bloom (New York: Oxford, 2001), 155.

12. "CIA Report: Restless Youth (September 1968)," in *The Global Revolutions of 1968*, ed. Jeremi Suri, 216–38.

13. "KGB Memorandum to the Council of Ministers of the Soviet Union," November 5, 1968, The Wilson Center, https://digitalarchive.wilsoncenter.org/document/report-relayed-andropov-cpsu-central-committee-students-and-events-czechoslovakia.

14. For example, an entire section of one anthology on 1968 is titled "Tet and Prague: The Bipolar System in Crisis" in *1968: The World Transformed*, eds. Carole Fink, Phillip Gassert, and Detlef Junker (Cambridge: Cambridge University Press, 1998), 31–216.

15. Michael Kidron and Ronald Segal, "The Student Sixties," in *The State of the World Atlas*, eds. Michael Kidron and Ronald Segal (New York: Simon & Schuster, 1981), 64.

CHAPTER 1

1. Anne Moody, *Coming of Age in Mississippi* (New York: Dial Press, 1965), 130.
2. Diana Trilling, "The Other Night at Columbia: A Report from the Academy," (original written 1958) in Diana quo in *Social Movements of the 1960s*, 23.

CHAPTER 2

1. Julian Bond, "The Movement We Helped to Make," in *Long Time Gone: Sixties America Then and Now*, ed. Alexander Bloom (New York: Oxford University Press, 2001), 11.
2. Quoted in Greg Palast, "How JFK Saved MLK's Life And So Won The Presidency," https://ibw21.org/commentary/how-jfk-saved-mlks-life-and-so-won-the-presidency/
3. Clayborne Carson, *In Struggle: SNCC and the Black Awakening of the 1960s* (Cambridge: Harvard University Press, 1981), 37.
4. Martin Luther King, Jr. "Letter from Birmingham Jail," (written April 16, 1963), King Institute, https://kinginstitute.stanford.edu/letter-birmingham-jail.
5. Medgar Evers, "I Speak as a Native Mississippian," in *Takin' It to the Streets: A Sixties Reader*, eds. Alexander Bloom and Wini Breines (New York: Oxford University Press, 4/e, 2015), 26–28.
6. John Lewis, "Wake Up America," in *Takin' It to the Streets*, 29–31.
7. Anne Moody, quopted in Burns, *Social Movements of the 1960s*, 23.
8. John D'Emilo, *Lost Prophet: The Life and Times of Bayard Rustin* (Chicago: The University of Chicago Press, 2003), 357. For a full discussion of Rustin and the march, see 326–57.
9. "Letters From Mississippi," in *Takin' It to the Streets*, 32.
10. Ibid., 35.

CHAPTER 3

1. Maurice Isserman and Michael Kazin, *America Divided: The Civil War of the 1960s* (New York: Oxford University Press, 2000), 172.
2. Terry H. Anderson, *The Movement and the Sixties* (New York: Oxford University Press, 1995), 59.
3. Louis Menand, "Change Your Life: The Lessons of the New Left," *The New Yorker*, v. XCVII, no. 5 (March 22, 2021), 46.
4. While a number of works focused on this theme, the most prominent was Daniel Bell, *The End of Ideology: On the Exhaustion of Political Ideas in the Fifties* (New York: The Free Press, 1960).
5. C. Wright Mills, "Letter to the New Left," in *Takin' It to the Streets: A Sixties Reader*, eds. Alexander Bloom and Wini Breines (New York: Oxford University Press, 4/e, 2015), 71–76.
6. James Miller, *Democracy Is in the Streets: From Port Huron to the Siege of Chicago* (New York: Simon and Schuster, 1987), 106.
7. Tom Hayden, *Reunion: A Memoir* (New York: Random House, 1988), 73.
8. Hayden, *Reunion*, 41. Hayden pursued Cason over the next year, and they married in 1961.
9. For a complete text of the Port Huron Statement, see Miller, *Democracy Is in the Streets*, 329–74.

10. Ibid., 216. For the fullest history of ERAP, see Wini Breines, *Community and Organization in the New Left, 1962–1968: The Great Refusal* (New Brunswick, NJ: Rutgers University Press, 1989).

11. Mario Savio, "An End to History," in *Takin' It to the Streets*, 105.

12. W. J. Rorabaugh, *Berkeley at War: The 1960s* (New York: Oxford University Press, 1989), 20. For a complete discussion of the Free Speech Movement, see 8–36.

13. Ibid., 22.

14. Savio, "An End to History," 105.

CHAPTER 4

1. Robert S. McNamara, *In Retrospect: The Tragedy and Lessons of Vietnam* (New York: Random House, 1995), 32.

2. Quoted in James S. Olsen and Randy Roberts, *Where the Domino Fell: America and Vietnam, 1945–1995* (New York: St. Martin's Press, 2/e, 1996), 22.

3. "The Vietnamese Declaration of Independence," in *Takin' It to the Streets: A Sixties Reader*, eds. Alexander Bloom and Wini Breines (New York: Oxford University Press, 4/e, 2015), 166.

4. "Geneva Accords," in *Takin' It to the Streets*, 167–70.

5. Olsen and Roberts, *Where the Domino Fell*, 62.

6. "The Pentagon Papers," in *Takin' It to the Streets*, 171.

CHAPTER 5

1. SDS Flyer, " ACall to All Students to March on Washington to End the War in Vietnam April 17, 1965," Students for a Democratic Society, https://michiganintheworld.history.lsa.umich.edu/antivietnamwar/exhibits/show/exhibit/item/154.

2. Paul Potter, "The Incredible War," in *Takin' It to the Streets: A Sixties Reader*, eds. Alexander Bloom and Wini Breines (New York: Oxford University Press, 4/e, 2015), 196.

3. "SNCC Position Paper on Vietnam," in *Takin' It to the Streets*, 204.

4. Terry H. Anderson, The Movement and the Sixties (New York: Oxford University Press, 1995), 147–48.

5. Stewart Burns, *Social Movements of the 1960s: Searching for Democracy* (Boston: Twayne, 1990), 71. Over the course of the Vietnam war, eight Americans committed ritual suicide in protest.

6. "The Fort Hood Three," in *Takin' It to the Streets: A Sixties Reader*, eds. Alexander Bloom and Wini Breines (New York: Oxford University Press, 4/e, 2015), 224–26.

7. "Jun 30, 1966: Fort Hood Three Release Public Statement of Vietnam Refusal," Zinn Education Project, https://www.zinnedproject.org/news/tdih/fort-hood-three/.

8. Oren Root, "Moving Tribute to the Fort Hood Three," October 14, 1966, Spectator Archive, http://spectatorarchive.library.columbia.edu/?a=d&d=cs19661014-01.2.16&.

9. "PrimeTime: Marrying to Avoid Draft," ABC News, https://abcnews.go.com/Primetime/story?id=132298&page=1.

10. Anderson, *The Movement and the Sixties*, 139–40.

11. "Channeling," in *Takin' It to the Streets*, 213–14.

12. Tom Wells, *The War Within: America's Battle Over Vietnam* (Berkeley: University of California Press, 1994), 106–12.

13. Anderson, *The Movement and the Sixties*, 145.
14. Daniel Bell, "The Mood of Three Generations," in *The End of Ideology: On the Exhaustion of Political Ideas in the Fifties*, ed. Daniel Bell (Glencoe, IL: The Free Press, 1965 [1960]), 302.

CHAPTER 6

1. Malcolm X, *The Autobiography of Malcolm X* (New York: Grove Press, 1965), 229.
2. "Playboy Interview: Malcolm X" (May 1963), Genius, https://genius.com/Playboy-playboy-interview-malcolm-x-annotated.
3. "The Hate That Hate Produced," Internet Archive, https://archive.org/details/PBSTheHateThatHateProduced. Wallace subsequently apologized for not fully understanding The Nation of Islam and Malcolm X.
4. Quoted in Stewart Burns, *Social Movements of the 1960s: Searching for Democracy* (Boston: Twayne, 1990), 34.
5. Malcolm X, "The Ballot of the Bullet," in *Takin' It to the Streets*, eds. Alexander Bloom and Wini Breines (New York: Oxford University Press, 4/e, 2015), 121–22.
6. Malcolm X, "Telegram to George Lincoln Rockwell (Leader of the American Nazi Party," 1965, http://www.malcolm-x.org/docs/tel_rock.htm. See Taylor Branch, *Pillar of Fire: America in the King Years, 1963–65* (New York: Simon and Schuster, 1999), 575–79.
7. "Malcolm X," King Institute, https://kinginstitute.stanford.edu/encyclopedia/malcolm-x.
8. Ossie Davis, "Eulogy for Malcolm X," in *Takin' It to the Streets*, 122–23.
9. *New York Times*, February 5, 1965, 15.
10. Amy Goodman, " 'I Felt Like I Was Going to Die':The Late John Lewis on Selma's 'Bloody Sunday,' " Truthout, https://truthout.org/video/i-felt-like-i-was-going-to-die-the-late-john-lewis-on-selmas-bloody-sunday/.
11. Lyndon B. Johnson, " 'And We Shall Overcome'—The American Promise: A Special Message to Congress," in *Takin' It to the Streets*, 94–95.
12. Branch, *At Canaan's Edge*, 170. For a complete discussion of Selma, see 5–205. In addition, see Isserman and Kazin, *America Divided*, 133–39; Burns, *Social Movements of the 60s*, 35–39; Terry H. Anderson, *The Movement and the Sixties* (New York: Oxford University Press, 1995), 115–19.
13. I. F. Stone, "SNCC Does Not Weish to Become a New Version of the White Man's Burden," *I.F. Stone's Weekly*, June 6, 1966.
14. "May 1966: Stokely Carmichael Elected as SNCC's Chair," SNCC Digital Gateway, https://snccdigital.org/events/stokely-carmichael-elected-snccs-chair/.
15. Quoted in Stewart Burns, *Social Movements of the 1960s: Searching for Democracy* (Boston: Twayne, 1990), 42; "Willie Ricks," SNCC Digital Gateway, https://snccdigital.org/people/willie-ricks/. The phrase "Black Power" had been used at times by others in the Black community, including novelist Richard Wright and Congressman Adam Clayton Powell, but it did not catch on as a popular phrase in the movement until this point.
16. Branch, *At Canaan's Edge*, 284–85.
17. Ibid., 297.
18. " 'Violence in the City—An End or a Beginning?': The McCone Commission Report on Watts," in *Takin' It to the Streets*, 126.
19. Branch, *At Canaan's Edge*, 501.

20. Quoted in Anderson, *The Movement and the Sixties*, 157.

21. Gene Roberts, "Rights March Disunity," *New York Times*, June 28, 1966, 23.

22. SNCC, "The Basis of Black Power," in *Takin' It to the Streets*, 122–24.

23. "(1966) Stokely Carmichael, 'Black Power,'" BlackPast, July 13, 2010, https://www.blackpast.org/african-american-history/speeches-african-american-history/1966-stokely-carmichael-black-power/. In 1967, Carmichael further expanded his analysis when he published, along with political scientist Charles Hamilton, *Black Power: The Politics of Liberation* (New York: Random House, 1967).

24. "'Black Power': Statement by National Committee of Negro Churchmen," *New York Times*, July 31, 1966, E5.

25. "The Black Panther Platform: 'What We Want, What We Believe,'" in *Takin' It to the Streets*, 142–43.

CHAPTER 7

1. https://www.npr.org/sections/thetwo-way/2013/03/11/174067341/book-news-hippies-were-dirty-and-liked-music-by-satanists-louisiana-textbook-cla

2. Diana Trilling, "The Other Night at Columbia: A Report from the Academy" (1958), in *Claremont Essays* (New York: Harcourt, Brace & World, 1964), 165–66, 158.

3. Damon R. Bach, *The American Counterculture: A History of Hippies and Cultural Dissidents* (Lawrence, Kansas: University Press of Kansas, 2020), 23.

4. Harrington, quoted in Dan Wakefield, *New York in the 50s* (Boston: Houghton Mifflin, 1992), 158.

5. Janet Maslin, "Bob Dylan," in *The Rolling Stone History of Rock 'n' Roll*, ed. Jim Miller (New York: Random House, 1980), 220.

6. Dylan quoted in Anthony Saputo, *Bob Dylan* (New York: Signet Books, 1973), 203–204; Wilson quoted in "100 Days That Shook the World" (The Psychedelic Beatles—April 1, 1965 to December 26, 1967). *Mojo* Special Limited Edition: London, 2002, 4.

7. Jacob Nierenberg, "Ladies and Gentlemen, The Beatles: When the Fab Four Met Ed Sullivan," Consequence, February 11, 2019, https://consequence.net/2019/02/the-beatles-appear-on-ed-sullivan/.

8. Sara Schmidt, "The Beatles on Sullivan Remembered," Meet The Beatles For Real, February 3, 2014, http://www.meetthebeatlesforreal.com/2014/02/the-beatles-on-sullivan-remebered.html.

9. Bach, *The American Counterculture*, 63.

10. http://www.meetthebeatlesforreal.com/2014/02/the-beatles-on-sullivan-remebered.html; https://www.nytimes.com/2014/02/08/nyregion/the-beatles-debut-on-ed-sullivan.html.

11. See Gael Graham, *Young Activists: American High School Students in the Age of Protest* (DeKalb, IL: Northern Illinois University Press, 2006); Gael Graham, "Flaunting the Freak Flag: Karr v. Schmidt and the Great Hair Debate in American High Schools, 1965–1975," *The Journal of American History* v. 91, no. 2 (September, 2004), 522–43; Tim Allen, "A Dilemma in Public High Schools: School Board Authority v. The Constitutional Right of Students to Wear Long Hair," *Louisiana Law Review*, v. 33, no. 4 (Summer 1973), 607–707.

12. "The Port Huron Statement," in *Takin' It to the Streets: A Sixties Reader*, eds. Alexander Bloom and Wini Breines (New York: Oxford University Press, 4/e, 2015), 68, 61.

13. Guy Strait, "What Is a Hippie?" in *Takin' It to the Streets*, 280.

14. Ibid.

15. Elaine Tyler May, *America and The Pill* (New York: Basic Books, 2010), 1–2.

16. Gary Snyder, "Buddhism and the Coming Revolution" and Malcolm Boyd, "Are You Running with Me, Jesus?" in *Takin' It to the Streets*, 262–66.

17. See Carlos Castaneda, "The Teaching of Don Juan: A Yaqui Way of Knowledge," in *Takin' It to the Streets*, 272–75. The truthfulness of Castaneda's narrative was later challenged by some researchers, but he always claimed that his story was true.

18. Donovan Bess, "LSD: The Acid Test," in *Takin' It to the Streets*, 270.

19. Robert C. Cottrell, *Sex, Drugs, and Rock 'n' Roll: The Rise of America's 1960s Counterculture* (New York: Rowman & Littlefield, 2015), 74.

20. Cottrell, *Sex, Drugs, and Rock 'n' Roll*, 87, 88.

21. Ibid., 90–94.

22. Tom Wolfe, *The Electric Kool Aid Acid Test* (New York: Farrar, Strauss and Giroux, 1968), 263. For many it was only with the publication of Wolfe's book that they learned about the breadth of the counterculture. See also, Bach, *The American Counterculture*, 82–84, and Charles Perry, *The Haight-Ashbury: A History* (New York: Random House, 1984), 44–50.

CHAPTER 8

1. *Women Workers in 1960*, Women's Bureau Bulletin 284 (Washington, DC: U.S. Department of Labor, 1962), vi, 13, 15; Mitra Toossi and Teresa L. Morisi, *Women in the Workforce Before, During, and After the Great Recession* (Washington, DC: U.S. Bureau of Labor Statistics, July 2017), 2.

2. S. J. Kleinberg, "Economic Activity During Boom, Bust, and War," in *Women in the United States, 1830–1945* (London: Palgrave, 1999), 207–32. https://link.springer.com/chapter/10.1007/978-1-349-27698-1_10.

3. These and other issues are poignantly described by the women interviewed for the classic documentary, Connie Fields, "The Life and Times of Rosie the Riveter" (1980). https://learn.sunyempire.edu/media/The+Life+and+Times+of+Rosie+the+Riveter/1_pdoydcgl/62990541

4. Ferdinand Lundberg and Marynia Farnham, *Modern Woman: The Lost Sex* (New York: Harper, 1947), 235. Interestingly, Farnham was a female physician, whose own life decisions appear to contradict the thesis of her work.

5. Ibid., 270.

6. Quoted in Terry H. Anderson, *The Movement and the Sixties* (New York: Oxford University Press, 1995), 20.

7. Edith M. Stern, "Woman Are Household Slaves," *The American Mercury*, v. 68, no. 301 (January 1949), 71, 76.

8. Rosie Germain, "Reading 'The Second Sex' in 1950s America," *The Historical Journal* v. 56, no. 4 (December 2013), 1045, 1046–49, 1053, 1055–56.

9. Clyde Kluckhorn, "The Complex Kinsey Study and What It Attempts to Do," *New York Times*, September 13, 1953.

10. See Marcia Gallo, *Different Daughters: A History of the Daughters of Bilitis and the Rise of the Lesbian Rights Movement* (New York: Seal Press, 2006), 62–63.

11. Frances Beal, "Double Jeopardy," in *Takin' It to the Streets: A Sixties Reader* eds. Alexander Bloom and Wini Breines (New York: Oxford University Press, 4/e, 2015), 453–56.

12. Carol Giardina, "MOW to NOW: Black feminism Resets the Chronology of the Founding of Modern Feminism," *Feminist Studies*, v. 44, no. 3 (2018), 737.

13. Quoted in Ibid., 743. See also the documentary film, "My Name is Pauli Murray" (2021).

14. Giardina, "MOW to NOW," 742.

15. Claudia Jones, "An End to the Neglect of the Problems of the Negro Woman!," *Political Affairs* (1949), New York, 4, 15.

16. Sherrie M. Randolph, *Florynce "Flo" Kennedy: The Life of a Black Feminist Radical* (Chapel Hill: The University of North Carolina Press, 2015), 44.

17. Ibid., 49.

18. Ibid., 52, 56–57.

19. Ibid., 56–57, 64, 72–73, 81, 84.

20. Dorothy Cobble, "More Than Sex Equality: Feminism After Suffrage," in *Feminism Unfinished: A Short, Surprising History of American Women's Movements*, eds. Dorothy Sue Cobble, Linda Gordon, and Astrid Henry (New York: Liveright Publishing, 2014), 47–52.

21. Giardina, "MOW to NOW," 745–48.

22. Randolph, *Florynce "Flo" Kennedy*, 85–95. WIMS groups returned to Mississippi in the summer of 1965. In 1966 its emphasis changed, as it became "Workshops in Mississippi," focusing on poor Black and white women and families.

23. Quoted in Isserman and Kazin, *America Divided*, 179.

24. Casey Hayden and Mary King, "Sex and Caste: A Kind of Memo," in *Takin' It to the Streets*, 43–44.

25. Mary King, "SNCC: Born of the Sit-Ins, Dedicated to Action," April 1988, https://www.crmvet.org/nars/maryking.htm

26. Anderson, *The Movement and the Sixties*, 313.

27. Pauli Murray and Mary Eastwood, "Jane Crow and the Law: Sex Discrimination and Title VII," *George Washington Law Review* v. 34, no. 2 (1965), 232–56.

28. Quoted in Stewart Burns, *Social Movements of the 1960s: Searching for Democracy* (Boston: Twayne, 1990), 120; Cobble, "More Than Sex Equality," 60.

29. Betty Friedan, "The Problem That Has No Name," in *Takin' It to the Streets*, 410–11.

30. See Daniel Horowitz, *Betty Freidan and the Making of the Feminine Mystique* (Amherst: University of Massachusetts Press, 1998).

31. National Organization of Women, "Statement of Purpose," *The American Women's Movement, 1945–2000*, ed. Nancy MacLean (Boston: Bedford/St. Martin's, 2009), 71–72.

32. "NOW Bill of Rights," in *Takin' It to the Streets*, 418.

CHAPTER 9

1. "Man Of The Year: The Inheritor," *Time*, Jan. 6, 1967. content.time.com/time/subscriber/article/0,33009,843150–11,00.html.

2. Quoted in "50 Years Ago Today, Muhammad Ali Was Told to Step Forward: He Refused," Washington Post, April 28, 2017, https://www.washingtonpost.com/news/morning-mix/wp/2017/04/28/muhammad-ali-50-years-ago-today-was-told-to-step-forward-he-refused/.

3. Quoted in Branson Wright, "Remembering Cleveland's Muhammad Ali Summit," *Cleveland Plain Dealer*, June 3, 2012. https://www.cleveland.com/sports/2012/06/gathering_of_stars.htmlURL uinbstead

4. John Hersey's 1968 bestseller, *The Algiers Motel Incident* (New York: Knopf, 1968), depicted all the brutality of the incident.

5. Don Oberdorfer, "The 'Wobble' on the War on Capitol Hill," *The New York Times Magazine*, December 17, 1967, 31.

6. Don Oberdorfer, *Tet: The Turning Point in the Vietnam War* (Baltimore: Johns Hopkins University Press, 2001 [originally published 1971]), 83–85.

7. Terry H. Anderson, *The Movement and the Sixties* (New York: Oxford University Press, 1995), 23–130.

8. Peter Doggett, *There's a Riot Going On: Revolutionaries, Rock Stars and the Rise and Fall of the '60s* (Edinburgh: Canongate Books, 2007), 123; Jon Kifner, "Hippies Shower $1 Bills on Stock Exchange Floor, *New York Times*, August 25, 1967, 23. See also Damon R. Bach, *The American Counterculture: A History of Hippies and Cultural Dissidents* (Lawrence, Kansas: University Press of Kansas, 2020), 125.

9. Doggett, *There's a Riot Going On*, 124–25.

10. Tom Wells, *The War Within: America's Battle Over Vietnam* (Berkeley: University of California Press, 1994), 191–92.

11. Michael Ferber, "A Time to Say No," in *Takin' It to the Streets: A Sixties Reader*, eds. Alexander Bloom and Wini Breines (New York: Oxford University Press, 4/e, 2015), 217–19.

12. Wells, *The War Within*, 192.

13. Ibid., 193–97.

14. Doggett, *There's a Riot Going On*, 124.

15. Bach, *The American Counterculture*, 125–26.

16. Norman Mailer, *The Armies of the Night* (New York: New American Library, 1968), 86–88.

17. Doggett, *There's a Riot Going On*, 85–86; Charles Perry, *The Haight-Ashbury: A History* (New York: Random House, 1984), 122.

18. Ibid., 125–26.

19. Helen Swick Perry, "The Human Be-In," in *Takin' It to the Streets*, 283–84.

20. "Bernard Weinruab, "10,000 Chant 'L-O-V-E,'"_*New York Times*, March 27, 1967, 1.

21. Doggett, *There's a Riot Going On*, 105–106; Bach, *The American Counterculture*, 118.

22. Mark Harris, "The Flowering of the Hippies," *The Atlantic*, September 1967, https://www.theatlantic.com/magazine/archive/1967/09/the-flowering-of-the-hippies/306619/.

23. Perry, *The Haight-Ashbury*, 139, 174.

24. Quoted in Charles Kaiser, *1968 in America* (New York: Grove Press, 1988), xxii.

25. Ibid., xxiii.

26. Ralph J. Gleason, "Like a Rolling Stone," *The American Scholar* v. 36, no. 4 (Autumn 1967), 555–63.

27. Hedrick Smith, "Westmoreland Says Ranks of Vietcong Thin Steadily," *New York Times*, November 22, 1967, 1.

28. Marilyn Young, *The Vietnam Wars: 1945–1990* (New York: Harper Perennial, 1991), 213–14.

29. *Washington Post*, January 1, 1968.

30. "Johnson's Popularity on the Upswing, Year-End Gallup Poll Discloses. *New York Times*, December 27, 1967, 1, 32.

CHAPTER 10

1. Don Oberdorfer, *Tet: The Turning Point in the Vietnam War* (Baltimore: Johns Hopkins University Press, 2001 [originally published 1971]), 3.

2. *New York Times*, January 30–February 2, 1968.

3. Sam Adams, quoted in Christian G. Appy, *American Reckoning: The Vietnam War and Our National Identity* (New York: Viking, 2015), 175.

4. *New York Times*, January 30–February 2, 1968.

5. Oberdorfer, *Tet*, 71.

6. Clark Dougan and Stephen Weiss, *The Vietnam Experience: Nineteen Sixty-Eight* (Boston: Boston Publishing Company, 1983), 9.

7. Christian G. Appy, *Patriots: The Vietnam War Remembered From All Sides* (New York: Viking, 2003), 302–303.

8. "Doris Allen," obituary, *New York Times*, June 28, 2024.

9. Dougan and Weiss, *Nineteen Sixty-Eight*, 10–11.

10. Oberdorfer, *Tet*, 152.

11. Ibid., 11–13.

12. Ibid., 28.

13. Ibid., 36–37.

14. Ibid., 33–36.

15. Appy, *Patriots*, 295.

16. Michael Herr, *Dispatches* (New York: Avon Books, 1978), 70.

17. Dougan and Weiss, *Nineteen Sixty-Eight*, 26–28.

18. Oberdorfer, *Tet*, 223.

19. Appy, *Patriots*, 303.

20. Tobias Wolfe, *In Pharoah's Army: Memories of the Lost War*. New York: Knopf, 1994, 138.

21. Appy, *American Reckoning*, 30.

22. Herr, *Dispatches*, 71.

23. Quoted in *Hearts & Minds*, directed by Peter Davis, documentary film (1974; Warner Bros). https://tv.apple.com/us/movie/hearts-and-minds/umc.cmc.pp7uw3yipzwd6lobamimzxyz

24. James S. Olsen, and Randy Roberts, *Where the Domino Fell: America and Vietnam, 1945–1995* (New York: St. Martin's Press, 2/e, 1996), 186–87; Ngo Vinh Long, quoted in Marilyn Young, *The Vietnam Wars: 1945–1990* (New York: Harper Perennial, 1991), 216.

25. Herr, *Dispatches*. 71, 73, 79, 101.

26. Oberdorfer, *Tet*, 175–77.

27. Michael Thomas and Peter Tautfest, quoted in Ronald Fraser, ed., *1968: A Student Generation in Revolt* (New York: Pantheon, 1988), 176–77.

28. "Clark M. Clifford Remembers His Post-Tet Questions," in *Major Problems in the History of the Vietnam War*, ed. Robert J. McMahon (Boston: Houghton Mifflin Company, 2003, 3/e), 331.

29. Clifford, quoted in Young, *Vietnam Wars*, 229.

30. Quoted in Davis, *Hearts & Minds*, documentary film, 1974.

31. James Reston, "Washington: The Flies That Captured the Flypaper," *New York Times*, February 7, 1968, 46; Joseph Kraft, quoted in Robert Cottrell and Blaine T. Browne, *1968: The Rise and Fall of the New American Revolution* (New York: Rowman & Littlefield, 2018), 49; *Wall Street Journal*, February 23, 1968; "After the Tet Offensive," *New York Times*, February 8, 1968, 42; *Time*, February 9, 1968.

32. Art Buchwald, "We Have the Enemy on the Run, Says General Custer," *Washington Post*, February 6, 1968, 17.

33. Quoted in Oberdorfer, *Tet*, 246–51.

34. David Halberstam, *The Powers That Be* (New York: Knopf, 1979), 716.

CHAPTER 11

1. Mark Memmott, "LOOKING BACK: RFK's 'Ripple of Hope' Speech," NPR, June 30, 2013, https://www.npr.org/sections/thetwo-way/2013/06/30/197342656/looking-back-rfks-ripple-of-hope-speech-in-south-africa.

2. Quoted in Lewis Chester, Godfrey Hodgson, and Bruce Page, *An American Melodrama: The Presidential Campaign of 1968* (New York: Viking Press, 1969), 111–12.

3. Quoted in Lawrence O'Donnell, *Playing With Fire: The 1968 Election and the Transformation of American Politics* (New York: Penguin Books, 2017), 90.

4. Ibid., 14–21.

5. Charles Kaiser, *1968 in America*. (New York: Grove Press, 1988), 82.

6. Ibid., 95; O'Donnell, *Playing With Fire*, 128.

7. O'Donnell, *Playing With Fire*, 130.

8. Kaiser, *1968 in America*, 105.

9. David Caute, *The Year of the Barricades: A Journey Through 1968* (New York: Harper & Row, 1988), 116.

10. O'Donnell, *Playing With Fire*, 172.

11. Ibid., 173, 174–75; Tom Wicker, "Kennedy Made Johnson Offer to Forgo Race," *New York Times*, March 18, 1968, 1, 50.

12. Kaiser, *1968 in America*, 116.

13. Ibid., 108–09.

14. "McCarrthy Spurns Help By Kennedy," *New York Times*, March 18, 1968, 1, 51; Kaiser, *1968 in America*, 117.

15. Caute, *The Year of the Barricades*, 121–22.

16. O'Donnell, *Playing With Fire*, 225.

17. Kaiser, *1968 in America*, 118.

18. Caute, *The Year of the Barricades*, 122.

19. Donald Janson, *"Mccarthy Vistory in Wisconsin Seen,"* *New York Times*, March 14, 1968, 31.

20. Steven Roberts, "Studernts Solicit McCarthy Votes*," *New York Times*, March 25, 1968, 44.

21. Roy Reed, "Johnson Aides Sees Loss in Wisxconsin, *New York Times*, March 27, 1968, 31.

22. Warren Weaver, "McCarthy Favored Over Johnson in Wisconsin Vte Tueday," *New York Times*, March 31, 1968, 58.

23. "Max Frankel, Johnson to Talk to Nation Tonight on Viatnam War," *New York Times*, March 31, 1968, 1, 38.

24. Kaiser, *1968 in America*, 128.

CHAPTER 12

1. Andrew Kopkind, in Charles Kaiser, *1968 in America* (New York: Grove Press, 1988), 139.

2. Martin Luther King, Jr., "Declaration of Independence from the War in Vietnam," in *Takin' It to the Streets: A Sixties Reader*, eds. Alexander Bloom and Wini Breines (New York: Oxford University Press, 4/e, 2015), 205–10.

3. Kaiser, *1968 in America*, 138; Tom Wells, *The War Within: America's Battle Over Vietnam* (Berkeley: University of California Press, 1994), 129–30; Taylor Branch, *At Canaan's Edge: America in the King Years 1965–68* (New York: Simon & Schuster, 2006), 595; "Dr. King's Error," *New York Times*, April 7, 1967, 36; "NAACP Decries Stand of Dr. King on Vietnam, April 11, 1967, 1, 17.

4. Martin Luther King, "The Crisis in America's Cities," August 15, 1967, https://www. crmvet.org/info/mlkcitys.htm.

5. Ibid.

6. Branch, *At Canaan's Edge*, 656.

7. Kaiser, *1968 in America*, 141–42; Robert V. Daniels, *Year of the Heroic Guerilla: World Revolution and Counterrevolution in 1968* (New York: Basic Books, 1989), 112.

8. Branch, *At Canaan's Edge*, 715–17.

9. Kaiser, *1968 in America*, 143.

10. Branch, *At Canaan's Edge*, 734.

11. Ibid., 738, 742.

12. Ibid., 744–45.

13. Ibid., 752.

14. Daniels, *Year of the Heroic Guerilla*, 98–99.

15. Kaiser, *1968 in America*, 146.

16. Daniels, *Year of the Heroic Guerilla*, 102–03.

17. https://archive.thinkprogress.org/how-lyndon-johnson-responded-to-baltimores-last-riots-f3c0378909c/

18. Jules Witcover, *The Year The Dream Died: Revisiting 1968 in America* (New York: Time Warner, 1991), 164–66.

19. "1968: The Most Racially Charged Oscars Ever," https://www.tumblr.com/benfalkyah oomovies/139382826969/1968-the-most-racially-charged-oscars-ever

20. Martin Luther King, Jr., "The Drum Major Instinct," sermon delivered at Ebenezer Baptist Church, Atlanta, Ga., February 4, 1968, http://www.mlkonline.net/speeches-the-drum-major-instinct.html.#1

CHAPTER 13

1. *New York Times*, March 11, 1968.

2. "Novotny Deposed as Party Leader; Slovak Gets Post"and "A New Prague Leader, "*New York Times*, January 6, 1968, 1, 6.

3. Harry Schwartz, "Prague's Revolution Within the Revolution," *New York Times*, March 31, 1968, 106, 404, 443–458.

4. Pavlina Morganova, "Action! Czech Performance Art from the 1960s to the 1970s," www.academia.edu/15102503/_Action_Czech_Performance_Art_from_the_1960s_to_the_1970s_, 6–7.

5. Milan Kundera, "Speech at the Fourth Congress of the Czechoslovak Writers," http://www.pwf.cz/rubriky/projects/1968/milan-kundera-speech-made-at-the-fourth-congress-of-the-czechoslovak-writers_897.html.

6. See Jeremi Suri, *Power and Protest: Global Revolution and the Rise of Détente* (Cambridge, MA: Harvard University Press, 2003), 195.

7. Petra James, "Listening to the 'Feverish Beat': Between Alienation and Creative Resistance—the Czech Reception of the Beats" in *Beat Literature in a Divided Europe*, eds. Harri Veivo, et al. (Leiden: Brill Rodopi, 2019), 64.

8. Jan Blüml, "Reception of the Rolling Stones in Communist Czechoslovakia," *Rock Music Studies* v. 2, no. 3 (2015), 257–279, 261–62.

9. Ibid., 261–68.

10. Quoted in Peter Doggett, *"There's a Riot Going On": Revolutionaries, Rock Stars and the Rise and Fall of the '60s* (Edinburgh: Canongate, 2007), 164.

11. Mark Kurlansky, *1968: The Year That Rocked the World* (New York: Random House, 2004), 31.
12. Quoted in Suri, *Power and Protest*, 195.
13. Kurlansky, *1968: The Year That Rocked the World*, 33.
14. Suri, *Power and Protest*, 198–99.
15. Kurlansky, *1968:The Year That Rocked the World*, 241.
16. Kieran Williams, *The Prague Spring and Its Aftermath* (Cambridge: Cambridge University Press, 1997), 67–70.
17. Quoted in David Caute, *The Year of the Barricades: A Journey Through 1968* (New York: Harper & Row, 1988), 193.
18. Zdenek Mlynar, quoted in Robert V. Daniels, *Year of the Heroic Guerilla: World Revolution and Counterrevolution in 1968* (New York: Basic Books, 1989), 200.
19. Caute, *The Year of the Barricades*, 195.
20. Kurlansky, *1968: The Year That Rocked the World*, 247.
21. Williams, *Prague Spring*, 13; H. Gordon Skilling, *Czechoslovakia's Interrupted Revolution* (Princeton, NJ: Princeton University Press, 1976), 849–50.
22. Jiří Suk, "The Utopian Rationalism of the Prague Spring of 1968," *The American Historical Review*, v. 123, no. 3 (2018), 765.
23. Caute, *The Year of the Barricades*, 195–98.
24. Williams, *Prague Spring*, 72–73.
25. Ibid., 73.
26. "The Action Programme of the Communist Party of Czechoslovakia," https://www.marxists.org/subject/czech/1968/action-programme.htm.
27. Daniels, *Year of the Heroic Guerilla*, 201.
28. Williams, *Prague Spring*, 73.
29. Kurlansky, *1968: The Year That Rocked the World*, 243.
30. Caute, *The Year of the Barricades*, 192.

CHAPTER 14

1. Jerry L. Avorn, *Up Against the Ivy Wall: A History of the Columbia Crisis* (New York: Athenaeum, 1970), 25.
2. Ibid., 25–27.
3. Charles Kaiser, *1968 in America* (New York: Grove Press), 1988, 155–56.
4. "Letter from Rudd and Freudenberg to Kirk (27/3/1968)," Columbia University, https://exhibitions.cul.columbia.edu/exhibits/show/1968/causes/ida.
5. Kaiser, *1968 in America*, 156.
6. Brian Flanagan, in Clara Bingham, "'The Whole World Is Watching': An Oral History of the 1968 Columbia Uprising," *Vanity Fair*, March 26, 2018, https://www.vanityfair.com/news/2018/03/the-students-behind-the-1968-columbia-uprising.
7. "MLK Button: I Have a Dream," Columbia University, https://exhibitions.cul.columbia.edu/exhibits/show/1968/causes/mlk.
8. Michael Stern, "Student Demonstrators Take Over Hamilton Hall; Administration Refuses to Talk 'Under Coercion,'" *Columbia Spectator*, April 24, 1968, 1–2.
9. James S. Kunen, *The Strawberry Statement: Notes of a College Revolutionary* (New York: Random House, 1969), 21.
10. Kaiser, *1968 in America*, 159.

11. Stuart Gedal, in Bingham, "The Whole World Is Watching."

12. Mark Rudd, "The Missing History of the Columbia '68 Protests," *New York Times*, April 22, 2018, https://www.nytimes.com/2018/04/22/opinion/-missing-history-columbia-protests.html; Bingham, "The Whole World Is Watching."

13. David Wyatt, *When America Turned: Reckoning With 1968* (Amherst: University of Massachusetts Press, 2014), 188.

14. Frank da Cruz, "Columbia University, 1968." http://www.columbia.edu/cu/computinghistory/1968/.

15. Kunen, *Strawberry Statement*, 26.

16. da Cruz, "Columbia University, 1968."

17. Tom Hurwitz, in Bingham, "The Whole World Is Watching"; da Cruz, "Columbia University, 1968."

18. Hilton Obenzinger, in Bingham, "The Whole World Is Watching."

19. James Branch, in ibid.

20. Eleanor Stein, in ibid.

21. Sherrie M. Randolph, *Florynce "Flo" Kennedy: The Life of a Black Feminist Radical* (Chapel Hill: University of North Carolina Press, 2015), 150.

22. Quoted in Alexander Bloom, *Prodigal Sons: The New York Intellectuals and Their World* (New York: Oxford University Press, 1986), 346.

23. David Caute, *The Year of the Barricades: A Journey Through 1968* (New York: Harper & Row, 1988), 171.

24. George Pataki and Vaud Massarsky, in Bingham, "The Whole World Is Watching."

25. da Cruz, "Columbia University, 1968."

26. Ibid.

27. Michael Rosenthal, in Bingham, "The Whole World Is Watching."

28. Nancy Lieberman, in ibid.

29. Ed Kent, in da Cruz, "Columbia University, 1968."

30. Pataki, in Bingham, "The Whole World Is Watching."

31. Mike Reynolds and Gary Beamer in Ibid.

32. Pataki and Massarsky, in ibid.

33. da Cruz, "Columbia University, 1968."

34. Stephan Salisbury, in Bingham, "The Whole World Is Watching."

35. Sydney H. Schanberg, "Panel Says Raiding Police Wielded Excessive Force," *New York Times*, October 6, 1968, 1, 82.

36. da Cruz, "Columbia University, 1968."

37. Tom Hayden, "Two, Three, Many Columbias," in *Takin' It to the Streets: A Sixties Reader*, eds. Alexander Bloom and Wini Breines (New York: Oxford University Press, 4/e, 2015), 346–47.

CHAPTER 15

1. Quoted in Marcin Zaremba, "1968 in Poland: The Rebellion on the Other Side of the Looking Glass," *AHR Reflections*, v. 123 no. 3 (2018), 769–772.

2. Jerzy Eisler, "March 1968 in Poland," in *1968: The World Transformed*, eds. Carole Fink, Phillip Gassert, and Detlef Junker (Cambridge: Cambridge University Press, 1998), 237–51; Mark Kurlansky, *1968: The Year That Rocked the World* (New York: Random House, 2004), 76–77.

3. David Caute, *The Year of the Barricades: A Journey Through 1968* (New York: Harper & Row, 1988), 81–85.

4. Ibid., 75–81.

5. Kurlansky, *1968: The Year That Rocked the World*, 154.

6. Stuart J. Hilwig, "The Revolt Against the Establishment," in *1968: The Year That Rocked the World*, 332.

7. Ronald Fraser, ed., *1968: A Student Generation in Revolt* (New York: Pantheon, 1988), 194.

8. Kurlansky, *1968: The Year That Rocked the World*, 154–56; Caute, *The Year of the Barricades*, 99–104.

9. Petros Markaris, "Greece: The Other Side of 1968, " in *1968: Memories and Legacies of a Global Revolt*, eds. Philipp Gassert and Martin Klimke (Washington, DC: German Historical Institute, Supplement 6, 2009), 209–12.

10. Félix Allueva, "Venezuela: A Sociological Laboratory," in ibid., 67.

11. Andy Stafford, "Senegal: May 1968, Africa's Revolt," in ibid., 129.

12. Želimir Žilnik, "Yugoslavia: "Down With the Red Bourgeoisie!" in ibid., 181.

13. Jeremi Suri, *Power and Protest: Global Revolution and the Rise of Détente* (Cambridge, MA: Harvard University Press, 2003), 186.

14. Kirk Anderson, "Song 'Adaptations' and the Globalisation of French Pop, 1960–1970," *French Cultural Studies*, v. 26 no. 3 (2015), 331–32.

15. Kurlansky, *1968: The Year That Rocked the World*, 215–17.

16. Marianne Debouzy, "The Americanization of the French University and the Response of the Student Movement, 1966–1968," *American Studies International* v. 28, no. 2 (1990), 24.

17. Michael Seidman, *The Imaginary Revolution: Parisian Students and Workers in 1968* (New York: Berghan Books, 2004), 29.

18. "On the Poverty of Student Life," https://theanarchistlibrary.org/library/u-n-e-f-strasbourg-on-the-poverty-of-student-life.

19. Seidman, *Imaginary Revolution*, 21–22.

20. Kurlansky, *1968: The Year That Rocked the World*, 219.

21. Ibid., 219.

22. Ibid., 224.

23. Caute, *Year of the Barricades*, 211.

24. Quoted in Robert V. Daniels, *Year of the Heroic Guerilla: World Revolution and Counterrevolution in 1968* (New York: Basic Books, 1989), 150.

25. Ibid., 152.

26. Caute, *Year of the Barricades*, 216.

27. Ibid., 216–17.

28. Kurlansky, *1968: The Year That Rocked the World*, 227.

29. Ibid., 229.

30. Fraser, *1968: A Student Generation*, 205, 209, 216.

31. Ibid., 222.

32. Ibid., 207.

33. Ibid., 222.

34. Ibid., 212.

35. Kurlansky, *1968: The Year That Rocked the World*, 227–28; Seidman, *Imaginary Revolution*, 144–45; Paul Matthey, "1968: The Year of Two Student Springs. Czechoslovak and French Movements Compared," https://www.academia.edu/4386028/1968_The_Year_of_Two_Student_Springs_Czechoslovak_and_French_Movements_Compared, 24.

36. Seidman, *Imaginary Revolution*, 132–44.

37. Ibid., 145–49.

38. Caute, *Year of the Barricades*, 220.

39. Fraser, *1968: A Student Generation*, 224.

40. Seidman, *Imaginary Revolution*, 233.

41. Ibid., 175.

42. Ibid., 190.

43. Daniel Singer, *Prelude to Revolution: France in May 1968* (Cambridge, MA: South End Press, 2nd ed. 2000), 207.

44. Seidman, *Imaginary Revolution*, 225–26.

45. Ibid., 218, 250.

46. Caute, *Year of the Barricades*, 248.

47. Seidman, *Imaginary Revolution*, 259.

CHAPTER 16

1. Arthur Schlesinger, Jr., *Robert Kennedy and His Times* (Boston: Houghton, Mifflin Co., 1978), 857.

2. Charles Kaiser, *1968 in America*. (New York: Grove Press, 1988), 167–68.

3. Robert Kennedy, "To Tame the Savageness of Man," in *Takin' It to the Streets: A Sixties Reader*, eds. Alexander Bloom and Wini Breines (New York: Oxford University Press, 4/e, 2015), 379–80.

4. Lawrence O'Donnell, *Playing With Fire: The 1968 Election and the Transformation of American Politics* (New York: Penguin Books, 2017), 232.

5. Jules Witcover, *The Year The Dream Died: Revisiting 1968 in America* (New York: Time Warner, 1997), 183.

6. Thurston Clarke, *The Last Campaign: Robert F. Kennedy and 82 Days That Inspired America* (New York: Henry Holt, 2008), 203.

7. O'Donnell, *Playing With Fire*, 245.

8. Witcover, *The Year the Dream Died*, 294.

9. Kaiser, *1968 in America*, 169.

10. Clarke, *The Last Campaign*, 233.

11. Ben Stavis, *We Were The Campaign: New Hampshire to Chicago for McCarthy* (Boston: Beacon Press, 1969), 51.

12. Kaiser, *1968 in America*, 176.

13. Clarke, *The Last Campaign*, 81.

14. O'Donnell, *Playing With Fire*, 252.

15. Ibid.

16. Witcover, *The Year the Dream Died*, 171–72.

17. Lewis Chester, Godfrey Hodgson, and Bruce Page, *An American Melodrama: The Presidential Campaign of 1968* (New York: Viking Press, 1969), 162.

18. Clarke, *The Last Campaign*, 169, 187–88; Witcover, *The Year the Dream Died*, 177.

19. Witcover, *The Year the Dream Died*, 208; Clarke, *The Last Campaign*, 190.

20. Witcover, *The Year the Dream Died*, 217.

21. Chester et al., *An American Melodrama*, 300.

22. Clarke, *The Last Campaign*, 233.

23. Chester et al., *American Melodrama*, 302–303; O'Donnell, *Playing With Fire*, 260.

24. Witcover, *The Year the Dream Died*, 226.

25. Ibid., 234; Chester et al., *American Melodrama*, 334.

26. Clarke, *The Last Campaign*, 246–47.

27. Ibid., 250.

28. Ibid., 252–56.

29. Tom Wicker, "McCartrhy's Drive Began Last Week," *New York Times*, May 30, 1968, 14.

30. Witcover, *The Year the Dream Died*, 240–43; Clarke, *The Last Campaign*, 257–60.

31. Ibid., 266–67.

32. Witcover, *The Year the Dream Died*, 249.

33. Clarke, *The Last Campaign*, 269–70.

34. Witcover, *The Year the Dream Died*, 245; Clarke, *The Last Campaign*, 262.

35. Witcover, *The Year the Dream Died*, 172–73.

36. Clarke, *The Last Campaign*, 118, 205.

37. Ibid., 276; O'Donnell, *Playing With Fire*, 272.

38. Witcover, *The Year the Dream Died*, 256.

39. Chester et al, *American Melodrama*, 360.

40. Kaiser, *1968 in America*, 184–86.

41. O'Donnell, *Playing With Fire*, 273.

42. Tom Hayden, *Reunion: A Memoir* (New York: Random House, 1988), 286.

43. Ibid., 286–89.

44. Ibid., 289–90.

45. Tom Hayden, "On Robert Kennedy's 1968 Presidential Bid," PBS, https://www.pbs. org/opb/thesixties/topics/politics/reflections_1.html.

CHAPTER 17

1. Earl Caldwell, "March of Poor Sets Out from Memphis,"*New York Times*, May 3, 1968, 1, 24; Earl Caldwell, "The Poor People of the South: Why Some Want to Join March to Washington," *New York Times*, May 7, 1968, 36; Earl Caldwell, Poor March Into Montgomery, 2,000 Following Rights Leader, *New York Times*, May 8, 1968, 31; Amy Nathan Wright, *Civil Rights "Unfinished Business": Poverty, Race and the 1968 Poor People's Campaign*, Ph.D Dissertation, University of Texas, 2007, 265.

2. Arthur Marwick, *The Sixties* (New York: Oxford University Press, 1998), 656; William L. O'Neill, *Coming Apart: An Informal History of America in the 1960s* (New York: Quadrangle Books, 1971), 182.

3. Terry H. Anderson, *The Movement and the Sixties* (New York: Oxford University Press, 1995), 191–192, 279–280, 282.

4. O'Neil, *Coming Apart*, 182.

5. To this point, the single best source on the Poor People's Campaign is Amy Nathan Wright's 2007 PhD dissertation, cited above.

6. Gordon K. Mantler, *Power to the Poor: Black-Brown Coalition and the Fight for Economic Justice, 1960–1974* (Chapel Hill: University of North Carolina Press, 2013), 134–35.

7. Ibid., 123–26; "Hollywood Flashback: Barbra Streisand Sang for Civil Rights in 1968," *Hollywood Reporter*, June 2, 2016, https://www.hollywoodreporter.com/news/hollywood-flashback-barbra-streisand-sang-898675.

8. Mantler, *Power to the Poor*, 127.

9. Martin Luther King, Jr., "Showdown for Nonviolence," *Look* 32 (April 16, 1968), 23–25.

10. Chuck Fager, *Uncertain Resurrection: Dr. King's Poor People's Campaign, Washington, 1968* (Durham, NC: Kimo Press, 2/e, 2017), 4–5, 32.

11. Gerald D. McKnight, *The Last Crusade: Martin Luther King, Jr., the FBI, and the Poor People's Campaign* (Boulder, CO: Westview Press, 1998), 112.

12. Wright, *Civil Rights "Unfinished Business,"* 177.

13. Ibid., 194.

14. "The Goals of the Poor People's Plan, 1968, https://web.archive.org/web/20070308223806/https://www.pbs.org/wgbh/amex/eyesontheprize/sources/ps_poor.html.

15. Wright, *Civil Rights "Unfinished Business,"* 201.

16. Ibid., 201–202.

17. McKnight, *The Last Crusade*, 8.

18. See ibid., 22–28, 123–29.

19. Wright, *Civil Rights "Unfinished Business,"* 203–205.

20. Ibid., 205–08.

21. Ibid., 208–10.

22. See ibid., 205–17.

23. McKnight, *The Last Crusade*, 96–97; Mantler, *Power to the Poor*, 133–34.

24. Ibid., 145.

25. Ibid., 146.

26. Ibid., 148.

27. Cornelius Green in Wright, *Civil Rights "Unfinished Business,"* 358, 348.

28. Ibid., 406–407.

29. Mantler, *Power to the Poor*, 140.

30. Ibid., 140–41; Wright, *Civil Rights "Unfinished Business,"* 413–14.

31. Ibid., 377; Mantler, *Power to the Poor*, 141.

32. Wright, *Civil Rights "Unfinished Business,"* 385.

33. *Newsweek*, July 1, 1868, 20–21.

34. McKnight, *The Last Crusade*, 113–19.

35. Wright, *Civil Rights "Unfinished Business,"* 430–31.

36. Ibid., 429.

37. McKnight, *The Last Crusade*, 85–88.

38. Wright, *Civil Rights "Unfinished Business,"* 444–46; John D'Emilo, *Lost Prophet: The Life and Times of Bayard Rustin* (Chicago: The University of Chicago Press, 2003), 463–65.

39. Ben A. Franklin, "Over 50,000 March in Capital in Support of Poor," *New York Times*, June 20, 1968, 1, 30.

40. Fager, *Uncertain Resurrection*, 59.

41. *New York Times*, June 20, 1968.

42. Wright, *Civil Rights "Unfinished Business,"* 446–54.

43. *Newsweek*, July 8, 1968, 19.

44. Wright, *Civil Rights "Unfinished Business,"* 496.

CHAPTER 18

1. David Caute, *The Year of the Barricades: A Journey Through 1968* (New York: Harper & Row, 1988), 203.

2. Ludvik Vaculik, "Two Thousand Words: A Manifesto for Prague," https://www.marxists.org/subject/czech/1968/2000-words.htm

3. Kieran Williams, *The Prague Spring and Its Aftermath* (Cambridge: Cambridge University Press, 1997), 90.

4. Paul Hoffman, "For Those Under 30, Prague Seems the Right Place to Be This Summer," *New York Times*, August 12, 1968,13.

5. Williams, *Prague Spring*, 100.

6. Ibid., 108.

7. Caute, *The Year of the Barricades*, 207.

8. Williams, *Prague Spring*, 129.

9. Ibid., 128; Mark Kurlansky, *1968: The Year That Rocked the World* (New York: Random House, 2004), 296.

10. Ibid., 294.

11. Ibid., 292–94; Robert V. Daniels, *Year of the Heroic Guerilla: World Revolution and Counterrevolution in 1968* (New York: Basic Books, 1989), 191; Paul Matthey, "1968: The Year of Two Student Springs. Czechoslovak and French Movements Compared," https://www.academia.edu/4386028/1968_The_Year_of_Two_Student_Springs_ Czechoslovak_and_French_Movements_Compared, 25.

12. Daniels, *Year of the Heroic Guerilla*, 193; Caute, *The Year of the Barricades*, 333.

13. Williams, *Prague Spring*, 131.

14. Ibid., 137–43; Kurlansky, *1968*, 299–303; Caute, *The Year of the Barricades*, 339–41.

15. Williams, *Prague Spring*, 188.

16. Caute, *The Year of the Barricades*, 431–33.

17. Alvin Shuster, "Aeroflot Office Burned in Prague," *New York Times*, March 29, 1969, 5.

18. Joseph Rothschild and Nancy M. Wingfield, *Return to Diversity: A Political History of East Central Europe since World War II* (New York: Oxford University Press, 2000), 210.

19. "Charter 77," https://www.rferl.org/a/1083022.html.

20. Anna Sabatova, "From 1968 To Charter 77 To 1989 And Beyond," https://www.rferl. org/a/From_1968_To_Charter_77_To_1989_And_Beyond/1192331.html

21. Dan Bilefsky, "Czechs' Velvet Revolution Paved by Plastic People," *New York Times*, November 25, 2009, https://www.nytimes.com/2009/11/16/world/europe/16iht-czech. html; Peter Doggett, *"There's a Riot Going On"*: *Revolutionaries, Rock Stars and the Rise and Fall of the '60s* (Edinburgh: Canongate, 2007), 164.

CHAPTER 19

1. David Caute, *The Year of the Barricades: A Journey Through 1968* (New York: Harper & Row, 1988), 294.

2. Lewis Chester, Godfrey Hodgson, and Bruce Page, *An American Melodrama: The Presidential Campaign of 1968* (New York: Viking Press, 1969), 413.

3. Lawrence O'Donnell, *Playing With Fire: The 1968 Election and the Transformation of American Politics.* (New York: Penguin Books, 2017), 324.

4. Chester, *American Melodrama*, 416–17; Jules Witcover, *The Year The Dream Died: Revisiting 1968 in America* (New York: Time Warner, 1997), 282–84.

5. Ibid., 285.

6. O'Donnell, *Playing With Fire*, 335.

7. David Farber, *Chicago '68* (Chicago: University of Chicago Press, 1988), 78, 84.

8. Chester, *American Melodrama*, 514; Farber, *Chicago '68*, 12–14.

9. Ibid., 17.

10. Ibid., 22.

11. Ibid., 34, 213.

12. Ibid., 35.
13. Chester, *American Melodrama*, 519–20.
14. O'Donnell, *Playing With Fire*, 322–23.
15. Farber, *Chicago '68*, 148–49; Charles Kaiser, *1968 in America* (New York: Grove Press, 1988), 233.
16. Ibid., 233.
17. Farber, *Chicago '68*, 44, 97.
18. Chester, *American Melodrama*, 518–19; Farber, *Chicago '68*, 102, 157.
19. Ibid., 158.
20. Chester, *American Melodrama*, 521; Witcover, *The Year The Dream Died*, 316.
21. Farber, *Chicago '68*, 161–63.
22. O'Donnell, *Playing With Fire*, 325–26, 330–32; Chester, *American Melodrama*, 556.
23. O'Donnell, *Playing With Fire*, 333–44.
24. Witcover, *The Year The Dream Died*, 319; O'Donnell, *Playing With Fire*, 342–43.
25. Ibid., 340.
26. Ibid., 146.
27. Farber, *Chicago '68*, 165–66.
28. Ibid., 167; O'Donnell, *Playing With Fire*, 347; Witcover, *The Year The Dream Died*, 320.
29. Farber, *Chicago '68*, 170–75; Chester, *American Melodrama*, 522.
30. Farber, *Chicago '68*, 176–83; O'Donnell, *Playing With Fire*, 349–50; Chester, *American Melodrama*, 522–23.
31. Ibid., 564–76; O'Donnell, *Playing With Fire*, 351–56.
32. Ibid., 350–51; Witcover, *The Year The Dream Died*, 323–24.
33. Farber, *Chicago '68*, 185–87.
34. O'Donnell, *Playing With Fire*, 357; https://danratherjournalist.org/about-dan/controversies/punched-1968-dnc/video-1968-democratic-national-convention.html
35. O'Donnell, *Playing With Fire*, 356–58.
36. Farber, *Chicago '68*, 190.
37. Chester, *American Melodrama*, 578–80; Farber, *Chicago '68*, 191–94.
38. Chester, *American Melodrama*, 580; *New York Times*, August 29, 1968; O'Donnell, *Playing With Fire*, 361.
39. Chester, *American Melodrama*, 580–81; O'Donnell, *Playing With Fire*, 361–62.
40. Tom Hayden, *Reunion: A Memoir*, New York: Random House, 1988, 317. See Farber, *Chicago '68*, 197.
41. Hayden, *Reunion*, 319; Farber, *Chicago '68*, 196–97.
42. Ibid., 197.
43. Ibid., 200.
44. Witcover, *The Year The Dream Died*, 334–36; Hayden, *Reunion*, 319.
45. Witcover, *The Year The Dream Died*, 336; Chester, *American Melodrama*, 583.
46. Ibid., 584–85; O'Donnell, *Playing With Fire*, 367–68; Witcover, *The Year The Dream Died*, 336.
47. Chester, *American Melodrama*, 585–86; O'Donnell, *Playing With Fire*, 373.
48. Ibid., 368–71.
49. Chester, *American Melodrama*, 590.
50. Witcover, *The Year The Dream Died*, 339–41.
51. Chester, *American Melodrama*, 591; Kaiser, *1968 in America*, 243.
52. Chester, *American Melodrama*, 595–96; Witcover, *The Year The Dream Died*, 344.

53. Daniel Walker, "Rights in Conflict," in Alexander Bloom and Wini Breines, eds. *Takin'* *It to the Streets: A Sixties Reader* (New York: Oxford University Press, 4/e, 2015), 389: Alsop, quoted in Carole Fink, Phillip Gassert, Detlef Junker, eds. *1968: The World Transformed*, Cambridge: Cambridge University Press, 1998, 227.

54. Witcover, *The Year The Dream Died*, 344.

CHAPTER 20

1. George Gallup and Evan Hill, "The American Woman," *The Saturday Evening Post* v. 235, no. 46 (December 22, 1962), 16, 18.

2. Arland Thornton and Deborah Freedman, "Changes in the Sex Role Attitudes of Women, 1962–1977," *American Sociological Review* v. 44, no. 5 (October 1979), 832–33; Gallup and Hill, "The American Woman," 28.

3. Ibid., 32.

4. *Women Workers in 1960*, Women's Bureau Bulletin 284, U.S. Department of Labor, 1962, vi, 13, 15; Mitra Toossi and Teresa L. Morisi, "Women in the Workforce Before, During, and After the Great Recession," U.S. Bureau of Labor Statistics, July 2017, 2, https://www.bls.gov/spotlight/2017/women-in-the-workforce-before-during-and-after-the-great-recession/home.htm

5. Cecilia A. Conrad, "Racial Trends in Labor Market Access and Wages: Women," in *America Becoming: Racial Trends and Their Consequences: Volume II*, eds. N. J. Smelser, W. J. Wilson, and F. Mitchell (Washington, DC: National Academies Press, 2001), 124–51, https://doi.org/10.17226/9719.

6. Ann Popkin, "The Personal is Political: The Women's Liberation Movement," in *They Should Have Served That Cup of Coffee*, ed. Dick Cluster (Boston: South End Press, 1979), 189.

7. "NOW Bill of Rights," in *Takin' It to the Streets: A Sixties Reader*, eds. Alexander Bloom and Wini Breines (New York: Oxford University Press, 4/e, 2015), 417–18.

8. Douglas T. Miller, *On Our Own: America in the Sixties* (Lexington, MA: D.C. Heath, 1995), 314.

9. Mark Kurlansky, *1968: The Year That Rocked the World* (New York: Random House, 2004), 312.

10. Stewart Burns, *Social Movements of the 1960s: Searching for Democracy* (Boston: Twayne, 1990), 132–34.

11. Kurlansky, *1968: The Year That Rocked the World*, 311.

12. David Caute, *The Year of the Barricades: A Journey Through 1968* (New York: Harper & Row, 1988), 267.

13. Popkin, "The Personal is Political," 190–91; SDS women quoted in Burns, *Social Movements of the 1960s*, 118.

14. Linda Gordon, "The Women's Liberation Moment," in *Feminism Unfinished: A Short, Surprising History of American Women's Movements*, eds. Dorothy Sue Cobble, Linda Gordon, and Astrid Henry (New York: Liveright Publishing, 2014), 104.

15. Sherrie M. Randolph, *Florynce "Flo" Kennedy: The Life of a Black Feminist Radical* (Chapel Hill: The University of North Carolina Press, 2015), 101, 114, 116–17.

16. Quoted in Rosalyn Baxandall, "Re-Visioning the Women's Liberation Movement's Narrative: Early Second Wave African American Feminists," *Feminist Studies* v. 27, no.1 (2001), 234–35.

17. Ray Lewis White, "Eldridge Cleaver's *Soul on Ice*: A Book Review Digest," *CLA Journal* v. 21, no. 4 (1978), 556–66.

18. Obi Egbuna quoted in Peter Doggett, *"There's a Riot Going On"*: *Revolutionaries, Rock Stars and the Rise and Fall of the '60s* (Edinburgh: Canongate, 2007), 209.

19. Ashley D. Farmer, Review of "'Sisters Up in Here'": Women, Gender, and Party Politics" in Review of "'Sisters Up in Here': Women, Gender and Party Politics" in *The Revolution Has Come*," by Robyn C. Spencer, *Journal of Civil and Human Rights* v. 3, no. 2 (2017), 98–99.

20. Linda Gordon, "The Women's Liberation Moment," 95.

21. Popkin, "The Personal is Political," 192; Barbara Susan (Kaminsky), "About My Consciousness Raising," in *Takin' It to the Streets*, 429; Pam Allen quoted in Gordon, "The Women's Liberation Moment," 79; Charlotte Bunch quoted in Burns, *Social Movements of the 1960s*, 130.

22. Susan, "About My Consciousness Raising," 429–30.

23. Sara Evans, *Personal Politics: The Roots of Women's Liberation in the Civil Rights Movements & The New Left* (New York: Vintage Books, 1980), 203, 207.

24. Popkin, "The Personal is Political," 190; Evans, *Personal Politics*, 218.

25. Robert Cottrell and Blaine T. Browne, *1968: The Rise and Fall of the New American Revolution* (New York: Rowman & Littlefield, 2018), 202; Miller, *On Our Own*, 316.

26. *New York Times*, January 16, 1968; Daniel quoted in Kurlansky, *1968: The Year That Rocked the World*, 308.

27. Joy Press, "The Life and Death of a Radical Sisterhood," *New York Magazine*, November 15, 2017, https://www.thecut.com/2017/11/an-oral-history-of-feminist-group-new-york-radical-women.html.

28. Sarachild, Kathie, "Funeral Oration for the Burial of Traditional Womanhood." https://www.cwluherstory.org/classic-feminist-writings-articles/funeral-oration-for-the-burial-of-traditional-womanhood

29. Martha Weinman Lear, "The Second Feminist Wave," *New York Times Magazine*, March 10, 1968, 25.

30. Ibid., 53, 55.

31. Ibid., March 10, 1968, 60, 2.

32. Valerie Solanas, *The SCUM Manifesto* (New York: Olympia Press, 1968), 45, 47.

33. Atkinson quoted in Cottrell and Browne, *1968: The Rise and Fall*, 200.

34. J.C. Pan, "Trasher Feminism: Valerie Solanas and Her Enemies," *Dissent*, Spring 2014, https://www.dissentmagazine.org/article/trasher-feminism-valerie-solanas-and-her-enemies.

35. Hanish quoted in Cottrell and Browne, *1968: The Rise and Fall*, 206.

36. Roxanne Gay, "Fifty Years Ago Protesters Took on the Miss America Pageant and Electrified the Feminist Movement," *Smithsonian Magazine*, January 2018. https://www.smithsonianmag.com/history/fifty-years-ago-protestors-took-on-miss-america-pageant-electrified-feminist-movement-180967504/.

37. "No More Miss America!" in *Takin' It to the Streets*, 423–26.

38. Randolph, *Florynce "Flo" Kennedy*, 158.

39. Georgia Paige Welch, "'Up Against the Wall Miss America': Women's Liberation and Miss Black America in Atlantic City, 1968." *Feminist Formations* v. 27, no. 2 (Summer 2015), 76.

40. Ibid., 77.

41. Laura Tanenbaum and Mark Engler, "No More Miss America: A Collective Memory of Liberatory Action," *Dissent*, September 7, 2018, https://www.dissentmagazine.org/online_articles/no-more-miss-america-1968-pageant-protest-oral-history-women-liberation.

42. Flo Kennedy, *Color Me Flo—My Hard Life and Good Times* (New York: Prentice-Hall, 1976), 62; Randolph, *Florynce "Flo" Kennedy*, 157.
43. Lindsy Van Gelder quoted in Press, "The Life and Death of a Radical Sisterhood."
44. Art Buchwald, "The Bra Burners," *New York Post*, September 12, 1968, A25.
45. Shana Alexander, "Hooray! Getting Back to Normal," *Life*, September 20, 1968, 28.
46. Quoted in Press, "The Life and Death of a Radical Sisterhood."
47. Karina Brand, "A Miss America Protest Propelled the Women's Movement into National Spotlight," *USA Today*, October 12, 2018, https://www.usatoday.com/story/news/nation-now/1968-project/2018/10/12/miss-america-protest-womens-movement/1578111002/; Randolph, *Florynce "Flo" Kennedy*, 158.
48. Brand, "A Miss America Protest."
49. Ibid.
50. "There's Now Miss Black America," *New York Times*, September 9, 1968, 54.
51. Gay, "Fifty Years Ago Protesters Took on the Miss America Pageant."
52. Robin Morgan, *Going Too Far*, New York: Random House, 1977, 65.
53. Harriet Van Horne, "Female Firebrands," *New York Post*, September 9, 1968. https://dukelibraries.contentdm.oclc.org/digital/collection/p15957coll6/id/103/
54. Morgan and Sarachild quoted in Press, "The Life and Death of a Radical Sisterhood."
55. Popkin, "The Personal is Political," 204; Stewart Burns, *Social Movements of the 1960s: Searching for Democracy* (Boston: Twayne, 1990), 131–32; Cottrell and Browne, *1968: The Rise and Fall*, 208.
56. Freedman quoted in Welch, "Up Against the Wall Miss America," 79.

CHAPTER 21

1. Quoted in Celeste Gonzalez de Bustamante, "1968 Olympic Dreams and Tlatelolco Nightmares: Imagining and Imaging Modernity on Television," *Mexican Studies/Studios Mexicanos* v. 26, no 1, (Winter 2010), 2.
2. Rafael Rojas, *Fighting Over Fidel: The New York Intellectuals and the Cuban Revolution*, (Princeton: Princeton University Press, 2116), 142.
3. Paco Ignacio Taibo II, *'68: The Mexican Autumn of the Tlatelolco Massacre* (New York: Seven Stories Press, 1991), 20.
4. Elaine Carey, *Plaza of Sacrifices: Gender, Power and Terror in 1968 Mexico* (Albuquerque: University of New Mexico Press, 2005), 13–15.
5. Taibo, *'68: The Mexican Autumn of the Tlatelolco Massacre*, 20–21.
6. Mark Kurlansky, *1968: The Year That Rocked the World* (New York: Random House, 2004), 311.
7. Ibid., 332–33.
8. Ibid., 333.
9. Quoted in Eric Zolov, *Refried Elvis: The Rise of the Mexican Counterculture* (Berkeley: University of California Press, 1999), 4.
10. Ibid., 6.
11. Johnny Laboriel, quoted in Ibid., 38.
12. *Excelsior*, May 14, 1959.
13. Zolov, *Refried Elvis*, 58–60.
14. Ibid., 84.
15. Ibid., 93, 95.

16. Taibo, '68: The Mexican Autumn of the Tlatelolco Massacre, 21.

17. Salvador Martinez de la Rica, quoted in Kurlansky, 1968: The Year That Rocked the World, 330.

18. Zolov, Refried Elvis, 106–10.

19. Carlos Minivans, quoted in Ibid., 114.

20. Carey, Plaza of Sacrifices, 39–42.

21. Cited in Ibid., 44.

22. Kate Doyle, ed., "Tlatelolco Massacre: U.S. Documents on Mexico and the Events of 1968," https://nsarchive2.gwu.edu/NSAEBB/NSAEBB99/.

23. Quoted in Carey, Plaza of Sacrifices, 76.

24. Ibid., 97, 81–86.

25. Jamie Pontones, quoted in Zolov, Refried Elvis, 123.

26. Carey, Plaza of Sacrifices, 86–87.

27. Taibo, '68: The Mexican Autumn of the Tlatelolco Massacre, 46–48.

28. Carey, Plaza of Sacrifices, 105–106, 111, 112–13.

29. Ibid., 120–21.

30. Ibid., 122–28.

31. Quoted in Elena Poniatowska, Massacre in Mexico (Columbia, MO: University of Missouri Press, 1975), 210.

32. Ibid., 204, 209; Carey, Plaza of Sacrifices, 136–37.

33. Ibid., 140.

34. Fallaci, quoted in Michael K. Schuessler, "Mexico's Tlatelolco Massacre, and Its Echoes Today," The Nation, August 3, 2018, https://www.thenation.com/article/archive/mexicos-tlatelolco-massacre-echoes-today/.

35. Leonardo Femat, Francisco Correa, Diana Salmerón de Contreas, and Jorge Avilés, quoted in Poniatowska, Massacre in Mexico, 216, 218, 225–26, 226.

36. Poniatowska, Massacre in Mexico, 200–201.

37. Doyle, "Tlatelolco Massacre."

38. New York Times, October 3–6, 1968.

39. Taibo, '68: The Mexican Autumn of the Tlatelolco Massacre, 122; Manuel Cervantes Palma, quoted in Poniatowska, Massacre in Mexico, 316; Jorge Rodriguez Inzunza, quoted in Zolov, Refried Elvis, 131.

40. Quoted in Poniatowska, Massacre in Mexico, 316.

41. Richard Hoffer, Something in the Air: American Passion and Defiance in the 1968 Mexico City Olympics (New York: Free Press, 2009), 25–27, 53.

42. Harry Edwards, "The Revolt of the Black Athlete," in Takin' It to the Streets: A Sixties Reader, eds. Alexander Bloom and Wini Breines (New York: Oxford University Press, 4/e, 2015), 141.

43. Hoffer, Something in the Air, 53–54.

44. Ibid., 55–57.

45. Quoted in Robert Cottrell and Blaine T. Browne, 1968: The Rise and Fall of the New American Revolution (New York: Rowman & Littlefield, 2018), 185.

46. Hoffer, Something in the Air, 57, 60–61.

47. Ibid., 61.

48. "The Olympic Jolt," Life, March 15, 1968, 26.

49. Hoffer, Something in the Air, 62–63, 87–88.

50. Ibid., 66–68.

51. Bob Ottum, "Dolls on the Move to Mexico," *Sports Illustrated*, September 2, 1968.

52. Hoffer, *Something in the Air*, 116.

53. Edwards, "The Revolt of the Black Athlete," 142; Hoffer, *Something in the Air*, 161.

54. Cottrell and Browne, *1968: The Rise and Fall*, 187; Hoffer, *Something in the Air*, 161, 175.

55. Hoffer, *Something in the Air*, 180.

56. Bridget Bennett, "Months Before His Famous Jummp, Bob Beamon Was Kicked Off His College Track Team for Protestin Racism," October 28, 2018, https://andscape.com/features/bob-beamon-mexico-city-olympics-high-jump-kicked-off-utep-track-team-for-protesting-racism/.

57. Hoffer, *Something in the Air*, 194.

58. Ibid., 241; Joe Saraceno, "George Foreman: 'If I Had to Do It All Over Again, I Would Have Had Two Flags,'" October 26, 2018, https://andscape.com/features/george-foreman-american-flag-john-carlos-tommie-smith-1968-olympics/.

CHAPTER 22

1. Dan T. Carter, *The Politics of Rage: George Wallace, the Origins of the New Conservatism, and the Transformation of American Politics* (Baton Rouge: Louisiana State University Press, 2/e, 2000), 196–98.

2. "Wallace Faces Wisconsin Fight," *New York Times*, March 8, 1964, 76.

3. Carter, *The Politics of Rage*, 206–207.

4. Ibid., 208–209.

5. Ibid., 211.

6. Quoted in Robert S. McElvaine, *The Times They Were A-Changin': 1964, The Year The Sixties Arrived and the Battle Lines of Today Were Drawn* (New York: Arcade Publishing, 2022), 181.

7. Carter, *The Politics of Rage*, 215.

8. *Los Angeles Times*, February 2, 1964.

9. Lou Cannon, *Governor Reagan: His Rise to Power*, New York: Public Affairs, 2003, 107–108.

10. Ronald Reagan, "A Time for Choosing Speech, October 27, 1964," *Reagan Library*, https://www.reaganlibrary.gov/reagans/ronald-reagan/time-choosing-speech-october-27-1964.

11. Cannon, *Governor Reagan*, 139.

12. Ibid., 139, 144.

13. Quoted in Rick Pearlstein, *Nixonland: The Rise of a President and the Fracturing of America* (New York: Scribner, 2008), 114–15.

14. Gerald J. DeGroot, "Ronald Reagan and Student Unrest in California, 1966–1970," *Pacific Historical Review* v. 65, no. 1 (1996), 107.

15. Michelle Reeves, "'Obey the Rules or Get Out': Ronald Reagan's 1966 Gubernatorial Campaign and the 'Trouble in Berkeley,'" *Southern California Quarterly* v. 92, no. 3 (2010), 286, 289, 275.

16. DeGroot, "Ronald Reagan and Student Unrest," 110.

17. Ibid., 115.

18. Ibid.

19. Reeves, "'Obey the Rules or Get Out,'" 293; DeGroot, "Ronald Reagan and Student Unrest," 111.

20. Reeves, "'Obey the Rules or Get Out,'" 294–95.

21. Paul Goldberger, "Tony Imperiale Stands Vigilant For Law and Order," in *Takin' It to the Streets: A Sixties Reader*, eds. Alexander Bloom and Wini Breines (New York: Oxford University Press, 4/e, 2015), 326.

22. Ibid., 326, 328.

23. *Detroit Free Press*, July 9, 2020, https://www.freep.com/story/news/local/michigan/detroit/2020/07/09/donald-lobsinger-death/5399812002/

24. Goldberger, "Tony Imperiale," 327.

25. In 1970, Hicks won election to Congress, winning the seat of retiring House Speaker John McCormack.

26. Louise Day Hicks, U.S. House of Representatives Archive, https://history.house.gov/People/Detail/14986.

27. Carter, *The Politics of Rage*, 302; Tanner Tefelski, "Looking Back at Philadelphia's Notoriously Racist Mayor Frank Rizzo, June 15, 2020, https://hyperallergic.com/571133/amateur-night-frank-rizzo-documentary-philadelphia/.

28. Pearlstein, *Nixonland*, 73–74.

29. Art Buchwald, "Rub-a-Dub-Dub: All Those Demonstrators Oughta Be Dunked in a Tub," *Washington Post*, April 25, 1965, E7; Eisenhower quoted in Damon R. Bach, *The American Counterculture: A History of Hippies and Cultural Dissidents* (Lawrence, Kansas: University Press of Kansas, 2020), 86.

30. "Air Pollution," in *Takin' It to the Streets*, 337–38.

31. David A. Noebel, "Rhythm, Riots and Revolution," in *Takin' It to the Streets*, 340–42.

32. Pearlstein, *Nixonland*, 79.

33. Carter, *The Politics of Rage*, 293.

34. Pete Hamill, "Wallace," in *Takin' It to the Streets*, 315.

35. Carter, *The Politics of Rage*, 305, 339.

36. Hamill, "Wallace," 315; Robert Cottrell and Blaine T. Browne, *1968: The Rise and Fall of the New American Revolution* (New York: Rowman & Littlefield, 2018), 221.

37. Ibid., 225.

38. Lawrence O'Donnell, *Playing With Fire: The 1968 Election and the Transformation of American Politics.* (New York: Penguin Books, 2017), 378.

39. Quoted in Chester Lewis, Godfrey Hodgson, and Bruce Page, *An American Melodrama: The Presidential Campaign of 1968* (New York: Viking Press, 1969), 652.

40. Hamill, "Wallace," 313–14.

41. Pearlstein, *Nixonland*, 89.

42. O'Donnell, *Playing With Fire*, 145–46.

43. Richard Nixon, "If Mob Rule Takes Hold in the U.S.," in *Takin' It to the Streets*, 307.

44. Ibid., 307–10.

45. Pearlstein, *Nixonland*, 89.

46. Jules Witcover, *The Year The Dream Died: Revisiting 1968 in America* (New York: Time Warner, 1997), 290.

47. Ibid., 290–91.

48. Ibid., 300–301.

49. Ibid., 299; O'Donnell, *Playing With Fire*, 287, 288.

50. Witcover, *The Year The Dream Died*, 300.

51. O'Donnell, *Playing With Fire*, 290.

52. Pearlstein, *Nixonland*, 303.

53. O'Donnell, *Playing With Fire*, 310.

54. O'Donnell, *Playing With Fire*, 314.

55. https://www.presidency.ucsb.edu/documents/address-accepting-the-presidential-nomination-the-republican-national-convention-miami
56. Carter, *The Politics of Rage*, 359, 360–62.

EPILOGUE

1. Quoted in Poniatowska, *Massacre in Mexico* (Columbia, MO: University of Missouri Press, 1975), 316.
2. Annie Ernaux, *The Years*, trans. Alison L. Strayer (New York: Seven Stories Press, 2008), 99–102.
3. Quoted in Maurice Isserman and Michael Kazin, *America Divided: The Civil War of the 1960s* (New York: Oxford University Press, 2000), 278.
4. Daniel Patrick Moynihan, "Memorandum for the President," January 16, 1970, https://www.jstor.org/stable/10.7864/j.ctt7zsvxq.
5. Roman Hruska, "55 years ago today: NPR: On This Day In 1970: Hruska Links Judge To 'Mediocre'," https://fourthamendment.com/?p=59768.
6. Quoted in David Carter, *Stonewall: The Riots that Sparked the Gay Revolution* (New York: St. Martin's Press, 2004), 143.
7. "Bring the War Home," in *Takin' It to the Streets*, 402.
8. Quoted in James Miller, *Democracy Is in the Streets: From Port Huron to the Siege of Chicago* (New York: Simon and Schuster, 1987), 311–12.
9. Quoted in Charles Kaiser, *1968 in America* (New York: Grove Press, 1988), 256.
10. Jack Newfield, quoted in Tom Hayden, "On Robert Kennedy's 1968 Presidential Bid," PBS, https://www.pbs.org/opb/thesixties/topics/politics/reflections_1.html.

Note on Sources

A complete discussion of all the important sources on each of the topics and events covered in this book would result in a bibliographic essay as long as this book itself. Rather, it seems best to cite the crucial works on 1968 that I used as well as those of the overall topic of the 1960s. Beyond that is a listing of the various sources cited in these pages.

Works Cited

WORKS ON 1968

Caute, David. *The Year of the Barricades: A Journey Through 1968*. New York: Harper & Row, 1988.

Cottrell, Robert and Blaine T. Browne. *1968: The Rise and Fall of the New American Revolution*. New York: Rowman & Littlefield, 2018.

Daniels, Robert V. *Year of the Heroic Guerilla: World Revolution and Counterrevolution in 1968*. New York: Basic Books, 1989.

Fink, Carole, Phillip Gassert, Detlef Junker, eds. *1968: The World Transformed*. Cambridge: Cambridge University Press, 1998.

Fraser, Ronald, ed. *1968: A Student Generation in Revolt*. New York: Pantheon, 1988.

Gassert, Philipp and Martin Klimke. *1968: Memories and Legacies of a Global Revolt*. Washington, DC: Bulletin of the German Historical Institute, Supplement 6, 2009.

Kaiser, Charles. *1968 in America*. New York: Grove Press, 1988.

Kurlansky, Mark. *1968: The Year That Rocked the World*. New York: Random House, 2004.

Suri, Jeremi, ed. *The Global Revolutions of 1968*. New York: Norton, 2007.

Suri, Jeremi. *Power and Protest: Global Revolution and the Rise of Détente*. Cambridge, MA: Harvard University Press, 2003.

Vinen, Richard. *1968: Radical Protest and Its Enemies*. New York: HarperCollins, 2018.

Witcover, Jules. *The Year the Dream Died: Revisiting 1968 in America*. New York: Time Warner, 1997.

Wyatt, David. *When America Turned: Reckoning With 1968*. Amherst, MA: Univ. of Massachusetts Press, 2014.

"Introduction." *American Historical Review* v. 123, no. 3 (June 2018), 706–09.

WORKS ON THE 1960S

Anderson, Terry H. *The Movement and the Sixties*. New York: Oxford University Press, 1995.

Bloom, Alexander, ed. *Long Time Gone: Sixties America Then and Now* New York: Oxford University Press, 2001.

Bloom, Alexander and Wini Breines, eds. *Takin' It to the Streets: A Sixties Reader*. New York: Oxford University Press, 4/e, 2015.

Burns, Stewart. *Social Movements of the 1960s: Searching for Democracy*. Boston: Twayne, 1990.

Chalmers, David. *And the Crooked Places Made Straight: The Struggle for Social Change in the 1960s*. Baltimore: Johns Hopkins University Press, 1996, 2/e

Gitlin, Todd. *The Sixties: Years of Hope, Days of Rage*. New York: Bantam Books, 1987.

Isserman, Maurice and Michael Kazin. *America Divided: The Civil War of the 1960s*. New York: Oxford University Press, 2000.

Marwick, Arthur. *The Sixties*. New York: Oxford University Press, 1998.

McElvaine, Robert S., *The Times They Were A-Changin': 1964, The Year the Sixties Arrived and the Battle Lines of Today Were Drawn*. New York: Arcade Publishing, 2022.

Miller, Douglas T., *On Our Own: America in the Sixties*. Lexington, MA: D. C. Heath, 1996.

Miller, James. *Democracy Is In The Streets: From Port Huron to the Siege of Chicago*. New York: Simon and Schuster, 1987.

SOURCES CITED

Anderson, Kirk. "Song 'Adaptations' and the Globalisation of French Pop, 1960–1970," French Cultural Studies, v. 26, no. 3 (2015), 330–42.

Appy, Christian G. *American Reckoning: The Vietnam War and Our National Identity*. New York: Viking, 2015.

Appy, Christian G. *Patriots: The Vietnam War Remembered From All Sides*. New York: Viking, 2003.

Appy, Christian and Alexander Bloom. "Vietnam War Mythology and the Rise of Public Cynicism." In *Long Time Gone: Sixties America Then and Now*, edited by Alexander Bloom. New York: Oxford University Press, 2001, 47–74.

Bach, Damon R. *The American Counterculture: A History of Hippies and Cultural Dissidents*. Lawrence, KS: University Press of Kansas, 2020.

Baxandall, Rosayln. "Re-Visioning the Women's Liberation Movement's Narrative: Early Second Wave African American Feminists." *Feminist Studies* v. 27, no.1 (Spring 2001), 225–45.

Bingham, Clara. "The Whole World Is Watching: An Oral History of the 1968 Columbia Uprising." *Vanity Fair*, March 26, 2018. https://www.vanityfair.com/news/2018/03/the-students-behind-the-1968-columbia-uprising.

Bloom, Alexander. *Prodigal Sons: The New York Intellectuals and Their World*. New York: Oxford University Press, 1986.

Blüml, Jan. "Reception of the Rolling Stones in Communist Czechoslovakia." *Rock Music Studies* v. 2, no. 3 (2015), 257–79.

Branch, Taylor. *At Canaan's Edge: America in the King Years 1965–68*. New York: Simon & Schuster, 2006.

Branch, Taylor. *Pillar of Fire: America in the King Years, 1963–65*. New York: Simon and Schuster, 1999.

Brand, Karina. "A Miss America protest propelled the women's movement into national spotlight," https://www.usatoday.com/story/news/nation-now/1968-project/2018/10/12/miss-america-protest-womens-movement/1578111002/.

Brewster, Claire. "The Student Movement of 1968 and the Mexican Press: The Cases of 'Excelsior' and 'Siempre!'" *Latin American Research* v. 21, no. 2 (2002), 171–90.

Buchwald, Art. "Rub-a-Dub-Dub: All Those Demonstrators Oughta Be Dunked in a Tub." *Washington Post*, April 25, 1965.

Buchwald, Art. "The Bra Burners." *New York Post*, September 12, 1968.

Buchwald, Art. "We Have the Enemy on the Run, Says General Custer." *Washington Post*, February 6, 1968.

Callahan, Mat. *The Explosion of Deferred Dreams: Musical Renaissance and Social Revolution in San Francisco, 1965–1975*. Oakland, CA: PM Press, 2017.

Cannon, Lou. *Governor Reagan: His Rise to Power*. New York: Public Affairs, 2003.

Carey, Elaine. *Plaza of Sacrifices: Gender, Power and Terror in 1968 Mexico*. Albuquerque: University of Mexico Press, 2005.

Carpenter, Victoria. "Tlatelolco 1968 in Contemporary Mexican Literature Introduction." *Latin American Research* v. 24, no. 4 (2005), 476–80.

Carter, Dan T. *The Politics of Rage: George Wallace, the Origins of the New Conservatism, and the Transformation of American Politics*. Baton Rouge: Louisiana State University Press, 2/e, 2000.

Chester, Lewis, Godfrey Hodgson, Bruce Page. *An American Melodrama: The Presidential Campaign of 1968*. New York: Viking Press, 1969.

"Clark M. Clifford Remembers His Post-Tet Questions." In *Major Problems in the History of the Vietnam War*, edited by Robert J. McMahon. Boston: Houghton Mifflin, 2003, 3/e, 329–31.

Clarke, Thurston. *The Last Campaign: Robert F. Kennedy and 82 Days That Inspired America*. New York: Henry Holt, 2008.

Cobble, Dorothy Sue, Linda Gordon, Astrid Henry. *Feminism Unfinished: A Short, Surprising History of American Women's Movements*. New York: Liveright Publishing, 2014.

Conrad, Cecilia A. "Racial Trends in Labor Market Access and Wages: Women." In *America Becoming, Vol. 2: Racial Trends and Their Consequences*, edited by Neil J. Smelser, William Julius Wilson, and Faith Mitchell. Washington, DC: National Academis Press, 2001, 124–51. https://doi.org/10.17226/9719.

Cottrell, Robert C. *Sex, Drugs, and Rock "n" Roll: The Rise of America's 1960s Counterculture*. New York: Rowman & Littlefield, 2015.

D'Emilio, John. *Lost Prophet: The Life and Times of Bayard Rustin*. Chicago: The University of Chicago Press, 2003.

da Cruz, Frank. "*Columbia University, 1968*." http://www.columbia.edu/cu/computinghistory/1968/.

DeGroot, Gerald J. "Ronald Reagan and Student Unrest in California, 1966–1970." *Pacific Historical Review* v. 65, no. 1 (February 1996), 107–29.

Doggett, Peter. "*There's a Riot Going On*": *Revolutionaries, Rock Stars and the Rise and Fall of the '60s*. Edinburgh: Canongate, 2007.

Dougan, Clark, and Stephen Weiss. *The Vietnam Experience: Nineteen Sixty-Eight*. Boston: Boston Publishing, 1983.

Doyle, Kate, ed. "Tlatelolco Massacre: U.S. Documents on Mexico and the Events of 1968." https://nsarchive2.gwu.edu/NSAEBB/NSAEBB99/.

Ernaux, Annie, *The Years* (tr. Alison L. Strayer). New York: Seven Stories Press, 2008.

Evans, Sara M. "Women's Liberation: Seeing the Revolution Clearly," *Feminist Studies* v. 41, no. 1 (2015), 138–49.

Evans, Sara, *Personal Politics: The Roots of Women's Liberation in the Civil Rights Movements & The New Left*. New York: Vintage Books, 1980.

Fager, Chuck. *Uncertain Resurrection: Dr. King's Poor People's Campaign, Washington, 1968*. Durham, NC: Kimo Press, 2017.

Fahs, Breanne. "Ti-Grace Atkinson and the Legacy of Radical Feminism." *Feminist Studies* v. 37, no. 3 (Fall 2011) 561–90.

Farber, David. *Chicago '68*. Chicago: University of Chicago Press, 1988.

Farmer, Ashley D. "'Sisters Up in Here': Women, Gender and Party Politics in *The Revolution Has Come*." *Journal of Civil and Human Rights* v. 3, no. 2 (Fall/Winter 2017), 98–101.

Gallo, Marcia, *Different Daughters: A History of the Daughters of Bilitis and the Rise of the Lesbian Rights Movement*. New York: Seal Press, 2006.

Gallup, George, and Evan Hill. "The American Woman." *The Saturday Evening Post* v. 235, no. 46, (December 22, 1962), 15–32.

Gay, Roxanne. "Fifty Years Ago Protesters Took on the Miss America Pageant and Electrified the Feminist Movement." *Smithsonian Magazine*, January 2018. https://www.smithsonianmag.com/history/fifty-years-ago-protestors-took-on-miss-america-pageant-electrified-feminist-movement-180967504/

Germain, Rosie. "Reading 'The Second Sex' in 1950s America." *The Historical Journal* v. 56, no. 4 (December 2013), 1041–1062.

Giardina, Carol. "MOW to NOW: Black feminism Resets the Chronology of the Founding of Modern Feminism." *Feminist Studies* v. 44, no. 3 (2018) 736–65.

Gleason, Ralph J. "Like a Rolling Stone." *The American Scholar* v. 36, no. 4 (Autumn 1967), 555–63.

Gonzalez de Bustamante, Celeste. "1968 Olympic Dreams and Tlatelolco Nightmares: Imagining and Imaging Modernity on Television." *Mexican Studies/Studios Mexicanos* v. 26, no 1 (Winter 2010), 1–30.

Hayden, Tom. *Reunion: A Memoir*. New York: Random House, 1988.

Herr, Michael. *Dispatches*. New York: Avon Books, 1978.

Hoffer, Richard. *Something in the Air: American Passion and Defiance in the 1968 Mexico City Olympics*. New York: Free Press, 2009.

Horowitz, Daniel. *Betty Friedan and the Making of "The Feminine Mystique": The American Left, the Cold War, and Modern Feminism*. Amherst, MA: University of Massachusetts Press, 1998. 2019.

Jones, Claudia. "An End to the Neglect of the Problems of the Negro Woman!" *Political Affairs*, June 1949, 3–19. https://libcom.org/article/end-neglect-problems-negro-woman

Kendi, Ibram. "Inside the Gun of the Black Panther Party." *Journal of Civil and Human Rights* v. 3, no. 3 (Fall/Winter 2017), 113–16.

King, Martin Luther. "The Crisis in America's Cities." August 15, 1967. https://www.crmvet.org/info/mlkcitys.htm.

King, Mary. "SNCC: Born of the Sit-Ins, Dedicated to Action." April 1988. http://maryking.info/?page_id=1074#mk-women\.

Kleinberg, S. J. "Economic Activity During Boom, Bust, and War." In *Women in the United States, 1830–1945*. London: Palgrave, 1999. https://link.springer.com/chapter/10.1007/978-1-349-27698-1_10.

Kluckhorn, Clyde. "The Complex Kinsey Study and What It Attempts to Do." *New York Times, Book Review*, September 13, 1953. 3.

Kreydatus, Beth. "Contesting Miss America: The Boardwalk Protests of 1968." *Pennsylvania Legacies*, v. 18, no. 2 (Fall 2018), 20–25.

Lear, Martha Weinman. "The Second Feminist Wave." *New York Times Magazine*, March 10, 1968. 24, 50–62.

Lundberg, Ferdinand, and Marynia Farnham. *Modern Woman: The Lost Sex*. New York: Harper, 1947.

MacLean, Nancy, ed. *The American Women's Movement, 1945–2000*. Boston: Bedford/St. Martin's, 2009.

Mailer, Norman. *The Armies of the Night*. New York: New American Library, 1968.

Mantler, Gordon K. *Power to the Poor: Black-Brown Coalition and the Fight for Economic Justice, 1960–1974*. Chapel Hill: University of North Carolina Press, 2013.

Matthey, Paul. "1968: The Year of Two Student Springs. Czechoslovak and French Movements Compared." https://www.academia.edu/4386028/1968_The_Year_of_Two_Student_Springs_Czechoslovak_and_French_Movements_Compared.

May, Elaine Tyler. *America And The Pill: A History of Promise, Peril, and Liberation*. New York: Basic Books, 2011.

McKnight, Gerald D. *The Last Crusade: Martin Luther King, Jr., the FBI, and the Poor People's Campaign*. Boulder, CO: Westview Press, 1998.

Melton Barry. "Everything Seemed Beautiful: A Life in the Counterculture." In *Long Time Gone: Sixties America Then and Now*, edited by Alexander Bloom. New York: Oxford University Press, 2001, 145–58.

Menand, Louis. "Change Your Life: The Lessons of the New Left." *The New Yorker*, v. XCVII, no. 5 (March 22, 2021), 46.

Mickenberg, Julia L. "'The Way We Were': Eve Merriam and the Hidden History of American Feminism." *Ms*, October 21, 2023. https://msmagazine.com/2023/10/21/the-way-we-were-movie-eve-merriam-american-feminism/?fbclid=IwAR03y_uSAOlG-jmUJPHCSzDmkpNoyTXL2klBcdjzwrnllrDPwvWxdIxaoq5Q.

Morganova, Pavlina. "Action! Czech Performance Art from the 1960s to the 1970s." www.academia.edu/15102503/_Action_Czech_Performance_Art_from_the_1960s_to_the_1970s_.

Murray, Pauli. "The Negro Woman in the Quest for Equality," speech to the National Council of Negro Women Convention, Washington, DC, November 14, 1963. cademic.oup.com/mississippi-scholarship-online/book/22504/chapter-abstract/182819173?redirectedFrom=fulltext

Murray, Pauli, and Mary Eastwood. "Jane Crow and the Law: Sex Discrimination and Title VII." *George Washington Law Review* v. 34, no. 2 (December 1965): 232–56.

Oberdorfer, Don, "The 'Wobble' on the War on Capitol Hill." *The New York Times Magazine*, December 17, 1967, 30–31, 98–107.

Oberdorfer, Don, *Tet: The Turning Point in the Vietnam War*. Baltimore: Johns Hopkins University Press, 2001 [originally published 1971].

O'Donnell, Lawrence. *Playing With Fire: The 1968 Election and the Transformation of American Politics*. New York: Penguin Books, 2017.

Olsen, James S., and Randy Roberts. *Where the Domino Fell: America and Vietnam, 1945–1995*. New York: St. Martin's Press, 2/e, 1996.

"On the Poverty [Misery] of Student Life." https://theanarchistlibrary.org/library/u-n-e-f-strasbourg-on-the-poverty-of-student-life.

Pan, J. C. "Trasher Feminism: Valerie Solanas and Her Enemies." *Dissent*, Spring 2014, https://www.dissentmagazine.org/article/trasher-feminism-valerie-solanas-and-her-enemies.

Pearlstein, Rick. *Nixonland: The Rise of a President and the Fracturing of America*. New York: Scribner, 2008.

Perry, Charles. *The Haight-Ashbury: A History*. New York: Random House, 1984.

Podhoretz, Norman. "The Know-Nothing Bohemians." *Partisan Review*, v. 25, no. 2 (Spring 1958), 315.

Poniatowska, Elena. *Massacre in Mexico*. Columbia: University of Missouri Press, 1975.

Popkin, Ann. "The Personal is Political: The Women's Liberation Movement." In *They Should Have Served That Cup of Coffee*, edited by Dick Cluster. Boston: South End Press, 1979, 181–222.

Press, Joy. "The Life and Death of a Radical Sisterhood." *New York*, November 15, 2017. https://www.thecut.com/2017/11/an-oral-history-of-feminist-group-new-york-radical-women.html.

Randolph, Sherrie M., *Florynce "Flo" Kennedy: The Life of a Black Feminist Radical*, Chapel Hill: The University of NC Press, 2015.

Reeves, Michelle, "'Obey the Rules or Get Out': Ronald Reagan's 1966 Gubernatorial Campaign and the 'Trouble in Berkeley,'" *Southern California Quarterly* v. 92, no. 3 (Fall 2010), 275–305.

Rojas, Rafael, *Fighting Over Fidel: The New York Intellectuals and the Cuban Revolution.* Princeton: Princeton University Press, 2016.

Rorabaugh, W. J. *Berkeley At War: The 1960s.* New York: Oxford University Press, 1989.

Roth, Betina. "Second Wave Black Feminism in the African Diaspora: News from New Scholarship." *Agenda: Empowering Women for Gender Equity* no. 58 (2003), 46–58.

Rothschild, Joseph, and Nancy Wingfield. *Return to Diversity: A Political History of East Central Europe since World War II.* New York: Oxford University Press, 2000.

Rudd, Mark, "The Missing History of the Columbia '68 Protests." *New York Times*, April 22, 2018.

Sabatova, Anna. "From 1968 to Charter 77 To 1989 and Beyond." https://www.rferl.org/a/ From_1968_To_Charter_77_To_1989_And_Beyond/1192331.html

Sarachild (Amatniek), Kathie. "The Funeral Oration for the Burial of Traditional Womanhood." https://www.cwluherstory.org/classic-feminist-writings-articles/funeral-oration-for-the-burial-of-traditional-womanhood.

Schlesinger, Arthur, Jr. *Robert Kennedy and His Times.* Boston: Houghton Mifflin, 1978.

Sideman. Michael. *The Imaginary Revolution: Parisian Students and Workers in 1968.* New York: Berghan Books, 2004.

Simons, Thomas W. Jr. *Eastern Europe in the Postwar World.* New York: St. Martin's Press, 2/e, 1993.

Singer, Daniel. *Prelude to Revolution: France in May 1968.* Cambridge, MA: South End Press, 2nd ed. 2000.

Solanas, Valerie. *The S.C.U.M. Manifesto.* New York: Olympia Press, 1968.

Soloman, David, ed. *LSD: The Consciousness Expanding Drug.* New York: G. P. Putnam's Sons, 1964.

Stavis, Ben. *We Were The Campaign: New Hampshire to Chicago for McCarthy.* Boston: Beacon Press, 1969.

Stern, Edith M. "Woman Are Household Slaves." *The American Mercury* v. 68, no. 301 (January 1949), 71–76.

Suk, Jiří. "The Utopian Rationalism of the Prague Spring of 1968." *The American Historical Review* Volume 123, Issue 3, 764–68.

Taibo, Paco Ignacio II. *'68: The Mexican Autumn of the Tlatelolco Massacre.* New York: Seven Stories Press, 1991.

Tanenbaum, Laura, and Mark Engler. "No More Miss America: A Collective Memory of Liberatory Action." *Dissent*, September 7, 2018. https://www.dissentmagazine.org/online_ articles/no-more-miss-america-1968-pageant-protest-oral-history-women-liberation.

Thornton, Arland, and Deborah Freedman. "Changes in the Sex Role Attitudes of Women, 1962–1977." *American Sociological Review* v. 44, no. 5 (October 1979), 831–42.

Toossi, Mitra, and Teresa L. Morisi. *Women in the Workforce Before, During, and After The Great Recession.* Washington, DC: U.S. Bureau of Labor Statistics, July 2017.

Touraine, Alain. *The May Movement: Revolt and Reform.* New York: Random House, 1971.

Trilling, Diana. "The Other Night at Columbia: A Report from the Academy." In *Claremont Essays.* New York: Harcourt, Brace & World, 1964. (Originally published in *Partiosan Review* v. 26, n.2 [Spring 1959], 214–230.)

Welch, Georgia Paige, " 'Up Against the wall Miss America': Women's Liberation and Miss Black America in Atlantic City, 1968." *Feminist Formations*, v. 27, no. 2 (Summer 2015), 70–97.

Wells, Tom. "Running Battle: Washington's War at Home." In *Long Time Gone: Sixties America Then and Now*, edited by Alexander Bloom. New York: Oxford University Press, 2001, 75–98.

Wells, Tom. *The War Within: America's Battle Over Vietnam*. Berkeley: University of California Press, 1994.

White, Ray Lewis. "Eldridge Cleaver's 'Soul on Ice': A Book Review Digest." *CLA Journal*, v. 21, no. 4 (June, 1978), 556–66.

Wicker, Tom. "Lyndon Johnson and the Roots of Contemporary Conservatism." In *Long Time Gone: Sixties America Then and Now*, edited by Alexander Bloom. New York: Oxford University Press, 2001, 99–122.

Williams, Kieran. *The Prague Spring and Its Aftermath*. Cambridge: Cambridge University Press, 1997.

Wolfe, Tobias. *In Pharoah's Army: Memories of the Lost War*. New York: Knopf, 1994.

Wolfe, Tom. *The Electric Kool Aid Acid Test*. New York: Farrar, Strauss and Giroux, 1968.

Women Workers in 1960: Geographical Differences. Women's Bureau Bulletin 284. Washington, DC: U.S. Department of Labor, 1962.

Wright, Amy Nathan. "Civil Rights 'Unfinished Business': Poverty, Race and the 1968 Poor People's Campaign." PhD diss., University of Texas, 2007.

Young, Marilyn. *The Vietnam Wars: 1945–1990*. New York: Harper Perennial, 1991.

Zolov, Eric. *Refried Elvis: The Rise of the Mexican Counterculture*. Berkeley: University of California Press, 1999.

Index

For the benefit of digital users, indexed terms that span two pages (e.g., 52–53) may, on occasion, appear on only one of those pages.